THE BEST
HOME
BUSINESSES
for People 50+

Other Books by Paul and Sarah Edwards

Best Home Businesses for the 21st Century

Changing Directions Without Losing Your Way

Cool Careers for Dummies, 2001
(with Marty Nemko)

The Entrepreneurial Parent
(with Lisa Roberts)

Finding Your Perfect Work

Getting Business to Come to You
(with Laura Douglas)

Home-Based Business for Dummies
(with Peter Economy)

Home Businesses You Can Buy
(with Walter Zooi)

Making Money in Cyberspace
(with Linda Rohrbough)

Making Money with Your Computer at Home

The Practical Dreamer's Handbook

Secrets of Self-Employment

Teaming Up
(with Rick Benzel)

Working from Home

Why Aren't You Your Own Boss?
(with Peter Economy)

THE BEST HOME BUSINESSES
for People 50+

*Opportunities for People
Who Believe the
Best Is Yet to Be!*

Paul and Sarah Edwards

JEREMY P. TARCHER/PENGUIN
a member of Penguin Group (USA) Inc.
New York

Most Tarcher/Penguin books are available at special quantity discounts for bulk purchase for sales promotions, premiums, fund-raising, and educational needs. Special books or book excerpts also can be created to fit specific needs. For details, write Penguin Group (USA) Inc. Special Markets, 375 Hudson Street, New York, NY 10014.

Jeremy P. Tarcher/Penguin
a member of
Penguin Group (USA) Inc.
375 Hudson Street
New York, NY 10014
www.penguin.com

Library of Congress Cataloging-in-Publication Data

Edwards, Paul, date.
Best home businesses for people 50+ : opportunities for people who believe the best is yet to be! / Paul & Sarah Edwards.
p.   cm.
ISBN 1-58542-380-7
1. Home-based businesses.   2. Home-based businesses—Management.   3. Self-employed.   4. Older people—Employment.   5. Home-based businesses—United States.   6. Home-based businesses—United States—Management.   7. Self-employed—United States.   8. Older people—Employment—United States.   I. Title: Best home businesses for people fifty plus.   II. Title: Home businesses for people 50+.   III. Edwards, Sarah (Sarah A.)   IV. Title.
HD2333.E338   2004   2004051618
658'.0412—dc22

Printed in the United States of America
1   3   5   7   9   10   8   6   4   2

Book design by Lee Fukui

ACKNOWLEDGMENTS

We wish to express gratitude to Mitch Horowitz, our editor, who first suggested this book, our publisher, Joel Fotinos, Ashley Shelby, Allison Sobel, Kelly Groves, Katie Grinch, Jean-Marie Pierson, and the others at Tarcher/Penguin who have helped to make this book come to life. We also acknowledge the helpfulness of our agents, Bob Diforio, Marilyn Allen, and Colleen O'Shea.

We owe special appreciation to Dave Fuller, Tim Talevich, and Anita Thompson of *The Costco Connection* who enabled us to use our column to identify many of the people whose stories appear in the snapshots, which helped assure that the book reflects the individual creativity that people employ in creating fifty-plus businesses for themselves. Similarly we thank Dottie Walters and Ivan Misner, whose vast contacts led us to other interesting people in this book. We thank Deborah Russell, Director of Economic Security, AARP for insights she generously provided.

We happily acknowledge April Durham and her husband, Bryan Gorrie, whose thousands of phone calls and e-mails helped to locate most of the people whose experience is reflected in the business profiles. We also thank Rick Benzel and April Durham for their editorial support in helping us organize the volume of information we gathered.

Finally, we thank the hundreds of people who allowed us to interview them. They shared their experience and expertise as well as insights, wisdom, cautions, and inspiration that helped us appreciate the possibilities for living the life you want to live while doing work you want to do after fifty.

CONTENTS

HELPING INDIVIDUALS AND FAMILIES

TURNING YOUR HOBBY INTO INCOME

WELCOME TO THE REST OF YOUR LIFE . . . YOUR WAY

Not long ago an AARP magazine cover featured a smiling, vibrant photo of fifty-plus model Lauren Hutton; the headline read "60 Is the New 40!" We would add, fifty is the new thirty-five. Now that growing numbers of us can expect to live to a hundred, fifty is truly midlife. But instead of being midlife at thirty-five with the many personal, work, and family obligations that age brings, those of us at or around fifty-plus are looking ahead to a second half of life we can pretty much shape, design, and structure as we wish.

Whether our jobs are being snatched from under us by layoffs and off-shoring or our interest in them is simply waning, many of us at this stage of life are beginning to think about new possibilities. And, indeed, there is a whole new world of possibilities that weren't open to our parents and grandparents, and probably wouldn't have been of interest to them anyway.

When we began writing about working from home over twenty years ago, our personal motivation was to better balance our work and family life, but even then we thought perhaps having a home-based business would be an appealing option for people approaching retirement age. So, when the first edition of *Working from Home* came out, we arranged to speak to a number of preretirement groups. Although we were personally well received—attendees thought we were a "cute couple"—their message was clear: The last thing these fifty-plus folks wanted to do was any kind of income-producing work, even as their own boss. They wanted to travel, spend time with their grandchildren, and pursue their favorite leisure-time activities.

But that has changed dramatically. The idea of a home-based business has become enticing to many folks approaching or beyond fifty, probably for one or more of the same reasons that you've picked up this book.

What's your motivation? Why are you attracted to a home-based career or business at a time when in the past people your age would be thinking about booking a cruise or joining a golf club? Here's what others tell us.

Why a Home-Based Business at Fifty-Plus?

1. Lots of us like to work. Boomers, both male and female, have always been career-oriented "free agents." And this is not changing just because we're hitting fifty. In fact, for many of us this stage of life is the chance we've been waiting for. We may have wanted to be our own boss for some time, but it just wasn't practical. For us, now could be the time. But even for those of us who've never thought of being our own boss, the idea is increasingly attractive, for as Joseph F. Coughlin, head of the Age Lab at the Massachusetts Institute of Technology, has observed, "Retirement is increasingly an historical artifact rather than a reality."[1]

In his book, *Good Business, Leadership, Flow and the Making of Meaning,* Mihaly Csikszentmihalyi points out that this is "an age in which business and work have replaced religion and politics as central focuses in contemporary life."[2] We saw Jack Nicholson's painful portrayal of retirement in *About Schmidt,* and perhaps we've watched our parents or grandparents go through similar struggles. And it's not an appealing scenario. As one fifty-plusser put it, "I don't want to be put out to pasture," or as another said, "I'm not ready for the rocking chair."

In fact, the older a worker is today, the more attractive continuing to work is. Only 31 percent of those aged eighteen to thirty-four say they want to stay employed indefinitely. Forty-one percent of those aged thirty-five to forty-nine intend to keep working. But nearly half of people over age fifty say they want to work until they are physically unable to do so.[3]

In fact, among people we interviewed for this book, many had already retired once or twice, only to find it boring. Others felt a need for more flexibility and freedom than a job allows, but that didn't mean they were not interested in working. They still wanted to work, but on their own terms.

---

1. Issues in Science and Technology Online, Fall 1999, *www.issues.org/issues/16.1/coughlin.htm.*
2. *Good Business: Leadership, Flow, and the Making of Meaning,* Mihaly Csikszentmihalyi (Penguin [USA], 2004. ISBN: 014200409X.
3. Gallup/UBS survey Index of Investor Optimism poll, January 2002.

2. We're concerned we will need to work. Many people fifty-plus share a growing concern about their future financial security. In fact, the number-one financial concern of Americans of all ages is whether they'll have enough savings to maintain a good quality of life when they retire. More than half of people over fifty say they are either very worried or moderately worried about not having enough money for retirement.[4] Seventy-four percent of people who haven't retired yet say they live comfortably now, but only 59 percent expect to live comfortably when they retire. Nearly one out of six anticipate a diminished standard of living after retirement . . . unless they do something different.

And it looks as though they're right. Most experts say we need to replace 75 to 80 percent of our preretirement income to live comfortably when we leave the workforce, but a study by New York University economist Edward N. Wolff shows that 40 percent of households headed by workers age forty-seven to sixty-four haven't saved enough to replace even half of their preretirement income, and that number is growing. In fact, even more concerning, nearly 20 percent don't have enough set aside to keep themselves above the poverty line.[5]

So finding a flexible way to continue earning an income after retirement age is becoming not only an appealing option but also a compelling one.

3. Unexpected problems have sidetracked our plans. Lots of us thought we'd planned adequately for our retirement, but unexpected circumstances have intervened to jeopardize our best-laid plans. For example, a divorce, illness, or death of a spouse can require a complete rethinking of one's future.

The dramatic collapse of the stock market in the 1990s pulled the rug out from under a lot of our plans. People aged fifty-five to sixty-four had almost twice as much money invested in stocks during those years as the average American. Syndicated columnist Robert J. Samuelson points out that this has created a social crisis for many. "People in their late fifties and sixties are postponing retirement or, if already retired, returning to work," he explains. "Their savings have been devastated. They can't afford not to work."[6]

---

4. Gallup's annual poll on Americans' personal finances, April 2002. Allstate Insurance surveys show the number of boomers worried about having sufficient retirement funds rose from 29 percent in 2001 to 50 percent in 2002.
5. *Retirement Insecurity: The Income Shortfalls Awaiting the Soon-to-Retire*, Edward N. Wolff, (Economic Policy Institute, 2002). ISBN: 1932066012.
6. *Los Angeles Times*, July 31, 2002.

The average length of time investors expect to delay their retirement because of recession-related losses is 4.4 years.[7] In fact, nearly a quarter of people forty-five and over are planning to postpone retirement.[8] But that doesn't change the fact that they're still ready for more flexibility and control over their daily lives than a traditional job provides.

The rising cost of health care is another unexpected surprise that's affecting our income needs. Just at an age when we might expect a few medical needs to arise, out-of-pocket costs of health care for seniors have increased nearly 50 percent and more employers are cutting back or eliminating health benefits for retirees, raising health-care costs even more. But while these costs are going up, the median net worth of boomers has been decreasing. So finding a reliable, yet flexible, supplementary source of income can provide a much appreciated sense of security.

4. We want to try something new, stimulating, and challenging. In interviewing people for this book, we found that interest in starting a home business often sprang from a desire to do something new, interesting, and exciting. This isn't really surprising because continuing to challenge ourselves is rapidly being recognized as an integral part of staying "healthy" as the years advance. Certainly this isn't a new idea. Oliver Wendell Holmes advocated that anyone over sixty should change careers every few years. He believed exploring something new rekindles our life force.

But we boomers don't think of ourselves as old anyway. Polls show that "old" is being defined as progressively later in life. People turning fifty-five won't consider themselves "old" until they're seventy-six. Just five years ago, "old" was seventy. Five years from now, "old" may well be eighty, and so on. In this spirit, as you will see from upcoming examples, many of the self-employment careers we're choosing are quite novel indeed, often things we could never have imagined ourselves doing when we were younger.

5. We're living longer, healthier lives. We're realizing that we have a lot more years to plan for than we might have expected. When Social Security was created in 1935, the average life expectancy was sixty-three years. But today the life expectancy in the United States is 79.6[9] and there are close to seventy thousand living centenarians, (people over 100). In coming

7. Gallup/UBS survey Index of Investor Optimism poll, January 2002.
8. Retirement Confidence Survey.
9. Paul Hodge, "Greenspan Is Right," *Los Angeles Times,* February 26, 2004.

decades that number will balloon.[10] Conservative demographers predict there will be ten times the current number of centenarians by 2050 when the last boomers hit that age.

Thanks to medical breakthroughs in cancer and heart disease, the United Nations projects that nearly one in twenty Boomers will live to 100. The National Institute on Aging takes that projection even further, suggesting that supercentenarians, those 110 or older, will also be common by then. So, as Horace Deets, executive director of AARP, points out, there's a good chance an American who turns fifty today has more than half of his or her adult life remaining.[11]

At the same time that we're living longer, we're also wanting to "retire" earlier, in the sense of wanting to leave the confines of the 24/7 corporate world. Many of us are ready to retire from that lifestyle in our fifties, but based on life expectancy, retiring at age fifty-five today would be roughly the equivalent of retiring in our mid-thirties when Social Security was established in 1935.

On the flip side of this, though, health problems or disabilities can cause some fifty-plussers to end their salaried careers prematurely or place limitations on the kinds of work they can do during retirement years. Nearly 40 percent of people who are currently retired say they retired earlier than they expected, and half of these had to do so because of health problems or disabilities.[12] But just because we may be suffering from a disability doesn't mean we don't want or need to continue working. As you will see from examples in this book, even if we can't do what we were doing in our salaried career, there are plenty of interesting and financially rewarding careers we can pursue at home on our own.

Clearly it's no wonder so many of us intend to work into our sixties and seventies and beyond. Even retiring at seventy, we might have over thirty more years to make sure we can support ourselves comfortably.

6. Ageism is a reality. While most people would rather work for a salary than create their own job, what is the job market really like for those of us with gray hair, wrinkles, and age spots? Seniors across all ranks from clerks to upper management complain that they are patronized, or made

---

10. Social Security Administration.

11. Address by Horace B. Deets to the National Press Club, Washington, D.C., September 8, 2000.

12. 2003 Retirement Benefit Survey, cosponsored by the Employee Benefit Research Institute.

to feel invisible, by younger co-workers, says Clare Hushbeck, who handles workplace discrimination cases for the AARP.

"The real issue," he explains, "is that in our society we do not respect the honor and beauty of people growing into their own skin." In fact, a 2003 AARP study found that 67 percent of those interviewed for jobs believe age discrimination is a fact of life in the workplace.[13] Age is viewed as so critical to employees that it was listed along with education as more important to how workers are treated than gender, race, sexual orientation, or religion.

The *New York Times* reported that "over the last two fiscal years, age-discrimination complaints filed with the Equal Employment Opportunity Commission have risen more than 24 percent." A poll by Yahoo and Hot Jobs found that nine out of ten job seekers report that interviewers hold age against them. To improve their prospects of getting hired, 63 percent of applicants say they would leave dates off their résumés and 18 percent would have plastic surgery.[14]

The History Channel recently shipped producers "visual guidelines" that urge them to "give younger experts a chance on camera" and emphasize finding interview subjects who "look good" on TV, even if they're not leading authorities in the field. If gray hair and wrinkles won't fly on the History Channel, where aside from as smiling Wal-Mart greeters are we acceptable? Our answer, as others are finding, is—in your own business! We found without exception that age and maturity are an asset in the businesses we've profiled.

7. We want to spend our second half "our way." As we have been throughout our lives, fifty-plus boomers want to handle this phase of life differently than preceding generations. We want to do something fresh and original. So we're especially attracted to the idea of designing a new independent career or business when we retire.[15]

Nearly one in five preretirees say they want to start their own business after retirement.[16] This number is consistent with AARP's *1998*

---

13. "Staying Ahead of the Curve: The AARP Work and Career Study," conducted for AARP by RoperASW, 2002.

14. Reported in *USA Today*, January 21, 2003.

15. Barbara Caplan, Yankelovich partner at the 2002 National Association of Home Builders Senior Housing Symposium. This was a subset of the 67 percent of boomers who want more novelty and change in their lives.

16. Work Trends series of the Rutgers University Heidrick Center for Workforce Development and the University of Connecticut's Center for Survey Research and Analysis, 2000.

BoomerSurvey of a somewhat different age group—those aged thirty-four to fifty-two—which found that 17 percent said they would start their own business.

One of the most noteworthy patterns you will notice throughout this book is the variety of ways people are tailoring their lifestyles to fit their goals and preferences in ways salaried jobs rarely make possible. Some are working part of the day, week, month, or year. Others work full-time, but are selective about with whom they will work and what kind of work they will do. Still others are keeping their salaried jobs, full- or part-time, and starting an appealing business on the side. Many are pursuing similar work to what they enjoyed when employed, while others are staking out entirely new, independent careers.

So the trend has begun. As Csikszentmihalyi says in his book *Good Business*, while 80 percent of adults say they would work even if they didn't have to, the majority can't wait to leave their jobs and get home.

What Makes These the Best Home Businesses?

There is no list of ideal home businesses for any age. The best home business is the one you can do successfully that not only supports you comfortably but also enhances your life. So that means the best business is a highly personal matter. Fortunately once we get past fifty we have a lot more flexibility to actually find and create that ideal career from the literally hundreds of possible home businesses. Our goal in selecting these seventy "best" businesses is to point you toward some of the most appealing options others fifty-plus have found to be reliable, both in terms of being able to generate income without undo effort and risk and in terms of fitting well with the priorities many of us have for the second half of life.

You've undoubtedly heard about and seen a lot of work-at-home scams. Your e mail in-box is probably deluged with such schemes. You've also probably heard about business failure rates, maybe even known someone whose business attempt failed, or suffered such a disappointment yourself. So in this book we feature only legitimate careers and businesses that large numbers of people fifty-plus have been successful at and that you can reasonably expect to continue to be good second-half careers into the future as well.

In researching and selecting these seventy businesses, we used specific criteria men and women fifty-plus tell us are the issues that matter most to them. For a business to be included in this book, our research needed to prove not only that it can be done successfully and practically at or from home, but also that it has been.

- Longevity. People fifty-plus can continue working in the business for at least ten to fifteen years.

- Flexibility. The hours worked each day or days worked each week can be structured to allow time for family, travel, and other priorities in life.

- Accessibility. No additional advanced academic degrees are required.

- Widespread. Geographically suited to a wide variety of locations in the United States and Canada.

- Popularity. Considered to be appealing, enjoyable, and rewarding by lots of people.

Are there other criteria you would add for the home-based careers you would consider? Keep them in mind as you review the businesses in this book.

Fifty-Plus Join the Ranks of New Professionals

While none of the seventy home-based careers we profile require additional advanced degrees, some people fifty-plus are deciding to return to school to enter a new degreed profession. Charles Haseltine of Santa Rosa, California, for example, had been an entrepreneur in the appliance-repair business for twenty-five years when he "retired" at fifty and went back to school to become a licensed clinical social worker. "When the last of our five children moved out, we decided we didn't need to have maximum income driving our lives," he explains. "In a sense I'm living that old dream, 'I wish I were twenty years younger and knew what I know now.'" He finds that his maturity provides insights and novel resolutions in helping his clients. "I used to help people fix their machines. Now I help people fix their lives."

William Benedetto worked as a marine investigator for twenty-eight years before pursuing his fifty-plus career as an attorney-at-law. After thirteen years of part- and full-time course work, he opened a solo law practice in Beaverton, Oregon. Operating on a shoestring for the first few years, he practiced law for twenty years before embarking on his third career at seventy-four as an author. "Starting a new profession in midlife was truly exciting," he recalls. "I was suddenly out there with a whole new set of challenges to occupy my energies. I looked forward to going to work."

In compiling the list, we drew first on our own experience. We have been teaching and coaching people in how to select and run a successful home business for nearly twenty-five years. Over those years through thousands of interviews, workshops, and coaching sessions, we have tracked businesses that can be run successfully from home to keep our pulse on what can stand the test of changing times.

In addition, during the past year we have interviewed hundreds of people fifty-plus who had started successful home businesses and reviewed trends affecting all the businesses we were considering to determine if there is evidence that the field will remain viable despite predictable changes in the economy and expected social, cultural, and global trends. We discarded many businesses that some people have run successfully and probably still could. But we only wanted to select businesses we feel confident can provide opportunities for many others to be successful in as well.

Which Business Is Best for You?

Because the "best" business is so highly personal, we designed this book to help you go right to the options that are most appealing to you and best meet your needs and lifestyle preferences. You'll notice, for example, that the businesses are divided into four sections based on whom you want to work with and the nature of the work you want to do.

Which would be most appealing to you?

- Serving the business world.

- Serving businesses and consumers.

- Helping individuals and families.

- Turning your hobby into income.

In addition, we have created icons to help you look for the kind of work you're looking for or want to be sure to avoid:

- People work . People skills are important to all businesses for marketing and good customer service, but in each profile we have indicated the proportion of time a person can expect to spend working directly with clients and customers in the process of doing the work of the business.

- Brain work ▨. Each profile also indicates the percentage of time a person can expect to be engaged in brain- or skill-based work involving little or no contact with clients or customers.

- Telephone ✆. A substantial portion of the work in these businesses is done on the phone.

- Deskwork ⌗. Most of the work of these businesses is done at a desk.

- On your feet ⋔. There's not much desk work in these businesses.

- Face-to-face interaction ⋈ is a large part of these businesses.

- Geographically transferable ⊕. You can pick these businesses up and take them with you just about anywhere.

- Indoor work ▨. You'll be indoors most of the time in these businesses.

- Outdoor work ♣. Much of the work in these businesses is done outdoors.

- Inventory required ▨. These businesses involve having stock or supplies on hand that must be stored in your home or elsewhere. Beware that some local zoning ordinances and common interest development CC&Rs (Covenants, Codes and Restrictions) prohibit stocking inventory in a home.

- Need staff ⋔⋔⋔⋔. To make a full-time income in these businesses you'll need to have one or more assistants at least some of the time.

- Part-time potential ☾. These business need not be done full-time.

- Physical stamina required ⋔. These business include physical labor or long hours.

- Solitary work ⬒. While virtually all work is done with the customer in mind, these businesses involve significant periods of working alone.

- Work at home ⌂. While usually all businesses involve some errands or marketing activities outside the home, the actual work of these businesses can be done without leaving home.

- Work from home 🚗. These businesses require leaving home to provide some or part of your service.

- Travel involved 💼. These businesses require some time traveling overnight away from home.

You'll see the applicable icons for each business in the **Business at a Glance** section of each profile.

The Profiles

Each of the seventy business profiles are organized in a concise, informative way to help you quickly get a realistic perspective of the nature of the business, what it involves, and what it offers. As you read through the following nine elements of each profile, you'll be able to weigh the pros and cons of each business in relation to one another and to your own personal needs and preferences.

Opening Overview

Each profile begins with a general description of the business, what makes it a good fifty-plus business, advice from experts for succeeding in that business, and specialties or customer and client niches in the field. However, in some profiles information on business niches appears in the Marketing Insights section.

Business at a Glance

Following the overview, you'll find a list of the icons that characterize the day-to-day nature of the business, along with a detailed chart that spells out some of the key questions most people have on their minds when considering a particular business.

	Minimal	Moderate	More than most
Start-up cost*	Under $2,500	$2,501–$7,500	over $7,501
Overhead	Under 20%	20–40%	Over 40%
Potential earnings	Under $20,000	$20,000–$50,000	Over $50,000
Computer skills required	Word processing, accounting software	Maintaining a Web site	Using specialized software for the business
Deadline pressures or, if appropriate, scheduling pressure	Few deadlines	Some deadlines	Frequent deadlines
Flexible hours	Not so flexible	Somewhat flexible	Very flexible
Overall stress	Rare stress	Some stress	Frequent stress

*Start-up cost does not include computer, printer, telephone, etc., as these are now standard in most homes.

Likely Transferable Skills, Background, Careers

This section of the profiles provides insights into who is best suited to go into this business, what kinds of background and experience are helpful, and what personal qualities are needed to succeed.

What to Charge

Knowing the ranges of what one can charge is always a tricky question for many home businesses, yet without this information it's hard to make realistic decisions about starting a particular business. This section provides price ranges from across the country, tips for how prices are typically structured, and common variations in fees among various niches and specialties in the field. All our pricing data are based on input from experts in that field or industry associations. It's important to note, however, that there is almost always variation in pricing from region to region and sometimes even within a single metropolitan area.

Best Ways to Get Business

Will I be able to get enough business? That's the number-one concern people have about any business that's attractive to them. And it seems that the more attractive the particular business is, the more concerned they are about whether it will be financially viable.

Everyone tells us word of mouth is the best way to get business, but when you're just starting out you will need other ways to get business coming in so you can then get word of mouth flowing from satisfied customers. Until then, you will need to have other ways to get the attention of your prospective clients and customers.

So in this section of the profiles we describe what experts and actual fifty-plus home-business owners tell us they have found to be the best ways to get business coming in. You will notice that some of the marketing methods are similar from business to business. This is because there are certain methods like having a Web site and networking that are vital to many businesses. But the list of marketing activities recommended for each business has been tailored to the actual methods used by those who have been successful in that business.

Marketing Insights

Because marketing is so important to success in your after-fifty business, we not only provide a list of what others have found to be the best methods; we have also gleaned key marketing insights and secrets from experts and successful fifty-plus business owners and we share them in this special section of each profile You may find this to be the most valuable information you get from this book because it's information you usually can learn only through actual experience, which can be both costly and time-consuming.

Where Next?

In this section of each profile you will find helpful books, organizations, associations, publications, training programs, and Web sites that can provide you with the information you need to take the next step when you're ready to get your business under way.

From the Home Front

This closing section of each profile features the heartfelt responses of successful fifty-plussers who share their insights into why they chose this business and their feelings about it.

The Snapshots

As you will discover, there are many variations in how people combine their skills, interests, and backgrounds into the kinds of business we profile, so in addition to our seventy business profiles you will also find forty snapshots of people who are running unique, related, or similar kinds of home businesses featured in the profiles. In the snapshots, others like you share their inspiring success stories and provide insights into how they went about creating their fifty-plus home-based careers. You'll notice that some stumbled into their business ideas. Others were responding to problems or hardships they were facing. Some were encouraged by friends and family. Still others are living long-lost dreams come true.

The snapshots also provide a peek into the broad range of ages, backgrounds, and goals of those of us who are starting fifty-plus home businesses. We found their stories inspiring, insightful, and informative and want to share them with you.

Here's to Your Success

We feel confident that this book will open your eyes to the many possibilities open to you and provide you with access to the information and tools you need to pursue them. If you have questions about how to proceed in the business of your choice or would like to consult with us, we invite you to write us at *www.workingfromhome* and would love to hear about your success story so we can share it with others.

SERVING BUSINESS CLIENTS

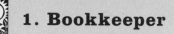

1. Bookkeeper

One thing that has remained constant from the time of ancient Babylonia to the global village of cyberspace is the need for businesses to have someone maintain the financial records of their business transactions. While accounting software has reduced the need for many smaller firms to have in-house bookkeepers, it has given rise to a need for independent bookkeepers who can do forensic work—that is, detecting and correcting problems that are inherent in or creep in with use into accounting software. Software also enables independent bookkeepers to handle more clients and broadband will soon allow home-based bookkeepers to work with their clients' records remotely, avoiding the need to physically transfer information.

"The demand for bookkeepers will remain strong, particularly among firms with fewer than five employees," says CPA Allan Bostrom of the Universal Accounting Center, because accountants are not trained to keep a set of books.

So if you're a "numbers person" who is comfortable dealing with details and can be counted on to be thorough, dependable, and accurate, and can communicate with clients, then bookkeeping can be a good source of income for you for many years.

You'll need to decide upon the scope of your services and whether you want to become certified. Some bookkeepers offer complete services; others stick to accounts receivable, accounts payable, auditing, or payroll. Some limit their payroll services to being an intermediary between their clients and payroll services. Still others combine bookkeeping with preparing tax returns for their clients.

Unlike accountants, bookkeepers do not need a professional license. But you can become certified, which may boost your confidence and be a meaningful credential for referral sources. Stephen Sahlein of the American Institute of Professional Bookkeepers, an organization that certifies bookkeepers, reports a recent instance that reflects the growing esteem of certified bookkeepers. An accounting firm added the name of one of their bookkeepers to the name of their firm upon his certification.

While bookkeeping can still be done using a ten-key calculator, we advise using a computer capable of handling a recent version of software like *Quickbooks* or *Peachtree*.

Bookkeeping at a Glance

📚 50% 🤝 50%

🪑 🌐 🗺 📦 👨‍👩‍👧‍👦 🌙 🧑‍🦽 🏠

	Minimal	Moderate	More than most
Start-up cost		X	
Overhead	X		
Potential earnings		X	
Computer skills required			X
Deadline pressures		X	
Flexible hours		X	
Overall stress		X	

Likely Transferable Skills, Background, Careers

Along with a good sense for math, many roles in a corporate setting can serve as a background for this business, i.e., working in accounting or financial record keeping or having administrative responsibilities involving any kind of number processing.

What to Charge

Most independent bookkeepers charge by the hour with fees ranging between $25 and $40 an hour. Some charge below $15, and a few can command more than $60 an hour depending on locale and the industries they work in. Some charge by the job or transaction—checks, invoices, deposits, purchases. Many bookkeepers find clients prefer being billed on a monthly or weekly basis. When using a flat weekly or monthly rate, be sure to have a letter of engagement that defines what you will be doing and when you will be charging for extra work.

Best Ways to Get Business:

- Networking face-to-face inside business and trade organizations such as the chamber of commerce and business referral organizations.

- Obtaining referrals and doing overload from CPA firms, other bookkeeping firms, and financial planners.

- Getting listed as a support service in referral services that professional associations maintain for their members.

- Having your own Web site with meta tags that identify your community so people using a search engine will find your site.

- Calling on retail stores and services within a twenty- to thirty-minute drive of your home.

- Listing in the Yellow Pages, which will enable you to be found on Web directories like *switchboard.com* and *anywho.com*. Consider placing ads on local directory sites like *Yahoo Get Local* and *SuperPages*.

Marketing Insights

- The key benefits you offer clients are providing a higher skill level than they can afford to employ and retain. By using your services they can spend more time serving customers and doing marketing, thus improving their focus and reducing their overall cost. As management guru Tom Peters advises business owners, "Do what you do best and outsource the rest."

- Your most likely clients are firms with five or fewer employees or with no employees other than the owner. Steven Kleinberg of Stoughton, Massachusetts, says, "Focusing on small businesses who cannot afford to have a bookkeeper on staff and are too busy doing business to do bookkeeping themselves will guarantee a steady flow of clients."

- Your age is an asset because keeping the books involves trust. Lurking in every business owner's consciousness are horror stories of employees running off with their companies' money. Kleinberg, who began his bookkeeping at fifty and has since brought his son into his practice, finds, "I am respected for my maturity and experience, something many of my younger clients must feel they lack."

- Times when larger firms are most apt to consider outsourcing their bookkeeping are when they are under financial pressure, relocating, or making significant personnel changes.

- You can specialize your practice to work with law firms, medical practices, construction companies, or any other industry well represented in your area. You can also specialize in doing forensic work.

Where Next?

- *How to Open Your Own In-Home Bookkeeping Service,* Julie A. Mucha. Available both in print and as an e-book: (619) 449-0675; *www.inhomebookkeeping.bizland.com.*

- Universal Accounting Center sells a video home-study bookkeeping and accounting course; *www.universalaccounting.com:* (800) 343-4827. The company provides a related site, *www.accounting-and-bookkeeping-tips.com,* which offers content, a message board, and a free newsletter.

- Over 150 links to free tax and accounting information: *www.aipb.org/accounting_bookkeeping_tax_links.php.*

TRAINING

- The American Institute of Professional Bookkeepers; *www.aipb.com;* (800) 622-0121. Offers certification exam, training materials, a telephone hot line, and a chat room/listserv that is open to nonmembers where a wide range of topics is discussed such as 1099 consulting, Canadian construction accounts, merchant account fees, and tracking a food-products inventory.

- The Sleeter Group trains in *QuickBooks* and *NetLedger* accounting software and maintains a database of bookkeepers on its site: *www.sleeter.com;* (888) 484-5484.

- The U.S. Department of Agriculture Graduate School offers distance learning courses in accounting: *http://grad.usda.gov;* (888) 744-4723.

- Many community colleges offer courses in accounting and a growing number of colleges offer distance learning programs.

Franchise

CFO *Today:* (888) 643-1348, (850) 681-1941; *www.cftoday.com.*

From the Home Front

Lynn Moran, of Livonia, New York, concluded, "There was no safety in corporate employment; the only safety was going to be in me," so she decided to be what she calls an "outsourced bookkeeper." In answer to the question "How long can you see yourself doing outsourced bookkeeping," Lynn, fifty, answered, "At least twenty years."

---

2. Consultant

You've spent twenty or more years in your field. Now either you're ready to go out on your own or changes in the economy are threatening the security of your job and your future. Can you package the experience and expertise you've acquired into a satisfying consulting practice? If you are a more-than-average performer in your field, the answer is probably yes.

Even if your industry is in decline, you may still be able to transfer your skills to consulting in another industry. For example, when Donna Blitzinger, a marketing veteran in the telecommunications industry, was laid off in the technology implosion of 2001, she was able to transfer her expertise into a successful consulting practice helping small businesses with their marketing campaigns.

Organizations and individuals engage consultants to help them accomplish goals and solve problems of all kinds. Consultants can specialize in hundreds and probably thousands of ways. The Institute of Management Consulting recognizes 279 types of management consultants. In addition to computer, engineering, and marketing consultants, there are consultants for industries such as aerospace, aviation, and agriculture; consultants for particular tasks like employee benefit planning, energy management, lighting, and security; consultants for special needs like charter schools and curriculum development; and consultants for rendering personal services like color and image consulting, health and fitness consulting, and wedding planning.

But what does it take to be a successful consultant? We asked Bill Mooney, who has taught and coached people entering this field for many years. Bill says consultants need both expertise and experience. He defines expertise as what you know and how to apply it. This is your knowledge base, but "it's not enough to get you hired," he explains "unless you've been employed as a university professor or researcher—in which case you may be hired by a company to do a 'brain dump.'" But most consultants are more than brains-for-hire. Increasingly consultants are called upon to implement what they recommend or whatever aspects of a project the staff decides to outsource to them.

That's where experience, the second prerequisite, comes in. "Experience allows you to respond to every prospective client's universal concern," says Mooney, "that you've solved problems like theirs before." So think of experience as a track record in using one's expertise to solve problems and in the process add value to a client's organization. Because of an increased emphasis on bottom-line results, adding value has become the measure of experience

If you've worked for one organization doing much the same thing over a long period of time, making yourself marketable as a consultant may mean volunteering to non-profit organizations in order to add breadth to your track record.

In addition to expertise and experience, every consultant must have first-rate communication and people skills to understand the human aspects that are part of every organizational problem. Consultants also need to be able to write clearly and present themselves and their findings to senior executives and managers. These skills are equally important in providing consulting to individuals.

Consulting at a Glance

 25% 75%

	Minimal	Moderate	More than most
Start-up cost		X	
Overhead		X	
Potential earnings			X
Computer skills required		X	
Deadlines pressures			X
Flexible hours			X
Overall stress		Less than employment in most industries	

Likely Transferable Skills, Background, Careers

Consulting is one business where the experience you bring is at the heart of the business. You may also be able to relate your expertise to emerging technologies and newly enacted regulations and laws, providing assistance with implementation and training.

What to Charge

Consultants usually bill either by the hour or the project. Hourly rates vary with the type of client, your field, and, of course, location. For small businesses and highly competitive fields, billing $75 to $150 an hour is common. For larger companies or specialties that are in high demand, expect to bill $150 and more. Experienced consultants are able to safely estimate the number of hours a project will require and can quote a project price, which is usually preferred over hourly rates by smaller businesses.

Best Ways to Get Business

- "Mine your past," says Bill Mooney. Make contact and meet with past employers and colleagues; invite their feedback on your plans for consulting. Mooney urges his clients not to do any typical marketing until they've fully explored the possibilities for work and/or referrals with people who already know them and what they can do.

- Face-to-face networking in organizations and groups. Consider participating in two types of organizations: (1) those whose memberships include potential clients and referral sources, such as industry and trade groups; (2) those such as professional associations, whose memberships include people in your own field with whom you may collaborate with in various ways—mutual-referral arrangements, cross-promotions, joint ventures, independent alliances, satellite subcontracting , consortiums, partnerships, and virtual organizations. We describe these types of affiliation in *Teaming Up: The Small Business Guide to Collaborating with Others.* Many people find that concentrating on only two organizations works best.

- If you're willing to bid your services at prices less than what you would charge a local client, check out Web sites like *elance.com, guru.com,* and *expertmarketplace.com* where buyers seeking services look for providers to bid on their projects.

- If you have a research and writing bent, "informational inquiries" can give you an opportunity to learn about a company or organization and form a relationship within the organization. Arrange for an interview with prospective clients for an article you will write on a subject of interest to them and your field. Ask non-threatening questions about whatever business or management problem you are researching. If your questions ring true, such interviews may lead to discussions of how you might work with them.

- Make sure your Web site highlights and confirms your credentials and value.

Marketing Insights:

- Because referrals and repeat business are going to be the most important sources of new business, you will need to consistently and continually nurture repeat and referral business. This means finding gateways into the awareness of key contacts. Having a regular newsletter or e-zine may accomplish this with some, but get filtered out by others. With the wholesale transition of most communication to e-mail, faxes and telephone calls get noticed when just a few years ago they wouldn't have. However, before using faxes to stay in touch, familiarize yourself with the requirements for having signed, written consent prior to transmitting any unsolicited faxes that are "commercial" in nature. If the gatekeepers who are important to your business predictably go to professional meetings or play golf, these will be the venues where you can best maintain contacts with them.

- As a consultant, you will be most valued for your clarity, including the ability to listen and translate what you hear and observe without wasting your client's time.

- If large corporations resist retaining you because they have a policy against hiring individuals whose income requires reporting on a Form 1099, consider affiliating with a group like SOHO Resources Group that acts as an intermediary.

- Because many people equate wisdom with age and it takes time to accumulate the experience and expertise you offer, your age should not be a barrier to most types of consulting. In fact, it can be a plus. Nonetheless, you will probably find it easier to get work from clients who are forty-plus.

Where Next?

ASSOCIATIONS OFFERING CERTIFICATION

- The Institute of Electrical and Electronics Engineers (IEEE) Consultants' Services: *www.ieeeusa.org/BUSINESS*.

- Institute of Management Consultants (IMC): (800) 221-2557; *www.imcusa.org*.

BOOKS

- *Consulting for Dummies,* Bob Nelson and Peter Economy (For Dummies, 1997). ISBN: 0764550349.

- *High-Impact Consulting,* Robert H. Schaffer (Jossey-Bass, 2002). ISBN: 0787960497.

- *How to Become a Successful Consultant in Your Own Field,* Hubert Bermont (Crown, 1997). ISBN: 0761511008.

- *Million Dollar Consulting,* Alan Weiss, Ph.D. (McGraw-Hill, 2002). ISBN: 007138703X. Other books by Alan Weiss include *Getting Started in Consulting* and

- *How to Establish a Unique Brand in the Consulting Profession.*

- *The Consultant's Toolkit: High-Impact Questionnaires, Activities and How-to Guides for Diagnosing and Solving Client Problems,* Mel Silberman (McGraw-Hill Trade, 2000). ISBN: 0071362614.

TRAINING

- How to Build & Maintain a Profitable Consulting Practice seminar, William Mooney Associates: (310) 324-2386; *www.consultantcoach.com.*

WEB SITE

- Consulting Central Web portal: *www.consultingcentral.com.*

From the Home Front

Peter Fulton of Los Angeles has developed a consulting practice specializing in marketing to fifty-plussers, and he's enthusiastic about his work, "I absolutely love what I do," he says. "I'm seventy years old and will do this until they carry me out of here."

Snapshot: Donna Blitzinger, Marketing Consultant

When Donna Blitzinger of Berkeley, California, was in her twenties, she said she wanted to run her own business someday. It wasn't until fifty-plus, though, that losing her corporate job became the impetus to actually pursue that lifelong goal. At first Donna began sending out résumés hoping to land another job, but when she found no one was hiring at her salary level in her area of expertise, she decided to forget the job search and create her own marketing consulting company, Dyer Stephenson.

Donna's expertise was in telecommunications, but that industry had suffered from the technology collapse of the late nineties, so she realized that she would have to re-create herself to serve a new industry. To succeed in her business, she drew on her knowledge and skills instead of the years of industry experience gained on the job.

One year later, she was living her youthful dream. She had paying clients and a plan for how to grow. Her advice: "Believe in yourself. You've learned a lot more over the years than you realize. So call on what you know and what you do best and make sure it's something you love to do."

Snapshot: Dr. James Hodges, Leadership by George!

James Hodges of Bellaire, Texas, has been a lifelong student of George Washington, but at age sixty-four he decided to *become* George Washington. James makes appearances and speaks as our first president. "I dress as George and I speak as George," he explains, right down to wearing an exact authentic replica of the buff-and-blue army uniform Washington wore throughout the war, complete with a black, tricornered hat, boots, and sword.

At six foot six, James bears a remarkable resemblance to the founding father who was six foot four. Like Washington, he has pure white hair and has let it grow out so that he can pull it back into a four-inch queue and tie it with a ribbon just as Washington did. He so resembles Washington that young audiences will sometimes whisper among themselves incredulously that they thought George Washington was dead, and people of all ages readily refer to him as George when they engage him in conversation.

James's clients include schools, business groups, clubs, and societies, both patriotic and historical. He doesn't use notes, a podium, or anything else that might make his presentations seem staged. "I never give the same speech twice," he adds, "I tailor my remarks to the particular group I'm addressing."

James can speak easily as Washington because, having read over a hundred books about our first presidents, he says, "I know almost every detail of George Washington's life." He recounts compelling stories and anecdotes that illustrate leadership skills and how Washington's ethical principles enabled him to lead in the creation of our country, and he helps the audience use these principles to improve their own leadership effectiveness.

Topics of his presentations include character, virtue, communication, vision, honesty, creating leaders, trust, spirituality, integrity, team building, and responsibility. James has also written a book on George Washington's ethical leadership style.

James hasn't quit his day job as a CFP (certified financial planner) wealth adviser with a major Wall Street firm but says, "This new business is keeping me young. I never felt more alive than now. My mission is to bring George back to life, with his inspiring messages of living life to the fullest. For Washington, and for me, this means helping others get what they want."

 ## 3. Desktop Publisher

An eye for layout, a creative feel for design and typography, a penchant for problem solving, along with proficiency in using desktop illustration and layout software are the essential ingredients of a home-based desktop publishing business. With these, a desktop publisher turns clients' intentions into multiple kinds of print and electronic documents, such as handsome catalogues, manuals, directories, brochures, and résumés that are ready to be posted on the Web or to go to the printer. For each publication, desktop publishers produce a design, lay out the pages, format the text, and add images.

The Bureau of Labor Statistics declares desktop publishing to be one of the fastest-growing vocations, forecasting the number of desktop publishers to grow from 38,000 in 2000 to 63,000 in 2010, an increase of 67 percent.

While most of this growing number of desktop publishers will not be self-employed, solo desktop publishers who add value to their service in the form of being able to edit the clients' words, focus their message, or even write copy for them have an edge over what a Kinko's or many in-house support personnel can provide.

Desktop Publishing at a Glance

 70% 30%

	Minimal	Moderate	More than most
Start-up cost		X	
Overhead		X	
Potential earnings		X	
Computer skills required			X
Deadline pressures			X
Flexible hours			X
Overall stress			X

Likely Transferable Skills, Background, Careers

Graphic design, Web site design, writing, and the production side of publishing.

What to Charge

Desktop publishers charge by the hour, by the page, or by the job. Sometimes they vary their method of pricing depending on the client and the job. Hourly rates vary between $15 and $75. Page rates, appropriate for shorter publications like newsletters, are between $25 and $50, but some desktop publishers are bidding jobs on *elance.com* at $2 to $4 a page. Pricing by the job accommodates clients who prefer to pay a fixed price. Here are some sites on the Web that provide pricing information:

- Brenner Books conducts national surveys and posts hourly rate ranges by state at *www.brennerbooks.com*.

- The Editorial Freelancers Association posts rates as reported by members at *http://www.the-efa.org/services/jobfees.htm*.

Best Ways to Get Business

- Specializing in an industry or an interest group. At the age of fifty-one Helen Garfinkle moved from New York to Tucson and began her desktop publishing business. While she tried multiple approaches to developing clients, what she found worked best was volunteering to do the desktop publishing chores for an environmental group. Satisfied with her work, a member proposed paying her. With that organization as a client and work she got through other members she met there, her business was under way.

- Getting listed in referral services that professional associations maintain for their members.

- Exploring possibilities for work from companies and nonprofit organizations you know by contacting them and showing them samples of your work.

- Participating in a business-referral organization in your community where members refer business to one another. If your community is large enough, network in publishing-related organizations.

- Bidding on local, state, and federal government work. School districts also use desktop publishing services.

- Bidding for work on *elance.com* and *guru.com*. However, because of highly competitive bidding, you will probably have to reduce your fees in order to win against competitors.

- Getting listed in on-line directories, such as that of the Editorial Freelancers Association, *www.the-efa.org*; (866) 929-5400.

Marketing Insights

- Kinko's and other chains like Alphagraphics and Insty-Prints are listed in most communities under "Publishing—Desktop" in virtually every telephone directory, both on line and in print. They charge about $50 an hour. Whether you underprice them or not, you will have an edge on them if you offer copyediting and proofreading as well as expert consultation on design choices, because these stores only provide layout services.

- The key benefit you offer to clients is producing top-quality work on time. The more editorial skill you have to make the document you produce both read and look good, the more apt you are to be able to attract and keep clients.

- Local small-business clients may require more hand-holding, that is, time you spend talking with them to define what they need. Your willingness and ability to provide this person-to-person support and encouragement will be one of your strongest advantages over the chain stores.

Where Next?

BOOKS

Dozens of books have been written about how to do desktop publishing, including a number by designer and writer Chuck Green. An extensive collection of books on desktop publishing is available at *www.desktoppublishing. com/bookstore*. One book that focuses on starting a business at home is Louise Kursmark, *How to Open and Operate a Home-Based Desktop Publishing Business* (Globe Pequot Press, 2002). ISBN: 0762722509.

WEB SITES

- A portal for desktop publishing along with forums: *www.desktoppublishing.com/open.html*.

- DesktopPublishers, an outgrowth of the now defunct Desktop Publishing Journal: *www.desktoppublishers.com*.

- Author Chuck Green's large list of links for designers and marketers: *www.jumpola.com*.

- The Open Directory project's listings: *http://dmoz.org/Computers/ Desktop_Publishing*.

TRAINING AND CERTIFICATION

- Courses on how to use desktop publishing software and related drawing, photo editing, and Web-page design programs are taught widely at community colleges; computer, trade, and art schools; and in continuing-education programs. Many of these programs issue certificates.

- Courses in how to use major desktop software programs are provided, sometimes free, by the companies making these products:

  - Adobe: *www.adobe.com/misc/training.html.*

  - QuarkXPress: *www.quark.com* or (800) 676-4575.

From the Homefront:

In answer to the question "Can you see yourself doing this in five years?" Helen Garfinkle, now fifty-eight, replied "I'll do this as long as I can see and clients hire me."

 ## 4. Editing and Other Editorial Services

If you're reading this particular profile, chances are you enjoy the written word and if you'd like to participate in the publishing world, doing editing or one of the other editorial services, like indexing or proofreading, can be a rewarding after-fifty career. Thanks to the Internet, you will find few home-based businesses with greater flexibility for when and where you can do your work than editorial services. You can work with clients from virtually anywhere, as long as you have Internet access. You can even do your work while traveling.

The kind of editorial work you can do also varies widely. As Hilary Powers, a freelance editor in Oakland, tells us, "What I do falls into every editorial category depending on the requirements of the job and what the client is willing to pay for." From proofreading to indexing, editors, particularly those with some background in the publishing industry, can provide one or all of the following editing services:

- Project editing: managing the editing process. Project editors co-ordinate the writing process for a book or other type of publication from beginning to end: hiring the other types of editors and other editorial specialties needed to produce the work. While this type of editing is typically an in-house staff function, some publishers and organizations are also contracting for editorial project management.

- Developmental editing: working one-on-one with their clients, usually authors, to develop or rework initial concepts into a logical, well-organized manuscript. These editors may help an author plan the sequence of chapters or sections, develop ideas for supplemental content, do research, shape and sometimes even rewrite portions of a project. Heavy substantive copyediting, however, is often done by the next kind of editor.

- Line editing: substantive editors, rewriting actual lines of copy. These editors may be hired when an author or publisher wants a project to be completed but knows it needs substantial reworking.

- Copyediting: done after a manuscript is considered complete and is being prepared for publication. Copy editors check facts, make corrections and style improvements, reword to correct grammar or improve clarity, and double-check for consistency and cross-references.

- Proofreading: reading manuscripts word for word after the book has been printed in galley form, comparing the copyedited manuscript to the galley to make certain changes have been made correctly. Proofreaders check for typos, misspellings, incorrect punctuation, and mistakes in word usage and such. Self-published authors need to use proofreaders, and commercially published authors may also hire proofreaders, now that some publishers have reduced the amount of editorial attention invested in manuscripts.

- Indexing: creating the alphabetical lists at the back of nonfiction and professional books and reference materials as well as for Web sites. Indexing for the Web is a growing specialty, and arguably more challenging than back-of-the-book indexes typical in most nonfiction books. Of the editorial services described in this profile, indexing is the most specialized and demands a different set of skills than other aspects of editing. The indexer needs to have a feel for how readers look for information and what topics and words they will most likely want to look up.

If you're breaking into editing as a new career without publishing experience, copyediting and proofreading are your best bets. Copy editors should be prepared to pass a screening test when seeking to contract with a publishing house or large organization.

Editors may further specialize their service a number of ways:

- The type of clients they serve: general and textbook book publishers, university presses, book packagers, government agencies and nonprofit organizations, advertising agencies, and law firms.

- The type of content they work on: fiction, nonfiction, translated materials, art, business/financial, children's, education, cookbooks, health, etc.

Editing at a Glance

75%   25%

	Minimal	Moderate	More than most
Start-up cost	X		
Overhead	X		
Potential earnings		X	
Computer skills required		X	
Deadline pressures			X
Flexible hours			X
Overall stress		X	

Likely Transferable Skills, Background, Careers

Many people who have worked in education, corporations, and governmental agencies must develop editorial capabilities in the process of what they do, and for some, editing just becomes a habit. So even if you've never worked in the publishing industry, if you're one of those people who automatically edits whatever you're reading, you may be well suited to this career.

What to Charge

Editors differ in whether they charge by the hour, by the project, or by the page. Often clients prefer flat-rate pricing by the project. But some editors believe you "get burned" with a flat rate. Others prefer charging by the project. The more experienced you are at knowing how long a project will take, the better able you will be to quote a flat fee that's based on an accurate assessment of what a given project will involve, in which case a flat rate price can be more profitable for you if you're able to work both quickly and accurately and the client does not present difficulty.

- Here are representative rates:

    - Project editing: $40 to $65 an hour.

    - Developmental editing: $30 to $65 an hour.

    - Line editing: $30 to $100 an hour.

    - Copyediting: $20 to $60 an hour.

    - Proofreading: $20 to $35 an hour.

    - Indexing: $3 to $12 per page or $25 to $60 an hour. (Indexing lends itself to a per-page rate.)

- Factors that influence what you can charge include special expertise you have, the industry you're in, the complexity and particular demands of the job, and turnaround time needed.

- The Editorial Freelancers Association posts rates as reported by members at *http://www.the-efa.org/services/jobfees.htm*.

Best Ways to Get Business

- For working with publishing houses, companies, and agencies, making personal contact with the person in charge of hiring freelancers. Begin by contacting them in writing, describing what you do, relating it as closely as possible to what they publish. Then follow up, usually by phone.

- Maintaining your own Web site; consider it your electronic brochure. One way to increase traffic to your site is to get listed in directories on sites like *www.writers.net*.

- Face-to-face networking in organizations related to the industry or profession you specialize in or the kind of customers you are targeting.

- Getting listed in referral services that professional associations maintain for their members.

- Bidding for work on Web sites that post projects for freelancers, such as *elance.com, guru.com, www.the-efa.org, and www.freelanceonline.com.*

Marketing Insights

- Freelance opportunities for editors are expanding because of the increasing numbers of self-published authors and Web sites that constantly need new content. Also since 9/11, many publishing houses and magazines have reduced staff, so editing has become more of a freelance industry.

- Two or three publishers or other major clients who have steady work can be enough to keep you busy. Once you get work with one organization, if your work is valued, word-of-mouth referrals can help attract additional clients.

- As outsourcing grows, developing and maintaining contacts with others in the editing field is an increasingly important source of referrals.

- Henry Krawitz, who specializes in editing for academic presses, says the key benefits you offer your clients are reliability and dependability. "It's not enough just to deliver your work on time," he advises. "Clients expect a quality piece of work that doesn't require additional cleaning up."

Where Next?

BOOKS AND NEWSLETTERS

- *The Copy Editor's Handbook: A Guide for Book Publishing and Corporate Communications,* Amy Einsohn (University of California Press, 2000). ISBN: 0520218353.

- *Copy Editor:* (888) 626-8779, *www.mcmurry.com.*

- Check out the publications published by the professional associations below.

ORGANIZATIONS AND RESOURCES ON THE WEB

- American Society of Indexers: (303) 463-2887; *www.asindexing. org.* This site has information on indexing, a list of publications on the indexing business, and a list of local chapters.

- The Association of Art Editors: (952) 922-1374; *www.artedit.org.*

- Editorial Freelancers Association: *www.the-efa.org;* (866) 929-5400. This site includes a listserv, information on health insurance, a job list, and publications.

- *Editorium.com.* Since most editing is being done by computer now, the add-ons for Microsoft available on this site can make the editor's life easier. Society for Technical Communication, *www.stc-va.org.* This site has Special Interest Groups (SIGs) for technical editors and indexers.

- This listserv discussion group of freelancers in the publishing industry, *http://peach.ease.lsoft.com/archives/freelance.html,* includes archives of resources for editors dating from 1998.

TRAINING

- Distance education courses in editing, proofreading, and indexing are available from the United States Department of Agriculture's Graduate School: (202) 314-3670; *http://grad.usda.gov.*

- Classroom courses as well as an increasing number of distance education programs are available from community colleges and university journalism departments.

From the Home Front

Hilary Powers, who started her freelance editing career almost a decade ago at age fifty, sagely advises: "If you're going to survive as a freelance business, you have to free yourself of the idea you're the last defender of the English language." She adds, however, that she thoroughly enjoys what she does. "As long as I don't succumb to repetitive stress injuries or Alzheimer's, I don't see myself ever stopping. In this business I can control the work flow by just saying 'no' to a few more projects."

 ## 5. Information Broker

Information brokers are also called information professionals, desktop on-line searchers, and information retrievers. Under these varied names, they fulfill a need that thousands of companies and organizations of all types and sizes have today: to obtain and analyze huge amounts of information. Like investigative reporters or market researchers, practitioners of this art track down and locate many types of specific information, including:

- Background research for business plans or grant proposals.

- Information pertaining to new product designs or concepts.

- Patent searches.

- Competitive information about companies producing related products.

- Information and analysis related to pricing.

- Market demographics

- And more.

Large corporations usually have in-house libraries and researchers on staff, but they often hire information brokers for special projects or to handle overload work. Most businesses, however, don't have in-house research capabilities and need to hire information professionals from time to time in fields such as science, technology, health care, and banking. Other types of work that information brokers frequently perform include:

- Researching for advertising, marketing, and PR agencies who need help preparing business proposals or creating an advertising or marketing campaign.

- Tracking down information for lawyers preparing for a trial such as determining if a product has a history of defects in a product-liability case.

- Assisting management consultants who are working on complex business projects.

- Doing background research for corporations contemplating a merger or acquisition.

- Working for private investigators who are involved in civil or criminal cases.

Given how valuable information is in the world today, there is in fact no limit to the variety of clients you might have and the types of questions they might need answered.

Information brokers do their research work in several ways, including:

- Interviewing people in person or by telephone.

- Going to libraries and city halls to research books and public records.

- Searching on the Internet.

The Web, of course, has greatly altered this profession because it provides access to billions of pages of information. However, professional information brokers also need to use one or more of the seven thousand specialized computer databases accessed via the Internet that are available only by subscription, such as Dialog, LEXIS, NEXIS, and Westlaw. These databases contain abstracts, or the full text articles, from thousands of publications around the world, including newspapers, magazines, newsletters, professional journals, and books, thus making it possible to find just about any news item or research result within seconds rather than days or weeks.

Increasingly, clients want information brokers to do more than simply find information. Jane John, who began her company, On Point Research, in Brunswick, Maine, at age fifty, comments that "the field is going more toward value-added services. Clients want more and more analysis, not just a list of sources or a data dump. Most clients have already done some information gathering on their own; they've already looked on the Web, and now they're looking for us to provide a complete solution, including organizing large amounts of information." Jane specializes in gathering, filtering, and analyzing information for technology-focused companies, as well as having a second line of business working with Maine entrepreneurs who need help doing market research.

Marcy Phelps of Phelps Research in Denver, Colorado, and Debbie Bardon of Bardon On Call Research in Oakland, California, also entered the information search business after other careers. Marcy began her business at age fifty after working in information-related aspects of health care. She is often hired to do research for marketing and business plans related to launching new products, or for investigating the competitors and trends in a client's field.

Debbie Bardon says she fell into the field when her neighbor started an information-brokering business and needed help with phone interviews. Debbie's background in sales and marketing made her the perfect candidate, and after a few years, her neighbor retired and Debbie took over the business. She gets most of her work from other information brokers who subcontract with her to do marketing-research-related projects.

As these three people exemplify, information professionals frequently find themselves specializing more and more in certain types of research. Some may focus on marketing, business plans, or patents, while others work in researching the environment, pharmaceuticals, or biomedical engineering. Specializing has several advantages: You develop a reputation for high-quality work in that area and can become more proficient at your research. This increases your chances of obtaining successful results at a lower cost, which is what clients want. Specializing does not mean turning down all unrelated work, but it does mean presenting a coherent image and focusing your marketing effort on your niche.

The opportunity to do intellectually challenging work appeals to many people, and the information profession is one that demands constant problem solving and curiosity. If this is your penchant, you may find a satisfying career in this evolving field.

Information Brokering at a Glance

 50% 50%

	Minimal	Moderate	More than most
Start-up cost			
Overhead			Subscriptions to databases
Potential earnings		X	
Computer skills required			X
Deadline pressures			X
Flexible hours		X	
Overall stress		X	

Likely Transferable Skills, Background, Careers

Once the special calling of librarians, information professionals now come from many careers, though it helps to have a background in the area of research you want to specialize in, such as law, medicine, chemistry, engineering, journalism, or sales and marketing. Whatever your prior career, you need to be highly detailed oriented and you must revel in the "chase" to find complete and accurate answers. Mistakes are costly. Speed-reading skills also help since you often need to read quickly and skim huge amounts of data.

What to Charge

Information professionals typically charge by the hour, averaging about $85 per hour, although experienced professionals may earn as much as $200 or more per hour. Expenses such as charges for on-line databases and printed copies of articles are either billed at cost or the bill is marked up by 15 to 20 percent.

Best Ways to Get Business

- Advertising in trade journals if you are in a specialty field.

- Collaborating with consultants and other information professionals to subcontract for specialized work or take on work that others cannot handle because of their being overloaded.

- Getting listed as a support service for members of professional associations in the industry whose members you are targeting as clients.

- Getting media publicity about your business and/or novel information searches you have done (with the approval of your client, of course).

- Having your own Web site with testimonial letters and articles you have written along with a toll-free number makes you accessible to clients anywhere in the world.

- Networking and making personal contacts in companies and organizations such as chambers of commerce and trade associations and professional organizations, particularly in industries or fields in which you have experience.

- Speaking and offering seminars on information research at meetings and trade shows.

- Writing articles for magazines or newspapers or starting your own newsletter.

Marketing Insights

- Many clients think they can find everything they need on the Internet, so you need to educate people that there's more available out there that a specialist such as you know how to find. Iuliana Pop, of ICAR Consulting, suggests that you offer to do a free search on some topic a potential client has already researched to demonstrate how much more data you can provide them than they can find.

- Clients often need information quickly at any time, thus you need to be flexible in your work hours and could find yourself offering virtually 24/7 service.

- The sheer quantity of information in the world doubles every seven years or less, so keeping up with your field will cut into both your research and marketing time.

Where Next?

ASSOCIATIONS

- Association of Independent Information Professionals: (225) 408-4400; *www.aiip.org*.

- Society of Competitive Intelligence Professionals: (703) 739-0696; *www.scip.org*.

- Special Libraries Association: (202) 234-4700; *www.sla.org*.

BOOKS

- *Building & Running a Successful Research Business,* Mary Ellen Bates and Reva Basch (Cyberage Books, 2003). ISBN: 0910965625.

- *The Invisible Web: Uncovering Information Sources Search Engines Can't See,* Chris Sherman and Gary Price (Independent Publishers Group, 2001). ISBN: 091096551X.

- *Super Searchers on Competitive Intelligence,* Margaret Metcalf Carr, Reva Basch, and Jan P. Herring (Cyberage Books, 2003). ISBN: 0910965641.

- *Super Searchers Make It On Their Own,* Suzanne Sabroski and Reva Basch (Cyberage Books, 2002), ISBN: 0910965595.

MAGAZINES AND NEWSLETTERS

- Information Today, Inc., publishes a number of magazines and newsletters, including a number that were previously independently published: (609) 654-6266; *www.onlineinc.com*.

TRAINING

- Amelia Kassel offers various training programs: (800) 544-5924, (707) 829-9421; *www.marketingbase.com*.

- Many colleges and universities of library science have courses on information searching open to outside students. Information Professionals Institute: (972) 732-0160, offers seminars with industry leaders: *www.burwellinc.com*.

From the Home Front:

"I was originally looking for a part-time second career, and now I love doing this exclusively. I never turn down work, and sometimes I work more than forty hours a week. If I wanted to do even more, I know I could. I don't see any reason to stop as long as I can do this from my home. I recently brought my sister into the business, and she's a doctor of molecular biology."

—Debbie Bardon, 57

 ## 6. Interim or Contract Executive

If you have prior experience as a CEO, COO, CFO, management executive, engineer, IT (information technology) professional, or a work history in other leadership roles, your next job may literally be right around the corner. Thousands of companies are seeking out "interim," "contract," or "short-term" executives. Often hired for one to three years on a part-time or sometimes full-time basis, such executives are in demand for their expertise and experience. They may be hired to:

- Bring new creativity and innovation into a company.

- Get stalled new projects off the ground.

- Act as additional manpower during unexpected surges in business.

- Realign corporate strategy.

- Bring costs under control.

- Contribute to unsolved technical problems.

- Teach in-house people a technology or expertise they don't have.

In the past, retired executives and professionals were often sidelined because corporations believed the "old folks" were not able to keep up with changing technologies or new business strategies. However, more and more organizations are recognizing that today's older workers have valuable skills to offer and often understand the leading edge of technologies better than many of their current employees.

The "interim executive" role has been more fully developed in the United Kingdom, according to Bill Vick, co-director of PhoenixLink, a talent management site and service: "In the U.S., people are more apt to think of themselves as a contractor or a consultant, but it's different," says Vick, in that as a contract executive you are far more involved and vested in the outcomes than a typical consultant.

Rick Lewis, an interim executive in Memphis, points out that while consultants come in and tell companies what to do and then depart, the interim executive stays on the job and completes the execution of the plans. Rick has had contract positions lasting from six months to three years. He advises that the best opportunities are with companies with revenues of $20 million or less, because "they're struggling to do battle with the big guys."

Marketing yourself in this area can actually be quite easy, because there are numerous employment agencies focused on representing former executives, technical experts, and marketing and financial gurus. In fact, Procter & Gamble Co. and Eli Lilly & Co. launched a job-placement firm matching retired scientists and engineers with companies in search of their know-how. The company, YourEncore Inc., was created to sign up thousands of retirees interested in working on short-term projects, with a focus on research and development. The company's motto is the catchy phrase "People don't retire anymore; they just go on to do other things."

But you don't need to go through an agency to get work in this field. You can also market yourself by networking extensively with executives and companies in your area, and by building your own Web site describing your talents and offering testimonials about the quality of your work. For example, Robert Goodman runs CEO Resource out of his home in Clearwater, Florida. He works at the CEO level, "slaying those dragons," as he puts it, that some CEOs simply don't want to handle or don't have the experience to handle. He has done this since 1986, working with clients in a wide variety of industries both in the USA and abroad. His Web site offers "quizzes" for companies to assess themselves and determine if they need him.

Goodman notes that many people over fifty are starting businesses, but they don't have experience in certain strategic areas, which is why they need to hire him. He finds that many CEOs are simply overwhelmed. "There're only twenty-four hours in a day but they need thirty. Since they can't afford a full-time COO, they come to me."

After a long career with Brunswick at its Chicago headquarters, C. Robert Ledbetter began doing contract work at age fifty-seven, working with smaller companies that need to establish policies and procedures in the human resources area. During the time he works for a company, he becomes the HR department. He finds it's possible to hold two and sometimes more positions at the same time.

Though some interim executives over the age of fifty use this path as a way to land new corporate jobs, many of them simply prefer the flexibility and variety that contract work offers. So, if you will be satisfied helping a company for a few months to a few years without the security of a golden handshake at the end of the path, this work could be your next best move.

Interim or Contract Executive at a Glance

60% 40%

	Minimal	Moderate	More than most
Start-up cost	X		
Overhead	X		
Potential earnings			X
Computer skills required		X	
Deadline pressures			X
Flexible hours		X	
Overall stress		X	

Likely Transferable Skills, Background, Careers

This work requires significant prior experience in an executive or advanced technical position. You must also have the skills to quickly understand issues and blend in with your client's culture and environment so permanent staff members don't see you as a threat or outside maverick.

What to Charge

Interim executives typically charge on a project-by-project basis, or they use a daily or monthly rate, depending on the assignment. You can typically obtain fees that are higher than your previous salary, especially if you are not receiving other employment benefits and are treated as an independent contractor or, possibly better for tax purposes, as a corporation.

Best Ways to Get Business

- Registering on employment sites like *http://www. thephoenixlink.com* and others that represent high-level executives seeking temporary contract work.

- Joining business groups such as the chamber of commerce in order to develop relationships with executives in your community to let them know about your skills and availability. In many major cities, you can also find interim executive networking groups.

- Teaching courses at community colleges that might attract start-up business owners and entrepreneurs.

- Offering to sit in on one or two meetings with a potential client to provide advice for free. You may end up proposing ideas they like but need you to handle.

Marketing Insights

Interim executives make it possible for companies and organizations to get top talent on a temporary basis while keeping their costs down.

- Robert Goodman's experience suggests it's possible to do all one's marketing via the Internet.

- A "tombstone ad" in the Yellow Pages "offers no compelling reason for anyone to do business with you and thus is of little value." Rick Lewis.

Where Next?

BOOKS

- *A New Brand of Expertise, How Independent Consultants, Free Agents, and Interim Managers are Transforming the World of Work,* Marion McGovern and Dennis Russell (Butterworth-Heinemann, 2001). ISBN: 0750672927.

- *Executive Temping,* Saralee Terry Woods (John Wiley & Sons, 1998), ISBN: 0471241571.

- *Free Agent Nation,* Daniel H. Pink (Warner Books, 2002). ISBN: 0446678791.

PLACEMENT ORGANIZATIONS

- The Phoenix Link: (972) 612-8425; *www.thephoenixlink.com.*

- Resources Connection: (714) 430-6400, *www. resourcesconnection.com.*

- YourEncore, Inc.: (317) 226-9301; *www.yourencore.com.*

From the Home Front

"As a lifestyle this business is great. I just got back from the Bahamas. If I had been working full-time, I couldn't have done that."

—Richard Lewis, fifty-four

Snapshot: Howard Parker, Greeting Card Rep

After thirty years in a successful career as a dancer/choreographer/director in New York City, Howard Parker set out for a cross-country trip and ended up in Tucson, Arizona. At fifty-three with no real retirement benefits to fall back on, he had to start bringing in some income and he had three goals for doing so: 1) be his own boss; 2) no start-up expenses; and 3) no monthly overhead.

Having started and aborted a greeting card company before leaving New York, Howard had some positive dealings with sales reps. The possibility of being an independent rep for greeting card manufactures seemed like a promising idea. The only expense would be the cost of a business card. He began contacting manufacturers from across the country and secured five small greeting card lines he could represent in Arizona.

You would think having performed on Broadway for years that walking into a store with bags of card samples to show would be a snap for Howard, but he says, "It was an entirely different matter. It scared me to death." He did it nevertheless and wound up writing eleven orders from three appointments on his first day out. Before long, other greeting card and gift manufacturers were contacting him to represent them.

Five years of success later, Howard took on an associate who expanded their business to New Mexico. Two years later, they expanded to Hawaii. Eventually Howard moved to San Diego and now travels from there to Phoenix five times a year to call on his accounts while his associate continues to handle the business in other states. His advice: "I don't think starting a business is ever easy, but if I can do it, anybody can do it!"

 ## 7. Mailing List Service

The mailing list business, like so many others, is undergoing consolidation and technological change. Your daily e-mail probably surpasses the first-class letters you receive, but your mailbox may still be crammed with direct mail—most of which comes to you from large mailing operations. In other words, as Eric Casey, Vice President of the Mailing & Fulfillment Service Association, points out, "Mailing services are now commodities." So is there anything left for a home-based mailing list service to do? We say yes.

First, according to Shelly Blake of Moonlight Mailing Service, the "do not call" ban on telemarketing has already resulted in an increase in direct-mail marketing. Looking down the road with this in mind, we doubt electronic mail will become a substitute for telemarketing because consumers have highly negative reactions to spam. We think there's a future for home-based mailing list services that will work with small businesses, professionals, and associations.

Small businesses have always been the primary customers for home-based mailing list services. and they need help in creating their own mailing lists or putting lists they already have in some form into usable database formats. They also still need help getting mailings. Doing a mailing involves adhering to a labyrinth of postal regulations, which are not always interpreted the same way; thus part of the value you can provide is to specialize in knowing the regulations and developing relationships with post office personnel so you can save money for your clients as well as improve the results of their mailings.

Let's review the three primary services a mailing list service provides:

1. Creating and maintaining a mailing list database. This service involves designing a customer's list and specifying in what format the addresses will be stored along with any other data the client wants to include. For example, let's say the client is a clothing store that already has the names of some customers stored in various nonmatching formats. You might begin by determining a standard format in which to keep the list. You might also advise them how to improve the value of their list by storing additional information about their customers such as their birth date, color preferences, and even their spouses' e-mail addresses so you can send a reminder when it's time to buy a birthday gift. Once you set up the database, you can either turn it over to your client to maintain themselves or you can offer to maintain it for them.

2. Doing mailings. Clients such as retail stores, hotels, businesses, and organizations provide you with their database and with the printed materials they want to be mailed—then it's your job to get the mailing out. You print out the labels, do all the folding, stuffing, licking, and collating. If you plan on providing this service, consider getting a machine that folds, inserts, and seals envelopes at the rate of thirty or more pieces a minute. For other than small jobs, Eric Casey recommends partnering with a printer who has the necessary equipment.

Doing mailings is actually the most complex aspect of this business. The U.S. Postal Service (USPS) has made major efforts to automate and computerize the delivery of all bulk mail, so you use software that prints bar codes, sorts, and categorizes mail following strict regulations. Mailing pieces must be sorted so that the pieces are eligible for greater discounts if they meet the USPS requirements of "saturation walk sequence," or "carrier route," or "automated walk sequence/delivery point bar code."

By following the regulations, you can perform a bulk mailing for 5 to 10 cents less for each piece than the cost of first-class postage, which adds up to a significant savings if your client mails thousands of pieces regularly.

3. Creating customized or localized mailing lists. While you won't be able to compete with large mail-list companies that sell millions of names categorized in thousands of ways, you can create your own specialized lists tailored to your city, area, or particular client needs. Large mailing houses often don't handle small requests, so a home-based business is sometimes the only chance that a small business has to purchase a list of two hundred to five hundred targeted names.

For example, some businesses want to mail only to all owner-occupied homes in a ten-square block. So you could create your own mailing list by buying print directories of residents in your city and typing the names into a database just for that area. You might create other localized lists based on public records, such as a list of new businesses in your city, new homeowners in your area, sole-practitioner chiropractors, newlyweds, and so on. You can rent out your lists to companies interested in promoting their products or services to your list and sell monthly updates. To increase the value of your lists and monthly reports, be sure to call the entries to obtain additional information that could be helpful to your clients such as: contact names, titles, whether it's male, female, and/or minority owned, as well as the number of employees a company has.

Technology is also creating opportunities for new services, such as maintaining databases for sales reps who use contact management software programs like ACT!, GoldMine, and Maximizer. Serving clients like these involves sending out scheduled follow-up mailings, faxes, and emails, which these programs make possible. Yet another type of niche service is helping large mailers keep their mailing lists up-to-date by providing a same-day change-of-address service. Getting this done so quickly is only possible because of the Internet.

Another way to generate income as a mailing list service is to consult or tutor small businesses that prefer to do their own mailings. You might teach your clients how to use mailing list software, how to comply with U.S. postal regulations, and how to use their lists to generate leads, obtain orders, or build store traffic. Clients may also ask you to locate and select the mailing lists best suited to their objectives. In such cases, you act as a broker between list sellers and list buyers.

You can perform as many or as few of these tasks as you like. A mailing list service is also a good business to combine with desktop publishing, because many businesses need help designing their flyers or brochures in addition to handling their database and doing the mailings.

Originally in the printing business, Raymond Frost began as a home-based business in the small city of Gadsden, Alabama. At the age of sixty-seven, his printing business slowed so he began providing mail services, too. He currently handles everything for his clients from designing the flyers to taking the mailings to the post office.

If you are detailed oriented, enjoy working with software, and don't mind some physical labor, a mailing list service can be a challenging but satisfying part-time or full-time business.

Mailing List Service at a Glance

 60% 40%

	Minimal	Moderate	More than most
Start-up cost		X	
Overhead		X	
Potential earnings		X	
Computer skills required			X
Deadline pressures			X
Flexible hours		X	
Overall stress		X	

Likely Transferable Skills, Background, Careers

A background doing most kinds of administrative work or perhaps having worked for the post office prepares you well to run a mailing list service. But more than a particular background is the ability to pay an enormous attention to detail, and a willingness to learn about the specific U.S. postal regulations. Being able to type accurately and to master the software needed for the services to be provided are important.

What to Charge

- For keying names into a mailing list database, 6 to 7 cents per line of input.

- For printing out labels, 3 to 5 cents per label (including the label stock).

- For printing envelopes, 10 to 12 cents per envelope printed.

- Purging a list, 1 to 2 cents per name.

Best Ways to Get Business

- Face-to-face networking inside business and trade organizations such as the chamber of commerce and business-referral organizations.

- Seeking work from printers and desktop publishers.

- Directly approaching personnel of locally owned stores to ask how they handle their mailing lists because they may need help turning these names into mailing lists.

- Calling associations, clubs, churches, and hotels in your area to see if any of them are interested in having you maintain their mailing lists or handle their mailings.

- Contacting professionals who may need help in sending out newsletters to their clients.

- Having your own Web site with testimonial letters and key words that identify your community so people using a search engine will find your site.

Marketing Insights

- Communities with many independently owned businesses are the markets for a mailing list service.

- Helping salespeople from all kinds of fields use contact management software is a growing area. Consultants who are certified by contact management software companies can be gatekeepers to help you reach this type of business.

- Clients are apt to be nervous about outsourcing their proprietary information, so establishing your credibility and trustworthiness is essential.

Where Next?

The resources available for this business are geared to larger mailing operations. Unfortunately the one book for home-based mailing services (*Mailing List Services on Your Home-Based PC,* by Linda Rohrbach, ISBN 0830644741) is out of print. While references to technology are dated and postal operations have changed, this book still has useful insights and is available on sites like Amazon.

ORGANIZATIONS

- Mailing and Fulfillment Services Association is the trade association for this industry but has few or no home-based members. Its publications are geared to its membership, but its *Forms Manual* may be of interest: (800) 333-6272, (703) 836-9200; *www.masa.org.*

- National Postal Forum assists the United States Postal Service in building relationships with large mailers. Audiotapes of past conferences may provide you with useful information: *www. nationalpostalforum.org.*

WEB SITES

- ACT! Certified Consultants (ACCs) in your area can be located from the directory at *www.act.com/community;* Maximizer's at *www.maximizer.com/services.*

- The United States Postal Service's site provides post office publications, business forms, mailing tips, and software tools: *www.usps.com/ncsc.*

From the Home Front

"Nothing in the business has really gone by the wayside, but it is changing constantly."

—Shelly Blake, Palatine, Illinois

---

8. Medical Billing

Medical billing has been around for more than a decade as a profitable home-based business with an expanding market. As a result, in some urban areas, the field is crowded, making entry difficult unless one buys the practice of an already established service. We continue to consider medical billing a good home business for people over fifty because in many communities there are still pockets of opportunity that are worth exploring for those with knowledge of medical insurance and good computer and accounting skills.

If medical billing is new to you, here is a brief explanation. The profession emerged in 1990, when federal law required doctors to submit claims for Medicare reimbursements on behalf of their Medicare patients rather than having the patients file the claims themselves. While some doctors' offices purchased the software and trained their staff to do this billing, many physicians turned to outside services to handle their billing. This created a boon for small home-based services. The industry was given a further boost when Medicare began requiring that most claims be submitted electronically rather than mailed in on paper forms and then again when private insurance companies also began preferring electronic billing directly from doctors.

As a result, many software companies jumped into the business, producing sophisticated software programs that allowed doctors or their billers to key in the necessary information for medical claims and send them by modem directly to Medicare, Medicaid, or "clearinghouses" (intermediaries that check claims and forward them for processing to the various private insurance companies).

In the 1990s, scores of vendors began selling medical billing "business opportunity" packages with software and a few days of training, touting the profession as the easiest way to make gobs of money. As a result, large numbers of people were oversold on medical billing, and some business opportunities were proven to be outright scams. The Federal Trade

Commission even brought action against several of the "biz op" vendors for falsely advertising how much money a medical biller can make.

If doing medical billing appeals to you, it is important to have a realistic view of the skills needed to operate this business, including the challenge involved in getting doctors or other health providers to sign up with your service. A good deal of study is needed to develop a sufficient familiarity with medical coding to recognize a likely mistake you need to check with your client about. You also need to become versatile in insurance claims processing and the financial operation of medical practices. This includes the Health Insurance Portability and Accountability Act of 1996 (HIPAA), which contains certain provisions about patient privacy and security to which medical billers must adhere. Also needed is good business sense, knowledge of bookkeeping or accounting, and a devotion to marketing your own business.

Generally, creating a full-time income in medical billing requires four or more doctors as clients, and sometimes as many as ten depending on how many claims each doctor files per month. Many billers extend their services beyond keying in of medical codes and electronically filing claims by getting involved in the more lucrative area of "full practice management." In this role, they advise doctors on such matters as which managed-care plans to join and how to improve their billables, collection rates, and recapture of overdue accounts.

One area of confusion about the medical billing business concerns the growth of managed-care plans such as PPOs and their impact on doctors. Some people have surmised that when doctors participate in a managed-care program, they no longer need to file claims. However, Merry Schiff, who has been involved in medical billing for forty-five years and is the founder of the National Electronic Billers Association (NEBA), states that managed care still requires that doctors submit claims to insurance companies, even when the plan pays the doctor a fixed monthly stipend (called a capitated plan) rather than reimbursements on a per-claim basis for "fee-for-service."

"Basically, every provider *must* report to the managed-care plan when a patient was seen," affirms Merry. "The patient pays a co-payment, the doctor gets a little bit of money at the end of the month, *and* they still have to generate the claim." In Merry's view, the fact that there is still so much busywork for doctors is what keeps the profession of medical billing alive.

Bob De Leon and his wife, Nancy, began their medical billing business after being in the railroad-car leasing business for twenty-five years.

Bob was fifty-five when they decided they wanted to "go into a different industry and meet new people." Their business has grown from its start in 1998 to having four employees. Bob continues to do his part of the work at home and says, "I enjoy helping doctors grow their businesses." Bob's pride in his work reflects how important the billing function is to every health provider.

In addition to claims billing and practice management, some services also handle other tasks in the daily operation of a doctor's office, such as invoicing patients, keeping track of past-due accounts, taking phone calls from patients about their bills, and sometimes patient scheduling. Additional fees can be charged for each of these extra services.

Medical Billing at a Glance

 50% 50%

	Minimal	Moderate	More than most
Start-up cost		X	
Overhead	X		
Potential earnings			X
Computer skills required			X
Deadline pressures			X
Flexible hours			X
Overall stress		X	

Likely Transferable Skills, Background, Careers

CPAs, nurses, and people with experience as back-office personnel in medical offices or hospitals have excellent transferable knowledge and skills for this business. If you don't have experience in the medical field, you can take a community-college or adult-education course in medical billing. Note that you do not need to learn to do coding, because this must be done either by the health-care provider or a certified medical coder. You can also attend various Medicare-sponsored classes about electronic claims processing for Medicare claims. You can contact the Medicare office in your area for information about these classes.

What to Charge

The most common way for billing services to charge is on a per-claim basis, usually ranging from $1.50 to $3.00 per claim, depending on competition and location. However, "Fees go up with expertise," says Merlin Coslick, who has operated a medical billing service since 1990 and teaches and writes about it. Billers who do full-practice management often charge a flat fee of 7 to 10 percent of the total claims they collect. Working on a percentage basis can also be used for collecting old claims that were previously denied by commercial insurance companies.

Best Ways to Get Business

- Canvassing medical office buildings and going door-to-door selling your service. Be prepared for the office manager to tell you that the doctor cannot see you, but you can leave literature about your service.

- Creating and mailing out brochures that explain how you can solve problems with billing, collections, and frequently changing office staff.

- Getting referrals from doctors who refer you to their colleagues. Begin by seeking referrals or contacts from your own doctor and other health-care providers you know and those of friends and family. Bob De Leon got his first client based on a lead from a co-worker of his daughter whose mother worked in a chiropractic office.

- Having your own Web site with its own domain name and testimonial letters.

- Partnering with pharmaceutical sales people who see doctors all the time. You can offer to pay them a commission if a doctor signs with you following their introduction to you.

Marketing Insights

- Medical billing is sold unlike almost all other businesses in that it's procured based on need only and not on any other benefits you offer. As Merlin Coslick told us, "Unless a doctor has a need, it doesn't make any difference how great a service you provide."

- Consider specializing in one or two medical specialties, like cardiology or osteopathy. Bob De Leon, for example, specializes in chiropractic offices. His company slogan is "Chiropractic Is Our Specialty and Your Cash Flow Is Our Priority."

- Besides doctors and health clinics, other health providers who do third-party billing, include:

  Acupuncturists

  Cardiac profusionists

  Chiropractors

  Commercial ambulance companies

  Dentists

  Home nursing services

  Massage therapists

  Nursing services

  Occupational therapists

  Optometrists

  Osteopaths

  Physical therapists

  Physician assistants

  Podiatrists

  Psychologists and other mental-health professionals

  Respiratory therapists

  Speech therapists

- It's vital to be able to make health-care providers and their office staffs feel comfortable with your trustworthiness. They need to feel confident that you will process their claims without errors or glitches. When Bob De Leon met his first client, he was asked about his experience. He replied honestly that he had none and asked to be given a chance, offering to do the first month free. Later he asked, "Why did you hire me?" and the doctor said, "Because you were so honest."

- In addition to practice management, revenue can be generated by providing other services of value to health-care providers, such as remote data backup and digital scanning and archiving of medical records.

Where Next?

ASSOCIATIONS

- Electronic Medical Billing Network of America, Inc., offers a course and certification: (908) 470-4100; *www.medicalbilling network.com*.

- National Electronic Billers Alliance (NEBA), offers a home-study course and certification as a Healthcare Reimbursement Specialist: (650)359-4419; *www.nebazone.com*.

BOOKS

- *7 Steps to Getting into the Medical Billing Business,* Rick Benzel (ClaimTek Software, 2004), *www.claimtek.com*.

- *A Guide to Health Insurance Billing,* Marie A. Moisio (Delmar Learning, book and CD-ROM, 2000). ISBN: 0766812073.

- *Medical Billing,* Claudia A Yalden (CAY Medical Management, 1999). ISBN: 0739203614.

- *Medical Billing Marketing Success,* Merlin B. Coslick (Electronic Medical Billing Network of America Inc., 1998). ISBN: 189397801X. Coslick has other spiral-bound titles: *Setting Up Your Medical Billing Business,* ISBN: 1893978052, and *Medical Billing Home-Based Business,* ISBN: 1893978044.

- *Start Your Own Medical Claims Billing Service,* Rob Adams and Terry Adams (Entrepreneur Media Inc., 2003). ISBN: 1891984802.

TRAINING

- In addition to the home-study courses offered by the associations, community colleges have classes, which require about a year.

WEB SITES

- Consumer claims of medical billing scams: *http://pub1.ezboard.com/bmedicalbillingscamwatch.*

- Medicare. Designed by the government for seniors, it has publications available for downloading: *www.medicare.gov.*

From the Home Front

"Why would I want to retire if I'm managing the business and it's making a profit? I enjoy this business too much. I enjoy helping doctors grow their business."
—Bob De Leon, sixty

 ## 9. Medical Coding

Medical coding is the process of translating the diagnoses and procedures performed by health-care providers into codes. It's a career for the meticulous at heart and in deed. Whenever a patient sees a health-care practitioner in an office or hospital, various notes are created that spell out the diagnosis and the procedures performed. These notes must then be translated into two or three types of codes that insurance companies need to process the billing. The codes are also used for record keeping and health-care statistical measurement by hospitals and various government agencies.

The three types of codes are:

- Procedural codes: The Current Procedural Terminology (CPT®) determines how much Medicare or the private insurance company should pay. These codes are published by the American

Medical Association, which owns their copyright and earns a royalty from their publication in manuals.

- Diagnostic codes: Originally developed by the World Health Organization, these codes have been modified by the United States National Center for Health Statistics (NCHS) for use in indicating clinical diagnosis. The code set currently in use in the United States is called the International Classification of Diseases, Ninth Revision, Clinical Modification (ICD-9-CM).

- Additional Procedure Codes: The National Center for Health Statistics maintains a supplementary set of codes that cover procedures not included in the CPT codes. It is called the Healthcare Common Procedure Coding System (HCPCS).

    Using the notes or chart from the doctor or hospital, the coder must enter the accurate and consistent codes called for on the insurance form. For example, the diagnosis and procedures codes must match. Coding an operation on the wrist if the diagnosis code indicates a problem with the forearm won't fly. Incorrectly coding for more than the actual treatment provided is called "up-coding" and can result in fines from Medicare or reimbursement to the insurance company. Similarly, coding for too little, or "down-coding," results in losing income and hurts the client's cash flow at a time when many health-care providers are in financial distress. Another error is "unbundling." It means that the coder has used too many separate procedure codes instead of choosing a more appropriate single code for one comprehensive procedure.

Medical coders typically work on site in hospitals and clinics, but many also work at home either independently or as contractors for large medical-coding companies. In addition to doctors' offices and hospitals, coders are hired by medical researchers, government agencies, managed-care organizations, nursing homes, social-service agencies, health clinics, emergency clinics, home-health agencies, ambulatory and outpatient surgical centers, and long-term care facilities. Another coding specialization is as a "nosologist," someone who extracts information from death certificates for mortality (cause of death) statistics.

Paula Styck, of St. Anne, Illinois, began her coding business at age fifty-four, after having been a licensed practical nurse. A heart attack at age forty-eight forced Paula to rethink her work, and she decided she wanted to do something different. She studied for three months to become a coder, and then trained with her daughter, who was also a coder. Paula now works for a company that gets contracts with physicians' groups. She specializes in emergency room coding. Her physician drops off charts, and Paula does the coding according to a template that he provides her. Paula says, "Coding is not easy; there are many controls over how you do it. You need to code accurately so doctors can get paid at the maximum rate, but you can't overbill or underbill either."

The good news for this career is that the coding profession is expected to grow significantly. In the year 2000, professional medical coders accounted for 136,000 jobs, but it is predicted that employment of medical-records and health-information technicians will increase 36 percent through 2010, due to rapid growth in the number of medical tests, treatments, and procedures that are increasingly scrutinized by third-party payers, regulators, courts, and consumers. Although most coders work in hospitals, it's expected that there will be an increasing demand for detailed records in physicians' offices and clinics. Rapid growth is also expected in nursing homes and home-health agencies.

A coder needs to be able to decipher handwritten doctor and non-physician provider notes, which can be written by physician assistants, nurse assistants, etc., who enter services in the medical record. When you don't understand something, you must be willing to call to get clarification. And you must know the coding well enough so that you don't waste time looking up codes in the manuals. This doesn't mean memorizing thousands of codes, but being sufficiently familiar with them to easily find the correct code when you need to.

Medical Coding at a Glance

80% 20%

	Minimal	Moderate	More than most
Start-up cost	X		
Overhead	X		
Potential earnings			X

	Minimal	Moderate	More than most
Computer skills required—writing codes on copies of charts		X	
Deadline pressures			X
Flexible hours			X
Overall stress		X	

Likely Transferable Skills, Background, Careers

Coding is a suitable career for former medical personnel such as nurses, medical transcriptionists, and others who have clinical backgrounds or basic knowledge of anatomy and physiology. If you do not have a medical background, training to become a coder can take a year to eighteen months of classes at a community college, or through an organization or a home-study program. Enjoyment of detailed work with numbers and researching is needed regardless of background.

What to Charge

Hourly rates for coders range from $20 to $45. Some coders are paid per chart—from fifty cents to a dollar a chart. Piece rates apply in writing insurance company appeals, which range from $5 to $10 a case and for hospital work at a dollar per item. Rates for coders vary by region, specialty (for example, an orthopedic coder may earn more than the general office coder), education, years of experience, and certification. Salaries of coders who hold four-year degrees and are certified in coding are higher.

Best Ways to Get Business

- Cold-calling by phone or in person to doctors' offices and other health-care facilities. Be prepared to show samples of what you can do or to take a test on the spot.

- Finding out who does the coding for hospitals and clinics in your area and calling to see if they are willing to outsource.

- Obtaining referrals from working coders in your community who already have enough work.

Marketing Insights

- Good coders are highly marketable. A well-trained, knowledgeable coder can bring in (depending on the specialty) an additional $100,000 to $200,000 for a hospital or doctor's office because good coding maximizes the payments without introducing errors that delay payment or result in fines.

- It is easier to obtain work and be paid if you are certified.

Where Next?

ASSOCIATIONS

- American Academy of Professional Coders provides education and certification: (800) 626-2633; *www.aapc.com.*

- American Health Information Management Association (AHIMA). Web site lists educational organizations it accredits: (312) 233-1100; *www.ahima.org.*

BOOKS

- *Codebusters,* Patricia T. Aalseth (Jones & Bartlett Publishers, 1999). ISBN: 0834213176.

- *Code It Right,* 2002, Staff Medicode Inc. (Medicode Inc, 2001). Published annually. ISIN: 1563373920.

- *Independent Medical Coding,* Donna Avila-Weil (Rhonda Regan Rayve Productions, 1998). ISBN: 1877810177.

- *Step-by-Step Medical Coding,* Carol J. Buck (W. B. Saunders, 2002). ISBN: 0721693334.

COURSES

- Many local community colleges offer courses in medical coding.

- At-Home Professions: (800) 359-3455; *www.at-homeprofessions.com*

10. Medical Transcription

If you watch a doctor or other health-care provider in a hospital, clinic, or office for any length of time, you'll see them dictating or otherwise making notes about what they've done with each patient—assessments, workups, therapeutic procedures, courses of clinical action, diagnosis, and prognosis. These mostly verbal notes must be transcribed into a clearly worded and typed medical record. This is what medical transcriptionists do.

Medical transcriptionists interpret and transcribe dictation from health-care providers. Transcriptionists must have expertise in medical language and health-care documentation, as well as excellent grammar and punctuation skills. They must be able to listen carefully to the spoken word in order to understand and spell the vocabulary used, and then format the document correctly into the required report.

The growing complexity of medicine and the possibility of litigation have turned medical transcription into a $50 billion industry. Virtually every institution involved in health care—from private doctors to multibillion-dollar hospitals—must keep patient records for a variety of purposes. A patient's medical record is used first as a reference point for continuing care. The record is also vital to a health-care provider's cash flow, because transcribed reports are often required before insurance firms will pay physicians or hospitals. Transcribed copy also supplies health-care providers with the necessary documentation in the event that legal evidence is required in a lawsuit over the quality of patient care as well as in other cases, particularly personal injury. Finally, medical records are used for research and statistical purposes.

Medical transcriptionists may be employed on site by hospitals, clinics, physician offices, transcription services, insurance companies, home health-care agencies, and other locations where dictation of health-care documentation requires transcription. However, many transcriptionists work in their homes as independent contractors or subcontractors, working for large outsourced transcription agencies, or as home-based employees, or simply independently taking overload work from hospitals.

The demand for qualified transcriptionists has been rising for years. In fact, the demand for transcription is so great that many agencies have begun farming out dictations to overseas countries such as Barbados, India, Ireland, the Philippines, and Pakistan, where lower labor costs are a huge added incentive.

The technology for medical transcription has changed over the years. Formerly, transcriptionists picked up audiotapes from their clients and played them on bulky transcribers with foot pedals to control the speed. Today, doctors can call in their dictations to a computer where the dictation is stored digitally. Transcriptionists can then download the dictation at any time onto their computers and type their reports from the digital file.

Use of voice-recognition software is emerging. Although it was originally believed that this new generation of software would do away with human transcriptionists, this has not proven to be true. The resulting text still needs editing, but doctors' time is too valuable to use in this way and in many cases, doctors' spelling is too poor. As Carrie Boatman of the American Association for Medical Transcription said to us, "If docs are spending time editing their notes, who's caring for patients?" So with voice recognition, the transcriptionists' work shifts to editing the documents on screen.

This puts a premium on editing skills rather than typing speed. Editing may range from minimal to extensive, depending on the quality of the speech-recognition software and the dictating habits of the originator, and may include correction of content as well as punctuation, grammar, and style. Being an editor limits the risk of developing repetitive motion injuries that result from keyboarding and other injuries associated with medical transcription like hearing loss and lower-back injuries.

Gale Sutphin entered this career after age fifty. Having worked for a software company in the accounting department and customer support, Gale decided to change careers when her son was injured in an auto accident. She wanted time to take care of him while also keeping abreast of changes in the medical field. She began by taking courses in medical terminology at a regional occupational program in Sacramento, California, then followed up with courses in medical transcription. After an externship in orthopedics, Gale was able to land a full-time job, but her chance to work independently came when a manager resigned and someone began outsourcing transcription work to her. Today, she has several clients, the largest being a workers' compensation doctor who handles a large number of cases for which transcription is needed. She also does work for a general surgeon, and an allergist, as well as chiropractors and general-practice physicians.

Gale believes that being over fifty is an asset in the medical transcription business. "You need a broad range of knowledge to do this job. It's life experience that helps you comprehend what doctors are saying. You need to be able look at the scenarios doctors give you and decide if they make sense to you." Gale also states that what distinguishes transcriptionists is the quality of their work. "I'm not the fastest transcriptionist, but I deliver a quality document."

Medical Transcription at a Glance

 90% 10%

	Minimal	Moderate	More than most
Start-up cost		Equipment	Technology
Overhead			X
Potential earnings		X	
Computer skills required			X
Deadline pressures increasing			X
Flexible hours		X	
Overall stress			X

Likely Transferable Skills, Background, Careers

Historically, people in this profession have not come from nursing or court reporting where many skills are transferable. The most common identifying factor is that transcriptionists are often women, typically young mothers who want to work at home. However, more and more transcriptionists have switched into the career following a midlife career change from a variety of industries like accounting, airlines, and teaching. Be aware that the training can take more than a year, but clearly, if you have any type of medical background, such as nursing or pharmacy, your learning curve will be far shorter.

What to Charge

Transcriptionists typically charge by the line of type they produce, which currently ranges between twelve to sixteen cents per line. What constitutes a line depends on the line length and font size, but these are mostly standardized. Transcriptionists need to guarantee twenty-four-hour turnaround.

Best Ways to Get Business

- Advertising in medical society publications.

- Advertising in the Little Blue Book (*www.thelittlebluebook.com*) for your area. This is a pocket-sized directory of doctors and health-care resources, also published in PDA and PC versions.

- Checking out agencies that contract out medical transcription work. Because of the Internet, geographical nearness is no longer the factor it was, which is also why so much agency work is being outsourced abroad.

- Directly soliciting work from private physicians' offices, hospital medical-records departments, emergency rooms, clinics, attorneys, pathology offices, medical examiners, coroners, radiology offices/imaging centers—anyplace there is a patient encounter. Directories of physicians such as Doctor Directory (*www. doctordirectory.com*) or the American Medical Association's Doctor Finder (www.ama-assn.org) can be used to identify doctors by specialty and location. You can also use state Web sites that list all doctors and others licensed in the state.

- Obtaining overload or referral business from other transcriptionists, whom you can meet and develop relationships with by participating in a professional organizations at both national and local chapter levels.

- Listing in the Yellow Pages, which will enable you to be found on Web directories like *switchboard.com* and *anywho.com*. Transcriptionists typically do not have Yellow Page listings, so those few who do can get the business from health-care providers that other transcriptionists miss out on.

Marketing Insights

- To be competitive, you may need to offer extra services, such as pickup and delivery to those doctors still using tapes or seven-day-a-week service, or a phone-in dictation system. The demand for fast turnaround creates time pressure and at least occasionally the need to work nights and weekends.

- Eighty percent of the work done by independent transcriptionists is done for small clinics and group practices, according to Linda McIntyre, a former electrical engineer who now teaches transcription. She finds that most people entering the field are doing so as a second or third career. She knows transcriptionists who are still working in their seventies.

- Agencies that farm out transcription work pay lower rates than you can get if you obtain your own clients.

- Radiology is one of the highest-paying specialties for transcriptionists because of the need for turnaround within hours. Orthopedics and workers' compensation work may also pay better.

Where Next?

ASSOCIATIONS

- American Association for Medical Transcription (AAMT) offers certification: (800) 982-2182, (209) 527-9620; *www.aamt.org*.

- Association for the Sensible Method of Acquiring Rates for Transcription (ASMART): *www.transcribing.com/asmart*. Primarily a Web site; membership is free.

- MT Daily, an on-line networking center: *www.mtdaily.com*.

BOOKS

- *The AAMT Book of Style for Medical Transcription*, Peg Hughes (American Association for Medical Transcription, book and CD, 2002). ISBN: 0935229388.

- *How to Become a Medical Transcriptionist*, Gordon Morton (Medical Language Development, 1998). ISBN: 0966347005.

- *The Independent Transcriptionist*, Donna Avila-Weil and Mary Glaccum (Rayve Productions, 2002). ISBN: 1877810525.

- *Medical Keyboarding, Typing and Transcribing: Techniques and Procedures*, Marcy Otis Diehl and Marilyn Takahashi Fordney (W.B. Saunders Company, 1997). ISBN: 0721668585.

- *The Medical Transcription Career Handbook*, Keith A. Drake (Prentice Hall, 1999). ISBN: 0130115401.

NEWSLETTER

- *The Latest Word: The Bimonthly Newsletter for Medical Transcriptionists*: (800) 460-3110; *www.elsevier.com*.

TRAINING

- To learn medical transcription, you can do one or a combination of things: Take a home-study course or enroll in classroom training at a vocational or technical school, community college, or hospital. Many people also take entry-level positions to obtain on-the-job training. You can evaluate educational programs based on the length of the program; whether actual physicians' voices and dictation are included on practice tapes; and how wide a variety of specialties, voices, and accents are covered. If you have a medical background, you can get an indication of your current proficiency by taking tests available on the Web at sites like *www.transcribeboston.com* and *www.cnctranscription.com*.

Among the dozens of courses to choose from, the following are some of the better-known ones:

- At-Home Professions, 2001 Lowe Street, Ft. Collins, CO 80525: (800) 359-3455; *www.at-homeprofessions.com.*

- Health Professions Institute: (209) 551-2112. Offers the SUM program. *www.hpisum.com.*

- MT Monthly newsletter has a training program: (800) 951-5559, (816) 628-3013; *www.mtmonthly.com.*

- M-Tec Education Center: (877) 864-3307, (330) 670-9333; *www.mtecinc.com.*

- Career Step, has a special Canadian career center: (800) 246-7837; *www.canscribe.com.*

From the Home Front

"I love this work. It is addicting. There is so much mental challenge and opportunity to learn new things every day. I love to learn. It's part of the allure of this profession. But be aware this is a very detailed job. Your accuracy rate is expected to be 98–99%."
                                                              —Gale Sutphin, fifty

---

 ## 11. Secretarial and Office-Support Services

Office-support services is a catch-all phrase for a wide variety of contracted work, including word processing, transcription, editing and proofreading, business writing, preparing spreadsheets or databases, maintaining contact management programs, bookkeeping, billing, notary services, desktop publishing, graphic design, multimedia presentations, office management and organization consultation, answering services, mailing preparation, résumé writing, Web-site design, and Internet research. You can specialize in one or several of these areas, or you can become a jack-of-all-trades, depending on your skills, interests, and what the needs are in the area in which you live.

Office-support services typically market to a variety of clients. One large market includes brand-new business, small businesses, and self-employed individuals who do not have full-time secretarial assistance. For example, your clients could be consultants, real estate and insurance agents, doctors, attorneys, private investigators, or any business where the proprietor or professional has little time or desire to do his or her own administrative work. According to industry veteran Nina Feldman, many independent consultants and professionals rent office space in "executive suites" (a upmarket name for shared office space) and then use independent office services, e-mailing them raw data or documents for transcription, formatting, proofing, editing, publishing, etc.

Other possible markets for office support services include:

- Technophobic individuals who have no ability or interest in learning how to use computers for their work. (Yes, they still exist!)

- Sales reps and traveling executives (often called "road warriors") who need database or contact management updating or document typing while they are on the road.

- Graduate students who need dissertations, theses, or moot court briefs formatted and sometimes typed.

- Job seekers who need résumés.

- Product-research companies who conduct "focus groups" on new products and need their interviews transcribed.

- Writers and authors of all kinds who need formatting and editing of their manuscripts.

Competition in the office-support field can be stiff, but tailoring your business to a few specific markets is the best way to carve out a niche for yourself. Some specialties, such as database work or transcribing legal and medical materials, pay better than others but require more specialized training. Rates for simple manuscript typing are generally less.

The key to success in this business is to ensure that you are detailed oriented, can work quickly, and produce work of impeccable quality. You must also build a reputation that you are able to meet all deadlines. To be competitive, it helps to offer pickup and delivery (some services charge for this and some don't), though much of your work may be transmitted to you electronically. Some cautions about secretarial work are that it can be fatiguing, particularly if you're being pressed by a deadline, and there is a risk of developing repetitive-motion injuries.

One very positive aspect of this business is that you can work at it until you are ready to quit. Bev Mahrt, of Spokane, Washington, began her service at age fifty-nine in 1980 and she's now eighty-two. Relying on her expertise in grammar and her lightning-fast 120-words-per-minute typing speed, Bev serves a wide range of clients, including lawyers, grad students, and people wanting résumés. Bev can also type in several foreign languages (German, French, or Spanish). She still works twenty-five to thirty hours per week.

Note: Many people who in the past would have called their business a secretarial service are now positioning themselves as "virtual assistants." (See the separate profile.) To be sure, the work of these two businesses does overlap, but the fact is that many potential customers for these services do not know the term *virtual assistant*, so they look in the Yellow Pages, on line, or otherwise, for "secretarial service." On the downside, virtual assistants tend to serve a narrower and more upscale clientele, so they are usually able to charge higher hourly rates and thus realize higher earnings.

Secretarial and Office Support at a Glance

50% 50%

	Minimal	Moderate	More than most
Start-up cost	X		
Overhead		X	
Potential earnings	X		
Computer skills required			X
Deadline pressures			X
Flexible hours		X	
Overall stress— clients waiting until the last moment.		X	

Likely Transferable Skills, Background, Careers

Administrative and executive assistant, office manager, word processor, and other administrative staff experience. Since people are expecting you to create documents they can't prepare themselves, you need much above average knowledge and familiarity with various software packages from word processing and desktop publishing to graphic design, database, spreadsheet, and presentation software. Your background should reflect your dedication to details and meeting deadlines. Since a good portion of this business involves working closely with people, it also helps to be reassuring, confident, and punctual.

What to Charge

Hourly rates range from a low of about $20 an hour to $50 an hour. Services such as desktop publishing, graphic design, database and spreadsheet work, or writing/editing bear higher hourly rates, as much as $75 per hour. Before setting your rate, calculate your overhead and find out what other secretarial services located within thirty minutes of you are charging.

To charge by the job, you can use the *Industry Production Standards* guide for estimating time. (See Books, Manuals.) When applied to your hourly rates, this guide enables you to estimate and calculate time and charges for a wide range of services.

Don't sell yourself short by undercharging, and be sure to find out if your state requires you to collect sales tax on word processing and other work you do.

Best Ways to Get Business

- Participating in one or more business networking groups or referral organizations

- Having a Web site. Because your business is local, be sure to use the name of the community or communities you serve on your home page, in key words, and if possible in your domain name. List your services and provide copies of testimonial letters.

- Listing in the Yellow Pages, which appear in print and on directories like *switchboard.com* and *anywho.com*. Test listing under multiple categories such as Secretarial Services, Word Processing, Desktop Publishing, and Résumé Service. Also consider listing on local directory sites like *Yahoo Get Local* and *SuperPages*.

- Advertising in university newspapers and church, club, and chamber of commerce bulletins, especially those published by organizations of which you are a member.

- Approaching hotels and office business centers (often called executive suite offices) about offering your services to their guests and clients.

- Contacting other office-support services and virtual assistants about doing overload or work you specialize in that they do not. You can set up reciprocal referral agreements where you send them the kind of work you don't do and vice versa.

- For attracting graduate student business, post notices or flyers with tear-off phone numbers on bulletin boards at colleges and universities and in facilities used by students, such as Laundromats. Advertise in campus papers. Register with department heads and thesis librarians, and communicate with others in the same business about helping with their overflow.

Marketing Insights

- Find out how other secretarial services in your city are specializing with an eye to determining if there is an unmet need you can supply.

- As businesses and individuals increasingly incorporate technology into their businesses and homes, success in office support becomes more dependent on specializing in doing things that clients don't like to do, can't learn on their own, or find too unprofitable.

- Get certified in the Microsoft Office Suite (MOS certification) to add credibility to your skills. (See Resources below for information.)

- Name your business to appeal to your market. Pick a name that clearly connotes what you specialize in.

- Offer discounts on future work to clients and others who refer clients to you.

Where Next?

ASSOCIATION

- International Association of Administrative Professionals (formerly Professional Secretaries International): (816) 891-6600. Offers certification: *www.iaap-hq.org*.

CERTIFICATION

- Microsoft Office Certification: *www.microsoft.com/traincert*.

BOOKS, MANUALS

- Nina Feldman Connections sells the useful *Industry Production Standards (IPS)*, pricing manuals and guides, formerly published by the ABSSI, Inc: (510) 655-4296; *www.ninafeldman.com*.

- *How to Start a Home-Based Secretarial Services Business,* Jan Melnik (Globe Pequot Press, 1999). ISBN: 0762705159.

- *Industry Production Standards* guide, Office Business Centers Association International: (800) 237-4741; *www.officebusinesscenters. com*. An annual report presents graphs, charts, and rates and other data categorized by firm size and geography.

From the Home Front

When asked how long she foresees operating her business, Bev Mahrt, eighty-two, unhesitatingly replied, "Until they pass me out."

Snapshot: Vic Blumenthal, Network Organizing Franchisee

Vic Blumenthal had retired for the second time when his daughter Linda pestered him into attending the local Business Networking International (BNI) meeting where she was a member. Linda thought BNI, an international franchise organization where business owners and professionals network and provide referrals and support to one another, would be a natural fit for Vic.

Networking was a talent Vic had learned well while directing large profit centers for thirty years before he retired at fifty-five and then again when he came out of retirement to oversee the turnaround of a family business before retiring again at sixty-two. "Dad," she told him, "every time you bump into one of my friends, you are always offering to help them with their businesses, giving them the phone number of a key contact and having them mention your name. You've been performing BNI for many years!"

As Linda predicted, after going to a BNI meeting, Vic was indeed interested. "I always loved working with a people to help them grow their businesses," he says. So he came out of retirement again and purchased the BNI franchise for Southeastern Massachusetts and Cape Cod with an option for Rhode Island.

Vic grew the franchise from nine small chapters with about 150 members to 34 groups with more than 700 members. At age sixty-five, he began transferring the business to Linda and her husband, who took over all the chapters when he retired once again, this time to spend half the year in Boynton Beach, Florida. Vic just turned seventy and still works with the kids when he's in Massachusetts from May to November.

"I do chapter visits, help start new chapters, and do business planning," he says. "Working with young people and seeing them succeed has been the most satisfying aspect of my BNI business."

12. Technical Writer

If you like to write and are good at understanding and explaining technical things, you can be well paid as a technical writer. That's because whenever any new product involving technology is introduced, there's usually an immediate need for some type of material to document or explain it. Depending on the item, what you write may be either a design-specification document, an instructional aid that explains how to use or assemble it, a marketing piece such as a brochure, a magazine or journal article about the item, or a press release for the media.

The audience for your writing might be buyers of the product, users (who may be different from buyers), installers or repair people, salespeople, or the press. Many items need more than one type of technical document from the above list.

The technical writer's job is to make the information clear and easily understood for the intended audience. For this reason, the writer must have a solid comprehension of the product and sometimes of the entire area, category, or field in which the product fits.

Most technical writers, therefore, specialize in some area such as engineering, chemicals, information technology, or hardware and software in order to ensure that they can stay on top of the latest technical issues. Many technical areas are so complex today that some writers specialize in very specific subcategories of a field, such as microwave technology or medical or financial software.

Technical writing encompasses a wide variety of writing styles and methods of publication, depending on the document you are hired to create. Some examples include:

- Articles for magazines, trade publications, or journals that are published in print and Web formats.

- Hardware or software documentation produced as robohelp files on a computer.

- Policy manuals for government agencies or employment manuals for businesses that must adhere to approved formats.

- Product specifications and how-to instructions published on the Web.

- Publicity materials such as press releases that follow specific formats.

- Training courses or "e-learning" that are produced for the Web or on CD-ROM.

- User or product manuals that get published in standard printed form.

The technical writer must understand the publishing and design issues for whichever format is required and have the technology and software to produce the document in the manner desired. In many cases, this requires nothing more than standard word-processing software, but in others, you may be asked to produce your document as a Quark, PDF, HTML, Powerpoint, Visio, or Robohelp file. You therefore need to be able to conceive of your work in the context of its final design and publishing medium, and to write precisely to that specification.

Once a technical writer works successfully on a project and learns about the product or item in great detail, he or she often becomes an invaluable resource to the hiring company since they don't want to take the time to train another writer. For instance, André Sharp of Manhattan Beach, California, was able to get a wide range of assignments from a database software company for years because he knew their software inside and out from having been hired initially to write their user manuals. His initial assignment expanded into writing on-line help files, marketing documents, internal documents, and sales materials, and doing research for the company.

One large market for technical writing is in-house policy manuals for businesses. These tend to cover business operations and regulatory issues, so getting into this line of work can be easier. Martha Collins of Tampa Bay, Florida, got a start in this area when in her late forties, she got a job with GE as a technical writer, though she had never done this before. She parlayed that experience into being a documentation specialist on policies and procedures for Price-Waterhouse. After retiring, she started her own technical writing business, focusing on operational procedures for financial service industries.

Whatever your specialty, technical writing never becomes formulaic. Thomas Barker, co-chair of the Society for Technical Communication's SIG for Consulting and Technical Writing, points out that even writing a simple product manual entails gaining extensive knowledge just for that project. He recommends that to get the necessary training people wanting to enter this field take courses in technical writing offered at universities and extension school programs.

Technical Writing at a Glance

 70% 30%

	Minimal	Moderate	More than most
Start-up cost		X	
Overhead		X	
Potential earnings			X
Computer skills required			X

	Minimal	Moderate	More than most
Deadline pressures			X
Flexible hours		X	
Overall stress			X

Likely Transferable Skills, Background, Careers

A background in any specific technical field will give you a leg up on getting into this business. If you came from engineering, chemicals, IT (information technology), or financial services, your knowledge may be highly prized and land you assignments quickly. Retired teachers, businesspeople, and government workers who have organizational skills and the ability to teach others can also transition into technical writing. However, you need superior writing and software skills to produce documents in the format required.

What to Charge

The Society for Technical Communications (STC) conducts regular salary surveys of employed technical writers and in 2001 found that the lowest end of the pay scale was $25 per hour for those who obtain work through an employment agency and $30 for sole proprietors, while some writers earn up to $85 per hour. The average hourly rate was $44 to $62 per hour.

Best Ways to Get Business

- Posting your résumé on on-line job banks and searching them for assignments. Most states and cities have on-line job sites where technical writing may be listed.

- Contacting agencies that place temporary technical personnel, including technical writers.

- Directly soliciting work from companies you want to write for. Some firms may advertise assignments on their Web sites, so you should search through sites for companies to contact.

- Participating in a visible way in trade associations and computer user groups.

- Looking for classified ads for technical writers on sites like *elance.com* and *guru.com* and in newspapers.

- Placing ads in the trade publications read by your prospective clients in the fields in which you work.

- Offering to write a column for a specialty trade publication in order to get your name out in the field and build a portfolio of work.

- Creating a Web site where you place testimonial letters and samples of your work. Linda Gallagher of Denver cites her Web site as inspiring several clients to contact and hire her.

Marketing Insights

- Note that this field is growing, but also becoming more competitive. One out of four technical writers is self-employed. The Bureau of Labor Statistics projects there will be 347,000 technical writers by 2006, up from 286,000 in 1996. These numbers may be reduced as some corporations are outsourcing technical writing outside the U.S.

- Technology is changing at a faster and faster pace, so to stay up-to-date in this profession, you must always be ready and willing to learn new things about your field.

- Get ahead of others by being the first to take the initiative to learn about a new cutting-edge technology. Learn as much as you can about a new field or product area to make yourself invaluable to the companies and media involved.

- Begin by developing a portfolio of work, possibly by taking a class, or if your current employer has a need for technical writing offer to take on assignments to build up a collection of work.

- If you're not a great writer, consider taking advanced classes in one or more methods of document publishing or illustration so that you can become an expert in producing documents or graphics. You may land work as a technical-design or publishing specialist.

Where Next?

ORGANIZATIONS

- American Medical Writers Association: (301) 294-5303; *www.amwa.org*.

- Institute for Electrical and Electronics Engineers' Professional Communications Society: *www.ieeepcs.org*.

- International Society for Performance Improvement: 301-587-8570; *www.ispi.org*.

- Society for Technical Communication: (703) 522-4114. The Society has local chapters: *www.stc.org*.

BOOKS

- *Handbook of Technical Writing*, Charles T. Brusaw (St. Martin's Press, 1997). ISBN 0312166907.

- *How to Become a Technical Writer*, Susan Bilheimer (Optimus Publishing Company, 2002). ISBN: 0970196415.

- *The Tech Writer's Survival Guide*, Janet Van Wicklen (Facts on File, 2001). ISBN: 0816040389.

COURSES

- The United States Department of Agriculture Graduate School offers courses in technical writing and writing skills at locations throughout the U.S.: (888) 744-GRAD, (202) 314-3670, (888) 744-4723), (202) 314-3300; *www.grad.usda.gov*.

From the Home Front

"As long as I am healthy, I don't have the desire to stop working at any point. I do a project and then take a few weeks off and then do another project. When I worked, I spent an hour and a half to get to work some days. Now I walk, do weights, and stretch. My blood pressure has gone down tremendously. I'm working because it's something I enjoy doing."

—Martha Collins, sixty-five

13. Virtual Assistant

Virtual assistants (VAs) are miracle workers to their clients, who are typically doctors, coaches, authors, financial advisors, attorneys, consultants, entertainers, ministers, speakers, realtors, start-up companies, and small-business owners or professionals who don't require a full-time in-house employee. VAs provide a variety of personal and office support services that their clients don't have time to do or can benefit from delegating.

VAs' hourly or daily rates are higher than those of most office-support professionals because they generally handle the more complex tasks needed by high-end professionals and businesspeople. So if you are a problem solver with keen communication skills who can always be counted on to get things done in a way that makes your clients look good and feel better, you could be a great VA.

When working as a virtual assistant you may be performing general administrative tasks, making necessary customer or patient contact, doing market research, scheduling client appointments, writing proposals, editing and formatting documents, sending out marketing materials, thank-you notes, and gifts, setting up and maintaining databases, handling the billing and bookkeeping, planning and coordinating meetings, making travel arrangements, creating e-zines, or updating your client's Web site. For a start-up company, you may be busy serving as a purchasing manager finding sources of insurance or outfitting an office on a minimum budget. Or you may be helping your clients manage their hectic lives, arranging for pet-sitting, calling a plumber, scheduling doctors' appointments, planning a family reunion or wedding, or coordinating a move.

Depending on your personality and your clients, you may be on call much like a fire company ready to respond on demand to any alarm, but more typically you will have the autonomy of setting your own schedule. In all cases, you're virtual—that is, you're on your own premises apart from that of the client, whether that's in the same community, on another continent, or traveling in your RV.

You and your clients communicate by e-mail, phone, fax, and real-time on-line messaging. Virtual assistants also communicate via video conferencing. You and your clients may even access one another's computers with software like *PC Anywhere* or jointly coordinate your work tasks via software housed on Web sites.

Virtual Assisting at a Glance

50% 50%

	Minimal	Moderate	More than most
Start-up cost	X		
Overhead	X		
Potential earnings		X	
Computer skills required		X	
Deadline pressures			X
Flexible hours			X
Overall stress		X	

Likely Transferable Skills, Background, Careers

Administrative or executive assistant, office manager, customer service, small-business owner.

What to Charge

Typically between $30 to $45 an hour. The more upscale your clientele, the more you can charge. Some VAs' rates approach $100 an hour.

Best Ways to Get Business

- Serving past employers.

- Networking among or with the type of clients or industry you wish to serve.

- Encouraging referrals from current and past clients.

- Selecting a niche based on your experience and expertise. Stacy Brice, founder of Assistu.com, says, "Aim for the top 10 percent of performers in your chosen profession, occupation, or industry. They're the people who need you." Stacy herself began by working for best-selling authors.

- Bidding for projects on Web sites like *elance.com* and listing yourself on sites like *freeagent.com* and *guru.com*. Note: You will earn less per hour when bidding for piecework.

Marketing Insights

- The best revenue stream comes from having several key clients willing to enter into retainer arrangements who need you regularly for ten to twenty hours a month. Consider offering them a daily rate, calculated below your hourly rate.

- Your key benefits for your clients are that they (1) get someone with skill sets they probably wouldn't be able to attract, keep, or otherwise afford; (2) only pay for the time they need; (3) don't pay for fringe benefits or office space, and thus (4) can get the assistance they need for a fraction of the cost of a full-time employee, (5) without the need for supervision, (6) increasing your clients' profitability and accelerating their growth.

- You may make yourself more valuable to your clients by offering more specialized skills such as writing, editing, marketing, desktop publishing, Web design, and bookkeeping, but if one of these is what you primarily do, consider positioning yourself in that particular business instead of as a VA. In this way, you may be able to charge more and focus your marketing more precisely.

Where Next?

TRAINING AND CERTIFICATION

- *www.assistu.com*—twenty-week training from one of the founders of the field with high admission standards.

- International Virtual Assistants Association, *www.ivaa.org*.

- Virtual Assistance U (VAU), *www.virtualassistanceu.com*.

WEB SITES TO LINK TO OTHER VIRTUAL ASSISTANTS AND THE VA INDUSTRY

- *www.adminprof.com/associations.htm.*
- *www.allianceforvirtualbiz.com.*
- *www.work-the-web.com.*

From the Home Front

"For forty years, I worked as a secretary or executive assistant. I was in a serving position. This is very different—now I can serve myself. My clients are all in their fifties, but I could serve younger clients even better." In answer to the question "Can you see yourself doing this in five years?" Lynne gave a definite "yes." In ten years? Lynne wasn't so certain.   —Lynne Kleeger, fifty-nine

SERVING
BUSINESSES
AND
CONSUMERS

14. Caretaking

Years ago, when people traveled, they found a relative or a neighbor to take care of their homes while they were away. Now relatives are scattered, people don't know their neighbors, and they can't easily find someone who wants to take on the responsibility of caring for someone else's home, which may include watering plants and feeding pets. Of course, some homeowners have tried enlisting nephews and neighborhood kids home from college only to find ruined carpets, evidence of wild parties, or dead pets when they return. Enter the paid caretaker or house-sitter.

Many caretakers serve wealthy people who have several homes. This is particularly true since 9/11 because insurance companies will no longer provide homeowner insurance on vacation property that's vacant for months at a time. Even less-than-wealthy people feel concerned about leaving a vacation home vacant.

Caretaking provides the possibility of living in beautiful places with plenty of freedom to pursue other interests. It can be an opportunity to leave an area you don't want to live in any longer, or it can be a way to afford remaining in an area you don't want to leave.

Caretaking is a field that favors mature individuals, particularly couples, according to Gary Dunn, publisher of the *Caretaker Gazette*. "With maturity, there are just fewer fly-by-night rip-off artists." At least 50 percent of the subscribers to the *Caretaker Gazette* are over fifty. Couples are favored because they are regarded as more stable. They're apt to remain in a position longer and have each other for company.

When they lost their jobs in the electronics industry in the early nineties, Patricia Roukens and Pat Frost, both just past fifty, decided to move to Arizona. They saw an ad in a local paper for a caretaker with light handyperson skills high in the Arizona mountains. To get to the property, they had to cross a river and go up a mountain for the interview. They got the job and at the time we interviewed them had lived in this isolated spot, taking care of the property, for twelve years. Like many caretakers, Patricia is able to earn additional money while she is caretaking. She's a sculptor and has been able to produce additional cash income from selling her work.

Don Cole closed his Houston architectural practice when he found the administrative demands of the practice were depleting his creativity. He describes himself as having been a "slave to my practice." So in 1996, he found himself divorced and with his children out of the house. He began looking for some way to live well without a lot of expense. At first he looked at three Houston "home tending" companies that placed people like him. But they required their caretakers to pay them $600 to $700 a month. He found this unappealing, so he started his own company at the age of sixty.

Don deals only with owners of investment properties or people who have moved away without having sold their homes. He emphasizes that this is not a landlord-tenant relationship, though he pays for utilities and takes care of upkeep. He requires that the house be emptied of belongings. Don then photographs the empty house so he has no liability for the possessions. He also provides documentation of the condition of the house via a condition statement that includes photographs and sometimes a video. He then fills the house with his own furniture and art work.

Don doesn't have a home of his own. In between homes, he uses a storage warehouse for his belongings and finds the ebb and flow of "stuff" he owns to be less stressful than the responsibility of owning a houseful of things. "I look at this as a lifestyle, a way of living well for less," he says. It also provides time for him to take on his choice of creative architectural projects and do some writing, golfing, and socializing.

While most caretakers love their caretaking experience, Paul Dietz's experience in Florida was an exception. He wasn't particularly satisfied with his position. He took a position that entailed using a tractor and a chainsaw to clear the land of trees. Then he was to keep trespassers from encroaching on the cleared land. He received free rent but no money. He recounts with grim humor, "I guess bullets bouncing off the tractor and tree branches, eleven cases of malaria within a one-mile radius, twelve murders in twelve months, including a body that showed up on the property I was caretaking, wouldn't be good fodder for an inspirational book." Although we are certain his experience was a rare one!

So it's important to check carefully into the expectations of the owner and the condition of the property and the community and surrounding area to be sure you know what you're undertaking.

House-sitting assignments can be short-term or long-term, up to six months or more, and they can be as varied as the lifestyles of people on this diverse planet. Gary Dunn estimates that about 50 per cent of jobs are long-term. For basic house-sitting, particularly if no care for plants or pets is involved, the physical stamina required can be minimal. If one specializes in being a household manager—a new term for "butler"—or an estate manager, which requires a business background and involves supervising other staff, the demands and stresses are similar to those of a salaried position.

Caretaking at a Glance

 50% 50%

	Minimal	Moderate	More than most
Start-up cost	X		
Overhead	X		
Potential earnings	X	X	X
Computer skills required	X		
Deadline pressures but sometimes household schedules must be observed	X		
Flexible hours but your regular presence is required			X
Overall stress	X		

Likely Transferable Skills, Background, Careers

People can and do come from all walks of life, and there are caretaking assignments for just about any combination of interests and preferences.

What to Charge

In this field, it's important to determine if you are wanting to make a career of caretaking or simply looking to live rent-free so you can afford to pursue another business or avocation. Fees are based on what you are re-quired to do beyond living in the home. Wealthy property owners will of-fer some sort of compensation, but it usually comes attached to duties such as providing animal care, housecleaning, lawn and plant care, snow removal, household repairs and maintenance, or supervising other con-tractors involved in maintaining the home. Household managers earn $35,000 to $75,000 a year; estate managers $85,000 to over $200,000 a year.

Best Ways to Get Business

- Registering on sites like *www.caretaker.org*. You post "situation wanted" ads providing information on your background and references so people seeking caretakers can find and respond to you.

- Listing on the Craiglist for your city—*www.craiglist.org*.

- Using employment agencies, such as Auspicious Gatekeeper in San Mateo, California, for short-term placement. Going through an agency provides homeowners with a greater sense of security.

Marketing Insights

- Gary Dunn, publisher of the *Caretaker Gazette* says, "Theft, main-tenance problems, vandalism, and insurance are the four horse-men that motivate having a caretaker.

- It's possible to fill your calendar from word of mouth with refer-rals from past clients, particularly for simple short-term (one week to three months) house-sitting. House-sitters get most of their work this way.

- Longer-term assignments, six months to five years, usually require more background information and the ability to be bonded. Homeowners often take care of the bonding through their property insurance.

- You'll find it easier to get assignments if you don't have pets and have a minimum of things to "move in."

- As one of the training programs says, you need to have a "service heart."

Where Next

PUBLICATION

- *Caretaker Gazette:* (715) 426-5500; *www.caretaker.org.*

TRAINING, CERTIFICATION, AND PLACEMENT

- Starkey International Institute for Household Management, Inc.: (800) 888-4904; *www.starkeyintl.com.*

- Professional Domestic Services and Institute: (614) 839-4357; *www.housestaff.net* (home study program).

- The International Butler Academy, located in the Netherlands. It is located on the site of the International Guild of Professional Butlers, *www.butlersguild.com,* which has a recommended reading list.

From the Home Front

"At this point, my life is about passion, art, and adventure," says Don Cole, sixty-eight, as he speaks of his philosophy for living a fluid life. "It's important to me not to get stuck."

---

15. Cleaning Service

People crave comfort and a clean home. In fact, when asked about what comfort means to them in a recent "State of Comfort" survey by the Karen Neuburger design firm, having a clean home ranked third for women and fourth for men, just below sleep, a healthy bank account, and, for men, making love.

Also respiratory illness has been linked to air pollution, and molds in air ducts and air filters and "sick" office buildings and homes have become commonplace. So more and more people are insisting on a clean environment, not just for the sake of appearance but for their health.

Yet housecleaning is one of the least liked tasks and the one harried people are most apt to ignore. So it's no wonder that more than one of six American households pays someone to do this work for them. This high demand makes starting a cleaning service one of the easiest home businesses to get under way.

Providing cleaning services of all kinds is one of the fastest-growing segments of the economy, with the number of residential and commercial cleaning services more than doubling in the last five years. The Bureau of Labor Statistics says there were more than half a million people doing cleaning for others in the year 2000.

Plenty of things besides homes need cleaning, too. Every office, apartment building, medical clinic, and other more specialized commercial facilities need attention. Usually people offering cleaning services choose between home or commercial cleaning and often specialize in one of more than two dozen specialities. This list, while long, is not exhaustive.

- Air ducts
- Apartment and rental property cleaning
- Auto detailing
- Carpet cleaning
- Ceiling cleaning
- Chimney cleaning
- Concrete floors/ceilings
- Construction cleanup
- Crime-scene cleanup
- Decontaminating "clean rooms" in high-tech manufacturing plants
- Disaster cleanup
- Drain cleaning
- Drapery cleaning
- Floor cleaning
- Furniture cleaning
- High-pressure or power washing
- Large commercial space (such as airports, arenas, schools, and supermarkets)
- Parking lot sweeping
- Pool cleaning
- Snow removal
- Stone and masonry cleaning
- Upholstery cleaning
- Venetian blind cleaning
- Window cleaning
- Yard and lawn maintenance

With so many people desiring to have things antiseptically scrubbed and polished, you may be able to dust off a niche that's just right for you. Consider, for example, if you love antiques. Dealers in your area may welcome your help cleaning newly acquired but tawdry in appearance items or in keeping what they already have in stock in tip-top form so it will fetch good prices.

Most commercial cleaning is classified as light duty today thanks to lighter and easier-to-use equipment. "Light cleaning tasks are a fertile area," says Stephen Gibson, regional vice president for Varsity Contractors, Inc. Any problems encountered in doing light cleaning are easily and inexpensively resolved, for example, by hiring others to do the taxing work. With the work only moderately physically demanding many over-fifty individuals can take on cleaning contracts themselves. Since she started her cleaning service business at age fifty, Roberta Baird of Naples, Florida, from Illinois agrees. She has attracted enough business cleaning vacation rentals and large homes that she's hired an employee and subcontractors to do the heavy work while she manages the jobs.

Roberta finds that her clients prefer her maturity, as it has a ring of reliability and lifelong knowledge. "They aren't interested in trusting the maintenance of their property to kids," she states. "There is very good money to be made, you're responsible because there are a lot of flakes in this business." Of course, hiring employees involves additional responsibilities and paperwork.

Green cleaning is an emerging fifty-plus niche. With allergies, asthma, and immune diseases rising at alarming rates, concerns about household chemicals and indoor pollution are creating a still small but growing market for services that use special nontoxic "green" cleaning supplies.

If you like to be outdoors, you can include cleaning decks, lanais, patios, and verandas in your services.

Cleaning Services at a Glance

📚 50% 🤝 50%

	Minimal	Moderate	More than most
Start-up cost	Homes	Commercial	
Overhead	X		
Potential earnings			X

	Minimal	Moderate	More than most
Computer skills required	X		
Schedule pressures			X
Flexible hours			
Overall stress	X		

Likely Transferable Skills, Background, Careers

For some people, cleaning things gets their feel-good endorphins flowing, and they're being well paid to do it. For others, it's something we've learned to do well and efficiently from a lifetime of experience.

Even if you don't feel adequately prepared, cleaning is one of the easiest businesses to enter. You can get free training from janitorial supply houses, and no particular background is better than another. Perhaps because of this, it's also one of the most popular businesses to franchise. But do you need a franchise? Don Aslett, longtime cleaning service operator and author, points out, "For a fee, of maybe $10,000 or $15,000, the franchise gives you a name, some forms, a few gallons of cleaner, some advertising info, and some secrets of success. In three months, with a little hustle, a sharp operator can accomplish the same thing independently." Bill Griffin, author and owner of Cleaning Consultant Services, Inc., says people don't need to buy a franchise so much today as they once did because software for running a cleaning service is commercially available and so is all the information one needs.

What to Charge

Housecleaning services can be priced by the hour or the job. If by the hour, the range is $12 to $35 an hour. Environmental or green-cleaning services can be priced at the high end of the range. If you charge by the job, you can establish a minimum of $50 or more for any-size job. Specialized work is usually priced by the square foot or by the item. Checking Web sites that post rates or phoning local services will help you determine current prices in your area. Commercial jobs are priced based on varying degrees of difficulty in terms of how much can be accomplished per hour and the proportion supplies will represent of your costs.

Best Ways to Get Business

- Taking out classified ads in weekly community newspapers. Find the local paper that produces the best results and advertise there indefinitely. Put clearly readable magnetic signs on the sides of your van or vehicle. Roberta Baird finds that people wave her down at stoplights to ask if she can give them a quote for cleaning jobs.

- Providing a cell-phone number on all your printed materials. Make sure you can answer calls yourself or forward them to a service so they can be answered twenty-four hours a day.

- Having your own Web site that is an electronic brochure for your service. Because you serve a local clientele, be sure to place the name of the community or communities you serve on your home page, in your key words, and, if possible, in your domain name.

- Having your phone listed in the Yellow Pages. It will be listed there as well as on Web directories like *www.switchboard.com*. Test out advertising on local search engines like *Yahoo Get Local* and *SuperPages*.

- Distributing flyers in neighborhoods or business districts.

- Calling directly on businesses that could use your services.

- If you operate as a green-cleaning service, letting doctors, particularly allergists, know about you.

- Offering some type of introductory discount with a direct-mail solicitation and then turning each customer you get into a regular weekly or monthly account.

- For types of cleaning that is done periodically like air-duct cleaning, keeping names of past clients in a database and contacting them at regular intervals.

Marketing Insights

- What you decide to name your business can be a way to distinguish your service from others.

- Reliability and impeccable-quality work make customers happy.

- Happy customers are the ones who will respond with your name when asked the perennial question overheard at neighborhood parties: "Do you know where I can find someone reliable to clean my house?" Don Aslett maintains that a cleaner who satisfies customers will get all the business she or he wants.

- Because people with allergies and multichemical sensitivities need to live free of toxic chemicals that harm them and many others want to protect the environment from harmful chemicals as well, you can cater to this market by using nontoxic, or green, products and vacuums with HEPA filters. Roberta Baird recommends using steam cleaners for carpets and upholstery as steam does not irritate the operator and leaves no smelly, lingering odor.

- It's wise to wait until you see what character your cleaning service takes before you invest in significant amounts of supplies and equipment. If you do commercial work, you can start as a sideline business because usually you will be working evenings and weekends. In contrast, residential customers expect cleaning to be done during weekday hours.

Where Next?

INFORMATION SOURCES

- Cleaning Management Institute, source of professional training and education, publishes magazines, which are archived on the Web site: (518) 783-1281; *www.cminstitute.net.*

- Contact Cleaning Consultants, Inc., publishes dozens of books, videos, and software and provides consulting services: (206) 682-9748; *www.cleaningconsultants.com.*

- Cleaning expert Don Aslett has authored a number of books about the cleaning business. He sells cleaning supplies, such as microfiber cloths, from his site: *www.donaslett.com.*

ASSOCIATIONS

- Building Service Contractors Association International, trade association for commercial cleaning firms: (800) 368-3414, (703) 359-7090; *www.bscai.org.*

- The International Window Cleaning Association, 7801 Suffolk, Alexandria, VA 22315; (703) 971-7771; *www.iwca.org*.

SPECIALTY MAGAZINES

- *American Window Cleaner:* (510) 233-4011; *www.awcmag.com*.

- *Cleaner Times* magazine, for pressure-cleaning/water-blasting businesses: (800) 443-3433, (501) 280-9111; *www.adpub.com/ctimes*.

BOOKS

- *Startup: Start Your Own Cleaning Service,* Jacquelyn Lynn (Entrepreneur Media, 2003). ISBN: 189198408X.

- *How to Start a Home-Based Housecleaning Business,* Melinda Morse and Laura Jorstad (Globe Pequot Press, 2002). ISBN: 0762722266.

From the Home Front

Roberta Baird proclaims: "I started this housecleaning business almost six years ago, and I love it! I make great money and work half the hours I worked before as an executive assistant. I know this business is not for the faint-hearted or the physically unfit, but for me, it has been the best job I've ever had."

16. Coach

How do you like the idea of turning around J. B. Priestley's lament, "When I was young there was no respect for the young, and now that I am old there is no respect for the old?" Do you find the idea of turning your years of experience into income appealing? And helping others in the process?

In the little more than a decade since Thomas Leonard founded Coach U in 1992, coaching has emerged as a distinct field, attracting tens of thousands of people. More of a right-brain intuitive process in contrast with consulting, which employs more left-brain analysis, coaching is an interactive process, says Timothy Gallwey, author of *The Inner Game of Tennis*. It's about "unlocking a person's potential . . . helping them to learn rather than teaching them." Thomas Leonard once said, "The less you say . . . the more successful you're being."

Clara Goldenhar, who styles herself as a "transition coach," was attracted to coaching after twenty-four years in commercial real estate and two years as a fine artist. "I thought my true calling was to become an artist, but I felt isolated in my studio; I missed interacting with people." So in 1998 at the age of fifty-five, Clara entered coaching. "I found my entire life from childhood on had prepared me for coaching. I had always been sought out for advice; problem solving was something I did well. Coaching has brought all my gifts and talents together."

Coaches need strong interpersonal skills, particularly the abilities to:

- Form a positive relationship with clients.

- Distinguish what clients mean, which is often different from what they say.

- Ask the kinds of questions that provoke clients to expand and clarify their thinking.

- Confront difficulties without being judgmental.

- Help with strategizing, prioritizing, and making plans.

- Provide support through change and growth.

Coaches typically work one-on-one with their clients, usually over the telephone. This means coaches can work while traveling. As Goldenhar says "You can design your practice around your life and not the other way around.

Coaches specialize by types of problems, by industry, and by outcome. They broadly fall into two categories: business and personal.

Personal coaches focus on career transitions, creativity, quality of life, health, and wellness, professional development, relationships, finances, balancing work with life, to name some of the common specialties. Business coaches may work with specific types or sizes of companies and may further focus on issues such as business planning, financing, strategic planning, conflict management, team building, partnership relations, and productivity.

Coaching at a Glance

 40% 60%

	Minimal	Moderate	More than most
Start-up cost	X		
Overhead	X		
Potential earnings			X
Computer skills required	X		
Deadline pressures	X		
Flexible hours			X
Overall stress	X		

Likely Transferable Skills, Background, Careers

Psychotherapy, small-business ownership, accounting, law, career counseling, human-resource development, management consulting, training, professional speaking, theater, financial planning, engineering, and sales all provide a background for coaching. As Goldenhar says, "What you bring to coaching are your life and work skills. The people you coach may be people from your industry."

What to Charge

Coaching fees range from $200 to $2,000 a month for three to four thirty-to-fifty-minute sessions a month. Lower fees are typical for newer coaches and for those serving consumers; higher fees, for business coaching and in established niches in which the coach has depth of experience. Four hundred to $600 a month are typical mid-range fees. For short-term or project-specific sessions, most typically with past clients, an hourly rate of $50 to $200 an hour is typical.

Best Ways to Get Business

- Identifying one or more niches or specializations that will help you attract clients. Ones based on your industry experience or extracurricular interests may offer you immediate contacts with gatekeepers.

- Offering sample (free) thirty-minute consultations.

- Making yourself visible by networking in organizations like women's, entrepreneurial, and artists groups where you are likely to meet people wanting to change or grow.

- Having a Web site that tells your specialization and approach along with client endorsements.

- Getting listed in directories like *findacoach.com* and the International Coach Federation's Coach Referral Service

- Speaking before groups, giving workshops and seminars.

- Writing articles about coaching for print and electronic publications, such as e-zines and newsletters. Some coaches produce their own publications, including booklets and tapes; others consider self-publishing too great a mental diversion from their work.

Marketing Insights

- The best revenue streams are one-to-one coaching by the month, group coaching by the month (by way of a corporate contract or groups you assemble), workshops, and teleclasses.

- Assessment tools such as the DISC system, Meyer-Briggs, may be helpful.

- The key benefit you offer clients is providing them with a high-quality relationship. Harriett Simon Salinger, who prior to becoming a coach at age sixty-two had been a practicing psychotherapist for over thirty years, says, "With the changes in family structure and the disappearance of long-term psychotherapy, coaching provides something missing in our culture." In another sense, coaching can provide typical citizens the kind of support star athletes, entertainers, and other performers routinely get.

- The best referrals come from your own clients who become your evangelists. Most likely clients are people in some form of transition, typically between the ages of thirty-five and fifty-five.

Where Next?

BOOKS

- *Coaching with Spirit*, Teri-E Belf (Jossey-Bass/Pfeiffer, 2002). ISBN: 0787960489.

- *Executive Coaching with Backbone and Heart*, Mary Beth O'Neill (Jossey-Bass, 2000). ISBN: 0787950165.

- *Getting Started in Personal and Executive Coaching*, Stephen G. Fairley and Chris E. Stout (John Wiley & Sons, 2003). ISBN: 0471426245.

- *Leading High Impact Teams: The Coach Approach to Peak Performance*, Cynder Niemela and Rachael Lewis (High Impact Pub, 2001). ISBN: 0971088802.

- *Masterful Coaching*, Robert Hargrove (Jossey-Bass/Pfeiffer, 2002). ISBN: 0787960845.

- *Personal and Executive Coaching*, Jeffrey E. Auerbach (Executive College Press, 2001). ISBN: 0970683405.

CERTIFICATION

The two leading organizations are the International Coach Federation (ICF): (888) 423-3131, *www.coachfederation.org,* which has many local chapters, and the International Association of Coaches, *www.certified coach.org.*

TRAINING

- See the chart comparing the many coaching schools at *www.coachingschools.org.*

- Among the best known schools are: Coach University, *www.coachu.com* or (800) 48COACH, (604)990-3545; Coachville, *www.coachville.com;* Academy for Coach Training: (800) 897-8707, *www.coachtraining.com;* and Life Purpose Institute, (858) 259-9345, *www.lifepurposeinstitute.com.* Important

considerations for a school are how long it's been operating and
how many graduates it has produced.

WEB SITE

- *CoachingMall.com*—a potpourri of services for coaches.

From the Home Front

In answer to the question "Can you see yourself doing this in five years?"
Clara Goldenhar said, "I can see myself doing coaching forever . . . as long as
my mouth, my brain and my heart work . . . as long as I can give to a client."

 ## 17. Computer Consultant

Would you like to turn the years of experience and the know-how
you've accrued mastering computer technology into an income? Or
maybe you've been the office guru everyone prefers to turn to and now
you'd like to get paid for doing what you've been doing for free. If so, computer consulting can be an ideal 50+ business.

Now that most homes and offices have computers and a passing
knowledge of how to use them, your task will be to identify a niche in
which you can shine as highly proficient and market yourself to a particular clientele. Steve Epner, a computer consultant for over twenty years
and past president of the Independent Computer Consultants Association, puts it this way, "You can't be everything to everybody—you need to
figure out where your expertise is."

Your niche might be working with a software product that while it's no
longer available anywhere except E-bay, companies continue to use and
rely on it. Now they need help to keep it up to snuff.

Or you might specialize in working with small and home businesses
that rely on readily available products like Windows and Office, but when
they change operating systems or equipment they run into compatibility
problems they can't handle. They can't afford to spend hours of time wad-
ing through help lines, but most consultants serving this market only have
superficial knowledge of installing new versions of Windows. So they will
gladly pay a consultant who will come to their office and make their systems work with a minimum of time and stress.

While in his forties, John Antaki started and then closed a computer consulting practice to take a turnaround job. He started consulting again at the age of fifty, having refined his niche. He takes on projects with corporations that spent millions trying to solve their computer problems but haven't gotten what they paid for. His motto is "We succeed where others fail."

A computer consultant must be more than technically proficient and specialized, however. Effective consultants need to understand what clients want to accomplish and be able to speak about problems in ways clients understand. They need to describe what they propose to do in a way that makes sense from the client perspective. Sometimes this involves recognizing the technical buzzwords clients have picked up and use but may not accurately describe their problem.

At fifty-nine Marty Klerkx of Detroit decided to do as a consultant what he had been doing for years for neighbors who sought his help. He often finds clients swamped by details and he brings another set of eyes to a situation, plus his forty years of technical experience

Computer consultants face competition from projects being outsourced abroad, but these are usually for million-dollar projects and sometimes they provide an opportunity for a solo consultant who can act as a U.S. local project manager. This is particularly true for a consultant who speaks the language of the country to which the work is being outsourced, typically Russia, India, Israel, and China. In part, the local consultant's role will be to help the overseas contractor understand the needs of the client. Of course, companies who have had unhappy costly experiences with outsourced projects are apt to look with favor on working again with a U.S. consultant.

Computer Consulting at a Glance

45% 55%

	Minimal	Moderate	More than most
Start-up cost		X	
Overhead			X

	Minimal	Moderate	More than most
Potential earnings			X
Computer skills required			X
Deadline pressures			X
Flexible hours		X	
Overall stress			X

Likely Transferable Skills, Background, Careers

Work in an information technology position or personal history helping people with computer problems.

What to Charge

The median hourly rate for computer consultants is $75 an hour, but some get under $15 an hour while still others charge as much as $250 an hour. Factors that influence rates include your specialization, what industry you work in, community size and location, the size and kind of clients you serve, the length of the project, and whether you work through a broker who finds work for you in return for 20 to 30 percent of your hourly rate.

Best Ways to Get Business

- Becoming known for your specialty, which can be done by writing articles for publications apt to be read by prospective clients, appearing as the speaker or a panelist at business organizations in your community, and personal networking in industry and trade associations and software user groups.

- Finding a specialty in which your clients need lots of hand-holding.

- Participating in business referral groups. For women, women's organizations can be helpful.

- Getting listed as a support service in referral services that professional associations maintain for their members.

- Having a Web site and using it effectively. Steve Epner observes that clients under thirty-five look on the Web but people over forty-five and in large organizations do not. They are more inclined to find a specialist from articles in business publications, or, of course through referrals. If your clientele is between thirty-five and forty-five, you need to use both approaches.

- Getting listed on sites that relate to your specialty. For example, Marty Klerkx got his first client by being listed on an Apple Consultant Network Web site.

- Getting work through brokers and job shops.

- Mounting a magnetic sign or decal on your vehicle featuring your service and displaying your phone number and Web site.

Marketing Insights

- The key benefit you offer clients is confidence that you can solve their problems without ripping them off.

- With companies that have an IT (information technology) staff, convey that you can relieve pressure on their staff.

- To help you generate repeat clients and referrals, deliver more than you promise.

- Once you have a client, you won't want to refer him or her to someone else if the client's needs exceed your specialty. So you need to know enough about the overall field to recognize when you should bring in a subcontractor and whom to choose.

- Bidding a fixed price for a job is risky until you have experience in pricing. Too high a bid is apt to scare off work, but too low a bid can cause heavy losses and lead to resenting your client, not the best attitude for developing a source of return and referral business.

Where Next?

BOOKS

- *The Computer Consultant's Workbook,* Janet Ruhl (Technion Books, 1996). ISBN 0964711605.

- *Getting Started in Computer Consulting,* Peter Meyer (John Wiley & Sons,1999). ISBN: 0471348139.

- *MCSE Consulting Bible,* Harry M. Brelsford (John Wiley & Sons, 2001). ISBN: 0764547747. You know doubt recognize MCSE as being Microsoft Certified Systems Engineer.

PROFESSIONAL ORGANIZATION

- Independent Computer Consultant's Association (ICCA): (800) 774-4222; *www.icca.org.*

WEB SITES

- Janet Ruhl's Computer Consultant's Resource Page, *www.realrates.com,* with tips, results of compensation surveys, and more.

- GovCon $_{SM}$. All about government contracting for computer consultants: *www.GovCon.com.*

TRAINING AND CERTIFICATION

- Training can be obtained from local colleges, universities, private training school, and vendors.

- Institute for Certification of Computer Professionals: (847) 299-4227, (800) 843-8227; *www.iccp.org.* As a rule, professional certification results in the ability to command higher fees, higher than vendor certifications.

- The Security Portal for Information System Security Professionals (INFOSYSSECT) has an extensive list of IT certification programs with links to them. *www.infosyssec.com/infosyssec/itcert.htm*

From the Home Front

"Don't be afraid to try something new."   —Marty Klerkx, sixty

18. Errand Service

Errand services do a variety of things that people and companies can't get done themselves. For example, there are nearly twenty-nine million two-career couples who have little time to do the many things they must do because they're both working long hours. Errand services pick up the slack for them, including fetching their kids after school and driving them to appointments and events, taking the family pet to the vet, getting the family car repaired, staying at the client's house or apartment to wait for a repairman or utility installer, delivering and picking up clothes at the cleaners, faxing or copying documents, mailing packages, or dozens of other tasks that the busy couple cannot squeeze into their tightly packed schedules.

Or there are many retired and elderly people who need a ride to the airport, the grocery store, a doctor's appointment, or who want to visit another senior friend. Some errand services deliver meals to seniors and the handicapped, since a food license is not required for delivering food. Some seniors hire an errand service to help them organize and pay their bills, move furniture around, or just to have some company once in a while. (See the profiles for Daily Money Manager and Eldercare elsewhere in this book.)

Some affluent (and sometimes not so affluent) individuals prefer to hire someone else to do tedious tasks they'd rather not do like shopping for a dinner party, picking up theater and sports tickets, selecting gifts for business contacts and friends, shopping for clothes, returning items to stores, dropping shoes off for repair, writing thank-you notes, or standing in line for registrations and license renewals. When working for well-to-do individuals, the role of the errand service evolves into that of a personal assistant or "concierge" service, willing and ready to do whatever their client asks, no matter how silly, such as driving to every button store in town looking for just the right color of blue button to match the woman-of-the-house's new dress.

Small- and medium-sized businesses also use errand services. Dry cleaners, pharmacies, advertising agencies, doctors, engineering firms, printing companies, auto dealerships, office buildings, apartment complexes, and nursing homes can all have the need to tap into "gofer" services once in a while for ad hoc deliveries and pickups. Such businesses often prefer not to hire a full-time employee for these types of services, since their needs are occasional, and they can save money by hiring an outside service on a contingency basis.

The fact is most errand services will do nearly anything that people will pay for. As one errand-service operator told us, "As long as it's legal, we do it. We take items back to stores to be returned or exchanged. We buy gifts. We take gifts to be wrapped. We make pickups and deliveries and do grocery shopping for small or new companies. We deliver wedding cakes for a bakery. Hiring us is cheaper than hiring a driver and leasing a truck."

Doreen Edwards (no relationship to us), who owns Let Honey Do It errand services in Los Angeles, began her business at age fifty-two after a divorce. From the start, she's done many types of errands, from personal clothes shopping to delivering summonses for attorneys to overseeing a half-million-dollar home remodeling job for a client. Her zaniest request was to drive thirty miles to a store and purchase a special pair of tennis shoes for a client from Texas. She recently became a notary and now brings her notary services to clients, often for home-loan signatures. Her company motto, "We never say no."

If it sounds fun, it is, but it's also challenging. Many newcomers to the business burn out or cut back to part-time. Those who succeed as a full-time professional service need to be constantly juggling the task of seeking new clients with carrying out the errands they've already been hired to do. This usually means being available 24/7 by cell phone or pager. So you need to have lots of energy and enjoy the stimulating fast-paced nature of this work. You need good and fast driving skills and the ability to read maps and get errands done quickly, all with a professional demeanor. As you might guess, this takes stamina, as often you will be behind the wheel or on your feet many hours a day, and could be called on to lift and carry packages and grocery bags.

Nevertheless, many people over fifty can enjoy this business for its variety of tasks and the sheer pleasure of helping other people get things done. And, of course, you can control how many and what kind of clients you want to take on. Being over fifty can have its benefits too in this business, as your clients may respect your ability to know how to get things done. As Doreen Edwards puts it, "I know how to take care of people and I intend to do this forever, till I die."

Errand Service at a Glance

 50% 50%

	Minimal	Moderate	More than most
Start-up cost	X		
Overhead	X		
Potential earnings	X		
Computer skills required	X		
Deadline pressures		X	
Flexible hours	X		
Overall stress		X	

Likely Transferable Skills, Background, Careers

People who have a background in a service industry, such as retail or banking, may have an aptitude for this business. You need organizational skills as well as a passion for helping others. You must be willing to do what your customers want done when they want it.

What to Charge

Errand services either charge a fixed rate or charge by the hour. Rates vary with location. Fixed rates can be calculated from zip code to zip code. Hourly fees range from $15 to $50 per hour, depending on the nature of the task, though $15 to $25 per hour is average. Rush or emergency services are priced 50 percent to 100 percent higher than normal rates and require a one- or two-hour minimum fee that covers drive time to and from the client's location. Transporting people such as on airport drop-offs and delivery is usually a flat fee depending on distance, but if you transport people for any service, you will need an endorsement or rider on your vehicle insurance to cover this. If you will be going into people's homes or offices where valuables are kept, it's wise to obtain business liability insurance. When you plan your fee structure, it's wise to take rising gas prices into account. Be prepared to add a gasoline surcharge as Federal Express does to accommodate increasing fuel prices.

Best Ways to Get Business

- Networking in chambers of commerce and business-referral organizations. Spreading the word about an errand service is one of the best way to get jobs. This is a top-of-the-mind business, in which having people think of you when they need an errand done is your key to success.

- Getting listed as a support service in referral services that professional associations maintain for their members.

- Calling on businesses or offices of the type or types you choose to specialize in serving. Talk with the secretary or office manager and leave behind an attractive flyer/brochure. It helps to have some fresh bagels or donuts to introduce yourself.

- Putting a sign on your car with the name of your business, your phone number, a memorable or cute logo, and your Web site. If you're bonded, indicate this.

- Getting referrals from satisfied customers is important. It helps to offer a discount on a future job if a current client refers someone to you. Discounts can also be used to stimulate repeat business and volume use.

- Listing in the Yellow Pages under Delivery Service, Messenger Service, and/or Shopping Service, which will enable you to be found on Web directories like *switchboard.com* and *anywho.com*. Consider ads on local directory sites like *Yahoo Get Local* and *SuperPages*.

- Having an informative Web site that can attract clients who are surfing the Web seeking errand services. Be sure to include on your home page and in your key words the community or geographic locations your prospective clients will use so a search engine will direct them to you.

Marketing Insights

- Frequent users of errand services include accountants, advertising and public-relations agencies, attorneys, auto dealers, doctors, escrow companies, realtors, hospitals, and nursing homes. It could help to specialize in one of these; however, be aware that if your specialization falters, so will your income.

- A key to getting established is finding one or more ongoing clients who have a enough work to keep you busy several days a week while you are building a reputation and clientele.

- Always consider yourself a convenience for your clients, which means that you must agree to their schedules and deadlines. The customer is always right.

- Getting bonded, in addition to having business liability insurance, will increase confidence in hiring you.

- Errand services are not suited to all communities. They work best in places where life seems hectic and complicated. They won't work, for example, where there is a mom-and-pop store handy on every corner or where parking is so limited that you'll spend your earnings on parking fees.

- Consider naming your business a concierge service. This may better position you to get corporate business and some wealthier customers.

Where Next?

ASSOCIATIONS

- *ErrandInfo.Com* provides a directory for site users to locate an errand service. The site also has information on starting an errand service: *www.errandinfo.com*.

- National Concierge Association: (612) 376-8013; *www.conciergeassoc.org*.

- International Concierge and Errand Association: (215) 743-5618; *www.iceaweb.org*.

BOOKS

- *How to Start and Operate an Errand Service*, Rob Spina (Legacy Marketing, 2001): (856) 778-6596; *www.legacymarketing.net*.

19. Gift Basket Business

Today gift baskets have become a popular choice for shoppers seeking something special to give friends and business associates. Companies are using gift baskets to show appreciation to customers, referral sources, and employees. Maybe it's the child inside of us that delights in getting a present filled with multiple treats, especially when they're items that tickle our personal fancy.

This gift basket boom is actually fairly new. As recently as a decade ago, it was not unusual to find people who didn't know what a gift basket was. But today you can find gift baskets in nearly every grocery store and at national merchandisers like Costco and Wal-Mart.

Given the prevalent mass merchandising of gift baskets, the best way for a home-based business to succeed is to specialize in creating unique and distinctive baskets. You can do this a number of ways. For example:

- Using unusual containers, such as Italian flower pots, colorful hat boxes, or straw baskets shaped like animals, sports gear, or children's toys.

- Going beyond the ordinary goods like jams, wines, or candies and filling your baskets instead with imported or unusual foods, specialty crafts from your region, fine soaps and cosmetics, or unique nonfood items you've created yourself such as jewelry, pottery, ceramics, soaps, weavings, and so on.

- Personalizing each basket for the recipient based on his or her occupation or interests: e.g., art supplies, cooking utensils, audiotapes, CDs, DVDs, or almost anything special.

- Making themed baskets for special target markets like wine lovers, chocoholics, hospital patients, or children at sleep-away camp where the basket might contain seven days' worth of individually wrapped gifts, one to be opened each day while the child is away.

Most gift basket businesses find that the year-end holidays, led by Christmas, Hanukkah, Kwanza, and New Year's, account for almost half of all their sales. Valentine's Day is the next most significant holiday for giving gift baskets, followed by Mother's Day, Secretaries' Day, Thanksgiving, Easter, Jewish holidays, and Father's Day. Birthdays are a significant source of business, too. Graduations, weddings, anniversaries, bridal and baby showers, and other special occasions provide more ways of generating income twelve months a year. Even death and divorce have become occasions for sending thoughtful gift baskets to cherished friends and relatives.

Enterprising gift-basket designers make a special effort especially to attract corporate buyers, since they are the most profitable segment of the market, followed by repeat individual customers. You can also develop other regular customers, such as wedding planners, resort hotels, real estate agents, meeting planners, and contest operators. Another option is to sell your baskets through retail locations such as coffee bars, postal receiving stores (such as Mail Boxes Etc.), hospital gift shops, nail salons, boutiques, and health-food stores. Such placements are often done on consignment, though, so you only get paid if the basket is sold and you must bear the risk of damage or spoilage.

Flora Brown, a gift basket expert who began her business following her retirement from teaching, believes that the Internet has given a boost to people in the gift basket business. Flora teaches classes in developing a gift basket business and she points out that having a good Web site allows you to compete with any retail store. Another benefit of having an effective Web site is that you can show high-quality photos of all your products, thus avoiding having to send out expensive brochures or sample baskets.

Both Flora Brown and Fran Civile, who started her gift basket business in Seattle when she was in her late sixties, shared the following advice for anyone interested in this business:

1. Avoid overpurchasing baskets and contents inventory; find local suppliers who can produce your containers and content items with only a few days notice.

2. Watch out for perishable items, or items that do not ship well, such as chocolate in the summertime.

3. Be prepared for seasonal rushes such as during the holidays when you may need assistance assembling large orders of baskets.

4. Try to ship to business addresses; shipping to residential addresses when no one is home during the day can result in spoilage or damage if your product ends up sitting in a shipping warehouse waiting for the recipient to accept delivery.

5. Stay in touch with your prior customers so you can turn them into repeat buyers.

Overall, the two keys to growing a successful gift basket business are to develop a highly distinctive look and feel to your baskets and to market as extensively as you can to build the largest possible loyal following. So if you have a good design sense, enjoy assembling things with your hands, and can develop a marketing approach that works, a gift-basket business could be an ideal business.

Gift Basket Business at a Glance

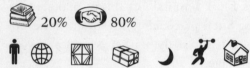

20% 80%

	Minimal	Moderate	More than most
Start-up cost	X		
Overhead	X		
Potential earnings		X	
Computer skills required		X	
Deadline pressures		X	
Flexible hours		X	
Overall stress		X	

Likely Transferable Skills, Background, Careers

In researching this field, Shirley Frazier, author of *The Gift Basket Design Book,* has found that many people come into this business from corporate America, where they worked as secretaries and receptionists, positions that require having a creative, artistic mind-set and excellent time-management, organizational, and business skills. Having a background in retail sales can also be useful if you have learned how to close sales.

What to Charge

The average gift basket sells for $25 to $45, though prices for customized baskets can go as high as $300, or whatever the buyer is willing to spend. Corporations favor gift baskets starting at $75. A formula for determining price is to double the wholesale cost for each item in the contents of your basket (including all the little extras that also go into wrapping your baskets, such as bows, ribbon, cellophane, grass, and so on). Then add an additional 20 percent to cover the time and labor of your making the basket. You can add to this price for unique and artistic design. Basket businesses typically give quantity discounts to corporate customers or for large orders.

Best Ways to Get Business

- Networking and developing personal contacts in organizations, such as trade and business associations, business referral organizations, and church groups, and periodically providing a basket for a door prize at their meetings. We've been told that donating baskets to nonprofit organizations, however, for fund-raisers in exchange for an acknowledgment in their printed materials does not produce new business.

- Making cold calls on corporations, hospitals, and other organizational buyers so you can show your portfolio and leave sample baskets or components for decision makers. Be sure to follow up quickly on any leads you develop. If you dislike cold calling, begin by using any connections you have or focus on only the industries you know best and are familiar with.

- Creating a well-designed informative Web site with photos of your baskets

- Networking with related businesses such as florists, party planners, and gift stores. They may want a sample basket from you for display, so be sure you don't bring baskets with perishable items.

- Organizing home parties similar to Tupperware parties and open houses at which you show your baskets and then take orders. Be sure to give a free basket to the hostess. This can be effective leading up to the holidays.

- Targeting ads in local papers that reach specific audiences, i.e., seniors and law-enforcement officers, and offering a 15 to 20 percent discount for members of that audience.

- Listing in the Yellow Pages, which will enable businesses to find you. Your listing will be found on Web directories like *switchboard.com* and *anywho.com*. Consider ads on local directory sites like *Yahoo Get Local* and *SuperPages*.

- Exhibiting at craft fairs and home shows.

- Developing your own mailing list of past customers and contacts and using it to send post cards or mailing tubes offering tips, news, or specials.

Marketing Insights

- Ancillary products can add to your sales. The industry has grown to include gift packs, individual keepsakes, imprinted specialties, and decorative accessories.

- Offering MasterCard, Visa, and American Express will increase your business.

- You can increase your profit with careful buying. For example, buying easy-to-store materials and supplies in large enough quantities that you can qualify for quantity discounts, but beware of stocking items that will go out of date quickly (like a calendar), spoil, or get stale.

Where Next?

BOOKS

- *The Business of Gift Baskets*, Cynthia McKay, Cynthia C. McKay, and Carol Dorris (1601 South Holdings, 1998). ISBN: 0966308301.

- *The Gift Basket Design Book,* Shirley George Frazier
  (Globe-Pequot Press, 2004). ISBN: 0762727950.

- *How to Start a Home-Based Gift Basket Business,* Shirley Frazier
  (Globe-Pequot Press, 2003). ISBN: 0762727624. Frazier is
  a major name in the gift-basket world. Her Web site is
  www.sweetsurvival.com, from which is available her annual
  Gift Basket Product Guide.

ORGANIZATIONS AND WEB SITES

- Autumn Winds' resources attract many Canadian basketeers:
  www.autumnwinds.com.

- Gift Basket Professionals Network, a trade organization started
  by Flora Brown, mostly of California basket businesses:
  http://www.giftbasketbusiness.org/. Related is Gift Basket Business
  World: *www.giftbasketbusinessworld.com.*

- National Specialty Gift Association and TeleGift Network:
  (813)671-4757; *www.nsgaonline.com, www.telegiftnetwork.com.*
  The TeleGift Network is a service for consumers similar to a floral
  wire service for the delivery of gifts.

MAGAZINE

- *Gift Basket Review:* (800) 729-6338, (904) 634-1902;
  www.festivities-pub.com.

From the Home Front

"I expect to do this forever. Putting together my gift baskets is now almost my sideline business. Working on my Web site has become the challenge."
—Fran Civile, late sixties

 ## 20. Makeup Artist

Makeup has been a significant part of human culture from prehis-
toric times, and applying it has been practiced as a vocation since
the time of the pharaohs. Today, our fascination for looking good, com-

bined with advances in the chemistry of makeup and a constant stream of new products, has created four major specialties for anyone who wishes to earn his or her livelihood as a makeup artist. You can specialize in any of these or do as many of them as you wish.

Beauty and Glamour Makeup Artist

This area focuses on helping people look good for special occasions. Clients include people having professional photographs taken; teenagers going to their proms; women wanting to look and feel great for a party or special family event such as an anniversary or bat mitzvah; and business-people wishing to learn how to apply makeup to look their best at business and social functions and on the job. More and more, this type of work requires knowledge of skin-care products as well as makeup because their clients may have a variety of skin-care issues.

To do this type of work, your state may require you to have a license as a cosmetician (also called aestheticians/estheticians) or a cosmetologist, which is a more inclusive license that includes styling hair.

Film, Television, Theater, and Fashion Makeup Artist

Though it is perhaps the most glamorous of careers, doing makeup for film, broadcast television, theater, or fashion photography is more challenging. Making actors, fashion models, and on-air personalities and their guests look natural and attractive under film or studio lighting takes significant knowledge of cosmetics and how they look on people's faces from behind a camera. These makeup artists need the ability to size up the features of actors or models quickly to determine which makeup products will work best on them given the conditions of the shoot. Then you must perform your work unobtrusively and professionally to the satisfaction of the photographer, director, producer, and executives.

Opportunities in this specialty include doing makeup for local television stations, for ad agencies shooting fashion and commercials in your area, for production crews shooting industrial movies, and of course for movie studios and independent film producers shooting box-office films and music videos who could be on location anywhere in the country.

According to Julie Shiffer, who owns the JLS Professional Makeup School in Hollywood, 15 percent of those in her classes are people over fifty. Julie, who started doing fashion makeup and then moved into films and videos, indicates that age has its advantages because film crews respect older people for their years of experience and artistic talent. Julie points out, however, that a drawback of working for commercials and movies is that shooting often begins early in the morning and continues until late into the night, so the hours are long. You should also be aware that working on movie sets requires admission to a union, which involves special training and passing a test.

Paramedical Makeup Artist

Paramedical makeup artists work with people who need to camouflage scarring from accidents, burns, and surgeries; skin disorders; the redness following cosmetic surgery; and laser resurfacing. This area of makeup work requires a solid understanding of the psychological aspects of the client's situation and its underlying physical nature. The artist must determine if the condition is temporary or something the client will have to deal with the remainder of her or his life. The artist must know if there is a conflict between the medical condition and the makeup to be applied. Paramedical makeup artists must also handle the detailed paperwork of patient documentation for insurance purposes.

Wedding Makeup Artist

Wedding makeup artists specialize in preparing the bride, bridal party, and even the groom for their joyous life event. Doing this type of makeup is no small feat, because people must look their best not only in person, but also for the formal photos and sometimes for a wedding video as well. The difficulty is that makeup that seems natural and vibrant in person can look washed-out in a photo or on video. However, if you apply extra makeup to highlight people's features for photos and video cameras, they may look overly madeup in person. The wedding makeup artist must therefore understand how to balance the two needs so that the bride and bridal party look their best in person and behind camera.

Wedding makeup artists must be prepared to work with all kinds of clients, from young brides who are getting married for the first time to older brides who are remarrying. They must have a good knowledge of skin types and be able to work around nervous brides and doting family members who often seek to supervise the makeup sessions.

Wedding artists typically structure their fees to cover two sessions. In the first session, before the wedding, the artist meets with the client to find out about the plans for the wedding, the color scheme, the number of people involved, and so forth, and to show the bride various possibilities. This session usually takes sixty to ninety minutes. Then on the day of the wedding, the makeup artist arrives at the wedding site very early, before the photos are taken, does the makeup for the entire bridal party, and puts on the bride's headpiece. At this point, the makeup artist may either leave or stay on hand to touch up the makeup at various times during the festivities. Assistants are needed to handle a large wedding party because you can't keep the wedding party waiting as you work on one person at a time.

Judy Stafford is a makeup artist who formerly worked in Hollywood but decided that her personality was more suited to the wedding makeup trade. "This is the most pleasurable thing I've ever done," Judy exclaims. In her San Diego business, Judy does hair and makeup for her clients, but she says she really helps them to stay calm and turn their big day into a pleasurable and memorable event. "The wedding is show time for the bride. She's the star of her movie that day." Judy indicates that her best form of marketing is her Web site, where she posts before-and-after photos of her brides that show the transformation she can bring about. "Brides-to-be will shop around, and you can't very well drive around to show them your books," she says.

Other Markets for Makeup Artists

In addition to these four major specialties, there are other special niches that makeup artists can work in:

- Body makeup for bodybuilders and performers called upon to expose more than their faces.

- Ethnic makeup serving the requirements of non-Caucasians.

- Law-enforcement makeup for officers doing undercover work who often need disguises and special effects.

- Funeral home restoration for open-casket wakes and burial services.

If working in makeup intrigues you, begin by finding out if your state requires that you be licensed as a cosmetician (aesthetician) or cosmetologist. If so, you can obtain the training you need for such a license from a cosmetology or beauty school or community college. A way to supplement what you learn in a school, particularly for working with different skin tones in different types of lighting, is by working with another makeup artist as an assistant or by working on student films.

Makeup Artist at a Glance

 50% 50%

	Minimal	Moderate	More than most
Start-up cost		Kit, tall chair, portable table	
Overhead	X		
Potential earnings			X
Computer skills required		Web site	
Deadline pressures			X
Flexible hours		X	
Overall stress		X	

Likely Transferable Skills, Background, Careers

Backgrounds in fashion, photography, or art can all be useful, because you need to have a basic knowledge of fashion and makeup trends. Whatever your background, you need a flair for color analysis and to know which colors blend together to produce a desired effect. Makeup artists must also have good interpersonal communication skills and be sensitive to their clients' needs.

What to Charge

In general, makeup artists charge between $25 and $100 an hour. However, for weddings, the fees are usually fixed, from $150 to $180 for the bride, around $65 for a bridesmaid, with the price including a meeting prior to the wedding. In addition, a fee can be charged for traveling to the site and for staying throughout the ceremony for touch-ups. By doing more than one wedding per weekend, makeup artists can earn $700 to $800.

For film and video make-up, typical pay rates are $300 to $750 per day. Industrial video is closer to the bottom of the range; studio movie work is closer to the top. In addition, artists can charge a daily "kit fee" to cover supplies.

Best Ways to Get Business

General Marketing

- Approaching photographers, funeral homes, studios, police departments, or ad agencies and letting them know you understand their needs and schedules and that they can count on you to work at their convenience. You will need a portfolio of photos showing off your work, which you develop once you are getting good results.

- Getting publicity about what you do. Because this is a glamour business, it lends itself to photo displays and demonstrations, such as before-and-after shots, and it's ideal for print media and TV.

For Film and Television

- Making a list of a dozen producers or production coordinators by name and sending them your biographical information. Then follow up with a phone call and contact them over and over.

For Weddings

- Putting your portfolio on your Web site, showing before-and-after photos of your clients.

- Networking in business organizations where other wedding services gather, and exhibiting at bridal trade shows, showing your photographs and doing makeovers in your booth.

- Advertising in local bridal magazines, with coupons included for specials.

For Paramedical

- Approaching plastic surgeons and others who do facial surgery about work that may be at least in part in their offices.

Marketing Insights

- Paramedical, funeral, and ethnic makeup are growing specialties. The size of the boom generation as well as the prior generation bodes well for funeral home restorators.

- To increase their income, makeup artists often go directly to manufacturers and arrange to have their individual label put on cosmetics and skin-care preparations, which they sell to their clients. These products can also be sold from a Web site.

- You may be able to do makeup for photographers in exchange for getting free samples of photos for your portfolio.

Where Next?

ASSOCIATIONS

- National Cosmetology Association offers certification: (312) 527-6765; *www.salonprofessionals.org*.

- Canadian Cosmetics Career Association offers a correspondence course: *www.cccacosmetics.com*.

BOOKS

- *The Business of Beauty,* Debbie Purvis (Wall & Emerson, 1994). ISBN: 1895131138.

- *The Complete Make-Up Artist: Working in Film, Television and Theatre,* Penny Delamar (Northwestern University Press, 2002). ISBN: 0810119692.

- *Making Faces,* Kevyn Aucoin and Gena Rowlands (Little Brown, 1999). ISBN: 0316286850. Aucoin is also the author of *The Art of Makeup.*

- *Makeup Your Mind,* Francois Nars (PowerHouse Books, 2002). ISBN: 1576870995.

- *The Technique of the Professional Make-Up Artist,* Vincent J.-R. Kehoe, (Focal Press, 1995). ISBN: 0240802179.

Also see the resources in the Facialist Aesthetician profile.

From the Home Front

"I love being part of a bride's life on her special day. I feel fulfilled because she's beautiful. I'm not doing makeup to create a pretty face, but rather to create a life event."   —Judy Stafford, who started at age forty-nine

---

 ## 21. Mediator

While some holdouts still consider mediation experimental, it has achieved broad acceptance as an alternative method of settling a conflict rather than having each party to a dispute hire lawyers and go to court. The growth of mediation has been explosive for several reasons:

- Clogged courts. Due to the burdens of criminal cases, tight budgets, and other factors, the court system is increasingly congested at both the state and federal levels. The saying "Justice delayed is justice denied" has never been truer.

- Attorneys costing an arm and a leg and your savings, too. The cost of hiring lawyers has risen enormously in the past decade. But you'll be glad to know lawyers' fees are subject to mediation.

- Nonadversarial emphasis. Mediation encourages people to act in a more cooperative and businesslike manner than litigation, which tends to be formal and adversarial.

- Preservation of privacy. Unlike disputes settled in court, the results of mediation are not published in public records. Hearings and rewards are kept private and confidential, which many people desire for their personal matters

- Finality. Mediation can be final, binding, and legally enforceable, subject only to limited review by the courts, which means no endless rounds of costly and emotionally draining appeals.

Mediation is actually one of two forms of conflict resolution (formerly called Alternative Dispute Resolution, or ADR), the other being arbitration. The difference between them is that under mediation, the parties themselves decide how they want to settle the case, whereas in arbitration, the arbitrator is empowered to decide who wins the case based on his or her sole judgment. Thus, mediators do not rule in favor of one of the parties over the other. Rather, they act in advisory and facilitating capacities, helping people on opposite sides find common ground, make compromises, and settle their claims. Mediators offer insights and suggestions, but the parties involved determine whether or not and how a dispute is resolved.

Mediation works best when the parties have roughly equal bargaining power. When power is unequal, traditional litigation may be more suitable, because litigation offers added protection to the weaker party. Mediation is commonly used for resolving workplace, business-to-business, consumer, contract, and domestic-relations disputes, among others. Millions of commercial contracts now contain clauses that provide for some form of non-court-based conflict resolution. At least forty-six of the fifty states require civil cases to go first to mediation or arbitration, and only if the parties can't reach an agreement does the matter go on to the courts. Divorce and child-custody disputes are exempted from this requirement.

Mediators do not need to be lawyers, but they must be skilled at helping people find compromise and understanding. They must receive some training, but at present there are no uniform nationwide standards for training or credentialing mediators. Only about a dozen states actually require mediators to be licensed; and in only one of those states, Florida, are mediators required to be attorneys. However, in order to become impaneled as an American Arbitration Association (AAA) mediator, you must meet certain specific requirements. The AAA and other groups will probably hammer out some national standards by the end of the decade as an alternative to state regulation, which many state legislatures are in various stages of considering.

The AAA's national roster of arbitrators and mediators lists more than twenty thousand individuals from diverse fields and professions. One mediator we spoke with emphasized that having a "background as a human being" was the most important criteria. It also helps to have significant experience or expertise in a particular field or industry, such as construction, human resources, real estate, or labor relations, so you can specialize in that area and attract clients more easily.

For example, when Samantha Winkler began her career as a mediator at age fifty-four, she began doing mediation as a volunteer. She became certified based on her work with community organizations and participates in a group practice where she now specializes in family mediation.

Mediators need to be good at consensus building, have calm and soothing personalities, be creative at solving problems, and act in a professional and dignified manner. A disadvantage of this type of work is that you are frequently dealing with people who are angry, so you have to be skillful at not getting caught in the cross fire. Endurance is important because sessions can be long, particularly the first sessions of intrafamily and divorce mediations. The mediator must be able to concentrate on multiple issues and agendas during these extended sessions. Of course, mediators also must be completely unbiased and come to the process free of any conflicts of interest.

While you may use your home office for business calls and administrative work, the mediation itself must take place in a formal, neutral, and controlled setting such as a conference room, which you may need to rent in an executive office suite.

Mediation at a Glance

40% 60%

	Minimal	Moderate	More than most
Start-up cost	X		
Overhead	X		
Potential earnings		X	
Computer skills required	X		
Deadline pressures—situational	X		
Flexible hours			X
Overall stress		X	

Likely Transferable Skills, Background, Careers

Lawyers easily find their way into mediation. Similarly, a prior career in social work or counseling could provide the necessary skills to help people understand their problems and resolve their conflicts. Substantive experience in a given area can be the basis for a career in mediation, because as T. K. Read of the Global Arbitration Mediation Association, Inc., told us, "Anyone who has expertise in an area will make a better mediator than someone who has just taken mediation training. Although this is not a nationally certified profession, getting some type of certification is important because in certain sectors of mediation it is a requirement. For example, if you are hired through a court system, you may need to show some sort of court-sanctioned certification. Such requirements vary by county."

What to Charge

Mediators usually charge by the hour or by the day, and by the number of parties involved. The fees normally are split by the disputing parties. Hourly rates vary from about $75 to $100 per hour if the mediation is court required. The fees for private parties hiring mediators run higher, $150 to $350 per hour if the mediator is an attorney. However, an important factor in what a mediator can charge is supply and demand. In some parts of the country, an abundance of mediators has depressed rates.

Best Ways to Get Business

- Developing referral relationships with people who are gatekeepers to clients, such as attorneys, accountants, and mental-health professionals. If your specialty is domestic relations, contacting the courts in your area.

- Doing pro bono work, particularly for churches.

- Face-to-face networking inside business and trade organizations such as the chamber of commerce and business-referral organizations.

- Having your own Web site with key words that identify your community and your specialty so people using a search engine will find your site; also getting listed on on-line directories. The Global Arbitration Mediation Association, *www.gama.com,* offers free listings.

- Listing in the Yellow Pages, which will enable you to be found on Web directories like *switchboard.com* and *anywho.com.* Consider ads on local directory sites like *Yahoo Get Local* and *SuperPages.*

- Speaking about mediation at business organizations that are pertinent to your specialty and community organizations such as Kiwanis and Rotary Clubs.

- Writing articles or a column on conflict resolution.

Marketing Insights

- Mediation is growing in acceptance because of the benefits it offers to parties in a dispute, including saving money, a less divisive atmosphere, and a tendency to work at preserving the relationship while solving the problem. Mediation also usually proceeds much faster than working through lawyers or court litigation. Mediators can often resolve conflicts in just three or four sessions.

- The field has many specialization possibilities: admiralty, architectural, professional fees, banking, business-industry, civil rights, commercial, construction contractor/subcontractor, debtor/creditor, domain name, education, elder care, energy, employer/employee, engineering, entertainment, environmental, equine, family law, franchising, homeowner association, intergovernmental, domestic relations (parent/teen, couples, siblings), insurance, international trade, Internet consumer, Internet service providers, labor relations, landlord-tenant, land use and zoning, maritime, motor carrier, parenting, partnership, Native American, pension and benefit, public policy, real estate (mortgages/financing, purchase/sale agreement), securities, shareholder, sports, tax, and technology. However, according to T. K. Read, the most promising arenas are family law and contract disputes between small businesses that involve small dollar amounts.

- To make a living as a mediator requires marketing intensively until establishing a self-sustaining practice; mediators can spend as much as 80 percent of their time marketing.

- Some mediation can be done over the telephone and by e-mail, but also, due to cost savings, it's anticipated that using videoconferencing with parties who are not in the same locale will be increasingly common. Many people, however, believe that nothing is as effective as in-person mediation.

Where Next

ASSOCIATIONS

- American Arbitration Association: (212) 484-4000; *www.adr.org*.
- Association for Conflict Resolution (ACR) has several publications: (202) 464-9700; *www.acrnet.org*.
- Global Arbitration Mediation Association, Inc. (GAMA): (770) 235-7818; *www.gama.com*.

BOOKS

- *Basic Skills for the New Mediator*, Allan H. Goodman (Solomon Publications, 1994). ISBN: 0967097304.
- *Mediation Career Guide,* Forrest S. Mosten (Jossey-Bass, 2001). ISBN: 0787957038.
- *The Mediation Process,* Christopher W. Moore (Jossey-Bass, 2003). ISBN: 0787964468.

TRAINING AND CERTIFICATION

- Community colleges offer degrees in mediation and conflict resolution.
- Some training can be obtained by interning at a local mediation or community-service program center in your community.

From the Home Front

"I can't imagine doing something at this point in my life if I didn't have a passion for it and couldn't be successful, not just financially, but in terms of knowing I have made a contribution."   —Samantha Winkler, fifty-nine

Snapshot: Miriam and Richard Zimmerman, Divorce Mediators

When Richard Zimmerman attended a workshop on divorce mediation over two years ago, he noticed the workshop leaders included a lawyer/therapist team. As he watched them work he thought, "My wife and I could do them one better." Richard is both a lawyer and an accountant, so he could handle the legal/financial aspects of resolving divorce issues. His wife, Miriam, is a communications specialist and counseling psychology professor; so she could handle interpersonal communication issues.

Richard came home excited with the idea that divorce mediation might be a way he and Miriam could embark on a second career path together. Both age fifty-five, he'd been working in corporate finance; she'd been teaching at the college level. Miriam liked the idea enough to attend the workshop herself and came home equally enthusiastic. "He can handle the substance; I can facilitate the process," she concluded. So, the Zimmermans took additional training in mediation and began volunteering at a community-based mediation center to gain experience.

They discovered they enjoyed both mediating and working together, so Miriam took a sabbatical from the university to launch Divorce Mediation Group, providing confidential and complete mediation services for the divorcing couple. Based in San Mateo, California, the couple now provide a full range of services including property division, spousal and child support, and parenting plans.

In talking of the benefits of working together in their new career, Miriam explains that "throughout over thirty years of marriage, I had never fully appreciated Richard's ability in quantitative analysis. He can look at a divorcing couple's complicated balance sheet and figure out many different ways to carve up the pie equitably." On the other hand, Richard has developed a fuller appreciation of Miriam's ability to help couples resolve conflicts and make decisions together.

By teaming up, they're able to help couples resolve the difficult legal, financial, and parenting process quickly, privately, and economically. It's a winning combination.

22. Mobile Notary

Every time we have an important document to sign—or even a not-so-important one—it needs to be notarized. Real estate and financial transactions as well as legal documents such as affidavits, jurats, acknowledgments, and wills all need to be notarized and all feed the demand for notary services. The mobile notary brings these services to the client's location. If you don't mind using a cell phone and driving from place to place, you can make a good living as a mobile notary while enjoying an autonomous and flexible schedule.

A mobile notary is a particularly valuable solution for people who cannot leave where they are, as well as those who do not have time to go to an office where a notary is. Clients range from home buyers needing loan documents notarized to businesses that regularly need customers to sign notarized documents. Persons in jail and patients in hospitals often need powers of attorney and property deeds notarized. Students need to sign residency forms.

Gerrie Pierre-Fleurimond, named Notary of the Year by the National Notary Association in 2003, started her notary service on a part-time basis to supplement her income from her corporate job. Her business thrived thanks to low interest rates and a booming real estate market. Pierre-Fleurimond's clients include legal organizations, nursing homes, and lenders. Now she also provides training for notaries in the New York–New Jersey area.

If you have a legal background, you might, like Dorothy Monigan, provide paralegal services in addition to notary services. Dorothy, of Ringwood, started her New Jersey–based mobile notary service at the age of fifty. While she specializes in loan signings, she also offers fingerprinting services.

Mobile notaries need to always be accessible by telephone and to be able to respond immediately to requests for service. Documents are always time sensitive, and it's mandatory to respond to requests without delay. Depending on the type of clientele, some periods of the month are busier than others. For example, loan signings are much heavier at the end of the month than at the beginning.

Some notaries travel up to a fifty-mile radius from their home offices; others choose to limit their service area to within five miles. Depending on where you are located and your client base, you can choose how much and how far you drive. Mobile notaries find it's important to schedule stops to get the most out of their driving time, but special last-minute trips are to be expected—especially if you are "on call" for a hospital.

To become a notary, you must pass a state examination. All states regulate their notaries, and requirements vary from state to state. Taking an exam-preparation seminar can better your chances of passing the first time. Also courses are available on loan signings and marketing a mobile notary service.

Mobile Notary at a Glance

 20% 80%

	Minimal	Moderate	More than most
Start-up cost	X		
Overhead		X	
Potential earnings		X	
Computer skills required	X		
Deadline pressures			X
Flexible hours			X
Overall stress		X	

Likely Transferable Skills, Background, Careers

Any work that demands close attention to detail and the ability to respond cheerfully to the requests of others. Having worked in a legal, real estate, or banking setting is helpful as is a Johnny-on-the-spot personality.

What to Charge

States regulate what notaries can charge. Ten dollars per signature is typical. Many documents require multiple signatures. Mobile notaries additionally can charge for travel, which some do on a mileage basis. Others charge a flat fee. For example, $35 might include travel and the first three notarized signatures. Some mobile notaries charge a premium for signings at airports because parking and security require more time. Fingerprinting charges run $10 per person plus $25 to $50 for travel.

Best Ways to Get Business

- Developing referral relationships with law offices, title companies, apartment complexes, realtors, and social-service directors of nursing homes and hospitals.

- Getting listed in hospital and nursing home service directories. For a fee, you may be able to get an exclusive listing, that is, be the only notary public listed.

- Having a Web site that lists your services and fees. Use key words that identify your community so people using search engines will find you. You may wish to collaborate on a Web site with other mobile notaries in your region, particularly if you each cover specific areas within a common region.

- Getting listed on sites like *www.123notary.com*.

- Listing in the Yellow Pages, which will enable you to be found on Web directories like *switchboard.com* and *anywho.com*. Consider ads on local directory sites like *Yahoo Get Local* and *SuperPages*.

- Walking around the neighborhood—that is, dropping in to introduce yourself and your service to local business establishments and leaving your card.

Marketing Insights

- Having a customer service orientation is key to developing the referral relationships that will create a sustaining business.

- Mobile notaries, in addition to offering quick service, can accommodate clients who wish to transact business at restaurants, hotels, or airports instead of at their homes or offices.

Where Next?

ASSOCIATIONS, SUPPLIES, AND TRAINING

- American Society for Notaries: (850) 671-5164; *www.notaries.org*.

- National Notary Association offers a home-study course: (800) 876-6827; *www.nationalnotary.org*.

BOOKS

- Publications are available from your state agency that appoints and commissions notaries public. Usually they're free.

WEB SITES

- Notary Public. Web site offers various services and links to the appropriate offices of all fifty states: *www.notarypublic.com*.

- Notary Signing Agent, affiliated with the National Notary Association to "help lenders, closing agents and signing services find reliable, mobile Notary Signing Agents": *www.signingagent.com*.

- Gerrie Pierre-Fleurimond's site: *www.notarytrainer.com*.

From the Home Front

"I enjoy meeting people and knowing that I'm helping them. Plus I have an anal personality and I like the detail aspects of the paperwork, too!"

—Dorothy Monigan, fifty-two

 ## 23. Mobile Screen Installation and Repair

Window and door screens, once a simple, functional necessity, are now part of home fashion and chosen as carefully as the windows and doors they cover. With the options for screens ranging from childproof, petproof, color coordinated, and disappearing, the potential for catering to a clientele desiring custom-tailored, top-quality screen designs is significant. But the core of this business remains installing and repairing screens.

Jim Red, a Silicon Valley engineer, has found the mobile screen repair business he opened at fifty-one in Las Vegas more recession proof than the high-tech world he came from. Living in Las Vegas, Red finds a strong demand for fiberglass sunscreens and sunshades to shield homes and businesses from intense sunlight. In many parts of the country, the threat of West Nile Virus, which is transmitted by mosquitoes, is motivating people to keep their screens in good repair and to screen any openings that lack them.

Mobile screen installation and repair is not just a guy business. Sondra Costa was one of the first women to become involved in the mobile screen business, starting after leaving a job she didn't care for as a hospital utilization officer. She said her job was to "kick out patients about three days before they were well. It was a thankless job. Both doctors and patients didn't like you." So when her brother invited her to take a look at his mobile screen repair business, she did, and ultimately decided to partner with another woman to buy the business, which they successfully operated for twenty years.

Sondra and her cohort became known in the San Francisco Bay area as the "Screening Grannies," after a TV station did a feature story about them. "We got our business up to $245,000 a year with one trailer," says Costa. At the time we spoke to Sondra, she had sold her San Francisco franchise and was consulting with other mobile screen businesses. She estimates that over 10 percent of screen repair and installation businesses are started by people over fifty, and Red asserts it is possible to do this work well into one's seventies.

In addition to installing and replacing screen doors and windows, you can also install pet doors and grilles, and replace window and door frames. You can also install and repair security screen doors, alarm screens, custom French-style screen doors, retractable screens and doors, sliding and swinging doors, patio doors, awnings, and various types of shade screens. Sites can include owner-occupied homes, rental houses, and businesses. What you can sell varies with the type of job. For example, homeowners might choose more customized designs to add value and beauty to their property, while rental agents want to keep tenants happy by making sure screens are in good repair.

This business is easier if two or more people work together. Costa described the fun she had working with her partner. Otherwise, Jim Red says, "You meet people but you work alone." Red's wife handles the phones while he does the installation work. In the busiest six months of the year, he hires a helper.

Mobile screening does not require that you have a workshop, but if you don't have a good-sized garage available you may need to acquire a storage unit for materials. All the work can be done from a properly outfitted van or truck that will accommodate you working on site. Franchises provide a customized thirty-five-foot trailer with the purchase of a franchise. The trailer requires a pickup truck to pull it, but it provides a work area and by painting your business's name on the sides of the trailer you in essence have moving billboards. You can expect to have new customers approach you when they see your trailer parked at a location where you're working and at restaurants where you're having lunch.

Screen repair and installation make moderate physical demands. Costa estimates that 25 percent of the work involves climbing ladders, although most upper-story windows can be accessed from inside a building. You also need to protect yourself from the risks of sun exposure, and while the tools are simple, the chop saw needed to make screens must be used with respect.

Mobile Screen Repair and Installation at a Glance

30% 70%

	Minimal	Moderate	More than most
Start-up cost			X
Overhead		X	
Potential earnings			X
Computer skills required	X		
Deadline pressures	X		
Flexible hours		X	
Overall stress		X	

Likely Transferable Skills, Background, Careers

Virtually anyone can learn to do this work. It involves using small tools, measuring, and fitting, some lifting and climbing. An average amount of business savvy is required to maintain schedules and keep records.

What to Charge

Charges vary regionally. Some materials, like solar screening, are priced by the square foot: $3 to $5. Insect screens are priced by the piece, around $27 for an average-sized window. If ladder work is involved, there is an up charge depending on the number of climbs. Thirty-five dollars is an average price to do installation or repair on the second story.

Best Ways to Get Business

- Calling on screen shops and handyman shops and offering to take overload or work they don't want.

- Contacting real estate agents to develop referrals. Offer to provide the agents with coupons they can give out to home buyers, good for one screen repair. One free repair can lead to more work and repeat customers.

- Having attractive signage on your truck and trailer.

- If you're independent as opposed to owning a franchise, having your own Web site, using it as an electronic brochure. Be sure to include your Web site on your signage, door hangers, coupons, and business cards.

- Listing in the Yellow Pages, which will enable you to be found on Web directories like *switchboard.com* and *anywho.com*. Consider ads on local directory sites like *Yahoo Get Local* and *SuperPages*.

- Soliciting door-to-door, leaving door hangers for people not at home stating that you'll be repairing screens in their neighborhood in the next two days.

Marketing Insights

- Offering a mobile service means convenience. By going to the customers' homes and businesses for every aspect of the service, customers feel you are saving them the time and the hassle of driving to a hardware store or screen shop, trying to describe what they need, and then scheduling another time for the work to be done.

- Once you establish customers, you can increase your revenue by recommending new products suited to their homes or businesses, offering preseason specials, and simply keeping in contact with them about their future needs. Sondra Costa says she always suggested a new door instead of rescreening an old one, pointing out the economy and adding, "There's nothing as tacky as an old screen door." When neighbors look at a new door, they order ones for themselves. She asserts that 95 percent of her business comes from these kinds of referrals.

- To help you create the desire for more work from your customers, you need to keep abreast of the latest developments in screen fashion and in protective materials.

- In seasonal climates, you may increase your off-season work by emphasizing other kinds of products, like security doors, window grills, alarm screen repair, pet grills, and pet doors.

- Whenever possible, show clients products that will enhance the look of their home. Appearances are important, especially if the screens are on the front of the house or business establishment.

- Red figures that for six months of the year he experiences extreme demand and the six other months are slow. Costa recommends using slower times to network and get new business.

- Though you don't need a contractor's license to install and repair screens, getting one will increase your credibility with prospective customers.

Where to Turn for Training

You either gain experience working with an existing company or purchase a franchise. One franchise offers six days of comprehensive training, including a "first time in business" course.

Franchises

- The Screenmobile: (866) 540-5800; *www.screenmobile.com.*
- The Screen Machine: (877) 505-1985; *www.screen-machine.com.*

From the Home Front

"This is so nontech. I threw away my PDA (personal digital assistant). I don't get on airplanes, so there's no hassle at airports. It's such a relief not to have all that. There's no traffic, less stress, and I like that. But I do check my e-mail. My wife and I enjoy each other more; we hardly saw each other before."

—Jim Red, fifty-seven, Las Vegas

---

24. Personal Historian and Scrapbooking

One consequence of our mobile society is that fewer family members, particularly the younger ones, are around their elders enough to hear the family stories. Even if they're not geographically separated, all generations of families are pursuing 24/7 lifestyles, and our family history and stories can get lost in the hustle. But many of us, especially as parents and grandparents age, realize our past could be lost forever and want to record it before it's too late. That's the role personal historians play in the lives of their clients.

Personal historians interview loved ones and record their stories and pull together treasured mementos and family photographs to create a living legacy in a book, audio, video, or family Web site. Some personal historians help prepare ethical wills and legacy letters by which family members pass on personal values and family traditions.

When Jan Lindgren's mother became ill, she realized she didn't know that much about her mother's childhood. Eager to fill this gap in her family history, she got out a tape recorder and began to interview her mother. "It took weeks to do," Jan explains, "because my mother's health was failing." But each night after teaching first-graders all day, Jan would ask her mother a question or two. Then after twenty-three years of teaching, Jan retired at fifty and began taping other personal stories. She runs her company, Life Reflections, from her home in Wheat Ridge, Colorado. Her motto is a quote from Alex Haley: "When an old person dies it's like a library burning." "Who is the librarian in your family?" she asks.

Ron O'Reilly, sixty-five, of Ringos, New Jersey, had enjoyed storytelling as an avocation and done some work in anthropology before he became a personal historian. As he sees it, his job is to create a smooth narrative of someone's history. He records family stories either on tape or with video cameras and then artfully edits out repetition and "ums" and "ers." He finds it helps when you know something personally about the experience of the individual, whether it's having served in a war or raised a large family. "That way you can fill in the details," he explains.

Kitty Axelson-Berry, founder and president of the Association of Personal Historians (APH), started doing personal history work at age forty-four but finds that more and more of her colleagues are older. She believes maturity gives them an advantage. "You need to have sensitivity for how much to push the project along and when to lay back." When interviewing clients, Kitty suggests involving other people in the community who share common backgrounds. She finds the interview process may be easier and more fluid when people feel they are with friends. "The final product," she says, "is the result of a combination of the desires of the client and your personal capabilities."

Scrapbooking is another approach to building a family memoir. Using special materials, family members create their own scrapbooks by gathering together visual and written family mementos into a "memory book." So as not to corrode photographs and other memorabilia, the materials used in scrapbooking need to be of archival caliber like those used in museums. So a huge craft products industry has grown out of this trend. Creative Memories, a company in Minnesota, uses home-based consultants to sell scrapbook products and offer workshops to help people create their own remembrance books.

In a similar do-it-yourself vein, Jan Lindgren has refined the questions she asks loved ones when taking personal histories into a kit she sells to family members who want to tape their own family stories. After recording one family's story, Lindgren stumbled onto another need for personal histories. Pleased with her interview of his grandparents, the son asked Jan if she would tape his young children's stories. He and his wife wanted to save their precious young voices for the future, so Jan adapted her interview questions to create a children's version of Life's Reflections and Kidviewz was born. She also sells it as a product a parent could use.

Families and individuals are not the only ones interested in their histories. Often corporations, organizations, communities, and cities want to document their progress, the changes that have happened over the years, and the how and why. Companies can use the information to help them in acquiring capital and for stockholders' information. Cities can use a history to increase tourism or to establish the particular community as a place where something important occurred, or as a place where everyday life is rich and interesting.

Personal Historian at a Glance

 40% 60%

	Minimal	Moderate	More than most
Start-up cost	X		
Overhead	X		
Potential earnings		X	
Computer skills required		print	visual
Deadline pressures		X	
Flexible hours		X	
Overall stress		X	

Likely Transferable Skills, Background, Careers

Writers and editors, teachers (particularly English teachers), social workers, therapists, lawyers, videographers, documentary-film producers, and media personalities transition well into this field.

What to Charge

Some personal historians bill by the hour; others by the project. Hourly rates range from $50 to $75. Some can bill by the week for as much as $7,000. It takes experience with ten to fifteen projects to be able to accurately quote a project price. The costs involve the technology used to create the final product (print, audio, video, Web site, etc.) also need to be accounted for in pricing. Experienced personal historians recommend obtaining a deposit and collecting progress payments.

Best Ways to Get Business

- Advertising in your college's alumnae/i press, many of which only take ads from alumnae/i.

- Doing "life writing" as a volunteer service.

- Face-to-face networking inside business and trade organizations such as the chamber of commerce and business referral organizations, particularly for organization history work.

- Getting publicity about your work in local papers and family-oriented newsletters and Web sites.

- Giving do-it-yourself workshops, which produce revenue and lead some in attendance to conclude they would prefer to use your services.

- Contacting funeral homes, high schools, colleges, veteran organizations about creating digital biographics for their members, alumni, customers. Funeral homes are doing this as a way of extending service to the living.

Marketing Insights

- The key benefit you offer clients is that you are helping them get their family story told, so loved ones can share what's been most important to them in life, and express their deepest reflections. But often family members make assumptions about common knowledge, thus leaving gaps in their own story. Your selling point as a professional who is not party to family struggles and issues can help bring out the full richness of their history.

- Other specialization possibilities include doing histories for class- and military-reunion projects, assisting lawyers in writing the life stories of plaintiffs for use during a trial, making photo quilts (photos are scanned onto transfer paper, then transferred using a hot iron onto pima cotton), preserving and restoring photos and other mementos, putting stories to music ("life songs"), using a particular "ethnic" tradition for storytelling, transcribing recorded material, rerecording audio and videos before they deteriorate, and transferring recorded materials to different formats, like DVD.

- While many family histories are funded by a well-to-do family member, other families share the cost.

Where Next?

PERSONAL HISTORIANS

- Association of Personal Historians (APH), directory of member services, links to oral history interview questions and topics: *www.personalhistorians.org.*

- Kidviewz: *www.kidviewz.com.*

- Soleil Lifestory Network, training workshops and supplies: (207) 353-5454; *www.turningmemories.com.*

SCRAPBOOKING

- Creative Memories sells supplies and is a multilevel direct-selling company: (320) 251-7524; *www.creative-memories.com.*

- *Simply Scrapbooks* magazine: (866) 334-8149; *www.simplescrapbooksmag.com.*

From the Home Front

"It is a dream come true to have a service that is so valuable, especially after loved ones are gone," she says. "I cherish my mother's voice and am forever grateful I can offer this service or opportunity to others."

—Jan Lindgren, seventy-one

25. Professional Investigator and Security Consultant

Security considerations are growing to be a routine part of everything from building design and employment background checks to preventing pirated goods. Terrorism, personal crime, stolen patents and copyrights, corporate espionage, counterfeited goods, insurance fraud, and missing persons are all unfortunate realities of the twenty-first century,

All these nefarious dealings, however, create a huge need for professional investigators (formerly called private investigators) and security consultants. So if you have an interest in these professions, you'll be welcome. You can train to work as either a PI or a security consultant in a wide variety of specialties, and you don't need to have a law-enforcement background. In fact, Dakota Michaels of the Spy Academy finds that unless they've been trained to do undercover work, cops don't make the best PIs. Here are overviews of the two professions.

Professional Investigator (PI)

Television, movies, and novels typically depict PIs working from downtown offices, but in fact, many of them work from home. Being a professional investigator is not necessarily a dangerous business, as most PIs have given up their guns for a computer, a camera, and a car. This is because a large amount of PI work today involves researching people and events via the Internet, tailing them by car to see what they do and where they go, capturing their sometimes shady activities on camera such as when someone who claims to be injured is out playing basketball.

One of the most common areas of PI work is background checking, fueled by the need of corporations to prescreen potential employees. Background checking has become commonplace because nearly one-third of résumés contain falsified information, often with serious-enough misrepresentations to cause a prospective employer to pass on an applicant. Corporations have another motivation for background checks these days: the fact that courts are holding companies negligent or liable in cases where employees have been guilty of wrongdoing or violence in the workplace and the company did not prescreen them adequately enough to identify these tendencies.

Background checking involves three types of possible investigations: 1) personal record checking, including credit and criminal history, driving record, lawsuits, and judgments; 2) reference checking to verify the past employers and references given by applicants; and 3) credentials verification, to verify a person's stated educational background.

Some companies have in-house staff that does this background checking, but in order to avoid potentially costly oversights and mistakes many prefer to outsource the work to a professional investigator or consultant who specializes in this work. Background checking is also used by people considering business dealings with another company or individual, by landlords screening tenants, and increasingly by couples who want to do a premarital check on their prospective mates.

There is a huge range of other types of PI work, too. Dakota Michaels, who trains PIs at his Spy Academy in Studio City, California, points out that PIs currently are being hired to:

- Locate assets that one spouse hides from another in a divorce case.

- Investigate and identify counterfeited goods such as DVDs, movies, software, clothing, handbags, watches, and cosmetics.

- Research insurance fraud, such as in workers' compensation where the person turns out to be healthy, or life insurance fraud when a person did not disclose his or her truthful medical records or died within two years after taking out a large policy.

- Trace a missing heir whose relative has died and left money.

- Prevent (or perform) corporate espionage to obtain secrets about what business competitors are doing.

- Retrieve information about prospective merger partners or acquisition targets.

Given the vast range of work, PIs are used by corporations, attorneys, accountants, insurance companies, employment agencies, collection agencies, and newspapers.

Michaels indicates that many of his students at the Spy Academy are over fifty, having come from a wide variety of backgrounds, and learn to use "backdoor" techniques, such as pretexting (fibbing) and surreptitious spying. His students have included journalists and grandmothers. The hardest task in this work, Michaels says, is learning how to tail someone in a car without being noticed. "You have to learn when to stay close by and when to drop back. This means you have to be a good driver."

Kenneth Variale is another PI who exemplifies the type of work you can do. After retiring from the Alcohol, Tobacco, and Firearms (ATF) division of the federal government at age fifty, Variale became a PI working for attorneys, insurance companies, and private parties. Originally much of his work focused on business intelligence in merger and acquisition cases. With age, though, he now tries to do most of his work from home using database searching rather than on-site surveillances and interviews. Variale points out that an awesome amount of data is available in public records that are searchable on the Internet or at county courthouses. As he says, "People hire me for what they can do themselves but don't know how." He advises newcomers who don't have a background in security to begin by doing surveillance work as a way to break into the field.

Robert Townsend, another self-employed PI who began his career after age fifty, says he often works in the area of product liability, being hired by the injured party's attorney to analyze the technology that caused the accident. He find his membership in the National Association of Legal Investigators valuable.

All but six states require PIs to be licensed, and some municipalities in nonlicensing states require them to register with the city or the police department. Some states also require that anyone doing background checking for a fee become licensed as a professional investigator. Licensing requirements vary but usually involve one to three years' experience in some sort of investigative work, such as law enforcement or claims adjusting. Sometimes this requirement can be met by having worked in a collection agency or having done investigative journalism. Note: Some states will do a background check *on you* when you apply to take the tests required for a license.

Security Consultant

Security consulting involves working for clients who want to protect their employees, property, client lists, or proprietary technology. There are several subspecialties, such as:

- Site consulting, evaluating the physical design of buildings and spaces.

- Systems design, specifying security needs at the design phase of construction and remodeling projects. This may also involve developing electronic security tools for use at the location.

- Technical security consulting, specifying, selecting, and installing specific security technologies and products.

- Forensic consulting, serving as an expert witness in trials in which security breaches are at issue, such as can occur with fires, thefts, break-ins, etc.

- Teaching, training law-enforcement officials and others about your specialization.

Security consultants are used by architectural firms, contractors, companies building new buildings, museums, banks, stadiums, city and municipal governments, schools and universities, computer facilities, and many other types of employers.

Unlike professional investigators, security consultants need not be licensed, though it helps to be certified by passing a rigorous examination given by one of the two associations listed below.

Process Server

A somewhat related field, legal process serving, involving serving suit papers and other legal documents that require personal service, has its own professional association, the National Association of Professional Process Servers, at *www.napps.com*.

Professional Investigator at a Glance

 20% 80%

Security Consultant

 60% 40%

	Minimal	Moderate	More than most
Start-up cost $5,000		X	
Overhead		X	

	Minimal	Moderate	More than most
Potential earnings			X
Computer skills required			X
Deadline pressures		Insurance work	
Flexible hours			X
Overall stress—if demanding clients. Stress the clients, not the cases.		X	

Likely Transferable Skills, Background, Careers

Often you can draw on your experience in whatever field where you've been working. Having had a career in a specialized technical field, for example, might help in developing a specialty in investigating product liability cases; accounting in divorce and forensic work; a background in an art field could be useful working with museums in art-theft prevention. First-rate computer skills are vital, as are creativity and intuition when it comes to knowing how to develop leads for a case.

What to Charge

Hourly fees for professional investigators range from $40 to $200, with the higher rates going for specialized technical work. Work done on a computer is typically priced on a project basis. PIs may also bill separately for any expenses incurred during an investigation.

Background checking is priced on a piece-rate basis, ranging from $20 for a tenant check to hundreds of dollars for national searches of criminal records or workers' compensation claims. Individual record searches such as credit reports, driving records, and education credentials range from $10 to $30. Reference checking ranges from $15 to $50 per reference.

Security consultants command between $100 to $250 per hour, with the higher fees for forensic work.

Best Ways to Get Business

- Directly soliciting trial lawyers and their office managers, insurance companies, and corporate personnel departments.

- Getting listed in bar-association directories of expert witnesses.

- Getting publicity about your work.

- Giving seminar presentations and speeches.

- Having a booth at conventions of industries you know about or wish to work in where you will meet potential corporate clients.

- Having your own Web page with its own domain name with testimonial letters and any articles you have written.

- Listing in the Yellow Pages is helpful for reaching the general public about PI work but not for corporate work.

- Participating in trade associations and professional organizations for the type of clientele you are seeking (industrial, law firms, educational, historic sites, etc.)

- Showing your expertise by writing articles and letters to the editors of newspapers and business journals. This can lead to being used as a source by journalists.

Marketing Insights

Age is a benefit to a professional investigator, according to Kenneth Variale, because "as you get older, people trust you more." He also believes it's easier for someone to get needed information from people. "We've had a lifetime of learning how to read people, develop rapport, and manage a conversation, all skills that are important to a professional investigator."

- The war on terrorism is resulting in the spending of billions of dollars in research and development of new security technology. It's important to keep up with changing technology as it becomes available to the private sector.

- Professional investigators network with one another over the computer on sites like *PICases@yahoo.com,* passing on work to each other, subcontracting specific tasks, and generally helping one another with cases.

Where Next?

ASSOCIATIONS

- Association of Certified Fraud Examiners: (800) 245-3321, (512) 478-9000; *www.cfenet.com*.

- ASIS International certifies security professionals: 703-519-6200; *www.asisonline.org*.

- National Association of Legal Investigators: *www.nalionline.org*.

- World Association of Detectives: *www.world-detectives.com*.

BOOKS ON PROFESSIONAL INVESTIGATION

- *The Complete Idiot's Guide to Private Investigating*, Steven Kerry Brown (Alpha Books, 2002). ISBN: 0028643992.

- *Complete Reference Checking Handbook*, Edward C. Andler, Dara Herbst and David Sears (AMACOM, 2003). ISBN: 0814407447.

- *Introduction to Security*, Robert J. Fischer and Gion Green (Butterworth-Heinemann, 1998). ISBN: 0750698608.

- *Private Investigation*, Bill Copeland (Absolutely Zero Loss Inc., 1997). ISBN: 0965765997.

  Public Records Online, Michael L. Sankey (Facts on Demand Press, 2003). ISBN: 1889150371.

- *Security Consulting*, Charles A. Sennewald (Butterworth-Heinemann, 1996). ISBN: 0750696435.

TRAINING

- Community colleges and four-year colleges offer degrees in security administration.

- The Spy Academy, operated by Dakota Michaels, interviewed for this profile, is an example of the many private schools for professional investigation in major cities: (661) 242-1788; *www.dmispy.com/spy_academy.htm*. A list of schools can be found at *www.infoguys.com*.

WEB SITES

- Investigators Anywhere: *www.investigatorsanywhere.com.*

- PI Mall: *www.pimall.com.*

From the Home Front

"I have many types of people in my classes at the Spy Academy. There's no age limit. I have grandmothers who want to be sleuths. Corporations are doing lots of surveillance work. The big studios are paying $100,000 to find counterfeiters and pirated goods."

—Dakota Michaels, Studio City, California

Snapshot: Edmund J. Pankau, International Security Expert

Edmund Pankau began his fifty-plus speaking and writing career as a security expert extraordinaire after having been a private investigator in The Woodlands, Texas. For thirty years, Edmund had specialized in financial investigation, security consulting, security negligence, and premises liability, among other security-related concerns.

"Learning and teaching have always been my goal," he explains. So when his investigation business slowed a bit, it was a natural shift for him to pursue speaking and writing about his expertise gained from investigating some of the nation's most publicized cases he'd worked on with attorneys, businesses, and U.S. Government regulatory agencies.

As the public became more aware that fraud is a major issue, the demand for Pankau's books and presentations grew. "The more speaking I did," he remembers, "the better I liked it." Soon his speaking fees rose to a point where he could afford to hire other investigators and devote his time to his new career. Over the past eight years he's become one of the nation's foremost speakers on security and privacy issues and has taught thousands of government and private investigators and auditors how to investigate fraud and white-collar crime.

With the security problems in the United States having spread to the Pacific Rim and the Caribbean, Edmund is a favorite with international audiences as well who want to know how to protect their companies from fraud, theft, and terrorism. Always ready to learn more, Edmund has also returned to school to get his Ph.D. Of his new career as international security expert he says, "It's a lot of fun and it's made a difference in my business, too."

26. Professional Organizer

The more stuff we have, whether it's possessions or information, the more help we need organizing it all. Few among us can keep up with the ever-increasing flow of mail, email, and other information flooding our lives. Despite growing square footage of homes most people simply have too much stuff and too little space to put it in, leaving us neatness-challenged, unable to get rid of things or to figure out how to better organize them. Our closets are full, our drawers are stuffed, and our computers and files are overflowing.

Coming to our rescue are professional organizers. They step into our homes and offices to help us take control and put our lives into operating order. Professional organizers help their clients organize everything from paper folders to computer files, from desktops to filing cabinets, from bookshelves to closets, kitchens, and garages. They help clients become more efficient, faster at finding what they need, smarter, and sometimes richer. In short, professional organizers help people turn raw data and information into knowledge, wisdom, and power.

Professional organizing is a relatively young profession, but the market demand for it has helped the profession grow at the incredible rate of 16 percent a year, according to Barry Izsak, president of the National Association of Professional Organizers (NAPO), which had nearly 2,000 members in 2003. Barry indicates that the profession has been able to capitalize on the acceptance of the notion that being disorganized is no longer shameful but chic. Using a professional organizer these days is almost a sign of hipness, like having a personal trainer or a therapist. Professional organizers have written books, and appeared on TV talk shows, with some almost as famous as Dr. Phil.

People who decide to become organizers come from many backgrounds. According to NAPO, 94 percent are women, with an average age of forty-six, 31 percent of the members being between fifty and fifty-nine, and

7 percent over age fifty-nine. And they are a smart bunch—the majority of members (71 percent have bachelor's, master's, or Ph.D. degrees).

Organizers can be generalists or specialists. Some work only in residential settings; others work exclusively in offices or corporations, such as banks, hospitals, schools, law offices, medical practices, and other business enterprises. Organizing home offices—a cross between residential and office work—is one of the fastest-growing areas of the profession. Other fast-growing specialists include organizing small business and corporate executive's offices.

Some organizers further refine their specialities by working with a particular type of problem such as computer documents or databases, collections, estate sales, filing cabinets, photographs and other memorabilia, garages, attics, basements, closets, kitchens, space designing, packing and moving, bill paying and finances, event planning, goal setting, relocation, project management, time management, and wardrobes. Some organizers focus on niche markets, working with specific types of clients such as well-to-do socialites, seniors and retirees about to become empty nesters, people with attention deficit disorder, teens, doctors, lawyers, and, finally, the "chronically disorganized" who constantly fail to understand how to control their clutter.

Sally Allen is a professional organizer in Golden, Colorado. She moved into the profession when she was fifty years old, and she is now seventy-two. Her company, A Place for Everything, is a "professional organizing business that helps individuals and companies to effectively arrange space and efficiently manage time by assessing environments and habits, by hands-on organizing services, and by creating systems and maintenance programs to keep on track in the home and office." Sally's Web site indicates that she gained her skills working with Marriott International Hotels and Resorts, the 1984 Los Angeles Olympic Committee, the 1996 Atlanta Committee for the Olympic Games, while moving her family nineteen times!"

Sally affirms that being over age fifty has its benefits in this profession. "If you have confidence, you will instill that confidence in your clients, and they'll recognize that you know what you're doing." She often sees herself as a coach, getting her clients to focus. Her speciality has been working with dental and small medical offices, where she has developed the expertise to help them learn how to store their files.

Sally has also done many other types of organizing, and often has more than a dozen clients per month, especially working in home offices where sometimes she acts more like a small business consultant *cum* organizer. As Sally says, "Home entrepreneurs have good ideas but they don't know how to organize a business. I help them identify their goals, think about their business plan, and work with them on many other details of their business. Sometimes I feel like an itinerant entrepreneur."

Depending on the speciality, the physical demands vary. For example, for an organizer who does residential move-ins and garage reorganization, there will be some moving furniture and heavy lifting; there's not as much, though, when dealing with paperwork, filing, time management, and corporate organizing.

Metropolitan areas provide the best opportunities for organizers because these areas have the largest market of people who have hectic overcrowded lifestyles and are juggling jobs, commuting, their families, and other obligations. But you can organize anywhere and anyone. As one organizer told us, "Disorganization has no age or location limit."

Professional Organizing at a Glance

 60% 40%

	Minimal	Moderate	More than most
Start-up cost	X		
Overhead	X		
Potential earnings			X
Computer skills required		X	
Deadline pressures		Relocation	
Flexible hours		X	
Overall stress		X	

Likely Transferable Skills, Background, Careers

Any career which required time and space management, such as administration and management, teaching, and secretarial work will serve you well. Other skills that are useful to have mastered are patience and an ability to teach and mentor people, a good spatial sense, as well as good grasp of computers since you often have to be dealing with documents and files that people have on their computer or other technology products like personal digital assistants, and cell phones.

What to Charge

Organizers charge in one of three ways:

1. Hourly rates of $35 to $200, depending on your location, experience, and expertise. The median is $65 to $85.

2. Project pricing, such as $1,000 to organize an executive's office and desk. An organizer might also charge a fixed fee to do an introductory training program, a needs assessment, a workshop, and a follow-up session.

3. Retainer fees, such as a few hundred to several thousand dollars a month to be available for a specified number of hours per month for any task desired.

Best Ways to Get Business

- Contacting developers and realtors who might agree to include closet organizing as a gift.

- Face-to-face networking in business and trade organizations such as the chamber of commerce and business referral organizations with the goal to making contact with professionals who work in industries related to your speciality, such as business consultants, interior designers, architects, realtors, movers, and tax professionals (accountants and enrolled agents.) Tax professionals see many people at tax time who are disorganized, bringing in their records in paper sacks and shoeboxes.

- Having your own Web site with key words that identify your community and speciality, so people using a search engine will find you. Things to include on your site are testimonial letters, articles you have written, and tip sheets. If you have a newsletter for past and potential clients, include copies of past issues.

- Listing in the Yellow Pages under "Organizing Services" or "Personal Services" will also enable you to be found on Web directories like *switchboard.com* and *anywho.com*. Consider ads on local directory sites like *Yahoo Get Local* and *SuperPages*.

- Obtaining publicity through news releases and by writing articles.

- Participating in the National Association of Professional Organizers where you get a listing in the membership directory which can be a source of some business. You also can join or form a local chapter.

- Speaking before community and business organizations. Organizers speak on virtually any topic by focusing on how to be organized or avoid being disorganized in the context of the topic. For example, a talk before a garden club could be about how to organize a plant collection.

- Teaching workshops and classes for community-college and adult-education programs

- Volunteering to work for friends, charity, or nonprofit organizations that will give you letters of recommendation.

Marketing Insights

- With creative marketing, professional organizers can do well during an economic downturn when the service can be positioned as a cost-saving way to trim fat and compensate for downsizing.

- Professional organizing is an evolving field, so constantly be on the lookout for new ways to apply your skills as technology changes, such as teaching people how to use new Palm devices like the Blackberry to organize their information.

- Most successful organizers specialize in some way. Look for a specialization that no other professional organizer is pursuing in your community.

- A specialty for upscale clients is lining drawers and closets with materials that are both attractive and scrubbable, such as velvet and luxe moiré.

Where Next?

ASSOCIATION

National Association of Professional Organizers: (847) 375-4746; *www.napo.net*.

BOOKS

- *Conquering Chaos at Work,* Harriet Schechter (Fireside, 2000). ISBN: 0684863146. Harriet Schechter is also the author of *Let Go of Clutter.* ISBN: 0071351221.

- *How to Be Organized in Spite of Yourself,* Sunny Schlenger and Roberta Roesch (Signet, 1999). ISBN: 0451197461.

- *Organizing from the Inside Out,* Julie Morgenstern (Owl Books, 1998). ISBN: 0805056491.

- *Organized to be the Best!,* Susan Silver (Adams-Hall Publishing, 2000). ISBN: 0944708609.

- *Organize Your Office!,* Ronni Eisenberg (Hyperion, 1999). ISBN: 0786883812.

- *Taming the Paper Tiger at Work,* Barbara Hemphill and Knight A. Kiplinger (Kiplinger Books, 2002). ISBN: 0938721984.

From the Home Front

"I love what I do because I can walk into a situation where someone's really frustrated and doesn't know what to do and make a difference. I can see things in component parts and how they should be put together to resolve their problem in one or two visits." —Sally Allen, fifty

---

27. Restoration Services

Many were better made than similar items today. Wrought-iron patio furniture, musical instruments, stoves, lighting fixtures and candelabra are just a few that come to mind. Frequently, restoring such things can be done at less than half than the cost of replacing them. Then, some people simply love old things quite apart from their cost. They love the history that comes with something that was the part. For them, it is much more interesting to refinish, restore, and rehabilitate something old than to furnish their lives with something new.

And why not? Old furniture can be repaired and resurfaced, the luster of its former beauty restored after years of hearty use. Porcelain plumbing fixtures and enameled iron can be restored. Old cars can be carefully reworked with original stock replacement parts and be as much fun as when they were driven off the showroom floor so long ago.

So if you are a lover of the old and would like to see it given renewed life, many niches in the field of restoration make good fifty-plus businesses. You might even start with old tractors, farm implements, or boats that are wasting away in the back of a garage or barn.

Dan Markel, of Marshall, Minnesota, started his antiques restoration business at the age of fifty. He specializes in restoring steamer trunks, often lined with cedar or vintage wallpaper, but he can also restore a wide variety of furniture. "I am a full-service provider," he states, and offers stripping, caning, staining, varnishing, and other forms of restoration including remaking missing parts. He knows he is often working with pieces that have great sentimental value, so he takes great pride in offering something more than just a refinish job.

Nelson Dale, of Restoration Services in Arlington, Massachusetts, works only with very expensive objects like Tiffany lamps and museum-quality paintings. With degrees in geology and archaeology from Harvard University and twenty years' experience as a figurative sculptor, he has developed a highly technical, specialized approach that has taken years to master. "People can bring in priceless pieces and I won't damage them," he says.

Nelson also collects antiques as a second career and understands that to make them saleable they too often need to be refurbished. "You can buy, strip, and refinish antique furniture pieces yourself," he says. He admits some restorers may not be willing to give away their "secret formulas" and will be unwilling to offer training, but some courses are available and you can talk to antique dealers to find out the standards for refurbishing a particular piece you'd like to work on.

The amount of space you'll need depends on the type of restoration work you do. Glenn Vaughn, fifty-five, is an award-winning auto restorer in Post Falls, Idaho. His company, Glenn Vaughn Restoration, Inc., requires lots of room for stripping, sandblasting, and pulling large pieces off the cars. He contracts aspects of his jobs to small independent restorers.

"I need a mechanic, a painter, an upholsterer and someone to work on the chassis . . . all of those skills rarely exist in one person," says Vaughn, who expresses keen interest in seeing small, specialized restoration businesses succeed. These specialties don't require much space and can usually be done from a home garage. But since most refinishing work requires some use of chemical products, the work space must be well ventilated. Some strippers also contain known cancer-causing agents so adequate precautions should be taken.

Any object with a history can be a vessel for valuable memories. Vaughn insists he remembers the people and the stories they tell more than the cars he restores. "It might be the car someone had your first date in or the one they used to rush their pregnant wife to the hospital," he says with a smile. "One of my finest moments was after restoring a Cadillac limousine for a client. He said, 'Glen, you've given me a part of my father back.'" Vaughn always focuses on the personal return more than the economic one.

While this profile focuses on things you can restore at home, there's burgeoning growth in all kinds of other restoration projects you can do from home ranging from rehabilitating beautiful old houses in older neighborhoods to disaster recovery projects after natural disasters like floods, earthquakes, and fires. Also rugs, old tiles, and enamel in older homes may need to be reworked or repaired; old floors can be stripped and restained instead of covered over with linoleum or carpet. Franchises are available for many kinds of restoration work that's done on client premises.

Another speciality is restoring "architectural salvage." Architects, antique dealers, interior decorators, builders, and consumers often buy fixtures and edifice parts from old buildings that are being torn down or remodeled. But these pieces need to be restored before they can be used in stylish homes, restaurants, offices, and other establishments. This work involves the touch of a skilled craftsperson or someone wishing to develop these special skills.

Restoration Services at a Glance

 40% 60%

	Minimal	Moderate	More than most
Start-up cost	Tools		Franchise
Overhead		X	
Potential earnings		Household	Commercial
Computer skills required	X		
Deadline pressures	X		
Flexible hours		X	
Overall stress		X	

Likely Transferable Skills, Background, Careers

Lots of people have tinkering skills. They've been tinkering all their lives. If you were a model builder as a kid, for example, you can build on those skills. Experts in this field say it's best to grow the skills and interests you already have.

What to Charge

Restoration work is done either on an hourly basis (around $35) or for a flat price. Parts and supplies like hardware are additional. Since unknown problems can arise, it's not uncommon to pad a flat price.

Best Ways to Get Business

- Developing referral relationships with architects and interior decorators who do restoration work.

- Getting work from antique dealers, who must clean and repair items they acquire before selling them. Make friends with antique dealers and you'll be on your way to long-term clients.

- Listing in the Yellow Pages which will enable you to be found on Web directories like *switchboard.com*. and *anywho.com*.

- Obtaining publicity such as about a particularly unusual item you've restored. Photos help. Make a practice of taking before and after shots or videos of your work. Publicity also provides credibility.

- Placing flyers posted on bulletin boards and kiosks, and in antique shops, hardware stores, and lumberyards; gas stations; and tear-off pads.

- Placing small or classified ads in small local newspapers. Don Markel gets business from his local HyVee Trader.

- Selling items in Web galleries like *www.architecturals.net*.

- Writing articles or a column on restoration for local newspaper or regional magazines and giving seminars and workshops on topics like how to decide if something is worth restoring, the various types of restoration methods available, the ways to prolong the life of wood, tile, enamel, floors, or whatever your specialty might be.

Marketing Insights

- Because there are cheap knockoffs of almost everything, it is possible to buy a look-alike something new for less money than it would cost to restore the real thing. So your customers will be those who want to pay for quality, history, and maybe even memories.

- Additional niches include restoring ceramics, Chinese porcelains, clocks, glass art, jewelry, leather, paintings, pottery, toys and dolls, textiles and paper, wood carving and wood turnings.

- The best revenue streams include commercial accounts with continuing work or large projects or consumers with projects that can be finished rapidly.

- Trust is the secret to success in this business. Customers must turn over their valuables to you.

- Having certification or special training can also give your promotional activities greater impact.

Where Next?

ASSOCIATIONS

- Association of Specialists in Cleaning and Restoration, offers training through five specialized institutes (ASCR): (800) 272-7012; *www.ascr.org.*

- Institute of Inspection, Cleaning and Restoration Certification (IICRC), offers training courses: (360) 693-5675; *www.iicrc.org.*

BOOKS

- *Furniture Repair & Refinishing,* Brian Hingley (Creative Homeowner Press, 1998). ISBN: 1580110061.

- *Restoration Recipes,* James Bain, Julia De Bierre, James Bain Smith, and Patrick McLeavey (Chronicle Books, 1999). ISBN: 0811825108.

- *Refinishing Old Furniture,* George Wagoner and E. George Wagoner (McGraw-Hill Professional, 1990). ISBN: 0830634967.

From the Home Front

"I take pride in transforming something that's in really bad shape into something that's parlor worthy. I'll keep doing this as long as I'm ambulatory."

—Dan Markel, fifty-six

---

28. Tax Preparer

One stark truth about the American tax system is that it grows increasingly complex and confusing for the average taxpayer. In 2003, the current Internal Revenue Code was over 17,000 pages and 6,900,000 words. Each year, there are hundreds of changes to the code that can impact the average citizen's taxes. Add to this complexity the fact that the tax forms themselves are redesigned nearly every year, and the end result is that nearly 60 percent of Americans are now hiring someone to calculate and file their taxes. That translates into millions of people seeking the services of a tax-preparation specialist.

But did you know that the IRS and most states don't require you to have a special license to prepare other people's tax returns? That's right; you don't need to be a CPA or have a college degree in accounting. In fact, many CPAs don't even know much about tax accounting because they specialize in other accounting areas. And, of course, many taxpayers who need help filing their taxes don't want to pay CPA fees.

This is not to suggest that you can just hang out a shingle and claim to be a qualified tax preparer. But the field is more accessible as a fifty-plus career than you may think. One of the quickest ways to start is to take tax-preparation classes such as those offered by the large tax firms like H&R Block. If you prove to be adept in the course, which lasts approximately eleven weeks, you could qualify for a full- or part-time position with the tax-preparation company, though you won't really know enough to open your own practice until you have more experience.

However, another route to a career as a tax preparer is to become an "enrolled agent." While the enrolled-agent (EA) designation is still not well known, it's been around since 1884 and is the only designation specifically granted by the federal government. No academic credentials are required to become an enrolled agent; you simply need to pass a rigorous two-day exam to demonstrate proficiency in handling tax matters.

Only 30 percent of exam takers pass, but if you pass, you are also entitled, like CPAs and attorneys, to appear before the IRS at hearings to represent your clients. Enrolled agents prepare for any entity with tax-reporting requirements. They can specialize in an area of taxation such as estate and financial planning or work with particular kinds of clients such as high-tech firms and thus draw a clientele from across the nation.

Harold Rosenfeld, in Rockville, Maryland, exemplifies both these paths to becoming a tax preparer. After having had surgery, Harold was on sick leave from the Veterans' Administration for six weeks, during which time he became fascinated with doing his own taxes. He decided to take the classes offered by H&R Block, and upon completion, worked for them part-time in the evenings for several years. When he retired from the government at age sixty-two, he took more accounting courses, joined the National Association of Tax Professionals, and got a Masters of Science degree in accounting. Although he did not pass the CPA exam, he became an enrolled agent.

Louise Clymer also decided to become an enrolled agent at age fifty-four, after which she purchased a tax-preparation practice from a CPA who burned out at age thirty-seven. Clymer points out that many CPAs refer business to enrolled agents. She finds being over age fifty is an advantage in this business for several reasons. First, the best market for tax preparers is people over fifty, since they often have the most complex taxes and are willing to pay for assistance. Second, Louise adds, "If you don't have a little gray in your hair, clients don't quite trust you. The older client isn't about to hire someone who looks a little green."

Although many software programs are now available that allow individuals to do their own taxes more easily, millions of people still prefer to hire a tax-preparer. As Michael Solomon, a tax-preparation expert in Los Angeles, finds, many people get burned by these software programs, when they discover they paid too much tax because they didn't get the advice of a professional.

Whatever your personal feelings are about taxes, they are an inescapable part of life. So if you enjoy making sense of numbers, tax preparation makes a good fifty-plus career.

Tax Preparation at a Glance

55% 45%

	Minimal	Moderate	More than most
Start-up cost	X		
Overhead		X	
Potential earnings			X
Computer skills required			X
Deadline pressures			X
Flexible hours		X	

	Minimal	Moderate	More than most
Overall stress		X	

Likely Transferable Skills, Background, Careers

Many tax preparers have prior careers in banking, the military, and government work where they can build on years of experience dealing with complex rules and financial information. However, as long as you enjoy working with numbers and like the challenge of mastering the federal and state tax codes, this profession is open to anyone.

What to Charge

Prices are either by the hour or a flat fee per return. For a simple 1040 return, rates range from $75 in low-cost areas of the country to $125 elsewhere. Complex tax returns are usually billed by the hour at rates ranging from $50 to $200 and can total several thousand dollars.

Best Ways to Get Business

- Advertising with your local "welcoming service" gives you access to new people moving into your area, including people moving from another state. Louise Clymer built her practice by advertising that specialized in working with people who need to file tax returns in multiple states, which means splitting income between states, possibly including income from partnerships and S corporations, deducting two mortgages, etc. You can purchase participation with a welcoming service by zip code.

- Conducting seminars or teaching tax principles for adult education and organizations.

- Contacting CPAs who do not work on taxes for referrals or to do overload work for those who do tax preparation work.

- Encouraging referrals from satisfied clients.

- Face-to-face networking inside business and trade organizations such as the chamber of commerce and business-referral organizations.

- Sending personalized mailings to people or new businesses that have moved into your area.

- Using free advertising such as in your local Recycler and on Craig's list (*www.craiglist.org*) on the Web.

Marketing Insights

- To gain experience, consider working for a tax-preparation company part- or full-time, followed by study for and taking of the enrolled agent examination. It's best, however, to avoid preparing taxes for your friends. It's essential to be impartial, ethical, and objective in doing taxes.

- An advantage of focusing on people moving into in area is that you are not taking a client from another practitioner in your area and are apt to get a repeat client who will return year after year. But you will need to invest in software that allows you to prepare multiple-state returns.

- You can save yourself headaches by choosing your clients carefully. You can often lose money by working with a picky client who excessively scrutinizes your work or is too disorganized.

- If you become an enrolled agent, you can eventually focus on representing clients who are undergoing tax audits, or working for lawyers and CPAs. These specializations allow you to charge double the rate for tax preparation.

Where Next?

ASSOCIATIONS

- National Association of Enrolled Agents (NAEA): (301) 212-9608; *www.naea.org*.

- National Association of Tax Practitioners provides training: (800) 558-3402, (800) 242-3430; *www.natptax.com*.

TRAINING

Training to prepare for the enrolled agent examination is provided by the associations as well as private schools. The California Tax Education Council provides a list of approved education providers, which includes home-study programs, at its site, *www.ctec.org*.

WEB SITES

- The H&R Block Income Tax Course: *www.hrblock.com/taxes*.

- Essential Links to Taxes: *www.el.com/elinks/taxes*.

- Jackson Hewitt Tax Resources: *www.jacksonhewitt.com/resources.asp*.

- Tax and Accounting Sites Directory: *www.taxsites.com*.

- Tax Information for Tax Professionals, provided by the Internal Revenue Service: *www.irs.gov/taxpros*.

- The Tax Resource Group's free access to tax research materials: *www.taxresourcegroup.com*.

From the Home Front

"I like the mental challenge of this profession, and dealing with people. If I just watched soap operas, I'd mentally melt away. I help people save money."

—Louise Clymer, sixty-seven

---

29. Writing Coach and Writer

There's no escaping the fact that the world depends on writing to express our thoughts, ideas, and feelings. Whether it's for e-mail, a memo, report, nonfiction book, novel, magazine, or copy for a Web site, people everywhere want, and in many cases need, to be able to write intelligently and persuasively. The problem is that most people don't learn to write very well or lack confidence in their writing skills. As a result, there's a growing need for writing coaches and consultants who teach others how to write, and in some cases, do the writing for them.

As a writing coach, you can specialize in several areas. Suzanne Beyer, fifty-seven, focuses on helping elementary-school children learn to write. She began her writing coach business by volunteering to teach third-graders how to create a book in memory of a school secretary. She then used this effort to transition into paying work teaching other children in the local schools and in their homes. "There's no way a classroom teacher can reach twenty-five to thirty children," she points out, indicating the opportunity for her coaching.

The increasingly competitive corporate environment drives the need for writing coaches by people who need to write for business reasons. This includes millions of people who have to write documents for their employers or businesspeople who wish to write a nonfiction book or articles to advance their professional careers.

Then there are tens of thousands of people who want to write as a means of creative expression to relieve the pressure of stressed lives, generally wanting to create fiction or poetry. San Francisco writing coach Cindy Shearer states that businesspeople are more inclined to seek out a writing coach because they are goal oriented in their desire to learn how to write better and to complete their projects.

Shearer compares being a writing coach with being a therapist, in that your goal is to help people express themselves. You need to assist them in discovering their ideas and finding a form to express them. You do not write for them, but rather teach and encourage them to engage in the writing process without fear and to find the best way to say what they are thinking. "The work of a coach or consultant is to make someone's expertise look good," Shearer concludes.

Another specialty area for a writing coach is helping people write their personal stories or memoirs. As America ages, more and more retirees are interested in writing down their life stories and publishing them for family and friends, but they don't have the skills to organize their ideas or write their stories down. They often seek out a writing coach to help them. If you think you'd like to specialize in doing this, read the Personal Historian profile in this book.

Writing coaches do not always remain on the sidelines; they often become ghostwriters working for the people who hired them when they discover that it takes more time and effort than they imagined to write something of quality. The transition from coach to writer can take you into a new level of higher fees.

Finally, since writing coaches are frequently writers themselves, they often spend some of their time writing their own books, novels, or magazine articles because they recognize that there's no point in wasting their own talent. But note that writing books or novels usually requires that you get a literary agent to represent you to publishing companies, and writing magazine articles requires that you learn the specific process by which to propose article ideas to magazine editors in order to get approval and a contract to write them. If you are new to book publishing or magazine writing, recognize that making money from your own writing may be more difficult, in fact, that being a writing coach.

Writing Coach at a Glance

40% 60%

	Minimal	Moderate	More than most
Start-up cost	X		
Overhead	X		
Potential earnings		X	
Computer skills required		X	
Scheduling pressures		X	
Flexible hours			X
Overall stress		X	

Likely Transferable Skills, Background, Careers

A background in journalism, teaching, or business writing is useful. Because you are working closely with people and their ideas, it is also important to know how to give advice and constructive feedback without hurting your client's feelings. Of course, you must have writing skills pertinent to your area of expertise (fiction, nonfiction, memoir, business writing, etc.)

What to Charge

The fees for writing coaches vary considerably, from $20 per hour for working with children (similar to a tutor) to $50 to $90 per hour for coaching adults on business writing or a book project. If you are ghostwriting an entire book or memoir, the usual practice is to negotiate a fixed fee based on how many days, weeks, or months you expect the work to take and the average rate you wish to receive for that time.

Best Ways to Get Business

- Creating a Web site for your business. You can attract clients from anywhere and work with them by phone or by e-mail.

- Getting listed in the referral service of support services maintained for members of the professional association you are targeting.

- Going to writing conferences where you can meet budding authors who might be seeking assistance from someone with writing expertise.

- Listing in coaching directories, such as *findacoach.com*.

- Listing in the Yellow Pages, which appear both in print and make you findable on on-line directories like *switchboard.com* and *any-who.com*. Consider listing on local directory sites like *Yahoo Get Local* and *SuperPages*.

- Networking with literary agents to get referrals to new authors who often need help with their manuscripts.

- Publishing articles on your area of writing expertise in your local newspapers and community newsletters.

- Teaching classes or workshops on writing at your local extension school or adult-education center. Or create your own workshop and rent a space in which to give it.

- Testing advertising in local publications that have readership among businesspeople.

- Volunteering to work with one author or businessperson so you can use the experience as a starting point to spread the word and get referrals.

Marketing Insights

- The benefit you offer clients is the ability to accomplish a goal—either to accomplish a specific project or to generally better express themselves in writing. Being a writing coach is more than being an editor. As Cindy Shearer says, it's like being a therapist. Your job is often to ask your clients questions, rather than to lecture them. The goal is to elicit your clients' ideas, help them to organize their thoughts, and to feel confident that they have something to say.

- You need to stay abreast of the writing field by reading books and magazines such as *Writer's Digest* and *Publishers Weekly* to see what's being published, what's hot, and what sells.

- As Cindy Shearer notes, many people have the desire to become writers but don't realize the effort and work it takes. As a result, despite your expert encouragement, they become discouraged and drop their coaching sessions after a month. So you will need to constantly generate new clients.

Where Next?

BOOKS

- *If You Want to Write,* Brenda Ueland (Graywolf Press, 1997). ISBN: 1555972608.

- *The Writing Coach,* Lee Clark Johns (Delmar Publishers, 2004). ISBN: 1401833284.

- *Writing Coach Strategies for Helping Students Develop Their Own Voice,* J. Grant (Pembroke Pub Ltd, 1992). ISBN: 0921217862.

- *Writing from the Inside Out,* Dennis Palumbo (John Wiley & Sons, 2000). ISBN: 0471382663

- *A Tutor's Guide: Helping Writers One to One,* Ben Rafoth (Heinemann, 2000). ISBN: 0867094958.

MAGAZINE

- *Writer's Digest.* Sold at bookstores: *www.writersdigest.com.*

TRAINING

See the resources for coach training in the Coach profile.

From the Home Front

"As a kid, I hated writing. Now when I leave a classroom after working with kids, I'm on cloud nine the rest of the day." —Susan Beyer, fifty-seven

---

Snapshot: Donna Beyer, Professional Writer and Writing Coach

Donna Beyer's after-fifty career began when she decided to sign up for a course at a technical college, on How to Get Published. She'd always loved writing and at the age of fifty-seven, with two overflowing notebooks to draw upon, she wrote her first query letter.

Her instructor had warned the class, "You will be able to wallpaper your living room in rejection letters," and, indeed, Donna started wallpapering. But the thought of being able to stay home with the kids, get paid, and do what she loved was enough motivation to keep her sending out more queries.

"The day I received my first letter of interest, I couldn't speak," she remembers. "A newspaper magazine wanted to print *my* article and would *pay* me fifty dollars. When I saw it in print, I ran around the neighborhood showing everyone my first published piece."

Through perseverance she was soon forming relationships with editors who knew they could count on her to meet deadlines and allow them to edit her pieces as they saw fit. Once her writing career was thriving, she wanted to inspire others with her love of writing, too, so she took her enthusiasm to the neighborhood elementary school and offered her first "Writing Coach" workshop to help a small group of fourth-graders improve their writing skills.

More writing classes have followed and, Donna reports, "I'm searching avenues for grant money and dreaming big about expanding my student writing classes to other schools." The rewards for her from working with young students have been many, including a wealth of inspiring experiences to enrich her own articles!

HELPING
INDIVIDUALS
AND
FAMILIES

30. Daily Money Manager

I ncreasing numbers of singles and older Americans need help managing their daily finances—making bank deposits, paying bills, balancing their checkbooks, reconciling bank, credit-card, and charge-account statements, organizing tax and other paperwork, and filing medical claims. Unlike in the past when adult children were nearby to manage their parents' affairs, many children now live too far away or simply don't have the time to help their parents with their day-to-day financial affairs. These hyper-busy middle-aged people as well as others like them who don't have the time or inclination to handle their own financial affairs are doing what movie stars have done for years, hiring daily money managers.

Patricia Manalio, president of the American Association of Daily Money Managers, says some of her clients are in deep trouble when they come to her. One woman told her, "If I have money and access to it, I spend it." So she turned the management of her money over to Manalio, both to pay her bills and to provide her with an allowance.

Such needs have given rise to a business that is distinct from accounting or bookkeeping, although sometimes accountants and bookkeepers add money management or bill paying as an add-on service to what they offer.

As a daily money manager, you will prepare checks to pay your clients' bills in a timely manner and deal with financial problems that arise, like calling creditors about incorrect bills and, when needed, negotiating with them. When your client's problems require professional help, you will need to make appropriate referrals to lawyers, investment advisors, and tax professionals.

Some daily money managers also become qualified as notaries; others handle payroll records for tax reports needed for clients who have domestic help, although the actual filing of the tax reports may be done by the clients' accountants or tax professionals.

To shine in this business, you need to enjoy working with details and numbers because that's the nature of what you'll be doing, but you need to have sufficient people skills to earn your clients' confidence and trust. You will need access to a car because most daily money managers pick up bills and papers from at least some of their clients and then return checks for them to sign. This level of service distinguishes you from the free or low-cost services available from some local governments and the AARP that have been established to serve low-income individuals.

Daily money managers do not render financial or investment advice or prepare taxes; thus at this time, no state requires them to be licensed. This means entry into the field is easy, but it makes obtaining professional liability insurance and bonding more difficult. For this reason, G. Ray Sims of San Antonio said, "I don't have access to my clients' funds," meaning that money managers do not become signatories to their clients' accounts. Some, however, do obtain power of attorney for Medicare transactions. Sims keeps track of important dates for his clients in his Palm Pilot and opens a separate *Quicken* account for each client.

Daily Money Management at a Glance

 50% 50%

	Minimal	Moderate	More than most
Start-up cost	X		
Overhead	X		
Potential earnings		X	
Computer skills required		X	
Deadline pressures		X	
Flexible hours			X
Overall stress	X		

Likely Transferable Skills, Background, Careers

Any previous experience that involved handling financial details, administering financial affairs, as well as dealing with people. Thus most relevant business, volunteer, or personal experience can be an adequate foundation.

What to Charge

Typically $25 or $35 an hour, but some daily money managers get as much as $60 an hour. Charging a minimum fee equivalent to two hours a month is not uncommon.

To keep your overhead low, establish that expenses like postage, long-distance calls made for clients, and mileage are reimbursable. Some daily money managers also charge for travel time.

Best Ways to Get Business

- For younger and middle-aged clients, personal networking in groups and with friends and contacts. Especially good contacts are professional advisors like financial planners, tax preparers, and mental-health providers. Lisa Berlin of Columbia, Maryland, finds that advisors will refer their clients when the clients tell them about events like getting a late notice about an unpaid bill they have no memory receiving or getting a notice about a bill that has been paid twice. Psychotherapists are frequent sources of referrals because as Patricia Manalio notes, "Depressed people often have difficulty handling their finances."

- For older people, calling on and making personal contact with:

  - Social workers in hospitals and those who work for large medical practices.

  - Pastors of larger churches.

  - State adult service agencies.

- Having a Web site where out-of-town adult children can easily locate you and learn what you offer.

- Having testimonials on your Web site.

- Staying top of mind with your referral sources by writing thank-you notes, sending appropriate thank-you gifts, and staying in touch through frequent contact.

Marketing Insights

- As a daily money manager, you'll be hired by the children of your clients, approximately three-quarters of whom will not live in the same city as their parents. Few older people will admit they can't handle their finances and seek you out.

- Often recent widowhood or divorce is the trigger for someone becoming a client.

- The key benefit you offer to adult children is the peace of mind that their parent's or loved one's affairs are being managed and their bills, paid. Thus your maturity is an advantage.

- Your clients will often be isolated or overwhelmed, so plan to provide TLC along with your services.

Where Next?

INFORMATION AND CERTIFICATION

- American Association of Daily Money Managers, Inc.: P.O. Box 8857, Gaithersburg, MD 20898; (301) 593-5462.; *www.aadmm.com*. Membership entails subscribing to the organization's code of ethics, which then entitles use of the association's logo.

TRAINING

- Learn to use the financial software of your choice, like *Quicken* or *Money,* before you begin serving clients.

From the Home Front

G. Ray Sims, fifty-eight: In answer to the question "Can you see yourself doing this in ten years?" Sims quickly replied, "I sure do. It's hard to find interesting things to do and it's a calling that enables me to give a little back to my community."

31. Direct Selling

Millions of Americans hate spending time at shopping malls. So they're choosing other ways to shop. On-line sales and direct selling, most of which is done face-to-face, are rising dramatically. Direct selling outpaces the growth in overall retail sales by about 1 percent a year and in less than ten years, direct sales have nearly doubled.

Home parties generate better than a quarter of all sales. While party-goers sip wine or coffee and chat with friends, they inspect the merchandise. The parties are thrown by a friend of the independent salesperson who invites other friends in the now-classic Tupperware model. But most direct selling—more than two-thirds of it—is done by calling on customers at their homes or offices personally to demonstrate products and take orders. Direct-selling companies call their salespeople by different names—distributors, representatives, or consultants—but by whatever name, they're all independent salespeople.

Just about everything anyone consumes is being sold these days through direct sales, including books, videos, CDs, computers, children's toys, artwork, kitchenware, cookware and cutlery, cleaning products, decorating items, small appliances like vacuum cleaners, men's clothing, luxury women's clothing, baby products, jewelry, health equipment, candles, air filters, water-treatment systems, Internet and telecommunications services, rubber stamps, plants, gift baskets, gift items, encyclopedias—and more. The diversity of products breaks down into these major categories, which are listed in order of volume of sales:

- Cleaning, cookware, cutlery, and other home products.

- Personal care, including cosmetics, skin care, and jewelry.

- Services such as benefit packages, insurance, Internet, and auto care.

- Nutrition and health /wellness.

- Leisure and educational items.

Bea Sherzer in Fern Park, Florida, exemplifies how direct selling can be accomplished by people of any age. Because of health challenges she faced, Sherzer began buying herbs. "They improved my health so much," she recalls "that everyone began asking me about them." So she started a career in direct sales when she was seventy; she is now eighty-three and has four sales associates working under her. Sherzer says, "This was the best thing that ever happened to me. Now my time is my own. I don't have to report to anybody and nobody's looking over my shoulder to see what I'm doing."

Sometimes couples decide to go into the direct-sales business together. This is what Fred and Julie Gladney of Laguna Niguel, California, did. Their business began when Julie discovered Noevir skin-care and nutritional products and loved them. So she began selling them part-time, while Fred, a senior vice president in a large computer company, traveled more and more on his job. He came to see that while his company offered less and less job security, his wife's business could offer him more time for himself and potentially greater rewards from the residual income that could be derived from the distribution network of other sales agents with them. So Fred resigned his executive position to work with Julie. They focus on what each does best—Julie sells the products and maintains contacts with their customers; Fred develops and trains their sales agents.

Rhonda Anderson, founder of Creative Memories, was teaching classes in how to make photo albums but found that the albums quickly fell apart. That was the beginning of her company, which markets photo albums and a wide range of products and training for families who want to create attractive, memorable scrapbooks and photo albums. Prior to founding Creative Memories, Rhonda sold Tupperware, so she established the party-plan approach for selling scrapbooking materials. She estimates that about 20 percent of the company's 80,000 sales consultants are over the age of fifty. Rhonda knows a sales agent who teaches workshops and sells products from her home, despite being paraplegic.

If you have an outgoing personality and love selling the products you represent, you can make money and enjoy direct selling. Keep in mind that in most companies, making money requires finding other people to join your "network" or "downline" of distributors who will also sell products to people they contact. Both you and they receive commissions from their sales. In turn, they also will try to find people for their downline to sell for them, for which all three tiers of people now receive commissions. Some distribution models allow you to get commissions down seven levels. This is why this type of direct selling is also called multilevel marketing.

Notice that all the people in this profile show extremely positive feelings about the products they represent, and that's what enables them to feel good about selling them. However, if you join a company that emphasizes spending most of your time developing the downline rather than selling the product, it may not be a successful venture. Direct selling needs to be primarily about selling something person to person.

Direct Selling at a Glance

 20% 80%

	Minimal	Moderate	More than most
Start-up cost	X		
Overhead		X	
Potential earnings	X	X	
Computer skills required	X		
Deadline pressures	X		
Flexible hours			X
Overall stress		X	

Likely Transferable Skills, Background, Careers

Many teachers and nurses, and others in people-oriented occupations, find a home in direct selling; though one can point out individuals from any and all walks of life and without any prior sales skills who have met their goals in direct selling. Companies provide sales training, though expect to pay for it. Prior sales training or team-building experience lends itself to companies that emphasize building a downline; party planning and showmanship skills are needed in party-plan companies. Direct selling enjoys its greatest popularity in the South.

What to Charge

Prices are determined by the direct-selling company. What you earn is based on the commission structure of what you are selling. Be sure you fully understand the commission structure.

Best Ways to Get Business

- For party plans, having friends willing to host parties for you. Make the parties fun.

- Attending events where you can meet people, such as craft fairs, Bible-study classes, senior-citizen centers, and mobile-home parks. Some direct sellers make contacts standing in lines and at bus stops. Because direct selling is face-to-face, be well-groomed and personable.

- Treating your customers as royalty. Gift them with extras; let them know about promotions on a monthly basis.

- Letting people know what you do so you can benefit from word-of-mouth referrals.

- Having a Web site can help, mostly to refer people to see your products. While only a small percentage of direct selling is done over the Internet, some people do manage to use their Web sites to make sales.

- Keeping in regular contact with your customers and down-lining via the phone, e-mail, postcards, and meetings.

- Incentivizing your downline with regular financial, travel, and other rewards that recognize achievement.

Marketing Insights

- Customers of direct sellers say the reasons for shopping this way are product quality, product uniqueness, and money-back guarantees.

- People who sign up with direct-selling companies do so to earn extra income, because they believe in the product, and to obtain items they use at discounted prices.

- For actually selling products, a passion for the product is more important than anything else.

- If you're naturally upbeat and treat people well regardless of how you feel, you're a candidate for direct selling.

Where Next?

ASSOCIATION

- The Direct Selling Association (DSA) is the industry trade association. Its Web site has a Membership Directory of companies that meet standards established by DSA and agree to its code of ethics. You will also find research about direct selling on the DSA Web site, *www.dsa.org.*

BOOKS

- *Network Marketing in the 21st Century,* Richard Poe (Prima Lifestyles, 1999). ISBN: 0761517529 . Richard Poe has written other respected books including *The Wave 4 Way to Building Your Downline.*

- *Secrets of Building a Million Dollar Network Marketing Organization From a Guy Who's Been There Done That and Shows You How to Do It Too,* Joe Rubino (Upline Press, 2000). ISBN: 1890344060.

- *Your First Year in Network Marketing,* Mark and Rene Reid Yarnell (Prima Lifestyles, 1998). ISBN: 0761512195.

From the Home Front

Says Bea Sherzer, eighty-three: "Being a weaver is an art and it wasn't hard to get myself to spend enough time doing my weaving, but direct selling is different. A day's work slips by without feeling like I've been working at all."

Snapshot: Evlyn Newell, Golf Stroke Counter

Evlyn Newell and her friend Peg Martin had taken up golf and needed a way to keep track of their strokes. But conventional stroke counters were large and bulky. They wanted something simple and unobtrusive. Not finding what they were looking for, they decided to create their own counter from a simple elastic cord with ten beads that attaches easily to a belt, a belt loop, or a golf bag. To keep track of their strokes, they would simply slide a bead down the string after each stroke and then count the beads at the bottom at the end of each hole.

As Evlyn and Peg began using their invention, members of the golf club kept coming up to ask "Where did you get that? I want one of those." So Evlyn and Peg gave away a few of their counters, and then the golf pro asked them to make some up for the pro shop. He sold several hundred and that was the beginning of their company, Greenway Golf Accessories. Soon The Golf Abacus® was being sold through a distributor.

Evlyn and Peg formed as a partnership and divided up the work of running the business based on their backgrounds: Peg's in book-keeping and finance, Evlyn's in administration and marketing. Nine years ago, Evlyn bought Peg's share of the business and moved with her husband to the Oregon coast. "The challenges of taking some-thing from a mere idea to a tangible product keeps me stimulated," Evlyn says, and "the bottom line is supplementing my Social Security. That's a positive." At seventy, she has five children, ten grandchildren, and a great-grandson, and still marvels at the whole scenario.

32. Doula

The word *doula,* pronounced DOO-la, has a Greek origin signifying a handmaiden or mother's helper. Today, doula services are a booming phenomenon for pregnant couples who want outside support and assistance before, during, and after the birth of their children.

Doulas don't deliver babies nor are they nannies. They are specifically educated to provide emotional and physical advice and support to mothers before and during childbirth, as well as information and assistance after the baby comes home. Unlike a midwife who only attends the delivery, a doula may assist the mother well before labor, at the delivery, as well as help out with postpartum care during the first one to four weeks of the baby's new life. Doulas often act as advocates for their clients in the hospital, making sure they get the attention and care they want in an era when doctors and nurses are usually overworked and not always available when patients need them.

While some doulas serve clients—not patients—both before and after birth, many are choosing to do one or the other. They find that being immediately available for a birth tends to be at odds with maintaining a schedule of regular postpartum care. Due to the unpredictable times a doula may be called to show up for a delivery and the long hours she must spend on her feet, awake all night (or for days) assisting clients in labor, experienced doulas find the postpartum schedules are less physically taxing—not that calming a crying newborn at night is not taxing.

Doulas truly help their clients. Research shows childbirth goes more smoothly with the help of a doula. Labor is 25 percent shorter, requests for pain relief drop by 60 percent, cesarean sections are reduced by 15 to 50 percent, and forceps deliveries go down by 40 percent. There's also a 60 percent reduction in epidural requests, a 40 percent reduction in oxytocin use, and a 30 percent reduction in analgesia use. In addition, women who have been assisted during labor when assessed two months after birth are found to be more sensitive, loving, and responsive to their infants.

Tracy Hartley, who started her doula practice, Birth Empowerment Support Team (B*E*S*T) Doula Service, at age fifty, says that the profession has gone from being a homespun movement to a respected and increasingly profitable career. As it becomes better known, doulas are also expanding their range of services or specializing. For example, some work with their clients as consultants to help them select their ob-gyn doctor and their hospital, or they teach their clients pain-coping methods of breathing, or breast-feeding. Some doulas offer hypnotherapy, massage therapy, music therapy (as in singing to the mother), or aromatherapy to calm the new mother and help her through the birth, or after the birth to regain her physical and emotional strength.

Insurance companies will pay for doula services if they are offered through a hospital, which is now more common because of new state laws that require insurers to pay for forty-eight hours of care after childbirth. Growing numbers of hospitals now have doulas on call twenty-four hours a day or are providing a certain number of hours of postpartum doula care as part of their child-birthing service.

Also the concept of doula services is expanding to a new area, hospice care. Some doulas who are using their "coming into life" skills to help dying people leave life behind. As Tracy Hartley says, "People need as much help going as well as coming." Another service doulas sometimes perform is going with clients getting mammograms, given how frightening this process can be for some women.

Doula at a Glance

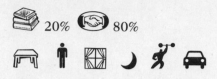

20% 80%

	Minimal	Moderate	More than most
Start-up cost	X		
Overhead	X		
Potential earnings		X	
Computer skills required	X		
Time pressures			X
Flexible hours	X		
Overall stress			

Likely Transferable Skills, Background, Careers

This is truly a profession for women who have had children and know what it's like. A background in medical care will add to your credibility. Furthermore, you need significant people skills such as compassion and empathy, the ability to listen and calm others, and a healthy amount of intuition to assess how your clients are feeling and thinking as they go through labor, delivery, and assume their new mothering role. You also need negotiation and management skills since you often need to rally nurses and doctors on behalf of your client.

What to Charge

Doulas generally charge a flat fee for birth services. Where you live influences what you can charge. For example, in the Midwest, fees run $400, but in Los Angeles, $1,500 is not uncommon. Some doulas charge based on a sliding scale related to income. For other doula services, hourly rates are appropriate. These range from $15 to $35 an hour. Your fees need to be high enough to absorb parking and travel expenses or be additionally billed. Some doulas charge a weekly rate for postpartum services. For other services, some doulas charge a three-hour or greater hourly minimum.

Best Ways to Get Business

- Advertising in the *Wet Set Gazette,* published through your local Dydee Diaper Service.

- Becoming a member of your local doula association and networking with other doulas. Doulas appear to be less competitive than many other professionals and frequently refer clients to one another, as couples may not like you and want someone else, or you may live too far away, or you may be unavailable the month they are expecting. Many doulas also team up in order to have a backup available for them in case the doula is unavailable or sick (doulas do not show up at the hospital with a cold or the flu).

- Creating relationships with doctors, childbirth educators, hospitals, and even yoga studios where pregnant women often go to learn breathing techniques in preparation for birth.

- Creating your own Web site, being certain to indicate where you are located, because couples want their doula to be able to get to the hospital within minutes.

- Listing in the Yellow Pages, which will enable you to be found on Web directories like *switchboard.com* and *anywho.com.* Consider ads on local directory sites like *Yahoo Get Local* and *SuperPages.*

- Speaking at women's groups.

- Wearing a T-shirt with your business name and a cute logo. This marketing technique often initiates conversation among women you pass on the street. Be sure to have some business cards with you to hand out whenever someone stops you to ask about your work.

- Writing articles in your local newspapers

Marketing Insights

- It may be easier to break in as a postpartum doula rather than a birthing doula. There is often a greater need and awareness of the role that a postpartum doula can provide

- Doulas are hired for any one of several reasons. In some cases, the woman does not feel confident that her mate will be physically or emotionally helpful at the birth or afterward. In other instances, a couple knows that the mate's job will prevent him from attending the birth. In still other cases, a couple does not feel comfortable as new parents and are willing to pay for personal advice and support to learn parenting and baby-care skills. Still other couples seek out a doula because they want a home birth and know they need a professionally trained person to assist in addition to a doctor or midwife.

- Aim to meet your clients as soon as possible in the pregnancy process so that you can get to know them better, offer more services, and spend more time with them.

- Consider a combination of services you can offer, such as a skill with breech babies, or being able to offer massage therapy or aromatherapy along with your postpartum care.

Where Next?

TRAINING AND CERTIFICATION

- Association of Labor Assistants and Childbirth Educators (ALACE): (888) 222-5223, (617) 441-2500; *www.alace.org.*

- Birthing from Within: (505) 254-4884; *www.birthingfromwithin.com.*

- Birthworks: (862-4784); *www.birthworks.org.*

- Childbirth and Postpartum Professional Association (CAPPA): 888-MY-CAPPA: *www.cappa.net.*

- Doulas of North America (DONA): (500) 448-3662; *http://www.dona.com.*

- International Childbirth Education Association (ICEA): (952) 854-8660; *www.icea.org.*

BOOKS

- *The Doula Advantage,* Rachel Gurevich (Prima Lifestyles, 2003). ISBN: 0761500588.

- *Ina May's Guide to Childbirth,* Ina May Gaskin (Bantam, 2003), ISBN: 0553381156.

- *Mothering the Mother,* Marshall Klaus, Phyllis Klaus, and John Kennell (Perseus Books, 1993). ISBN: 0201632721.

- *Special Women,* Paulina Perez and Cheryl Snedeker (Pennypress, 1994). ISBN: 0964115999.

- *The Thinking Woman's Guide to a Better Birth,* Henci Goer and Rhonda Wheeler (Perigee, 1999). ISBN: 0399525173.

WEB SITES

- On-line childbirth resources: *www.doula.com.*

- Childbirth.org has a section for doula information.

- Yahoo has a number of doula groups.

From the Home Front

"What's amazed me the most is the variety of people I work with, people you'd otherwise never get to meet. And you get to know them intimately very quickly. You're in their home, in their lives, cooking for them, shopping for them, everything. It's fun, exciting."　　　　　—Tracy Hartley, fifty-seven

---

33. Environmental Assessment and Inspection

Environmental inspections are becoming a must for nearly all real estate transactions, commercial and residential property, and new and old construction. Lenders require them because of the concern about potential liability created by the Comprehensive Environmental Response, Compensation and Liability Act (CERCLA), popularity known as the Superfund. This act mandates inspection and remediation of environmental hazards. Also as growing numbers of people are becoming more aware and concerned about environmental hazards, they too want the information environmental inspections provide.

Inspections can indicate conditions such as contamined soil, vegetation damage, or the presence of molds, mildew, allergens, lead paint, asbestos, radon, electromagnetic radiation, water leaks, or just old storage tanks lying beneath the surface. In order to avoid liability under CERCLA, a new property owner needs a report to establish that he or she has no reason to believe any hazardous substance has been discharged on the property.

At the same time as horror stories about mold-infested homes abound and homeowner insurance rates go up to cover huge mold losses, people are insisting on having their environments vetted for contaminants and molds. One reason mold has become a common concern is that in order to make homes and buildings more energy efficient, they're being built or remodeled with tighter construction that prevents air from circulating well enough to prevent molds and mildews from forming.

In addition, people are more aware of "sick building syndrome," in which trace elements of contaminants in the air, materials, soils, and water around a home are linked to a wide variety of ailments and illnesses.

Environmental assessments and inspections help us identify and protect ourselves from problems like these. There are three types, or "phases," of environmental assessment. Two of these, phases I and II, can be the basis of successful home-based businesses.

Phase I is a review phase and is done by someone who has been trained to use the specific steps prescribed by the American Society of Testing Materials for identifying whether hazardous substances and petroleum products may be present in the structure or in the groundwater, or surface water of a property. Four elements comprise phase I. These are:

- Reviewing records in government databases and historic, topographic, and hydrogeologic files and reports that concern the property.

- Visiting the site to determine if there are visual clues or observable evidence of problems.

- Interviewing past and present property owners, tenants, neighbors, and state and local regulatory agencies to determine their knowledge of problems.

- Writing a report of findings and making recommendations.

Phase II involves taking samples of possibly contaminated materials, surfaces, or subsurfaces and testing them, sometimes in a laboratory. The scope of tests may include soil testing, measuring the quantity and quality of well water, searching for volatile organic compounds around an oil tank, checking roofing and tiling materials for asbestos, confirming that painted surfaces do not contain lead, testing indoor air quality and sampling the air from air conditioning ducts, looking beneath the house and carpeting for live and dead mold, and many other tests.

Elements of phase II activities include:

- Defining the possible problems, determining the techniques for investigating them, developing a plan for sampling, and identifying the professionals and laboratories to do the testing.

- Testing samples and analyzing the results.

- Reporting the findings and making recommendations.

In states where they are licensed, some aspects of this phase must be performed by licensed geologists, but many tests can be performed by people who have a certification in the field for which they test.

Sometimes these tests are ordered by a new owner who wants peace of mind about the new property; other times by an owner with commercial plans who wants to know the anticipated risks of development.

Phase III consists of remedial activities to clean up the problems such as removing asbestos and PCBs, removing lead paint, cleaning up contaminated soil, and removing and disposing of hazardous waste. The contractors who do things of this nature are usually not home-based businesses.

Albert Snow of Stratford, Connecticut, began his mold analysis and inspection firm at age sixty-eight after his "third retirement." He describes the investigative process they use as looking like the procedures employed on the CSI television shows. He comes to a site wearing gloves, carefully takes samples, and sends the samples to an independent lab, taking care to assure an unbroken chain of evidence along the way. When the lab results come back, he interprets them to the owner and makes recommendations for remediation if it's needed.

Bill Conroy of Conroy Environmental, Inc., in Huntington Station, New York, finds a growing portion of this work involves identifying moisture leaks that result from mistakes made between the architect and the mechanical engineer. For example, he points out that many times architects do not leave enough room for air-conditioning ducts so the ones in-stalled lack ventilation, which leads to moisture building up and leaking out to eventually create the conditions for molds to grow.

Running this business takes good business skills, too, according to Conroy. He mentions, for example, that it is important to write your con-tracts with clients to allow for contingencies in the number and cost of lab tests that sometimes run far higher than expected.

As you might guess, in order do phase I and phase II assessments as a business, you need to obtain the required training, certification, and licens-ing. Since these requirements vary by state, check with your state about training you need to do environmental assessments. You can check the li-censing for your state on the Internet through links provided by the Council on Licensure, Enforcement and Regulation (CLEAR) at *www.clearhq.org/boards.htm*.

With new construction on a general upswing and old construction in a constant state of deterioration, environmental assessment can be a very good business for those with the right background.

Environmental Assessment at a Glance

 50% 50%

	Minimal	Moderate	More than most
Start-up cost		Certification	
Overhead		$1 million + E&O insurance	
Potential earnings			X
Computer skills required		X	
Deadline pressures		X	
Flexible hours		X	
Overall stress	X		

Likely Transferable Skills, Background, Careers

People who have done mechanical engineering, construction, maintenance, or worked for a utility can transition into this business smoothly. Alternatively, if you have an interest in environmental issues, architecture, and design, or you have mechanical aptitudes and enjoy "figuring things out," you can build on these interests and skills in this field. Note that reports are part of the work, so good writing skills are necessary.

What to Charge

Phase I services range from $1,500 to $2,500. Hourly rates for phase II consulting are $100 an hour and more. Sampling and other direct costs are additional. Reimbursable expenses are sometimes made subject to a 10 percent surcharge. Consider making your fees subject to renegotiation if there are delays not caused by you.

Best Ways to Get Business

- Developing relationships with attorneys, mortgage companies, and banks and other lenders.

- Obtaining referrals from home inspectors who do not have the certifications to do phase I or phase II work themselves.

- For Phase II inspection work, contacting reputable companies that do phase III remediation exclusively and offering to list their firms as among those you will give to clients needing work in exchange for their listing you as a firm that does phase II inspections with customers they get.

- For phase II inspection work, particularly mold inspection, developing referral relationship with allergists who will refer asthma and allergy patients who need their homes or offices tested.

- Having a professional-looking Web site that serves as an electronic brochure and includes your credentials and areas of specialization.

- Listing in the Yellow Pages showing your Web site.

Marketing Insights

- Referrals from professionals and companies involved in real estate transactions will be responsible for most of the work you get. Occasionally, owners of property will order an inspection unrelated to the property being involved in a current real estate transaction.

- Credentials matter, so the time and money you invest in getting them help both with credibility and your professional standing compared with those who don't have them.

- This is a profession in which specialization may help. For phase II work, select the one or two specialties that best fit your skills: water, air, soil, chemicals, molds, radon, electromagnetic radiation, lead paint, leakages, asbestos, etc.

- If this field interests you but your technical background is limited, at this time, it makes sense to focus on mold inspections, which is a growing problem. You can become a certified mold inspector in a short period of time through a number of certifying organizations.

- Consider beginning your business in an area where there is a lot of new construction going on or where there has been a known history of contaminants that might cause many home sellers and buyers to insist on having environmental assessments whenever property changes hands.

Where Next?

BOOKS

- *Environmental Assessment in Practice*, D. Owen Harrop and J. Ashley Nixon (Routledge, 1999). ISBN: 0415156912.

- *Environmental Site Assessment*, Phase I, Kathleen Hess and Kathleen Hess-Kosa (Lewis Publishers, 1997). ISBN: 1566702712.

CERTIFICATIONS OR DESIGNATIONS

- Environmental Assessment Association (EAA) offers five designations: (320) 763-4320; *www.iami.org*.

- Indoor Air Quality Association (IAQA) certifies indoor environmentalists and mold remediators and updates the Standards of Practice: (301) 231-8388; *www.iaqa.org.*

- Indoor Environmental Standards Organization certifies mold inspectors and updates the Standards of Practice: (800) 406-0256, (952) 928-7471; *www.iestandards.org.*

- National Ground Water Association: (800) 551-7379, (614) 898-7791; *www.ngwa.org*

FRANCHISE

- Professional House Doctors: (515) 265-6667; *www.prohousedr.com.*

From the Home Front

"What's most gratifying about this work is encountering problems and finding the solutions. It's exercising your brain. I see myself doing this for ten or fifteen more years."

—Albert Snow, sixty-nine

---

34. Elder Care

Given that you are approaching or over fifty, you know that America is aging. By the year 2020, one in every six people will be over age sixty-five and nearly seven million people will be over eighty-five. Fortunately, there's a positive outcome from aging—it creates a variety of home-based and small-business opportunities. Here are four emerging ones that can be done from home:

Certified Senior Advisor

If you are engaged in or have a background in any one of the following, you can become credentialed to specialize in working with seniors by becoming a Certified Senior Advisor (CSA):

- Accounting
- Businesses serving seniors
- Clergy
- Financial planning
- Home health care
- Insurance
- Law
- Long-term care
- Medicine,
- Nursing
- Pharmacy
- Real estate
- Reverse mortgage lending
- Senior housing
- Social work

The training for the CSA designation prepares professionals to help seniors understand and solve problems such as the social aspects of aging, distinguishing forgetfulness from dementia, physical and psychological changes, Social Security and Medicaid programs, end-of-life planning, and long-term care.

Geriatric Care Management

If you have a professional degree in nursing, social work, psychology, or gerontology, consider becoming a geriatric care manager. Geriatric care managers can work independently of an agency. They assess the needs of frail older people and arrange and coordinate a wide range of services so their clients can remain at home. Geriatric care managers are also called upon to intervene in crises management, and they may help to make financial arrangements. They handle the many difficult and time-consuming tasks of negotiating services from a complex array of public and nonprofit agencies, many of which have waiting lists.

In-Home Nonmedical Caregiver

As a caregiver you help seniors perform their "activities of daily living" (called ADLs) such as cleaning, cooking, grocery shopping, bill paying, grooming, laundry, medication reminders, errands and shopping, and driving them to medical appointments. Elder-care providers also provide companionship and may come in from a few hours a day, in which case they might serve several clients, to all day or all night every night seven days a week. The Administration on Aging estimates that nearly one in five elderly people needs help at home with nonmedical activities. Ruth Johnson of Buhl, Idaho, who is eighty-one now, began her elder-care home service from her home at seventy. She has enough clients to hire others who work for her and says, "Going into people's homes keeps them safe and helps them avoid going into nursing homes." She prepared herself for this work by going to school to become a certified nurse's aide, which she did in six weeks.

Although elder caregivers do not need to be medically trained, you do need to be bonded and have liability insurance if you are transporting people in your vehicle. While you don't need a franchise to enter this field, franchises are available and, in fact, require insurance and bonding. Franchises for nonmedical in-home elder care include: Comfort Keepers of Dayton, Ohio; Griswold Special Care of Erdenheim, Pennsylvania; and Home Instead Senior Care of Omaha, Nebraska.

Senior Relocation Service

Relocation specialists help seniors who are moving to smaller homes or assisted-living facilities. Because their children often live elsewhere, many older folks do not have family members available to help with their move and so are willing to hire a service that facilitates getting through the hassles and complexities of their relocation. Services include such things as sorting through the family's possessions to determine what the clients may want to keep versus what they may want to sell or donate, helping them pack and label boxes, arranging to hire a moving company, as well as taking care of discontinuing or setting up utilities and phone services. Following the move, there's the unpacking and completely setting up the new household, along with grocery shopping and other errands that people often don't have time to do when they move. Gentle Transitions, probably the first senior relocation service, was started in 1990 by Mercedes Gunderson at the age of fifty-five.

Elder Care at a Glance

 20% 80%

	Minimal	Moderate	More than most
Start-up cost	X		
Overhead	X		
Potential earnings	Caregiver	Elder relocation	Geriatric care manager
Computer skills required	Caregiver	Geriatric care manager	
Regular schedule			Caregiver
Deadline pressures			Elder relocation
Flexible hours			Geriatric care manager
Overall stress		X	

Likely Transferable Skills, Background, Careers

Many people have told us that their interest in an elder-care business was sparked by having been forced to help or take care of someone in their own family, so if you've had that experience, why not turn what you learned into your new business? In addition to personal experience, elder-care work is a great business for former teachers, nurses, social workers, and other people who have been in a helping profession and enjoy being with elderly people.

What to Charge

Relocation services charge $30 to $40 per hour, and can often end up with contracts ranging from $300 to $6,000 to help a senior couple move. The average move costs between $1,500 and $2,000. Elder companion services bill at $10 to $15 an hour, with the higher rates if they are transporting seniors to cover their liability insurance. Geriatric care managers earn from $70 to $200 an hour.

Best Ways to Get Business

- Seeking out referrals by developing relationships with the intake personnel at assisted-living/retirement homes, hospital discharge planners, physicians, realtors, and social agencies who come into contact with the elderly.

- Participating in a business-referral organization with the aim of meeting people who work with seniors, such as attorneys, banking and trust officers, health-care professionals, and social service providers.

- Creating two types of brochures:

  - A brochure for seniors so they can self-refer to you. Distribute these in senior centers and assisted-living homes, in doctors' offices, country clubs, and other recreational areas for seniors.

  - A brochure for adult children that you can use in hair salons, gyms, and community centers where you can reach adult children who likely have aging parents.

- Describing your services on a Web site. Since yours is a local business, be sure to place the name of the community or communities you serve on your home page, in meta tags, and if possible, in your domain name. Design the site for the children of seniors who will be searching for help.

- Getting listed in directories that enable prospective clients to phone or e-mail you. Caregivers can check out getting into the CareScout Provider database as a home-care provider: (781) 431-7033; *www.carescout.com.*

- Posting flyers on your local community center bulletin boards.

- Advertising in senior-oriented publications and community newspapers, although we recommend testing a publication with small or classified ads before spending significant amounts of money.

Marketing Insights

- Expect to be hired mostly by the children of your senior clients. Children in the sandwich generation are caught between job demands and the responsibility they feel to their parents. Many have children under eighteen living at home, which is the case for 41 percent of adults who are caring for their parents themselves. You provide peace of mind so these busy adults can attend to these other demands in their busy lives. For many, this means avoiding lost wages or burnout by trying to do too much.

- Your age is an advantage. Empathy, needed for any type of elder-care service, is apt to be easier for people over fifty.

- Stay abreast of the demographic trends for where people are retiring. If you wish to make a geographic move, you may be able to find an agreeable geographic location that is growing in popularity where you would have the best chance of being the first, or among the first, elder-care businesses to establish there.

Where Next?

LICENSING AND CERTIFICATION

- Geriatric-care managers need to be certified or licensed in their state in a field such as social work, nursing, psychology, or therapy. Some training, short of becoming a Certified Nurse's Aide, is required for reimbursement under Medicaid or Medicare.

- Society of Certified Senior Advisors: (800) 653-1785, (303) 757-2323; *www.societycsa.com*

BOOKS / NEWSLETTERS

- *The Caregiver's Essential Handbook,* Sasha Carr and Sandra Choron (McGraw-Hill/Contemporary Books, 2003). ISBN: 0071395199. More than 1,200 tips.

- *Eldercare 911,* Susan Beerman and Judith Rappaport-Musson (Prometheus Books, 2002). ISBN: 159102014X.

- *Handbook of Geriatric Care Management,* Cathy Cress (Aspen Publishers, 2001). ISBN: 0834216671.

WEB SITES

- Administration on Aging, resources of the Department of Health and Human Services: *www.aoa.dhhs.gov.*

- Eldercare Online, resources including a forum: *www.ec-online.net.*

- *The AARP Guide to Internet Resources Related to Aging:* www.aarp.org/cyber/guide1.htm.

- Transitions, Inc., a Minneapolis elder-care consulting firm, offers resources on its site and a business package: *(612) 978-1176; www.asktransitions.com/testimon.html.*

ORGANIZATIONS

- National Alliance for Caregiving: *http://caregiving.org.*

- National Association of Senior Move Managers: *www.nasmm.com.* Provides consumers with a directory to locate a senior move manager.

- National Association of Professional Geriatric Care Managers: (520) 881-8008; *www.caremanager.org.* Provides consumers with a directory to locate a geriatric care manager.

FRANCHISES

NONMEDICAL IN-HOME CARE

- Comfort Keepers: (937) 264-1933; *www.comfortkeepers.com.*

- Griswold Special Care: (888) 777-7630, (215) 402-0200; *www.home-care.net.*

- Home Instead Senior Care: (402) 498-4466; *www.homeinstead.com.*

SENIOR RELOCATION SERVICE

- Gentle Transitions: (952) 944-1028; *www.gentletransitions.com.* The company is anticipating offering franchises.

From the Home Front

"I enjoy elder care because I feel I'm helping people. In growing my business, I hire people who I wouldn't mind having to take care of me."

—Ruth Johnson, eighty-one

Snapshot: Eva Fry, Composer and Entertainer

Motivated by a troubled home life, Eva Fry had two dreams as a young girl: to be an entertainer and to make a difference in the world. Like so many of us, life stepped in and she stored those dreams away. She married young and became a stay-at-home mom, a role she thoroughly enjoyed. But that came to an abrupt end when her children grew up and left Eva with an empty nest and newfound time to retrieve her dreams, dust them off, and bring them back to life.

Eva returned to school, took speech, singing, and stand-up comedy classes, along with guitar and piano lessons and at age fifty-nine began writing music. Now sixty-three, she's living her dreams. She entertains at senior facilities and performs at fairs and other events in her community of Valley Center, California.

As Eva Fry Productions, she has produced two CDs of her original music, *Remember* and *Oh What Joy Christmas* and teaches an adult-education seminar on living your dreams. She's also making a difference in the world through her "Be a Winner in Life" presentations for youth organizations, and she's written a book called *You Must Have a Dream.*

"The senior years are the perfect time to live your dreams," Eva maintains.

35. Estate Sale Services

George Carlin's routine about the dilemma of having too much "stuff" struck a chord with tens of millions of people whose homes are so overstuffed that, weather permitting, we see a plethora of garage sales every weekend coast-to-coast and more recently a twenty-four-hour stream of auctions on *eBay*. To many people clutter has become a "dirty word" and recycling a cause, but for others the process of recycling stuff has become a career—managing estate and garage sales. While the term *estate sale* implies a death, other occasions prompt sales needing the services of a professional, such as moving and divorce.

When disposing of household contents, most people want to make some money in the process, and estate sales managers enable them to get more for their stuff than they could get on their own. Besides increasing sales, the professionals of this field, also called agents, do the time-consuming work of sorting, cleaning, repairing, organizing, arranging, showing, pricing, advertising, and selling, leaving the property "broom clean" and picking up and hauling off remaining trash and debris. The service may also involve disposing of unsold items in a number of possible ways, such as donating them to charity, selling them to a dealer or on *eBay*, or returning them to the owner. So clearly a professional estate-sale manager takes the stress out of disposing of items before a major move or after a death in the family.

Ed Tuten's wife thinks he's a pack rat, but he has been able to use this trait to his advantage. Tuten started Team Estate Sales in Memphis at age sixty-four, offering estate-sale services to seniors who are downsizing their homes, and selling items on consignment sales. When working with seniors, Ed goes through the house with the older person to identify the things that haven't been used in ten years and pave the way to scaling down the household while saving what's most important for the new home. In building this business, Tuten says, "You need to develop a customer base of collectors." You can do this by subscribing to collector associations and societies, which charge an annual fee, and developing your own collector database as you go. "A lot of collectors have come to me after seeing my Web site," mentions Tuten. He also places ads in the newsletters of different collector societies related to the kinds of items he has to sell, e.g., the American Pottery Club.

Kim Hoover of Web Estate Sales in Dallas approaches the estate sales she coordinates in steps. First she conducts a free, no-obligation interview and inspection with the responsible party. She provides honest feedback about the options for selling the items, as well as the likely costs and outcomes.

Once the client agrees to her conducting the sale, the cleaning and sorting begins. If anything needs to be repaired, organized, or arranged, this is the time to do it. The groundwork is put in place for a successful estate sale at this time, and personal or keepsake items are set aside for the family. Next all the items are researched as to value and priced. Tuten recommends doing this step with a family member present to prevent misunderstandings. The client gets a list of the inventory before and after the sale occurs. If you do not have experience with appraisal, you may want to take a course or hire someone to help with this as it is crucial to a successful sale.

Regardless of the preparation, the proceeds of a sale will not be what they could be if the sale is not advertised properly to people who are interested in what is being sold. Again, connecting the right buyers with the products they want is the real goal of this service. Estate sales can be advertised in local newspapers and trade magazines and are open to anyone who stops by. Sales also can be conducted on an "appointment only" basis—appropriate, for example, in gated communities. In this case, buyers can preview photos and descriptions of items at a "virtual estate sale" posted on a Web site or printed for distribution so only interested buyers actually come to the sale. The type of goods being sold to the buyer base and the location of the sale determine what will be the best type of sale to hold.

When a sale is in progress, especially if it is held at the client's property, security is important. Staff needs to be available to monitor each room and answer any questions. Finally after the sale is finished, there's cleanup and disposal of unsold items. The handling should be predetermined with the client. This, too, may require staff help. Then within seven days of the end of the sale, a settlement with a full listing of items sold is presented to the client along with a check.

No special training or certification is required to manage an estate sale. It is important, though, to have knowledge of the items you are dealing with. Some may be extremely valuable and others may not be. If you understand the worth of the commodities you are handling, you will have a better idea of where and to whom to sell them to make the most money for your client and yourself. Since an estate-sale agent links buyers to sellers, it is important to keep abreast of who is buying what and where. For example, a particular make of china may sell better through a collector's club or listing than it will on *eBay*. Your research and experience will help you figure out the best places to list the items you handle.

Estate Sale Services at a Glance

 50% 50%

	Minimal	Moderate	More than most
Start-up cost	Display tables and supplies		
Overhead		X	
Potential earnings		X	
Computer skills required		X	
Deadline pressures		X	
Flexible hours		X	
Overall stress		X	

Likely Transferable Skills, Background, Careers

Antiquers, art historians, and collectors with good organizing capability are naturals for this business. Professional organizer skills transfer well into estate-sales management. Since researching and familiarizing yourself with the market are mandatory, curiosity is an excellent attribute to have along with organizational skills.

What to Charge

Usually a commission of 25 to 40 percent of total sales is charged for this service. Advertising costs are subtracted before calculating the commission. Payment is made after the sale is finished. The commission varies depending on the quality and quantity of the stock as well as the amount of work involved to coordinate the sale.

Best Ways to Get Business

- Developing referral relationships with attorneys who handle probate and bankers who deal with trusts; their clients appreciate the relief from stress that a professional estate-sale services provides, but they may actually hire you. Other sources of referrals can be retirement home managers, pastors and rabbis, and charities; realtors also make referrals.

- Having a Web site with your services and contact information. Use key words that identify your community and specialties so people using a search engine will find your site. Webrings for collectors are good places to list your Web site. Webrings, which link sites with a common topic such as a type of collectible, will also help in generating traffic for your Web site. (A webring is a group of Web sites linked together by topic or interest to facilitate users to navigate between related sites.)

- Listing in the Yellow Pages, which will enable you to be found on Web directories like *switchboard.com* and *anywho.com*. Consider ads on local directory sites like *Yahoo Get Local* and *SuperPages*.

- Advertising in publications such as auction house catalogues, real estate journals, and trust fund magazines

Marketing Insights

- The key benefits you offer clients are a higher return on their goods, relief from stress, time savings, and convenience. Estate sales involve handling a lot of specialized details and can be overwhelming to anyone without the proper experience or organizing skill. An individual may miss things of value or incorrectly price costly items.

- Specialization possibilities include handling particular kinds of goods, like furniture, or dealing with particular situations, like downsizing. Ed Tuten offers a special "Senior Service," which includes planning for the new home with the help of an interior designer who helps the client select the best of his or her treasures and make a plan of where those things will go in the new home. They also pack, sort, and supervise the move in addition to conducting the sale.

- Being able to take credit cards and do instant check verification will increase sales. No-return policies are standard in this business.

Where Next?

ASSOCIATIONS FOR APPRAISERS

- The Appraisers Association of America has a certification process: (212) 889-5404; *www.appraisersassoc.org.*

- American Society of Appraisers offers accreditation: (703) 478-2228; *www.appraisers.org.*

- New England Appraisers Association: (802) 228-7444; *www.newenglandappraisers.net*

BOOKS

- *The Complete Guidebook to the Business of Tag and Estate Sales,* Mim Nagy (TLC Tag Sales and Publishing Co., 2002). ISBN: 0971314403.

- *Garage Sale & Flea Market Annual,* Beth Summers and Karen Smith (Collector Books, 2003). ISBN: 1574323229.

WEB SITES

- Garage Sale Zone, free listings, free printable signs, links to supply sources: *www.garagesalezone.com.*

- I Collector Live lists auctions and broadcasts them live on the Internet, *www.icollector.com.*

- This Vancouver estate sale service sells an "Estate Sale Business Starter Kit": *www.estatesales.bc.ca.*

From the Home Front

"We're addicts—I enjoy making discoveries. Rather than watch TV, I'll read about Heisey glass."   —Ed Tuten, sixty-six

36. Facialist/Aesthetician

While "beauty is only skin deep," there is no getting around the fact that beauty begins with the skin—or so feel millions of people who are increasingly turning to facialists (also called aestheticians or estheticians) to help them make their faces look young, fresh, and healthy. Facialists are increasingly in demand simply because we live in an aging society. In the year 2005, almost half of people in America will be over age thirty-five, which translates into well over 100 million men and women who have skin that shows signs of aging. Baby boomers especially are a generation that refuses to age ungracefully. More important, looking young or as close to ageless as possible helps one's career, whether one is employed or seeking clients for one's own business.

The services of a facialist are the next best thing to plastic surgery for slowing the inevitable aging process of the skin, averting wrinkles, and minimizing other types of skin problems. To keep the face looking as young and healthy as possible, facialists use chemistry, pressure, and electricity to offer an exotic array of treatments such as peels, waxing, collagen, seaweed, mud, oxygenating and lifting masks; facials using vitamins, glycolic acid, aromatherapy, and paraffin; lash and brow tinting; drainage massages; and treatments using cold, hot stones, ayurveda, herbology, lasers, cell abrasion, and crystal microdermabrasion.

Each facialist has her own point of view as to what works best and is healthiest for her clients, but they usually offer each client a wide selection of treatments from basic care to deep pore cleansing, rejuvenating and hydrating, with each session lasting roughly one to two hours.

Some facialists put their clients on antiaging regimens that involve weekly treatments over a period of six to eight weeks followed up with ongoing monthly sessions. Treatments may include applying oxygen to the skin and electric facial toning. Many clients continue their monthly followup treatments indefinitely.

Because people tend to hop from one facialist to another, constantly seeking new ways to keep their skin young, facialists generally need to periodically introduce new products and ideas to keep attracting new clients and retain old ones. Something new as of this writing is the use of crushed gemstones and minerals to create custom-blended skin products for clients. Permanent makeup is becoming popular. It involves providing permanent eyeliner, eyebrows, and lip color for clients using a tattooing process, micropigmentation. It also can be used to camouflage scars and create beauty marks.

On average, a busy facialist sees between three and five clients per day, because it takes time for clients to disrobe and dress again, and you need time to do the facial and counsel each client on proper follow-up care.

The main challenge to becoming a facialist is that most states require you to be licensed as a cosmetician (also called aesthetician/esthetician) in order to work with people's skin. While many states allow home and mobile salons, others do not and the zoning in some communities does not permit home-based salons. However, facialists can sometimes successfully apply to their local zoning board and receive approval to work from their homes, as long as they restrict their work to facials and don't do haircutting or styling. You will need to have business insurance to protect yourself in the event of any problems or accidents, although some facialists lessen their insurance costs by not doing higher-risk procedures like chemical peels or micropigmentation. Some simply sell products but don't apply them.

Facialists at a Glance

 40% 60%

	Minimal	Moderate	More than most
Start-up cost		Good chair, insurance	
Overhead			X
Potential earnings			X
Computer skills required	X		
Deadline pressures		X	
Flexible hours		X	
Overall stress		X	

Likely Transferable Skills, Background, Careers

In most states in order to get licensed, you must graduate from a school of cosmetology or aesthetics that is approved by the state agency that regulates this occupation. You can find training at private cosmetology schools and community colleges. Cosmetology schools are listed in the Yellow Pages, though they may be found under Beauty or Aesthetics. Training usually takes about six months, though community-college training may take longer. Training leads to certification, the requirement for licensing. Facialists who perform electrolysis have additional licensing requirements.

Facialists need to have a nurturing personality and to genuinely enjoy pampering people, including feeling completely comfortable touching and having close physical contact with clients. If your business will depend on product sales, you need to have or develop selling skills.

What to Charge

Facialists charge by the appointment, by service, or by time spent. A basic facial runs from $50 to $75 and sometimes more, depending on location. Additional services and products can add to a client's bill from 20 to 100 percent.

Best Ways to Get Business

- Giving clients complimentary gift certificates to hand out to their friends.

- Listing in the Yellow Pages under headings like Skincare and Treatment and Facial Cosmetology. Consider ads on local directory sites like *Yahoo Get Local* and *SuperPages*.

- Letting past clients know about new services by postal card or e-mail.

- Networking in business organizations, particularly women's business groups, attended by people who are likely users of facialist services, as well as informal networking among friends, social organizations, and at health clubs.

- Participating in one or more business-referral organizations.

- Providing complimentary or low-cost initial sessions to new clients.

- Working with a hair salon, but this will require you to work on their premises, although you remain independent and split the fees you receive with the salon.

Marketing Insights

- Prime sources of clients for facialists are women whose occupation requires them to have a youthful visual appearance or where looking their best is perceived as critical to their success. Executives, performers, service personnel, professional speakers, and airline attendants are just a few of the groups for whom appearance is a particularly important element. And because care of the skin is an ongoing process, satisfied clients often become regular customers.

- You may find opportunity in growing communities in arid climates, particularly popular western mountain communities, where dry air creates a demand for facial services.

- Creating a homey environment with music and refreshments like cappuccino helps make clients consider their facials a special treat they look forward to and are more apt to give as a gift.

- Facialists can also do makeup; see the Makeup Artist profile for more information.

- Specialization possibilities, in addition to the kind of services you provide, include targeting people with special concerns such as sensitive skin, smokers, etc.

- The benefits of permanent makeup include less hassle applying makeup, freeing time, a more youthful look, and being able to engage in activities like swimming without smearing makeup.

To increase profitability, facialists often sell skin-care products they have purchased wholesale and sometimes had relabeled under their own names.

Where Next?

ASSOCIATIONS

- Aesthetics' International Association: (877) 968-7539, (972) 932-8380; *www.beautyworks.com/aia/*.

- National Cosmetology Association: *www.salonprofessionals.org*.

BOOKS

- *The Business of Beauty,* Debbie Purvis (Wall & Emerson, 1994). ISBN: 1895131138.

- *Milady's Standard Comprehensive Training for Estheticians,* Janet D'Angelo, Paula S. Dean, Sallie Dietz, Catherine Hinds, Mark Lees, Erica Miller, and Alexandra Zani (Milady Publishing Company, 2002). ISBN: 1562538055. This company also publishes *Milady's State Exam Review for Professional Estheticians, Milady's Standard Textbook for Professional Estheticians, Milady's Standard: Fundamentals for Estheticians, Clinical Cosmetology,* and other titles.

- *Skin Secrets,* Nicholas Lowe and Polly Sellar (Sterling Publishing, 1999). ISBN: 1855856654.

MAGAZINE

- *Dermascope* magazine: (972) 226-2309; *www.dermascope.com*.

WEB SITES

- *Beautyworks.* Participants on this site include *Skin, Inc.* magazine, the Aesthetics' International Association, the International Guild of Professional Electrologists, and the American Society of Esthetic Medicine, Inc.: *www.beautyworks.com*.

- Links to the licensing boards in all states are provided at *www.beautytech.com/st_boards.htm*.

37. Family Child Care

The stay-at-home mom has gone the way of star-filled urban skies. Today, more than 70 percent of married women with children under six years of age work outside the home, as do the majority of divorced women who have preschool-age children. This new reality has created a surge in the need for high-quality child care.

Some large employers offer on-site child care, but most don't, so millions of parents are left to make their own arrangements for day care for their children. There are usually just two choices: large corporately owned or franchised child-care centers and "home-based family-style" day care. Large commercial child care tends to be more impersonal, often with as many as sixty children together in one commercial building, school, church, or temple. By contrast, home-based day care is more personal because states and cities regulate the size of these operations to no more than six to twelve children per home, depending on how many adults are present. So if you love children and feel that you can be dependable, responsible, and nurturing, you can offer a more appealing alternative to many, many parents.

Most states require a license or registration with a government agency if you intend to care for more than three children in your home. The licensing process usually requires an inspection of your home for adequacy, space, cleanliness, and safety. You must demonstrate that you have removed all dangerous chemicals, cleaning fluids, and other things that could be harmful to children. Some states also require that you take a training course in CPR, emergency care, and child development.

You will also need to check out your zoning. Your home may be located in an area that isn't zoned to allow family child care or that limits the number of children to no more than three or six. You may need to obtain consent from your neighbors to gain the needed approval from your city or community zoning board. Some states have passed laws superseding local zoning ordinances to allow home child care.

There are advantages to being fully licensed because you may be eligible for food subsidies from the U.S. Department of Agriculture to help pay for costs of breakfasts, lunches, and snacks you provide. Licensing is also needed for liability insurance, which protects your business and personal assets in the event of an accident. Finally, being fully licensed opens up the opportunity to become accredited by the National Association for Family Child Care, which will help you gain the trust and confidence that parents need to be attracted to your business.

The mark of high-quality family child care, according to the Families and Work Institute, is a strong commitment to create an environment in which children can be both nurtured and taught. You need to stimulate children's mental, physical, and social development by providing them with a variety of learning experiences. This means that you should have ample toys for children to play with both indoors and out that are suitable to their developmental level. Letting them watch videos or TV all day is absolutely forbidden.

In fact, an interesting new marketing concept is catching on among child-care centers: specialization. Debra McLaurin, who was forty-nine when she started her day-care business in Santa Clarita, California, specializes in "high-impact" teaching. "I learn how my children learn by observing them for ten days, allowing them to play by themselves. I document all daily activities and progress of each child. Then I design a program for them, with a special curriculum for each child." Debra's techniques are well appreciated by parents. According to Debra, parents are constantly telling her that their children are attentive, know how to share, can count and spell their names, and are always happy when they leave her facility. There's no better marketing than that.

Debra's commitment to high-impact learning has paid off. Her business was selected for a Community-Developed Initiative Small Grant of roughly $20,000 to assist in purchasing computers, software, a listening center group table, educational toys, books, arts and crafts material, early-education books, and a science and water table.

Shari Steelsmith, author of *How to Start a Home-Based Day-Care Business,* finds family day care is increasingly being done by husband-and-wife teams. "You can be there to spell each other and men and women interact and play a little differently with children, giving them a more well-rounded experience."

Steelsmith cautions, though, that "young children require a lot of energy, so it's important to take good care of yourself, getting enough sleep, exercise, and enjoy enough leisure activities to restore yourself."

Child care has traditionally been a low-paying career, but it provides a wealth of psychic rewards for someone who wants to earn an income at home and loves working with children.

Family Child Care at a Glance

30% 70%

	Minimal	Moderate	More than most
Start-up cost		X	
Overhead		X	
Potential earnings	X		
Computer skills required	X		
Regular schedule			X
Overall stress			X

Likely Transferable Skills, Background, Careers

Personal characteristics like being loving, nurturing, patient, and understanding matter most, though a background in early-childhood development or psychology, or having done teaching, nursing, or social work helps. You also need to be able to schedule, organize, and manage four or five things at the same time, because children are unpredictable and you never know what you may need to do on a day-to-day or even a minute-by-minute basis.

What to Charge

Child-care rates vary considerably with the age of the children you care for, the hours of care, and where you are located. The rate for infants is typically more than toddlers, preschoolers, and school-age children. Generally, rates are higher in the Northeast and California, less in the Midwest and South. Within a metropolitan area, rates may be double in one area what they are in another. If you hold a current early-childhood-development credential or your home is accredited by the National Association for the Education of Young Children (NAEYC), you may be eligible for higher reimbursements from your state. We recommend calling other child-care providers in your area to learn what they are charging as well as checking Web sites.

Best Ways to Get Business

- Getting listed with a referral agency.

- Befriending other family child-care providers and proposing an agreement to exchange overflow. Some may work with you only if you offer a referral fee.

- Placing notices on bulletin boards in supermarkets, Laundromats, retail locations.

- Listing in the Yellow Pages, which will enable you to be found on Web directories like *switchboard.com* and *anywho.com*. Consider listing on local directory sites like *Yahoo Get Local* and *SuperPages*.

- Going to your local elementary schools and telling them about your business. See if they will list you in their newsletter or on their bulletin board.

- Advertising in local parenting newspapers and magazines.

- Making up T-shirts and sweatshirts with the name and logo of your business and giving them out to your children to wear on weekends.

- If permitted, put a sign in your yard.

- Using a Web site as an electronic brochure. Because you serve a local clientele, be sure to use the name of the community or communities you serve on your home page, in meta tags, and, if possible in your domain name.

- Contacting corporations in your area and asking if you can post notices on their bulletin boards.

- Contacting small- to medium-size businesses in your area to find out if they might be interested in contracting directly with you to supply child care for children of their employees.

- Offering discounts to new clients, such as $50 for the first introductory week. Also offer a discount to any current client who refers a new family to you.

Marketing Insights

- The key benefit you can offer is high-quality and personalized child care that makes parents feel completely comfortable leaving their children with you. According to a five-year study by the Families and Work Institute, just 9 percent of family child-care providers in a sample survey were rated "good," while 56 percent were ranked only "adequate." This leaves a lot of room for new home child-care providers to prosper by committing themselves to providing the highest kind of safe and intellectually and socially stimulating environment for young children.

- Specializing can help you attract a specific clientele if you have a Web site or have developed referral sources. Possible specialties include serving a particular age group, after-school care, working with learning disabled, handicapped, or very bright children, having a specific curriculum such as preschool, infants, or religious. There's a kind of day care that's more difficult and complex, but there's a national support organization for it: National Association for Sick Child Daycare: (205) 324-8447; *www.nascd.com*.

- Particularly if you're in a crowded market, consider offering child care at nonstandard times. Millions of people work shifts around the clock. These one-third of all employed women have performed shift-work jobs, and 45 percent of these are single moms.

- Some ways to stimulate business are to:

  - Provide a discount for multiple children from the same family.

  - Offer a video camera hooked up to the Internet so parents can see their kids are safe and behaving well at any time from their work.

Where Next?

ASSOCIATIONS

- Canadian Child Care Federation: (800) 858-1412; *www.cccf-fcsge.ca.*

- National Association for the Education of Young Children: (800) 424-2460, (202) 232-8777; *www.naeyc.org*—accreditation program; site has a directory of links to many national organizations.

- National Association for Family Child Care, organization specifically for family child-care provider and its advocates; offers an accreditation program: (801) 269-9338; *www.nafcc.org.*

BOOKS

- *Family Child Care Marketing Guide,* Tom Copeland (Redleaf Press, 1999). ISBN: 1884834752. This is one of a series of Copeland books. Others include *Family Child Care Contracts and Policies* and *Family Child Care Record-Keeping Guide.*

- *How to Start a Home-Based Day-Care Business,* Shari Steelsmith (Globe Pequot, 2003). ISBN: 0762727616.

- *Start and Run a Home Daycare,* Catherine M. Pruissen (Self Counsel Press, 2002). ISBN: 1551804107.

WEB SITES

- National Association of Child Care Resource & Referral Agencies, national network of more than 850 child-care resource and referral centers: (202) 393-5501; *www.naccrra.net.*

- National Resource Center funded by the Maternal and Child Health Bureau, U.S. Department of Health and Human Services, HRSA. Links to all state licensing agencies: *http:nrc.uchsc.edu/STATES/states.htm.*

- Resources for Child Caring, a nonprofit resource and referral organization affiliated with Redleaf National Institute and Redleaf Press, publisher of curriculum, management, and business resources for early-childhood professionals: (651) 641-0305; *www.resourcesforchildcare.org.*

38. Feng Shui Practitioner

Perhaps it's the constant pressures of 24/7 lives, perhaps it's the growth in the number of "cultural creatives," certainly it's the growing number of Asian-Americans, but increasing numbers of people are using Feng Shui to evoke harmony in their surroundings. Feng Shui can be described as the art of understanding how the physical environment affects one's physical, mental, and emotional health and sense of well-being.

Feng Shui and related disciplines are methods for "clearing" and harmonizing both home and work spaces. There are several specific approaches to Feng Shui, but for the most part learning the basics plus applying one's own sensory awareness, aesthetic sense, and personal intuition can lead to a career helping others bring their lives and surroundings into balance.

At the heart of Feng Shui theory is "chi," or energy, the flow or interruption of which affects the people in their spaces. The practice of Feng Shui is devoted to opening the flow of chi in the environment so occupants experience a sense of calm, prosperity, and creativity.

According to Sheila Wright of Feng Shui Services (*www.fengshuiservices. com*), once you learn the theory, you can interpret it and establish your own way to apply Feng Shui. Sheila, who began her Feng Shui practice at the age of fifty, points out that when Feng Shui originated in China, people didn't have things like electricity to contend with. She says, "Practitioners need to develop their own approach and learn to discern what's right and what isn't in the moment. Certain rules apply, like with driving a car, but then there are ways we can deviate, like changing lanes."

Feng Shui consultants use color, shape, sound, and certain objects placed strategically to align with different areas in the building to affect various themes of the occupant's life: success, relationships, health, vitality, and contentment. Some use tools like the ba gua, a five-sided compass that locates the various themes in certain areas of the space. Other schools use the front door as the beginning point of reference.

Realtors, architects, and interior designers consult Feng Shui practitioners. Some real estate agents find that homes that have been subjected to Feng Shui principles are selling faster. Companies seeking to increase morale among their employees or to alleviate chronic downtime resulting from illness or low vitality among employees are using Feng Shui consultants to improve working environments. The *Los Angeles Times* on March 21, 2004, reported that top executives at Coca-Cola, News Corporation, Ford Motors, Hewlett-Packard, and Procter and Gamble are using Feng Shui consultants. Schools, city planners, and parks and recreation departments are also consulting Feng Shui experts.

Feng Shui is not the sole technology being used as an antidote to the stresses of contemporary life. Others are:

- Vastu shastra, the art of correctly placing yourself in a space to achieve maximum benefit from the five elements and magnetic fields. It takes some years to learn Vastu shastra. This Indian science of design is catching on in North America with training programs apt to follow.

- Bau-biologie or "building biology" is a movement promoting healthy building principles to make living and working spaces healthier places.

- Natural Systems Thinking is a process for learning how to live our daily lives in harmony with nature, even in the most congested metro areas where most of us live.

Feng Shui at a Glance

50% 50%

	Minimal	Moderate	More than most
Start-up cost	X		
Overhead	X		

	Minimal	Moderate	More than most
Potential earnings			X
Computer skills required		Web site	
Deadline pressures	X		
Flexible hours			X
Overall stress	X		

Likely Transferable Skills, Background, Careers

Healers, spiritually or metaphysically oriented people, interior designers, architects, naturalists, and real estate professionals are among the people finding their way into these fields. However, no particular background is required to be trained and engaged in a Feng Shui practice. Sheila Wright states, "I have been a student of spirituality over my adult life and Feng Shui is a natural progression in my learning."

What to Charge

While hourly fees generally ranging from $75 to $150 are frequently used, some practitioners charge flat fees; others, use square feet as the basis of their charges. Nancilee Wydra, a leading Feng Shui author and founder of the Feng Shui Institute of America, finds that Feng Shui consultants can charge midway between the going hourly rate for a massage therapist and a lawyer, so determining the rates of these in your area can help you determine your fee.

Best Ways to Get Business

- Making presentations to salespeople in real estate offices. Realtors need to be aware of Feng Shui principles where there are Asian buyers.

- Face-to-face networking in business and trade organizations and business-referral organizations.

- Giving free talks at public libraries and for service organizations. Often one or more people will be curious enough to talk to you more and schedule a consultation.

- Writing a series of articles for local papers.

- Providing a folio of information and trifold on types of services you provide.

- Giving workshops in community education, extension, noncredit courses.

- Having a Web site that serves as an electronic brochure with client endorsements and listing your services and fees.

- *Fengsuiservices.com; Energybalancingservices.com.*

Marketing Insights

- Target clients are the fifty million people Paul Ray and Sherry Anderson (*www.culturalcreatives.org*) have identified as "cultural creatives," people who seek less stress, better health, more spirituality, and more respect for the earth and are open to changing their environments to accomplish this.

- While people of all ages turn to Feng Shui, the typical client is in her mid-thirties.

- Niches in Feng Shui practice areas include color therapy and energetic cleansing. Color therapy, or auro-soma, uses color fields to invoke certain kinds of energy. Energetic cleansing is used to clear negative energy in a building. This is a service used by some real estate agents.

Where Next?

ASSOCIATIONS

- International Feng Shui Guild: (954) 345-3838; *www.internationalfengshuiguild.org.*

- The Feng Shui Association of Canada: *www.fengshuiassociationofcanada.ca.*

BOOKS

- *Aura-Soma,* Irene Dalichow, Mike Booth, and Joan M. Burnham (Hay House,1997). ISBN: 1561702919.

- *Feng Shui Principles for Building and Remodeling,* Nancilee Wydra and Lenore Weiss Baigelman (McGraw-Hill/Contemporary Books, 2002). ISBN: 0809297388. Nancy Wydra has authored six other books on Feng Shui, including *Designing Your Happiness,* ISBN: 0893468118.

- *Flying Star Feng Shui Made Easy,* David Twicken (Writers Club Press, 2000). ISBN: 0595099661.

- *The Modern Book of Feng Shui,* Steven Post (Dell, 1998). ISBN: 0440507685.

TRAINING

- The American Feng Shui Institute: (626) 571-2757; *www.amfengshui.com.*

- International Institute for Bau-Biologie & Ecology: (772) 461-4371; *www.bau-biologieusa.com.*

- The Feng Shui Institute of America (FSIA). Offers a home-study course and weeklong on-site professional certification program, which is the oldest in the country and is accepted by the American Society of Interior Designers: (888) 488-3742, (772) 388-2085; *www.windwater.com.*

- Geomancy/Feng Shui Education Organization: (415) 753-6408; *www.geofengshui.com.*

- International Institute for Bau-biologie offers on-line courses and home study: (727) 461-4371; *www.bau-biologieusa.com.*

- Project Nature Connect provides on-line training and certification in the Natural Systems Thinking Process: (306) 378-6313; *www.ecopsych.com.*

WEB SITES

- Feng Shui News, *www.fengshuinews.com.*

- Webrings. Enter Feng Shui at *http://dir.webring.com /rw.*

From the Home Front

"My practice is becoming transformed. There is a delicate balance between bringing our lives into focus and respecting nature and the energies present. I'll keep on doing this for the rest of my life."   —Sheila Wright, fifty-six

39. Financial Planner

If you're over fifty, you undoubtedly recognize how critical financial planning can be for a young family or for individuals as they grow older. Many in our age range wish they had had a financial advisor themselves, and so financial planning is not just for the young. The fact is our educations don't prepare most of us for the wide variety of financial skills we need to live the lives we want to live, including:

- Investing in a diversity of income and savings instruments (stocks, bonds, annuities, etc.) that offer growth and security.

- Buying health and life insurance to ensure decent care for oneself and family throughout life.

- Buying a home.

- Saving for a college education for our children.

- Planning and saving for retirement and financial independence.

Despite the desirability of financial planning, only about one-third of Americans prepare a long-term financial plan or use an accountant or financial planner, according to a 2003 Gallup survey. This means that there is a large, untapped market needing the help of a financial planner.

Financial planning includes several categories of work. You can work as a generalist, providing people with a wide range of advisory services such as developing college savings and retirement plans, or you can be a specialist focused on investments, estate planning, wealth management, insurance, or tax reduction.

Depending on which focus you choose, you will benefit from having a certification, and you may need a license to practice in your state. Although most states do not have statutes that regulate the qualifications for financial planners, and in most places people can legally use the term to describe themselves without completing any formal education in the field, you will have far more credibility if you have specific training and have passed an exam that allows you to call yourself a registered or certified financial consultant or investment advisor. Furthermore, if you intend to sell insurance products or any type of investment product such as securities (stocks and bonds), all states (except for Colorado, Iowa, Ohio, and Wyoming) require you to register with them as a broker or investment advisor, and the federal government also requires you to register with the Securities and Exchange Commission (SEC) for certain types of securities sales.

You have several options to obtain training and become certified in this field. We count over fifteen specialty certifications. The following two certifications represent knowledge of all aspects of financial planning:

- Certified Financial Planner (CFP)—This designation is perhaps the most general and useful for someone just starting out. Granted by the Certified Financial Planner Board of Standards, it requires a bachelor's degree, passing an exam, and experience. Educational requirements are specified by the College for Financial Planning.

- Chartered Financial Consultant (ChFC)—Most members have an insurance background, take eight courses from the American College, and must pass examinations administered by the college.

After attaining one of the above credentials, you can go on to obtain certifications in various specializations including:

- Estate planning (accredited estate planner)

- Insurance analysis (chartered life underwriter)

- Investment analysis (chartered financial analyst, chartered investment counselor)

- Investment consulting (certified investment management consultant, certified investment management specialist)

- Investment management (accredited asset management specialist)

- Mutual funds (certified fund specialist, chartered mutual fund consultant)

- Registered investment advice (registered financial consultant, registered investment advisor, registered financial planner)

- Retirement planning (chartered retirement planning counselor, chartered retirement plans specialist)

Financial planners are responsible for absorbing and understanding a continuing stream of changing information. To stay up-to-date in this field, you need to be an information junkie because you must keep track of economic and stock market news, as well as current events that affect investments.

At the same time, financial planners need good people skills, the ability to listen to clients about their needs on sensitive financial matters, conveying intelligence, knowledge, confidence, and trust.

To build a clientele, one needs good marketing and selling skills. You will probably need to be able to work evenings and weekends, since that is when many people are available for appointments to see you.

Jim Barnash, a financial planner in the Chicago area, notes that people who get into financial planning after the age of fifty are usually financially savvy and can enter the profession following a self-study program and passing a certifying exam. However, they must choose from among the many certifications and registrations available. "If you intend to provide advice as well as helping people implement that advice," he says, "you need to get the securities or insurance licenses." He indicates that he has found that people who have always tinkered with investing and who have good listening skills and can ask good follow-up questions are those who do best at finding and keeping clients.

A positive Jim Barnash has found for being over fifty in this field is that for many people your age carries an aura of wisdom. Financial planning also allows flexibility in your work hours on a day-by-day basis; Jim knows financial planners who work eight months a year or less, and earn decent incomes even working less than full-time during those months. Once you are established with clients, you can serve them from anywhere, so some planners split their time between two climates or move to a climate they like.

Financial Planner at a Glance

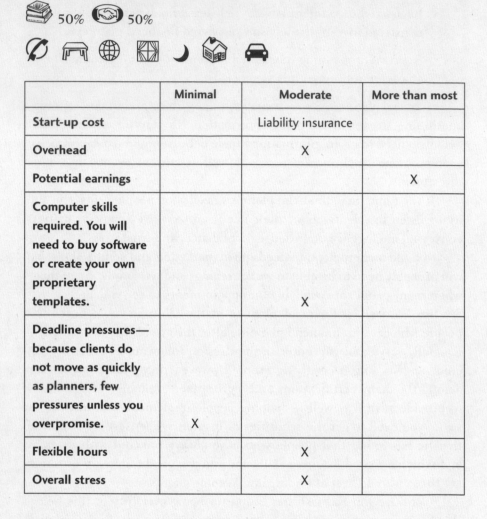

50% 50%

	Minimal	Moderate	More than most
Start-up cost		Liability insurance	
Overhead		X	
Potential earnings			X
Computer skills required. You will need to buy software or create your own proprietary templates.		X	
Deadline pressures—because clients do not move as quickly as planners, few pressures unless you overpromise.	X		
Flexible hours		X	
Overall stress		X	

Likely Transferable Skills, Background, Careers

A background in accounting, law, insurance, or banking is a natural lead-in to financial planning because you likely have some knowledge of planning and financial products. Licensed accountants and attorneys are able to do most aspects of financial planning with their existing licenses. Accountants can obtain additional certification as personal financial specialists (PFS) awarded by the American Institute of Certified Public Accountants.

What to Charge

Financial planners base their charges in one of three ways:

- Fee-only planners charge a straight fee for their services, based by the hour or on a monthly or annual retainer basis. Hourly rates range from $75 to $150, according to the National Association of Personal Financial Advisors, although a few planners charge as much as $350 an hour. There are other planners, however, who charge based on the value of the assets they manage. The charge for managing assets is typically from 0.5 percent to 1 percent of the assets managed.

- Commission-only planners do not charge for their time but receive commissions on the investment products they sell. Commissions depend on the products they are selling.

- The third fee structure is a hybrid, fee-and-commission planners, who charge hourly fees for their advice and get a commission on the products they sell.

In addition, some planners charge for an initial assessment, which includes a review of the client's assets and debts, and crafting a financial plan for a fixed fee ranging from $600 to $2,000.

Best Ways to Get Business

Getting referrals from your own family and friends to establish a base of clients from which you can use further referrals to expand.

- Teaching courses at local colleges, extension programs, and businesses, and speaking to local organizations such as Kiwanis Clubs, Rotary, and so on.

- Networking with attorneys, accountants, and insurance agents who specialize in estate planning or divorce law, who might be able to refer clients to you, if they do not handle the areas or products you sell.

- Writing a column or articles for publications or sending out your own print newsletter or e-mail newsletter, or you can purchase prewritten articles from the National Association of Personal Financial Advisors (NAPFA) to use in your newsletter.

- Creating your own Web site. Without a Web site, you will not get as many leads from database directories maintained by national organizations that refer consumers seeking a financial planning professional. Most "Find a Planner" directories provide the ability to link the consumer directly to your page.

Marketing Insights

- You can specialize your practice to service specific markets or needs, like college planning, premarital, divorce, tax strategies, retirement planning, small-business owners, planning for women or minority groups, helping families with children with special needs, or working with people in the same profession as your former one. Your reputation in a specialized area can go a long way toward facilitating your success in getting your practice known and finding new clients.

- Communicating to clients about the value of financial planning is best done by using personal stories, metaphors, and analogies. People often can be motivated to recognize the importance of financial planning in their own lives if they hear success and woe stories about others.

- Resistances potential clients have that must be overcome include: Is this someone I can really trust? Does he care about my welfare? Is she on my side? Can I count on him? Price sensitivity: Will I really get a better return? Has the planner worked with anybody like me?

- If you plan to have clients come to your home office, you need to make sure your office has the air of a prosperous professional. This may require relocating or redecorating your residence.

Where Next?

TRAINING AND CERTIFICATION

- American College has a distance education through its American College Online Services: (888) 263-7265; *www.amercoll.edu.*

- Certified Financial Planner Board of Standards (CFP®), The Web site provides a directory of education programs located throughout the United States that qualify for study needed for certification, including distance-learning programs plus examination information including sample questions: (888) 237-6275, (303) 830-7500; *www.cfp.net*.

- College for Financial Planning: (800) 237-9990; *www.fp.edu*.

BOOKS

- *Deena Katz on Practice Management for Financial Advisers, Planners, and Wealth Managers*, Deena Katz (Bloomberg Press, book and CD-ROM, 2001). ISBN: 157660084X.

- *Getting Started as a Financial Planner*, Jeffrey H. Rattiner (Bloomberg Press, 2000). ISBN: 1576600351.

- *Getting Started in Financial Consulting*, Edward J. Stone (John Wiley & Sons, 2000). ISBN: 0471348147.

- *So You Want to Be a Financial Planner*, Nancy Langdon Jones (AdvisorWorks, 2001). ISBN: 0971443610.

- *Storyselling for Financial Advisors*, Scott West, Mitch Anthony (Dearborn Trade Publishing; 2000). ISBN: 0793136644.

MAGAZINES

Financial advisors keep up with the popular financial publications, among them the *Wall Street Journal, Barron's, Forbes, The Economist, Kiplinger's Personal Finance, Money, Smart Money,* and *Worth*.

ASSOCIATIONS

Scores of associations serve the financial planning field, typically organized by specialty. Here are three representative associations:

- Financial Planning Association (FPATM); on-line new planner community: (800) 322-4237; *www.fpanet.org*.

- National Association of Personal Financial Advisors (NAPFA), fee-only planners: (800) 366-2732; *www.napfa.org*.

- Society of Financial Service Professionals (SFSP): (610) 526-2500; *www.financialpro.org*.

> ### From the Home Front

"You can continue as long as you want as a financial planner. Many great practitioners go on into their sixties and seventies, as long as they stay sharp and provide good service to their clients."   —Jim Barnash, fifty-plus

---

Snapshot: Russ and Diane Barberio
On-Line Real Estate Investment

The Barberios decided they wanted to change their work situation after Russ, fifty-eight, had been on the road for fourteen years selling computers and doing consulting and Diane, fifty-six, had just become a grandmother for the second time. They wanted to do something they could do together, something flexible so they could spend more time with their family. After taking a number of courses, they decided upon real estate investment.

In the process of finding property to buy, the Henderson, North Carolina, couple came across a lot of people whose homes were about to go into foreclosure, so their business soon became more than just buying and selling property. They began finding options, solutions, and resources for people who were pressed to sell their homes due to threats of foreclosure, transfers, divorce, or slow-moving property.

Russ and Diane offer alternatives both to those who want to sell their property and those who want to buy new property. By expanding beyond the parameters of conventional real estate investment, the Barberios have not only carved out a niche for themselves; they can also teach others how to use their unique approach.

"I always said I didn't want to retire," says Diane. "We love doing this business. It provides us with an income, a creative outlet, and we can do what we are doing for as long as we choose. I believe reaching our fifties means we're in the infancy of our next fifty years. At the very least, reaching fifty can be the beginning of a fresh, new adventure."

Snapshot: Jackie Waite,
Long-Term Care Insurance Specialist

At age fifty, after working as a legal secretary for over eighteen years and doing personnel management for many more, Jackie Waite of Spokane, Washington, needed a change. "I felt like a gerbil spinning in the same wheel every day," she remembers, "waiting for some vacation time so I could do something I like." But she didn't know what else someone like her without a college education could do until by happenstance she overheard a conversation that suggested an appealing alternative.

Someone was discussing how elderly people often lose their life savings to pay for nursing homes or assisted-living care because they don't know about the benefits of long-term care insurance. Jackie knew this was a situation she wanted to do something about, so she began looking into how she could become an agent to sell this type of insurance.

The first hurdle was getting an insurance license. That was almost enough to stop Jackie in her tracks. She hadn't been in school for what seemed like a thousand years, but she studied as if her life depended on it and got her license without difficulty.

Then she recalls, "It took great discipline at first to get on the phone every day, including Saturdays, make appointments, and travel to visit the homes of prospective clients." She also had to overcome her fear of public speaking so she could make presentations to groups. But despite the challenges she found being her own boss "was very freeing, because no one else was telling me what to do. I had total freedom to be successful on my own."

Now Jackie works mostly with referrals from satisfied clients. She's become a specialist in educating individuals, couples, and businesses about the options for handling the high costs of long-term care. She assists her clients in evaluating the best methods currently available for protecting their assets and has become known for her in-depth working knowledge of different plans and policies on the market, including Medicare supplements, eligibility factors, and the Elder and Tax Law pertaining to long-term care.

One of the added benefits of her field is that every time clients pay their insurance premiums, Jackie receives a renewal payment. "Much more than the financial reward, though," she says, "is the reward of having wonderful clients who appreciate my service. I have a sense of accomplishment knowing I'm contributing to freeing my clients from the overwhelming costs of long-term care."

Jackie no longer has to wait for her "vacation days" either. "I've created a life that allows me to set my own schedule," she explains. "How exciting after nine years to be the president of my own corporation, LTC Insurance Shoppers. Who could ask for anything more?" The best advice she can offer: "Never let anyone (especially yourself) say you can't change after fifty."

 ## 40. Fitness Trainer/Coach

Between 1999 and 2010, the fifty-five-to-sixty-four age group will grow 55 percent, more than double that of any other ten-year age bracket. Responding to the growing research that shows that fifty- to ninety-year-olds benefit from regular physical activity, fifty-plussers are turning to personal trainers and fitness clubs in great numbers. While many are encouraged by studies that show out-of-shape fifty-year-olds can restore their aerobic capacity to what it was in their twenties, others turn to fitness training to help fight specific conditions or diseases. The growing fitness field translates into numerous opportunities for fifty-plus home businesses.

You can join the field of fitness in any of several ways. You might become a personal trainer, teacher, coach, motivational speaker, or all of these rolled into one. You can work with clients of all sizes and shapes or you can focus on the huge fifty-plus population itself, or some other market like people in rehabilitation, people with diseases (such as arthritis, cardiac or musculo-skeletal problems, and diabetic conditions), people with disabilities, overweight people, executives and professionals with limited time, beginners, children, teens, or pregnant women.

You can practice as either a generalist or a specialist in any of several areas: aerobics, aquatic exercise, group fitness instruction, indoor cycling, diet and nutrition, Pilates technique, yoga, sports training, strength conditioning, or weight training.

In general, personal fitness trainers design workout routines for individuals or small groups and meet with their clients to guide them through workouts one to three times a week. Some trainers rent space in a gym, or they meet clients at a commercial gym, in which case they usually need approval or certification to teach at that gym. Some trainers have clients come to their own homes where they have the necessary equipment. Others go to their clients' homes because some people don't want to go to a public gym or don't have time in their day to go somewhere else. And finally, some trainers meet clients in a natural venue, such as at the beach, in a park, or up in the mountains.

Personal trainers usually love their work. Most will tell you that they are proud to have a positive effect on their clients' health and well-being. For example, Patricia Myers-Marano, had long been interested in helping people. After a career in personal coaching, she began a fitness training business at age fifty-one. Patricia specializes in weight training. She has clients come to her home, where she works with them either one-on-one or occasionally in twosomes when a pair of friends wants to motivate each other by taking a class together.

Patricia recently went back to school to get a master's degree in nutrition, which will allow her to discuss nutrition in depth with her clients. Patricia comments that her clients are often women in their sixties who see men looking good at that age and feel that they too want to remain active and vibrant in their middle age.

To break into the field, you need to be physically fit, since your own health and appearance are your best advertising for potential clients to literally see the results of your experience and knowledge. Being fit is also required because you need to demonstrate how to do an activity or often must work out alongside your clients. Assuming you look healthy, being over age fifty can be an advantage in your marketing, too, as younger potential clients may think, "Gee, I'd like to look that good when I'm at that age."

Though the fitness profession is not regulated by state or federal laws, many trainers get certified in their field through a professional organization that provides education, testing, and credentials. If you want to teach or rent space at a commercial gym, you usually need to show a certification, which we discuss in the Where Next section. You need expertise in the type of training you do as well as on safety and health issues. You can't afford to cause a client to get hurt, or to have a lawsuit on your hands due to injury.

The latest trend in fitness training is coaching by phone or Internet, driven by the irony that people seem to have less and less time to see a trainer in person. To solve this dilemma, they sign up with a coach, who meets them once in person for a background interview, medical history, lifestyle evaluation, and goal setting. The coach then prepares a plan for the client, and they stay in touch via weekly phone calls or e-mails to track progress and get ongoing motivation to overcome obstacles. Some coaches use heart-rate monitors, pedometers, or software to track clients' exercise and diet progress. It is predicted that the next development in long-distance coaching will tap into Webcam technology so that coaches can demonstrate their techniques, check that their clients are moving correctly, and even verify if the clients really look like they shed those extra fifteen pounds they claim they lost.

Fitness Training at a Glance

 20% 80%

	Minimal	Moderate	More than most
Start-up cost	X		
Overhead	X		
Potential earnings		X	
Computer skills required		X	
Regularly scheduled appointment			X
Flexible hours		X	
Overall stress		X	

Likely Transferable Skills, Background, Careers

If you're one of those people who say, "Exercise will always be a part of who I am," and you obtain the needed training to teach others and have good people skills, fitness is a business you can consider. A nursing or social-work background helps in that you understand the difficulties of getting people to think about themselves in a healthy way. Similarly, teaching can be a helpful background, since training and coaching require the ability to explain things to people.

What to Charge

Depending on their reputation and locale, fitness trainers charge from $25 to $200 per hour; $50 is typical, while $100 is common on the East and West coasts. By comparison, clubs charge an average of $50 per month for membership. Some trainers add to their income by selling equipment to their clients.

Best Ways to Get Business

- Making presentations in the form of workshops, seminars, and speeches in which you demonstrate what you do. Provide handouts that give basic information about fitness training or how to select a fitness trainer. You may find that local sports shops and health-food stores will allow you to do evening presentations.

- Developing relationships with chiropractors, orthopedic surgeons, cardiologists, and others who have patients who need the type of fitness training you do

- Creating publicity for yourself through articles in newspapers, including using before-and-after photos showing the effects of your training

- Having your own Web site, incorporating client testimonials that are specific about how your clients were helped: e.g., were able to stop taking pain medication, relieved back pain, lost weight, reduced blood pressure, etc.

- Being involved in community-outreach programs, causes, and fund-raising events.

- Donating some lessons to private schools in your area for their fund-raising auctions.

Marketing Insights

- Happy clients who tell and, importantly, show friends their progress and provide referrals are the key to building a busy practice, so encourage referrals. In markets that are glutted with trainers, like Los Angeles, seek a specialization that allows you to market to a specific group; like seniors, to lower their risk of everyday injuries and maintain their independence, or specific conditions, like people with AIDS, alcoholism/substance abuse, arthritis, chronic fatigue syndrome, depression, diabetes, eating disorders, emphysema, fibromyalgia, hemophilia, lupus, multiple sclerosis, organ transplant, osteoporosis, Parkinson's disease, or traumatic brain injury. If you work with special populations, you'll need additional training and experience to recognize contraindications. Secondary certification with a recognized credentialing organization may be needed to get referrals from professionals.

- In addition to choosing a training specialization for your work, consider adding other aspects of health care that enable you to present a holistic approach to wellness, such as nutrition counseling and stress reduction.

- In order to attract a clientele, you may find it helpful to work evenings and weekends.

- Expect also to have clients cancel on you at the last minute, so be sure to have a cancellation policy that protects you.

Where Next?

BOOKS

- *The Business of Personal Training,* Scott O. Roberts (Human Kinetics Publishing, 1996). ISBN: 0873226054.

- *The Personal Trainer's Business Survival Guide,* Craig Mastrangelo and Kirk Galiani (Exercise Science, 2001). ISBN: 1585184950.

- *The Personal Trainer's Handbook,* Teri S. O'Brien (Human Kinetics Publishing, book and CD, 2003). ISBN: 0736045015.

- *Start Your Own Personal Training Business,* Jacquelyn Lynn (Entrepreneur Media Inc., 2003). ISBN: 1932156003.

- *Fitness over Fifty,* National Institute on Aging (Hatherleigh, 2003). ISBN 1578261368.

ASSOCIATIONS AND CERTIFICATION

With over three hundred certifications for personal trainers available from many organizations, certification is relatively easy to get in this field. Are some certifications more recognized than others? Credentialing organizations that have been accredited by the National Commission for Certifying Agencies (NCCA), the certifying arm of the National Organization for Competency Assurance (NOCA), are more apt to be recognized by clubs, should you want to work with one, and if you're a veteran, you can use your GI benefits to pay for professional certification tests. At this writing only, a few organizations, even among these leading organizations, are accredited:

- American Council on Exercise: (858) 279-8227, (800) 825-3636, *www.acefitness.org.*

- Aerobic and Fitness Association of America (AFAA): (800) 446-2322, (818) 905-0040; *www.afaa.com.*

- American Fitness Professionals and Associates: (609) 978-7583; *www.afpafitness.com.*

- Fitness by Phone Coaches: (888) 714-4042; *www.fitnessbyphone.com.*

- International Dance and Exercise Association (IDEA): (800) 999-4332, (858) 535-8979. Education and insurance but does not certify.: *www.ideafit.com.*

- International Fitness Professionals Association: (813) 979-1925, (800) 785-1924; *www.ifpa-fitness.com.*

- National Aerobics & Fitness Trainers Association: (800) 925-6403; *www.nafta1.com.*

- National Federation of Professional Trainers: (800) 729-6378, (765) 447-3296; *www.nfpt.com.*

- National Strength and Conditioning Association: (888) 746-CERT, (402) 476-6669; *www.nsca-cc.org.*

From the Home Front

"In this field, it's never too early and never too late."

—Patricia Myers-Marano, fifty-one

Snapshot: Linda Kennedy, Waterproof Fanny Packs

Linda Kennedy, an avid water sports enthusiast, started her business one month before her fiftieth birthday. Having grown tired of feeling that her talents, intuition, and free spirit were being suppressed in a conventional job, she decided to turn an aggravating problem into an opportunity.

Three times Linda had lost valuables while enjoying underwater adventures. First, her money and credit cards were stolen from her hotel room while she was diving and snorkeling in the Caribbean. Soon after, they were stolen again on another trip, this time from her parked rental car near the beach. The third time, she was snorkeling off a desolate beach in Bermuda when she watched from a distance as someone approached her beach towel, rummaged through her clothing, and walked off with her driver's license, keys, currency, and passport.

That did it. Upon returning to her home in Midway, Utah, Linda set out to find a waterproof fanny pack she could dive with. To her surprise, there were none, not even at the most prestigious sporting-goods stores. So she decided to create one. But 390 phone calls later, after months of exploring waterproof fabric, seals, and glues, she was still being told, "It's not possible. There is no waterproof fabric."

Undeterred, Linda contacted the hazardous liquid industry and found a company that believed they could make her a bag. After rounds of testing, she found success at last! A waterproof fanny pack, better than she ever anticipated. Watchful Eye Designs, LLC, was born, supplying the world with waterproof bags that don't leak, even after being submerged in 130 feet of water for three hours.

First, though, Linda had to struggle through the process of getting a patent, obtaining nondisclosure agreements, resolving legal entanglements, and finally learning how to sell to the mass market. "I was laughed at by just about everyone I talked to at first," Linda recalls. "Even after I sent out free samples to try out, all they could say was, 'These are just very expensive Ziploc bags.'"

But now Watchful Eye Designs' clients range from big accounts like the Boy Scouts of America and Magellan's Travel Supplies to hundreds of mom-and-pop stores, as well as the military, law enforcement, and governments throughout the United States and worldwide. "I have learned much," Linda says, "and the company is 100 percent mine!"

41. Professional Gardening and Landscaping

Gardening is the number-one hobby in the United States and Canada, yet as much as almost everyone loves green laws and blooming plants, others find gardening onerous work or don't have the time to do it. So they'd rather hire someone to keep their lawns tidy and flower beds blooming. While large commercial companies offer generic "mow, blow, and go" services with a revolving cast of crew workers, many people are interested in using someone knowledgeable whom they can count on.

So if you enjoy gardening and have a green thumb instead of a brown one, you can join the many people who at fifty plus are turning their hobby into a full- or part-time income. Peggy Bowers of the American Horticulture Society says, "This can be perfect for a retired person looking for a career change."

The types of services you can offer range from simple maintenance to landscape design and installation. Many customers just want basic maintenance, raking up leaves, cutting grass, clipping hedges, and some pruning. Depending on the climate where you live, this can be a year-round or seasonal business, lasting from spring to early winter.

Depending on how much you are willing to devote to learning about growing requirements, microclimates, and design methods, you can expand lawn maintenance into custom design. David Streeter, sixty-two, of Coeur d'Alene, Idaho, started his landscape design business after retiring from carpentry work. He had experienced a bad accident doing construction and was off for a while. "So I decided to get into something I really enjoyed and had appreciated all my life," says Streeter.

Some states require a contractor's license to work above a stated dollar value, so if the services you provide include installation of plants, chances are you'll need to obtain a contractor's license, which involves a course and licensing exam. You may also want to take a course at a community college in computer-aided design if you plan to design landscapes or gardens.

Still, Peggy Bowers says being out in the field is the best teacher. "Start by volunteering at public gardens," she suggests. "Many people are avid gardeners all their lives; joining professional organizations is a great way to make contacts as you transition into this business." She also suggests an internship at a botanical garden. Some have three- to six-month programs, which are paid. Bowers also suggests attending lectures and learning as much as possible about plant material and growth requirements for your area.

Clients hiring a designer are probably interested in a garden that develops over time. Otherwise they can call in a commercial company and have a finished yard in a matter of a few days. Bowers indicates that a smaller business can offer a "more hands-on approach" to the development of a beautiful garden with consideration to individual lifestyles and upkeep needs.

David Streeter finds his competition to be targeting "generic tract developments" as the population in his area continues to expand. "I do custom design and construction," says Streeter, "no tract homes." Instead he focuses on fine details like waterfalls, interesting retaining walls, patios, arbors, and gazebos. He spends time consulting clients on the types of plants that will grow well, the level of maintenance and tending required, and how something will work in a particular garden.

Still another avenue to pursue in a passion for gardening is to grow varieties of plants that are in demand, like aquatic waterplants and cacti, and wholesale them to nurseries. For more about growing things for profit, see the Gardening and Growing Flowers, Food, and Herbs profile on page 362.

Gardening Services at a Glance

50% 50%

	Minimal	Moderate	More than most
Start-up cost		X	
Overhead	X		
Potential earnings		X	
Computer skills required	X	CAD software	
Deadline pressures		Weather dependent.	
Flexible hours	X		
Overall stress	X		

Likely Transferable Skills, Background, Careers

Many retired military personnel are seen in internship programs, but anyone who enjoys making things grow, has a customer orientation, and is in good enough physical condition to do what's required can provide gardening and lawn service.

What to Charge

Consulting and design of services go for between $60 to $100 an hour, depending on your market. Installation and maintenance work is about half the consulting rate. If installation is involved, the design may be free. For customers who want consistent, weekly or monthly service, it's better to provide a flat rate.

Best Ways to Get Business

- Face-to-face networking within your industry in organizations related to gardening, grounds management, and maintenance organizations. Peggy Bowers recommends, "Get with other gardeners." Larger companies will refer jobs for services they don't provide, particularly if the job is too small or it's a specialized service you do.

- Placing a tasteful contractor sign indicating your name and contact information on your job sites, with the permission of your customer.

- Having a Web site listing your services with client endorsements.

- Advertising in local papers, offering a discount for first-time customers.

- Posting fliers at garden centers.

Marketing Insights

- Personal attention, a reputation for reliability, and expert advice cause customers to choose self-employed gardeners over larger services. Word-of-mouth referrals are key to growing a gardening service.

- It's important to guarantee plants you install. Depending on the type of plant, the replacement period can run from six weeks to six months and be from 50 to 100 percent of the replacement cost of the plant. If you buy plants from a wholesaler versus a warehouse store, chances are the wholesaler rather than you will absorb the cost of the replacement plant.

- Specialization possibilities include focusing on a particular plant species like trees or roses, sustainable plantings, irrigation, and outdoor lighting design and installation.

Where Next?

ASSOCIATIONS

- American Association of Botanical Gardens and Arboreta (AABGA): (610) 925-2700; *www.aabga.org*. You can meet others devoted to gardening at meetings and events of member gardens.

- Associated Landscape Contractors of America. Certified Landscape Professional program: (800) 395-ALCA, (703) 736-9666; *www.alca.org*.

BOOKS

- *Making Gardens Works of Art,* Keeyla Meadows, (Sasquatch Books, 2002). ISBN: 1570613079.

- *Small Spaces, Beautiful Gardens,* Keith Davitt (Rockport Publishers, 2002). ISBN: 1564968316.

From the Home Front

"I have the freedom to design and create what I want and that it pleases the customer is a great reward." —David Streeter, sixty-two

---

Snapshot: Jim Giambruno, Landscape Lighting

After working for thirty-seven years at the local power company, Jim Giambruno of Reno, Nevada, retired at age sixty and realized he'd never had the time to do something he'd always wanted to do: pursue his artistic talents. So after much discussion with his wife, who was still working full-time, Jim took and passed the electrical contracting exam, obtained his license, got bonded, and opened his own business specializing in landscape lighting.

"This business affords me much pleasure," he reports. "I can pick and choose jobs, offer much needed advice on interesting lighting systems to my customers, and I'm my own boss!"

Jim attracts new residents of the area to his business through his Web site and considers the fact that he's a one-man business to be an advantage. "Unlike many larger companies in the Reno/Sparks area," he explains, "I do not turn down 'small' jobs unless I choose to.

"You're only as old as you feel," Jim advises. "You can start a whole new life after fifty. I started after sixty and I still have time to enjoy other activities like hiking, golf, and camping. No rocking chair for me!"

42. Handyman

In the life of any house, there comes a time for remodeling, but in between, before that time comes, there are a lot of little jobs that are too small for a professional contractor and too much for the busy homeowner. This is where the handyman (or woman) comes in. From adjusting a leaky faucet to putting a closet door back on the rail, doing odd jobs for homeowners can be a great business that will keep you as busy as you want to be. It requires some skill and know-how with tools, so if you have been fixing things around your own house for years and enjoy a variety of small jobs that can be finished quickly, offering handyman services could be an enjoyable full-time or part-time business for you.

Ron Peterson, sixty-five, a retired law-enforcement officer, was someone who had done fix-it jobs around his own house since buying his first home in 1963. "I got frustrated with people who did a slipshod job," he says. So a few years ago when a neighbor asked Peterson if he would fix her faucet when she couldn't find anyone who was willing to drive to their small community to repair it, he decided that offering a local handyman's services would be a pleasant way to make some extra money. He works four hours a day and stays busy enough in his small Southern California community of 1,800 residents doing the jobs that larger contractors won't do.

"My idea of a good job is where you're in and out in two hours and have done the lady's honey-do list, the one that's been around for months," says Peterson. He enjoys the variety and the challenge of solving unusual problems. Sometimes he's called because a licensed plumber or electrician someone hired didn't quite do the job correctly. "I look at it and let my mind work on it," he says. He's in demand because in addition to being right there in town, his fees are more reasonable than an electrician's or a plumber's. He may even find himself planting trees, because the owner has said, "I don't want to pay landscaper rates when you can do it just as well."

Jerry Alonzy has offered handyman services since 1987. Now he provides an Internet subscription service for handymen, *www.natural-handyman. com*. Many of his almost thirty thousand members are self-employed, offering services ranging from cleaning gutters to electrical work. "You need a broad set of skills and good learning ability," he emphasizes. He also finds that many people over fifty start and stay in this field and customers appreciate the sense of confidence that age and experience offer.

"Home-improvement contractors are the second source of consumer complaints," he states. "People want someone who will show up, be pleasant, and empathize with their problem."

As Peterson implied, as a handyman, you may find yourself doing almost anything you're willing to do, including hanging wallpaper, painting, installing flooring, electrical wiring, fixing decking, repairing roofs, cleaning gutters, and replacing tiles. You need to have all the tools required to do whatever services you provide. You should also carry small supplies like Spackle or the odd bolt just to save time and trips to and from the hardware store, but it's acceptable and probably good practice to have your customer purchase major materials like gallons of paint and significant plumbing parts.

Alonzy stresses the importance of knowing when a job is too big and telling the customer that he or she needs a professional. Peterson is willing to try to fix anything, and he suggests a motto for someone first starting: "If it's broke, I can fix it." But both he and Alonzo emphasize being honest about your skills. So if you haven't done a repair before, tell the client. If you're willing to try, offer to give a price break to cover your learning curve. "Don't be desperate for the job," Peterson comments. "If you don't know how to fix it, say so."

Licensing requirements vary from state to state. Some states have home-improvement laws that require you to register your business and have appropriate licenses for the services you offer if the job exceeds a certain dollar limit. In Massachusetts, for example, you can work on small appliances that are plugged in to electrical outlets without a license, but you are not authorized to run wire or install plugs unless you register with state agencies. Having professional liability insurance is a good idea.

Handyman at a Glance

50% 50%

	Minimal	Moderate	More than most
Start-up cost		X	
Overhead		X	

	Minimal	Moderate	More than most
Potential earnings		X	
Computer skills required	X		
Deadline pressures		X	
Flexible hours	X		
Overall stress		X	

Likely Transferable Skills, Background, Careers

People with experience in construction work are naturals, particularly as they age or, as someone told us, "when their knees have begun to ache." But anyone who is "handy," has the physical dexterity, and is a problem solver can become a handyman.

What to Charge

A rule of thumb is two-thirds the rates of plumbers and electricians, whose overhead costs are higher. There's a large variation from $15 an hour in low-cost areas to $80 an hour in New York City. The rate for emergency or after-hours service, if offered, may be up to double the regular hourly rate.

Best Ways to Get Business

- Letting people know what you are doing in your personal circles. One handyman, active in a local church, worked for half the people in the choir.

- Soliciting businesses in condominium complexes as often the owners don't have tools and equipment to do home improvement and repairs but they also don't have a landlord to call when things break.

- Calling on real estate offices and leaving fliers.

- Advertising in local shopper papers.

- Posting fliers, cards, and brochures on community bulletin boards.

- Having attractive signage on your truck or vehicle with your phone number and Web site visible.

- Listing in the Yellow Pages.

- Offering short courses on fixing household items through local adult-education programs.

- If you live in a resort area where people have second homes, soliciting mostly absent owners for off-season work. They will leave "to-do" lists.

Marketing Insights

- The key benefits you offer clients are availability and being less expensive than trade personnel.

- Trust is fundamental to this business. "There are not a lot of handymen around that people feel they can trust," state both Alonzo and Peterson. Customers need to be able to leave you a list and the key and know the job will be done and their house will be standing when they get back.

- Referrals are the number-one way to build a clientele and even if your work is satisfactory, people need to trust you to refer others to you.

- Give yourself time to develop a sufficient number of customers so that you're turning down work instead of looking for it.

- Dressing presentably and neatly separates you from the workers people are suspicious of when they see them in their neighborhoods.

- Because people feel pride in their homes, complimenting their house helps establish rapport.

- Making yourself indispensable to someone with a fixer-upper is one way to stay busy for several months or even years.

Where Next?

BOOKS

- *Handyman's Handbook,* David Koenigsberg (McGraw-Hill Professional, 2003). ISBN: 0071416706.

- *Buy It, Fix It, Sell It,* Kevin C. Myers (Dearborn Trade Publishing, 1997). ISBN: 079312610X. Buying, rehabilitating, and selling homes as a business

WEB SITES

- Guide and CDs: *www.handyman-business.com.*

- The Natural Handyman: *www.naturalhandyman.com.*

FRANCHISE

- House Doctors Handyman Service: (800) 319-3359, (513) 831-0100; *www.housedoctors.com.*

From the Home Front

"Your phone will ring off the hook with calls from homeowners, senior citizens, and others who don't want to fix it themselves."

—Ron Peterson, sixty-five

Snapshot: Skip and Linda Wilkinson, Electrical

Linda was fifty-five and Skip was fifty-seven when they retired to move to the "north country." Since they didn't have any retirement income, Skip decided to draw on his background in electronics to start an electrical contracting business. Linda assists him with all the business-related paperwork.

Their home business in East Tawas, Michigan, provides the Wilkinsons with sufficient income, keeps their minds challenged and their bodies active, and gives them control and flexibility over their schedule and their work hours. And says Linda, "Nobody writes us a performance review, except our customers."

When she hears people say, "I don't know what I would do with my time if I retired," Linda likes to tell their story. "There is no excuse for being bored after fifty or after full-time employment!" she assures them. "We both have never been busier or happier in our lives and we still have time to fully immerse ourselves in volunteer work in our church and our community."

Her advice to others is to keep a positive attitude, think about what you like to do, pray a lot, and have fun."

Snapshot: Dick Speer, Painting Company

Dick Speer of North Hollywood, California, was working as a painting contractor when tension on the job spurred him to start his own painting company at age fifty-two—but only after some long and hard thinking. Dick was apprehensive about the responsibilities involved in making such an extreme move. To get started he would have to borrow from his 401K, and the cost of insurance and bonds alone would pretty much deplete his life savings.

But Dick's past clients gave him the confidence to proceed. He'd had a reputation for dependability, fairness, and clean, neat crews. So when the customers he'd developed while on the job told him they were willing to continue with him, he felt honored and proceeded to apply for his license. He took the exam and passed. Five years later with twelve employees, he's well past his initial fears of failing and says of owning and running his business, "I'm glad I made the decision to move on."

Dick's advice to others: Research the business as much as possible beforehand, arrange to have the funds to sustain your costs for the near future, and believe in yourself. "You'll wish you had started sooner," he predicts.

43. Home Inspector

Home inspection got its start in the 1970s when mortgage institutions wanted to verify that the properties on which they were about to make loans were a good risk. Then as housing prices began to soar in the early 1980s, many buyers voluntarily chose to hire inspectors to protect the investments they were about to make. The demand grew for home inspection even after states like California, Florida, and Texas passed laws requiring sellers to disclose any existing problems with their home to prospective buyers and placing liability on real estate agents, too. So if problems weren't disclosed, sellers began using home inspectors as a way to predict what problems they would encounter in selling their homes and real estate agents recognized they could be protected by an adequate home inspection.

The home inspector objectively examines a residence to identify its structural soundness and the quality of all its systems. The goals are to detect any signs of failure, safety problems, or wear and tear, and to estimate the remaining useful life of the home's major systems and finishes. Formerly done by visual inspection, today's inspectors may use high-tech tools to examine the roof, foundation, attic, insulation, walkways, heating, air-conditioning, plumbing, and electrical systems. Some inspectors tote laptop computers in order to write up a formal report on the spot for the party that hired them with detailed explanations of any problems.

Often these reports play an important role in the sale of the home. If defects are found, the buyer may choose to accept the problems, obtain a larger mortgage to pay for fixing the problems, renegotiate the offer to make the seller correct the problems, or even decline the purchase. When working for the seller, the inspector's analysis can help the homeowner become aware of any defects that could affect the home's price or that might cause a deal to fall through.

Lee Benda, in Pinion Pines, California, started inspecting homes in 1999 at age fifty, drawing on his background in supervising and maintaining apartment buildings. Lee finds an increasing acceptance of home inspection among real estate agents, because agents recognize that an inspection is an "asset to the sale" in preventing hidden surprises that negate a sale at the last minute that they've worked so hard to obtain. For Benda, the key to his success is his thoroughness. "You've got to be as thorough as you can be, to protect both the buyer and seller."

Benda pointed out that an excellent growth area for inspections is new construction. Although you might not think brand-new homes need an inspection, Lee indicates that buyers today are wary of new construction, no doubt due to hearing horror stories about dissatisfied home buyers forced to sue home builders. Although contractors are required to have a city building inspector check their work at every major stage, the city inspectors are not as rigorous as home inspectors and they don't represent the buyer. As a result, many buyers of new homes bring in their own inspectors to confirm good-quality construction. This is becoming a specialization and is sometimes called "in-progress" inspection.

Getting into this field requires extensive up-to-date knowledge about home construction, building codes, and all the systems in a house. You can't have a fear of heights or claustrophobia, because you will need to go up on roofs and in crawl spaces beneath homes.

Home inspectors must be beyond reproach when it comes to ethics. The professional code of ethics of the American Society of Home Inspectors (ASHI) opposes inspectors doing any repairs they've recommended so as not to give the impression, or the opportunity, that they've drummed up repair business for themselves.

Working as an inspector requires errors-and-omissions insurance to cover potential liability for oversights and mistakes. This will be difficult to obtain until you have passed the ASHI test, but once you have, you will be able to purchase it through the association.

Be aware that the profession is saturated in some major cities, but the field will likely grow in regions where the population is expanding. Although there are no laws requiring a home inspection, it is estimated that roughly 70 percent of homes sold in affluent urban areas are inspected, making home inspections almost as common as termite inspections. In addition, the federal government may require home inspections as a condition for obtaining FHA and VA mortgage loans, which will further expand the market.

Home Inspection at a Glance

 60%  40%

	Minimal	Moderate	More than most
Start-up cost	X		
Overhead	X		
Potential earnings			X
Computer skills required	X		
Deadline pressures	X		
Flexible hours		X	
Overall stress		X	

Likely Transferable Skills, Background, Careers

Most new home inspectors have a background in the construction industry or in the maintenance field. Lee Benda points out, "Often inspectors are people who became tired of wearing a belt or have been injured on the job and need to do less strenuous work." However, if you are a serious hobbyist and have remodeled houses and would enjoy the freedom of not being bound by an office, with study you can learn what needs to be learned to succeed in this business.

What to Charge

The fee for a home inspection varies by region. In most cases, the fee ranges from $225 to $400, with $250 to $300 being the average in urban areas. Rural areas are lower. It takes about two hours to complete an inspection, plus additional time to write the report. Note: A busy inspector can do 200 to 250 inspections per year, averaging about one inspection a day.

Best Ways to Get Business

- Developing relationships with local realtors who are in a position to refer you to buyers and sellers.

- Giving lectures and training in real estate offices on topics such as how not to let inspection kill your deal and new areas of concern.

- Joining the American Society of Home Inspectors (ASHI), which refers potential clients to its members and has a "Find an Inspector" service on its Web site.

- Having your own Web site. The link will show on the ASHI listing.

- Joining your state or local chapter of home inspectors such as the California Real Estate Inspection Association (CREIA). If you specialize in the type of home inspection you do, you may develop referral relationships with other inspectors.

- Obtaining publicity in real estate sections of the newspaper and then using reprints in your promotional and sales materials to establish credibility.

Marketing Insights

- To meet real estate agents, call on them at Sunday open houses and meet them at industry-related business groups, such as the Board of Realtors, Women's Councils of Realtors, as well as business-referral organizations that include nonrealty people.

- Even if you're not lecturing at real estate offices, you can introduce yourself at weekly meetings before caravans (when agents go see properties that have been newly listed for sale). Anytime you can provide high-quality information face-to-face you will be appreciated. Getting in good with a popular agent in one office can set you up for many inspections.

- Specialization possibilities include forensic engineering, older homes (built before 1945), being expert witnesses in lawsuits, and becoming experts in environmental problems such as inspecting for molds or radon. If this interests you, see the Environmental Assessment and Inspection profile on page 194.

- In states where home inspectors are not yet licensed, people already in the field are apt to be automatically licensed or "grandfathered in" when licensing is adopted. Licensing increases demand and stature and limits competition. You can determine whether your state currently requires a license for home inspectors along with a summary of the regulatory legislation on the ASHI Web site at *www.ashi.com/inspectors/state.htm*.

Where Next?

ASSOCIATIONS OFFERING CERTIFICATION

- American Society of Home Inspectors (ASHI). The older and larger of the two national associations: (800) 743-2744, (847) 759-2820; *www.ashi.com*.

- National Association of Home Inspectors, Inc. (NAHI): (800) 448-3942, (952) 928-4641; *www.nahi.org*.

BOOKS

- *Become A Home Inspector!*, Michael A. Pompeii (Pompeii Publications, 2001). ISBN: 0971195404.

- *Home Inspection Handbook*, John E. Traister (Craftsman House, 1997). ISBN: 1572180463.

- *The Home Inspection Troubleshooter*, Robert Irwin (Dearborn Publishing, 1995). ISBN: 0793110912.

COURSES

Some community colleges offer courses in building inspection. Many companies offer courses in home inspection, such as:

- ASHI@Home Training System: (877) 332-7267; *homeinspection@dearborn.com*.

- Home-Tech: (800) 638-8292; *www.hometechonline.com*.

- Inspection Training Associates: (800) 323-9235; *www.home-inspect.com*.

FRANCHISES

- AmeriSpec Home Inspection Service: (800) 426-2270; *www.amerispecfranchise.com.*

- HouseMaster of America: (800) 526-3939; *www.housemaster.com.*

- Inspect-It 1st Property Inspection: (800) 510-9100, (602) 971-9400, *www.inspectit1st.com.*

- National Property Inspections Inc.: (800) 333-9807; *www.npiweb.com.*

- Pillar to Post: (877) 963-3129; *www.pillartopost.com.*

From the Home Front

"Realtors are realizing that if there's something in the home inspection that prevents a sale from the taking place, it's the property that's dictating the problem, not the report. I will continue doing this the rest of my productive life."   —Lee Benda, fifty-four

---

44. Image Consultant

Today more people than ever subscribe to the idea that you can positively affect your success in life by shaping your image. Businesspeople (men as well as women), educators, socialites, and politicians all recognize that the way you dress, style your hair, gesticulate, and talk can greatly impact how others perceive and accept you. As nearly every job in the world has become more competitive, people have come to understand that their confidence and personal power are often a function of "looking good" in the eyes of colleagues, customers, and the general public.

As a result, more people are hiring professional image consultants to help them learn how to improve their appearance and personal style. Corporations also hire image consultants to work with their executives, sales personnel, receptionists, and telemarketers to ensure that they present themselves visually and vocally in the best possible manner.

Image consultants may coach and train people about many different aspects of their personal impression. They may advise clients about the basics of clothing, helping people choose colors, shapes, and styles that best emphasize their personalities and figures. They may provide clients with advice about how to make a positive impression on others through eye contact, body language, voice quality, and etiquette. They may consult with corporations to design corporate dress uniforms, or help with a company's "branding" through its visual image and public-relations campaign.

Several other trends have also opened up new markets for image consultants, including:

- College graduates seeking to polish their image for job interviews in an increasingly competitive world.

- People seeking employment or changing fields, such as those who are downsized and need advice on the appropriate look and behavior to make a winning impression in a new field or community.

- Single people wanting to improve their success in dating by improving their self-confidence and learning how to meet potential partners while looking their best.

- The "active" aging population concerned with maturing elegantly and updating their image.

Image consultants use a variety of techniques to work with their clients:

- Accompanying them to business or social events and watching how they perform from a distance.

- Coaching one-on-one, the mode in which most consultants work.

- Going shopping to purchase clothing and makeup, which can be more physically taxing.

- Using software imaging programs and other audio-visual aids to help clients preview different types of clothing, makeup, hairstyle, speech, and body stance from which to perfect their desired look.

- Video- or audiotaping clients.

Joyce Knudsen, who has been an image consultant since she was a teenager and now operates a home-study mentoring program from her

Brentwood, Tennessee, home, observes that image consultants are tempted to do it all when first starting out, but later become specialized as they discover the areas they're best suited for and experience success doing.

Image consultants all agree that this profession is not superficial or superfluous. Coralyn Lundell, whose company Appearance Designers in Saratoga, California, typifies how seriously consultants take the value of their work. She came into the profession at age fifty-one, after raising her children. With a master's degree in fine art, she worked in retail, then studied color and style, and when she heard about image consulting, began teaching image classes. Now seventy-six, Lundell says about her work, "My responsibility is to help people realize their potential in how they look. I'm not talking about putting a façade on people; each person must be authentic within the framework of what's appropriate for them. After all, our visual impression is what others make their judgments on."

Lundell emphatically states that age is an advantage in this business. "People in their thirties and forties don't want someone in their twenties telling them what to do. People respect your life experience."

Carol Goldstein discovered image consulting in her late fifties. Goldstein formerly modeled and sold Mary Kay cosmetics. Now sixty-four, she agrees with Lundell about the value of age in this profession. "No matter what I'm doing, I find younger women respect my attitude. It's giving them a different slant on life. I give them inspiration for life down the road. They say, 'Look at her.'"

Image Consulting at a Glance

	Minimal	Moderate	More than most
Start-up cost		X	
Overhead	X		
Potential earnings			X
Computer skills required		X	
Deadline pressures	X		

	Minimal	Moderate	More than most
Flexible hours			X
Overall stress	X		

Likely Transferable Skills, Background, Careers

Likely past careers include retail, fashion, direct marketing of cosmetics or clothing, and on-air television, as well as teachers, people with public speaking experience, models, actors, and those with psychology or career-development backgrounds. Key attributes of image consultants include warm, extroverted, and nurturing personalities plus keen consciousness of the effect of dress, makeup, look, and style and the desire, plus the communication skills, to help clients develop confidence about every aspect of their personal impression.

What to Charge

For wardrobe consulting, according to the Association of Image Consultants International (AICI), hourly rates range from $50 to $250 with $150 being the average; for speech coaching, rates range from $75 to $300 an hour. Full-day workshops and seminars produce fees ranging from $750 to $5,000 per day, depending on the number of participants, the company, and the nature of the workshop (speech, wardrobe, and so forth). Some consultants negotiate annual retainers from corporations for working with a specified number of executives or employees each month.

Best Ways to Get Business

- Getting listed as a support service in referral services that professional associations maintain for their members.

- Having a Web site on which you place your photo, testimonial letters, and articles you have written.

- Offering complimentary consultations—as many as four to five a month—with key individuals who might be gatekeepers to potential paying clients and who are respected for their opinion.

- Participating in organizations like professional and business associations that give you the potential to meet prospective clients or corporations.

- Partnering and trading referrals with people in related businesses, such as public relations and media.

- Speaking and offering seminars to organizations with members apt to use your services, even if there is no fee, and using these as an opportunity to show off the dramatic results you can achieve; show slides or videotapes of your clients before and after. (Be sure you have obtained their written permission.) Groups for women with eating disorders are an example; sewing guilds, which exist in virtually every community, are venues to develop referral sources.

- Writing articles with your photograph included, then sending reprints of them to prospective clients.

Marketing Insights

- Advertising isn't usually effective for image consulting. You need to demonstrate your skills and build relationships with people before they will retain you.

- Conveying a first-rate image of yourself carries through to e-mail, for which you can use a program like *BrandMail (Letterclick. com)*, to enable you to use your letterhead for your e-mail.

- Direct-selling organizations dealing in cosmetics have diluted the profession by casting their sales representatives as image consultants but also are another avenue for someone who prefers this to developing a private practice, which entails training and certification. If you enjoy selling merchandise, you can also add to your income by selling clothing and makeup directly to your clients through appointments and with such devices as trunk shows.

- If you are going to pursue corporate work, target industries in which the appearance of the personnel plays an important role, such as hotels, entertainment facilities, health-care industries, and retail stores. Contact the human-resources director to discuss your doing a two- to three-hour introductory seminar. (You can usually find HR directors through the local chapter of the American Society of Training and Development.)

- Image consultants in the early days of the industry were prone to follow formulas and rules for how to dress for success; today the profession stresses bringing out an individual's strengths and supporting his or her goals within the boundaries of cultural expectations. Therefore, creativity and a having a visual orientation are critical talents.

- Letting clients pay you with credit cards will particularly help people seeking employment who may be low on cash.

- Specialization possibilities include "full-figured" women, corporate officers, on-air personalities, or book authors on how to give media interviews, or advising executives who are working overseas to help them learn the customs and etiquette of the country in which they are stationed.

Where Next?

ASSOCIATION AND CERTIFICATION

- Association of Image Consultants International: (877) 247-3319, (972) 755-1503; *www.aici.org*.

BOOKS

- *40 Over 40*, Brenda Reiten Kinsel (Wildcat Canyon Press, 2000). ISBN: 1885171420.

- *Image Consulting in the 21st Century*, Brenda York-McDaniel (Academy of Fashion & Image, 2000). ISBN: 0970359500.

- *The Perfect Fit: How to Start an Image Consulting Business*, Lynne Henderson Marks and Dominique Isbecque (FirstPublish LLC, 2001). ISBN: 1929925646.

- *The Triumph of Individual Style*, Carla Mason Mathis and Helen Villa Connor (Fairchild Publications, 2002). ISBN: 1563672693.

COURSES

Image consultants frequently teach their skills to others. Here are two such courses.

- Academy of Fashion and Image, Brenda York-McDaniel: (800) 450-5545, (623) 572-8719; *www.afiyork.com*.

- The ImageMaker, Inc. *www.imagemaker1.com* Distance-learning courses; also publishes a series of *Head to Soul* booklets—Daily Guides to Personal Style and Inner Self-Confidence: (888) 845-5600, (615) 309-8168; *www.imagemaker1.com*.

From the Home Front

"People want to feel better about themselves, but they cannot look at themselves objectively. An image consultant draws out their best points. I help people feel more confident about their purchases, about how they put themselves together, how they dress for the occasion. This is not a recreational sport; it is a disciplined activity."

—Coralyn Lundell, seventy-six

Snapshot: Dianne Bennett, Matchmaker (after-image consultant)

Dianne Bennett had been a Beverly Hills meter maid, an assistant to a Hollywood gossip columnist, and a syndicated investigative reporter for the music industry before starting her lucrative and glamorous fifty-plus business. From her position in the media, she noticed that even attractive women and wealthy men in Hollywood have a difficult time meeting the person of their dreams.

Drawing on her many contacts and an instinctive ability to match up the right men with the right women, Dianne began holding upscale singles parties, charging $12 a person. Soon other matchmakers were trolling her parties and reaping a wealth of new clients. Knowing that a matchmaker can charge fees in the five figures, she decided to start her own international introductory service, Beautiful Women; Successful Men, from her lavishly refurbished Hollywood home.

She attributes her success to a combination of an infectious personality, movie-star good looks, and sunny nature, combined with a commitment to do diligent research into all her clients, male and female. She thoroughly researches each client for moral fiber, life goals, careers, and salaries and holdings, and verifies everything. "I don't want any surprises," she says. "I don't want my gentleman clients or the awesome women to whom I introduce them to hear anything from me but the absolute truth. In this line of work my good reputation is everything, and I want to keep it that way."

Dianne claims a high number of marriages among clients from her rarified world of the rich and superrich, including models, actresses, movie stars, two college presidents, a brain surgeon, and an Asian head of state.

45. Personal Chef

Does everyone tell you what a great cook you are? Even better, do you love to cook? If so, you can put these two things together and become a successful personal chef. Personal chefs differ from private chefs in that they cook for multiple families or individuals instead of just for one household. They differ from caterers in that the cooking is done in their clients' kitchens. Personal chefs do the grocery shopping and bring their own utensils and equipment with them. Typically personal chefs cook for their clients once a month; the next most popular period is every two weeks, which is more typical for seniors, and then some cook weekly. Meals are packaged and stored in the refrigerator or freezer for use throughout the week or the month. Relationships begin with an initial consultation during which clients fill out a questionnaire about their food preferences.

The demand for personal chef services has been increasing steadily since 1998, according to David MacKay of the United States Personal Chef Association (USPCA). While more people are taking gourmet cooking classes, fewer and fewer people are spending time in the kitchen every day. This is another business that's growing to meet the needs of two career couples and 24/7 schedules.

When he was sixty, Jim Davis started The Really Good Food Company with his son. "I thought it would be easy because I love to cook," he says, but he finds he has had to develop his people skills more than his cooking skills. "You've got to sell your clients on being a little adventurous." Still he suggests keeping track of your clients' specific requirements and preferences, so each meal is absolutely customized to their tastes. Every client has different needs. One doesn't like garlic, one needs less salt."

Personal chefs are becoming specialized now, offering menus based on doctor- or self-prescribed diets, like diabetic, Weight Watchers, Atkins,

Zone, and blood type. MacKay also notes that offering a specialized service may require some training. Specialization can be more profitable as well as make finding customers or having them find you easier. Even with specialized diets, personal chefs still need to present menus for approval.

Cindy Holt is a personal chef who started at fifty-eight and has been working in this business for ten years. Formerly an interior designer who had "done a lot of kitchens," Holt concentrates on healthy cooking and specializes in individual dietary needs. "I'm always studying," she says, "but time is of the essence. I do everything that I can to make meal preparation simple, healthy, and fast." She usually cooks two weeks' worth of meals in one day. The clients then heat up the meals when they want them. "They like their own home-cooked food, the kind they can't get in a restaurant." She regularly checks to see what kind of seasonings her clients like and if they are in the mood for a particular taste for the upcoming week or period.

Sometimes Holt makes special treats like peasant bread or delivers flowers and wine with the meals. Sometimes she drops off things she's baked to her clients in between her cooking visits to give clients a little extra they use for a fill-in. She appreciates the immediate gratification when clients sit down to her meals: "It's an instant reward to make food that's healthy and good for people . . . and see that they love it."

Candy Wallace, executive director of the American Personal Chef Association in San Diego, started her association as a way to support personal chefs, especially women. She says of personal chefing, "The big difference between it and being a corporate executive is that when your feet hit the floor on Monday, you no longer say, 'Oh, hell.' For someone over fifty this career means working as little or as much as you want."

Personal Chef at a Glance

40% 60%

	Minimal	Moderate	More than most
Start-up cost ($1,000 plus initial marketing)	X		

	Minimal	Moderate	More than most
Overhead	X		
Potential earnings			X
Computer skills required	X		
Deadline pressures		X	
Flexible hours			X
Overall stress	X		

Likely Transferable Skills, Background, Careers

According to David MacKay, most personal chefs do not come from the food industry. Candy Wallace finds 50 percent of her members are self-taught. People who choose this field as second or third careers come from all walks of life—airline vice presidents, elementary-school teachers, architects, physicians, anyone who loves to cook.

What to Charge

Personal chefs earn $200 to $250 a day. Some charge a daily rate plus the cost of groceries. Some calculate their fees based on the number of servings per month, such as $295 for twenty servings; others charge a multiple of the cost of the food, typically double or triple. Prices for special diets are $25 to $50 a day higher.

Best Ways to Get Business

- Face-to-face networking inside business and trade organizations such as the chamber of commerce and business-referral organizations. Have a sample menu or brochure available if you are asked for it.

- Making educational presentations. David MacKay says, "You can't be shy. Speak at local health clubs, the Rotary, and senior centers," and any other venues where people might be interested in finding out about healthy eating.

- Having an attractive Web site that tells about your services, shows sample menus, and states your fees.

- Listing in the Yellow Pages. Consider ads on local directory sites like *Yahoo Get Local* and *SuperPages*.

Marketing Insights

- The primary appeal of having a personal chef is the convenience of having someone else do the shopping and planning, and the time your clients save as a result of not having to pick up meals or wait for deliveries. Then come the tasty meals.

- Keeping clients happy is key, which is enhanced by leaving a surprise treat with each visit, such as flowers, a bottle of wine, chocolate-chip cookies, or a gift certificate.

- The more affluent the client, the more frequent the service.

- Specialization makes sense as the growing connection between food and health, plus the availability of inexpensive and tasty quick restaurant food from places like Baja Fresh, becomes competitive.

- Teaching classes will both attract clients and be an additional source of revenue.

Where Next?

ASSOCIATIONS

- American Personal Chef Association: (800) 644-8389, (619) 294-2436; *www.personalchef.com*.

- Canadian Personal Chef Association: (877) 723-6722, (800) 995-2138; *www.cdnpca.com*.

- United States Personal Chef Association provides teaching, tests new recipes, and investigates local food service regulations: (800) 995-2138; *www.uspca.com, www.uspca.com,* and *www.hireachef.com* for consumers to search for a personal chef.

BOOKS

- *How to Open and Operate a Home-Based Catering Business,* Denise Vivaldo (Globe Pequot Press, 2002). ISBN: 0762724803.

- *A Personal Chef Cooks,* Cheryl Mochau (1st Books Library, 2003). ISBN: 1403329532.

- *Personal Chef Catering Business,* e-Book at *www.mymommybiz.com.*

From the Home Front

"Given my age, my clients think I should know what I'm talking about. I'll keep cooking as long as I can stand up to do it. I don't see any reason to slow down."
—Cindy Holt, sixty-eight

---

46. Pet Groomer

Even when allergies are not an issue, everyone prefers a clean pet. The house and the car are more pleasant and, overall, living with a clean pet is more enjoyable. So as the pet population grows, so does the amount of bathing, combing, clipping, brushing, and primping. But the fast-paced lives of so many pet owners leave little time to bathe and groom their pets, and many find it cumbersome to take their pets to a grooming shop.

So pet grooming, whether you do it part-time or full-time, from a mobile van or out of your home, can be one of the more profitable fifty-plus pet businesses. Although no federal or state license is required to be a pet groomer, training is available and strongly recommended.

Kathy Sanders started her grooming business in 1982 with $4,000 and a beat-up truck. She developed the business, added a school for training people in how to do grooming, and later sold them for around half a million dollars. Sanders now offers a correspondence course through her Groomadog Academy. According to her, 15 percent to 20 percent of people who train to be groomers are over fifty. Citing a woman who operates a mobile grooming service from a wheelchair, Sanders finds it's possible to do grooming at whatever level of physical stamina suits you. "They start out doing it for fun, and then they see how much money they can make."

Nancy Bouman honed her skills by grooming dogs she brought home from the local shelter. She believes, as a home-based or mobile groomer, you can assure your clientele higher-quality care than they'll find at a large establishment or a veterinarian's office where training may be minimal and injuries do occur. She believes it's important to show clients a certificate to demonstrate that you've had training.

Whether you operate at home or from a mobile van, you'll need a tub, a grooming table, clippers, blade assortments, scissors, towels, and an industrial-force dryer that dries in half the time. Groomers say it's better to start with a minimum of good-quality tools instead of an abundance of lower-cost ones.

Mobile grooming requires a van, but because of the extra convenience you're providing, you can charge more than if pets were brought to you. Sanders says it's only possible to groom four to five dogs a days in a mobile unit, which she prefers over grooming ten dogs in a shop. It's not unusual for mobile groomers to have a waiting list. Thus they can be choosy about their customers, refusing larger dogs or biters.

A used van outfitted to do grooming costs around $25,000; new units run about $55,000. They come equipped with a tub, grooming table, dryer, clippers, a water tank, and vacuum system so you don't breathe in the fur. The van should also have its own source of hot water, air conditioning, and heat, though if you can plug in to the electricity and water at your customer's home, you'll keep your costs down. If you already own a van, outfitting it can be done for about $5,000. Of course, the more customizing you do, the more you'll spend.

Many groomers will also clip and bathe cats, though they charge more for the equivalent of "hazard pay." Cats don't remain pussies at the sound of clippers. You may be asked to groom other animals, too. Nancy Bouman laughs when she says "I once shaved a cat, and I've even groomed a goat."

Pet Grooming at a Glance

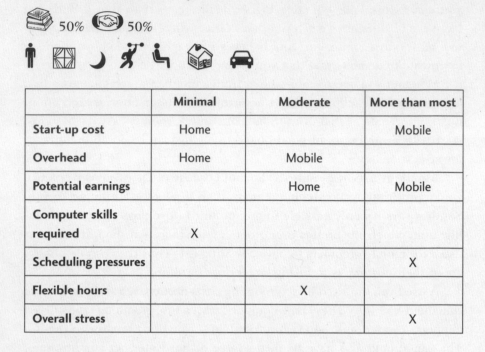

50% 50%

	Minimal	Moderate	More than most
Start-up cost	Home		Mobile
Overhead	Home	Mobile	
Potential earnings		Home	Mobile
Computer skills required	X		
Scheduling pressures			X
Flexible hours		X	
Overall stress			X

Likely Transferable Skills, Background, Careers

No particular background is required to become a dog groomer. You need to like animals, have patience, and, according to Nancy Bouman, a little artistic ability. "You need to know what a breed dog is supposed to look like and be able to visualize what the owner wants." Being able to establish good rapport with animals plus patience are needed. Bouman also says, "It takes a lot of patience." However, the more regular the customer, the more the dog learns what it needs to do. "It results in a well-trained dog," declares Bouman. In fact, Bouman finds both her customers and the dogs become well trained.

What to Charge

Grooming tends to range from $20 to $60 per animal, though mobile services in wealthier communities may be even more. Smaller short-haired dogs are at the low end of the scale; larger long-haired dogs at the high end. Matted dogs and cats are more. Charges are higher for mobile services. A grooming job that costs $35 in a shop might cost $50 in a mobile unit. Cat charges start at $40 and go up, depending on locale and the length of the coat.

Best Ways to Get Business

- Kathy Sanders says all you need are your first twenty-five to thirty customers, "and it's word of mouth from there." You can stimulate referrals by offering a free service to existing clients for referrals.

- Advertising in local papers, offering a discount for first-time customers.

- Having a Web site with photos of animals you've groomed and listing your services and fees.

- Placing ads on local Web community sites, such as *www.petwalk.com* in San Diego.

- If your community has local festivals, take a booth and have freshly groomed animals available for people to see. Pass out pet treats.

- If your community has a parade in conjunction with the festival, hire people to walk freshly groomed dogs in the parade while wearing T-shirts with your business name on it.

- Listing in the Yellow Pages with your calls going or being forwarded to your cell phone if you do mobile grooming.

- Having attractive signage on your mobile unit with your phone number and Web site visible.

Marketing Insights

- Your best customers are regular ones. This is more possible in an urban area where people are more apt to keep their dogs indoors and they want them clean. In the country, owners may bring pets for annual shaves. Owners of pure-bred pets are likely to visit more often and pay a higher price than owners of the Heinz fifty-seven variety.

- The more often a pet comes, the better it will do and look. It may take a couple of visits from a dog to get it accustomed to being groomed and to figure out its "figure flaws" and to camouflage them.

- You can specialize by offering precision grooming to breeders and others who show their dogs, though this is not done by most groomers. You might work with large dogs or long-haired cats.

- You can offer interim bathing and nail clipping at a lower cost than the entire grooming service. It takes less time to bathe a basically clean animal.

- With the rise of interest in "pampered" pet services, you can offer special services, such "gentle" or organic treatments that have appeal with some clientele, which increases revenue. You might team up with an aromatherapist to provide aromatherapy treatments for problems.

Where Next?

ASSOCIATIONS

- National Dog Groomers Association of America: (724) 962-1919; *www.nationaldoggroomers.com*. Offers certification.

- Scores of state and local associations can be located at *www.petgroomerdirectory.com/associations/S.htm*.

BOOKS AND VIDEOS

- *How to Start a Home-Based Pet Care Business,* Kathy Salzberg (Globe Pequot Press, 2002). ISBN: 0762710225.

- *Dog Groomer,* video (Delmar Publishers, 1998). ISBN: 0766853780.

- For books about aromatherapy for animals, see the list on page 320.

TRAINING

- You can apprentice yourself to a master groomer. Expect to pay several thousand dollars for two to three months of training.

- Groomadog Academy: (803) 337-3534; *www.groomadog.com*.

- *PetGroomer.com*. Amid the advertising is a school-near-you locator: *www.petgroomers.com*.

From the Home Front

"This is a great business for someone over fifty. My mom bathed dogs until she was seventy-five. For me, it's till death do us part."

—Kathy Sanders, forty-seven

47. Pet Taxi Service

Just like kids who need to go to the dentist, dance classes, and baseball practice during the day or after school, pets must get to their appointments at the vet, the groomer, and the dog park. But busy pet owners in both urban and rural areas have difficulty finding time to get their pets to these appointments, hence the demand for pet transportation services that are growing right along with the increasing number of pets in U.S. households. A successful pet taxi service requires only a van or SUV, a calm driver, and a good rapport with animals.

David Appell of Washington, D.C., created a niche for himself, starting the first and only pet taxi service in the area. He used to work as a collection agent for a major corporation earning a six-figure income. Now, he says, "I don't work for a living. I play with dogs all day." Appell transports more than dogs. "I take anything I can get into a crate, including a forty-foot python and a small Komodo dragon."

Appell lost his desire for corporate offices and tailored suits when his doctor told him he was in "heart attack country." The more relaxed lifestyle operating a pet taxi service suits him much better. "It's true, my salary is half, but my stress level is too." Appell figures he makes under $50,000 a year but he has more time to be involved with his community and help at local shelters, which he finds has its own reward.

Pet taxis provide three types of service:

- Regular pickups to weekly obedience training and occasional non-emergency transportation such as to the vet or the groomer.

- Emergency services that require you to be available twenty-four hours a day but which pay three to four times more than regular pickups. Appell gets two to three calls for an emergency pickup a week.

- Airport transportation, like a shuttle service for people, but includes submitting all necessary paperwork and ensuring that the pet is loaded safely on the designated flight. This also entails getting to know the airline personnel responsible for pets at each of the airlines.

The initial start-up cost for this business is fairly low and the monthly overhead can be kept to a minimum, though you will need to keep your vehicle well maintained so your clients can depend on you not to miss pickups. Your vehicle must be large enough to hold crates of various sizes, and if you decide to transport horses or small farm animals, you will need a truck and trailer. If you transport sick animals you'll need to have your vehicle regularly disinfected, which you may be able to do through a local car wash. Should you allow pet owners to ride with you, you'll need liability insurance to cover transporting people, which will increase your overhead.

David Appell finds technology is essential to running a pet taxi efficiently. He always has his cell phone on so he can get dispatches wherever he is and uses a headset to make and take calls. He links his PDA (personal digital assistant) to the Internet and calculates mileage charges with online mapping services. Using Act 2000, he has access to his database with clients and destinations in his PDA, and he uses a headset for cell-phone calls. He uses his Web site, *www.fetchapettaxi.com*, to attract business.

Pet Taxi Service at a Glance

 20%  80%

	Minimal	Moderate	More than most
Start-up cost (van, crates, insurance)			van
Overhead		X	
Potential earnings		X	
Computer skills required	X		
Deadline pressures			X
Flexible hours		X	
Overall stress	X		

Likely Transferable Skills, Background, Careers

A good driving record, a way with animals, and the ability to read a map and organize your day are about all it takes.

What to Charge

Prices vary from region to region just as passenger taxi service does, with charges based on mileage with an initial start fee like a taxi. Start fees range from $15 to $30. Emergency transportation is two to four times greater than normal fees. Some pet taxis base their charges on time. Airport transportation can be a flat fee if you are just dropping off the animal or more if you are providing check-in services.

Best Ways to Get Business

- Getting referrals from past clients is the best source of new business. David Appell figures 90 percent of his business comes from direct referrals.

- Parking in front of local pet-services store, especially large ones like Petco and Petsmart, and handing out fliers and business cards.

- Visiting veterinarians, animal hospitals, kennels, and groomers in your area regularly to develop referral relationships. Seek permission to place your brochures or cards in waiting rooms. David Appell makes a point of calling on the nearest vet office when he's on a transport to keep top-of-mind with the staff and to restock brochures. He also brings small gifts like bagels or donuts for the staff.

- Listing your service on community Web sites, particularly ones serving pet owners like *www.petwalk.com* in San Diego.

- Having a Web site listing your services, prices, and contact information. Include in keywords or metatags for your site the names of all the communities in the area you serve, terms like *pet taxi, pet cab,* and *pet transportation,* as well as the names of the animals—dogs, cats, horses, reptiles—you'll transport.

- Obtaining contracts with cities and counties to pick up animals, though these are not likely to be live ones.

Marketing Insights

- The animals likely to need transporting vary by region. In a rural or equine-oriented area, consider transporting horses as some people own them but do not have a trailer and must hire one if they move, take their animal to the vet or a breeder, or show their horses. If you face competition, consider specializing in particular kinds or sizes of animals. Someone's more apt to have difficulty finding transportation for her Saint Bernard than for her Pomeranian.

- In addition to having adequate liability insurance, it helps to be bonded and include this fact on your Web site and all printed material.

- To supplement your income, you can provide additional services, like food delivery and pet training.

- A significant proportion of your business is apt to come from customers of limited means, who don't have access to a vehicle for any purpose.

Where Next?

ASSOCIATION

- Independent Pet and Animal Transportation Association. Most members are focused on shipping animals by air: (903) 769-2267; *www.ipata.com.*

From the Home Front

"When I was doing corporate collections, the pressure was great. I noticed no one in this field was old. When my doctor told me I was a candidate for a heart attack, I had to ask myself, 'When I'm fifty years old, will I be able to take this pressure?'"

—David Appell, who started his pet taxi service instead at forty-six

---

Snapshot: Edna and Ross Andersen, Raising Peruvian Alpacas

Six years ago, when Edna was sixty-nine and Ross was seventy-four, the Andersens retired, but they didn't want "to be put out to pasture." They wanted adventure, excitement, and a feeling of accomplishment. Their retirement dream included five goals: an investment with a good return, great tax advantages, freedom to travel and enjoy life, a quiet peaceful country setting close to urban amenities, and light physical labor they could handle as they aged.

The Andersens believe they've met their goals. Living in Payson, Utah, a beautiful country setting just twenty miles from big-city amenities, they raise pure Peruvian alpacas. Their business is called Alpacas of Utah, and they report that alpacas are a good investment, each costing about the same as a new car. But, they point out, unlike a car that depreciates as soon as you drive off the lot, when a bred female alpaca has her first baby, your investment has doubled, and the male Peruvian alpacas make great studs. On top of that, thanks to their alpacas, the Andersens enjoy a farm tax advantage.

They find alpacas to be very hardy, but gentle and lovable creatures that require little care. Ten alpacas can share an acre of grass hay and some fresh water. Their fiber feels like silk but it's ten times warmer than wool, so the clothing they sell from the fiber doesn't overheat the body, but keeps it at body temperature. Edna and Ross have thirty pure Peruvian registered alpacas now, some for sale, some for stud services, and all, they say, compounding their investment.

48. Résumé Writer

Each year, millions of Americans change employers and hundreds of thousands of college graduates enter the job market. What's common to all these people is the need to have an impressive résumé that will win them the positions they want.

This need fuels a demand for professional résumé writers who can write top-notch competitive résumés that will lead to interviews. The résumé writer does something that no how-to book or software program can do: interviews the client to draw out and recognize what's special about his or her background, skills, accomplishments, strengths, and weaknesses in the context of the type of job for which he or she is applying. A résumé writer can organize this information in a concise and appealing way that highlights the clients' most noteworthy accomplishments and skills so they stand out from the crowd.

Résumé services often specialize in one or more specific areas, including IT (information technology), engineering, government, academic, medical, legal, finance, sales, middle- or executive-level management, midcareer change, recent college graduates, or military returning to the civilian workforce. Teena Rose, whose company, Résumé to Referral, in Huber Heights, Ohio, confirms that "businesses that focus on a niche clientele can find great success and high profits dealing with specific career challenges and how to handle them."

In addition to the basic résumé, most writers also offer other services to better their clients' chances at landing the jobs of their choice. These include: developing a salary history or reference list; writing cover letters and thank-you notes; designing a personalized letterhead; mailing, faxing, or broadcast e-mailing cover letters and résumés to prospective employers; uploading résumés to on-line job banks; sending résumés to executive recruiters; typing applications or forms; writing telephone scripts for job seekers to use in making calls; verifying information presented on the résumé (referred to as a verified résumé); and creating Web pages that clients can direct potential employers to. Of course, extra services mean extra revenue per client.

An increasing number of résumé writers are expanding into career coaching, which itself can involve ancillary services, including:

- Giving personality assessments and psychological tests to help clients better understand themselves.

- Helping clients in person, by phone, or over the Internet to define their life goals and how these translate into what type of jobs to seek.

- Teaching clients techniques to improve how they handle themselves in job interviews, presentations, and job conflicts.

- Strategizing with clients to help them obtain a salary increase.

- Coaching clients to present themselves on camera and for taping, and reproducing, and uploading video résumés to the Internet.

For example, Sally Shepherd Cofer of Modesto, California, began her résumé writing business at age fifty-one but has launched into many aspects of career coaching, including goal setting, interview training, and personality assessment. Similarly, Joyce Fortier, of Create Your Career in Michigan, conducts her business as a full-service career center, offering not just résumé writing but many types of career coaching. To lend credibility to herself as a career coach, she has passed numerous certification exams that have allowed her to become a Certified Career Management Coach (CCMC) and a Credentialed Career Master (CCM).

Résumé writing can be described as an evergreen business. Frank Fox, president of the Professional Association of Résumé Writers, states, "Résumé writing is a recession-proof business. When unemployment is low and people have good jobs, they want to create résumés to position themselves for better jobs. And when unemployment is high, people need great résumés in order to compete."

Résumé Writing at a Glance

 50% 50%

	Minimal	Moderate	More than most
Start-up cost	X		
Overhead		X	
Potential earnings			X
Computer skills required		X	
Deadline pressures		X	
Flexible hours		X	
Overall stress		X	

Likely Transferable Skills, Background, Careers

Prior experience in human relations, teaching, or secretarial services can be a stepping-stone to résumé writing. You need to be skilled at interviewing so you can help people open themselves up to their talents and what makes them special. While superior writing ability is required, you can improve this skill by studying books on résumé writing.

What to Charge

Résumé services often charge by the hour, billing between $50 for entry-level résumés to $150 and up per hour to create executive-level résumés. Many services include 25 to 50 copies as part of their base price, with additional copies or a copy on disk available for an added fee. Prices for add-on services also vary greatly. For example, the range in pricing cover letters goes from $30 to $65. You can obtain a pricing manual from the Professional Association of Résumé Writers (PARW).

It's best to post your prices on your Web site so clients know in advance what you charge. You will increase your business if you accept credit cards.

Best Ways to Get Business

According to the results of the Professional Association of Résumé Writers' membership study, the most successful methods for getting business are:

- Advertising in the Yellow Pages or Smart Pages.

- Creating a visually attractive Web site on which you list your services and prices, testimonial letters, and articles and tips you have written.

- Networking in professional, trade, and civic organizations and referral organizations.

- Maintaining a database of clients for one year and, prior to the end of the year, sending out an e-mail or letters to your clients suggesting they may want to update their résumés or have you work with them in career coaching.

- Getting referrals from print shops that print résumés and executive recruitment and placement firms.

- Creating a community identity so people recognize your name by giving workshops, seminars, and speeches on how to write a résumé; getting publicity and media attention, such as appearing on talk shows.

- Writing articles for magazines and e-zines.

Marketing Insights

- A Web site can attract clients nationwide.

- The key benefit you offer clients is the personal attention a book or software can't. Focus on giving unique, personal attention to your clients. People often have difficulty tooting their own horns, and your role is to help them learn to be confident and proud of their accomplishments.

- Always provide a sense that what clients tell you is confidential and that you have honesty and integrity.

- Writing résumés is not what it was thirty years ago. Today, as more employers seek on-line résumés and more on-line job sites abound, résumé writers must think about not only the print version of a résumé but also the electronic version. They must also know about all the on-line job banks and how to submit résumés to on-line services. Learn about the styles used today in résumé writing. Many résumé writers are now getting creative, no longer abiding by the old formulaic rules for résumés that are now considered stodgy.

- Be prepared to start out slowly. Bill Murdock of the Employment Coach, in Dallas, Texas, began his business at age fifty-one in 1991, doing only a handful of résumés per month. But after just a few years, he is working full-time and his business is still strong today.

- If you are offering career coaching, one of the keys, according to Sally Shepherd Cofer, is creating a safe atmosphere where your clients can release their pent-up emotions about their careers. "Offering true care and concern for people is one of my hallmarks, and this is done sincerely. Clients know this and respond with goals, hopes, and dreams that may have been hidden for a long time," says Cofer.

- Certifications in résumé writing and career coaching increase your credibility as people shop for a résumé writer.

- Job fairs at which you critique résumés for free as well as advertising in "throwaway" newspapers are apt to be disappointing.

Where Next?

ASSOCIATIONS AND CERTIFICATIONS

- Career Masters Institute at (800) 881-9972 offers a credential: *www.cminstitute.com*.

- The Professional Association of Résumé Writers & Career Coaches offers certification in résumé writing, employment interviewing, and career coaching: (800) 822-7279, (727) 821-2274; *www.parw.com*.

- The National Résumé Writers Association offers certification: (888) NRWA-444; *www.nrwa.com*.

BOOKS

Books about résumés and interviewing number in the hundreds. Here are some representative titles.

- *How to Start a Résumé Service,* Teena Rose. Emphasizes creating a nonlocal clientele. A downloadable book at *www.résumébiz.com.*

- *The Interview Rehearsal Book,* Deb Gottesman and Buzz Mauro (Penguin/Putnam, 1999). ISBN: 0425166864.

- *Résumé Magic,* Susan Britton Whitcomb (Jist Works, 1999). ISBN: 1563705222.

- *The Résumé Handbook,* Arthur D. Rosenberg and David V. Hizer (Adams Media Corporation, 1996). ISBN: 1558506160.

From the Home Front

"There's a feeling I get when a project is done and I've helped someone re-create their life. I've helped them become someone they didn't believe they were before . . . put them back in the game and given them another chance at life. I have found a profession and will do this for the rest of my life."

—Bill Murdock

---

49. Tutoring

Tutoring is on the rise for multiple reasons. Getting admitted to college is more difficult. Children are simply not keeping pace with their assignments due to increasingly difficult courses. As one tutor told us, "What used to be taught in college in the old days is now taught in high school." Also budget cuts and overcrowded classes are motivating some parents to seek out tutors to ensure that their children are learning what they need so they can get into private schools. In other instances, students are so busy with extracurricular activities, on-line chatting, or simply goofing off that they don't study as much as they should and begin failing their classes.

Children with learning disabilities or who are regarded as failing under the No Child Left Behind Act also need help. In these cases, tutoring is subsidized under federal law.

As a tutor, you can focus on elementary-, middle-, or high-school children, depending on your preference, though most tutoring is done at the middle- and high-school levels. Your educational background or professional work experience will play a role in determining which area of instruction you are most qualified to tutor in such as reading or writing skills, computer hardware usage or software skills, math, foreign languages, history, or one of the sciences. Consider, too, if you have musical skill or expertise in a sport, you can turn this into a niche for tutoring or teaching practice.

Parents usually want tutors to have at least a B.A. in the field they're tutoring. If you want to tutor children under one of the federal programs, you'll need teaching credentials, or a credential related to learning disorders.

If income is your primary objective, consider preparing high-school students for the tests nearly all college applicants are required to take—the PSAT, SAT I and II, and ACT. These tests are pivotal in determining which college the child will qualify to attend. An adjunct service to college test preparation tutoring is college admissions counseling, in which you help families research and select the most appropriate colleges for their children to apply to. Surprisingly, there is also test preparation tutoring for young children in large cities like New York and Los Angeles where the pressure to get into the "best" private school causes parents to hire tutors to help their kids prepare for the independent school entrance exam (ISEE) or even for a kindergarten interview.

In the past, independent tutors often competed for clients with large corporate tutoring centers such as Sylvan Learning Centers, Kaplan Test Centers, Princeton, and others. But according to Thomas Redick, president of the National Tutoring Association, the publicity and advertising from these large corporate tutoring companies has served to increase business for private tutors, because the fees and atmosphere at the large centers often drive parents to seek out less expensive, more personal tutoring.

Tutoring does not always have to focus on children or on academic subjects. You can also earn an income by tutoring adults or by teaching a sport or hobbyist skill, such as tennis, golf, dancing, carpentry, or plumbing. Dave Gorrie, for example, parlayed his career as a head coach into a profitable home-based business giving batting lessons to kids ages eight to eighteen. Operating out of his home in Carthage, Texas, Dave, who is now seventy-three years old, works with fifteen to twenty kids each week in forty-five-minute batting-practice lessons. While most people know how to use computers now, some computer tutoring is still being done.

Educational therapy that uses both educational and therapeutic methods is another option. Educational therapists help children with attention-deficit disorders, emotional problems, family issues, and learning disabilities that get in the way of learning. They are called learning disability specialists in some areas. Some universities offer Educational Therapy certification programs.

Tutoring can be an evergreen career because of its vast market and the fact that the level of knowledge that people must have today is ever-expanding. Private tutors will likely always be in demand because many people simply prefer individual instruction since it allows them to learn at their own pace, without the pressure of peers or authorities.

Tutoring at a Glance

 50% 50%

	Minimal	Moderate	More than most
Start-up cost	X		
Overhead	X		
Potential earnings		X	
Computer skills required	X		
Deadline pressures	X		
Flexible hours		X	
Overall stress	X		

Likely Transferable Skills, Background, Careers

A college degree in the field in which you are tutoring is sufficient as long as clients sense you care about helping students learn and succeed. For nonacademic fields, life experience can be enough. Overall, tutoring is easy to step into.

What to Charge

Academic tutors charge as little $15 and as much as $125 an hour, with most charging between $25 and $60 an hour. Rates vary with subject, grade of the students, experience, your community, and travel time required. Tutors working in their own homes usually charge less than tutors who go to students' homes. Nonacademic tutors can charge between $25 to $60 per hour, depending on the skill or hobby you are teaching.

Best Ways to Get Business

- Calling on teachers in the subject areas in which you specialize and communicating that you work with students having difficulty and whose parents are demanding more than the school can provide. Also talk with school office personnel, counselors, and principals, leaving behind an attractive brochure that features your qualifications.

- Getting to know psychologists and family counselors who are apt to see in their practices children with learning difficulties associated with the other problems children may have that cause them to see a mental-health professional.

- Posting flyers on bulletin boards in your community.

- Writing articles for community publications on topics that relate to your subject with your photo and byline, including how to contact you.

- Having a Web site on which you post testimonial letters from past clients. Be sure to place the name of the community or communities you serve on your home page, in metatags and, if possible, in your domain name.

- Teaching adult education classes in your local schools from which you might obtain private students who need further assistance from you.

Marketing Insights

- "Once a student, including A students, works with a good tutor, they recognize the value." Thomas Redick, president of the National Tutoring Association.

- Clients usually resent paying for your travel time, but if you go to students' homes instead of having them come to you, you need to figure this time into your hourly rate. You also need to calculate into your rate the time you will spend in parent consultations, discussions at school with teachers, and paperwork to keep track of your students.

- You need to get to know the curriculum followed in your local schools and buy the textbooks that are used. While you may sometimes teach your own curriculum, you usually need to coordinate with the specific textbook used in your client's classroom.

- As you build your tutoring practice, you can operate more like a referral service, combining the tutoring you do yourself with providing referrals for students you can't fit into your schedule or who need tutoring on subjects outside your area of expertise. You can either subcontract with other tutors or arrange to receive referral fees from the tutors you refer to.

Where Next?

ASSOCIATIONS

- Association of Educational Therapists: (800) 286-4267; *www.aetonline.org*.

- Music Teachers National Association: (888) 512-5278; *mmanet@mma*.

- National Tutoring Association: (866) 311-6630; *www.ntatutor.org*.

CERTIFICATION

While no states require licensing or certification to tutor students privately, if you wish to work with students whose tutoring is subsidized with government funds, you will need to meet the qualifications established by the school district that administers the money. A teaching credential will always fulfill the standard. The National Tutoring Association has a certification program.

BOOKS

- *The Accidental Trainer: You Know Computers, So They Want You to Teach Everyone Else,* Elaine Weiss (Jossey-Bass 1996). ISBN: 0787902934.

- *The Computer Training Handbook: How to Teach People to Use Computers,* Elliott Masie and Rebekah Wolman (Lakewood Publications, 1998). ISBN: 0943210372.

- *Tutoring Matters:,* Jerome Rabow and Tiffani Chin (Nima Fahimian, 1999). ISBN: 1566396956.

- *Tutoring as a Successful Business,* Eileen Kaplan Shapiro (Nateen Publishing, 2001). ISBN: 096723610X.

FRANCHISE

- Abrakadoodle®, (703) 871-7356; *www.abrakadoodle.com.*

From the Home Front

"I can't see myself quitting. I do get good results."
—Dave Gorrie, seventy-three

Snapshot: Dr. Michael J. Cohen, Educational Programs on the Internet

For twenty-seven years, Michael Cohen operated Outdoor Travel Camps, a conservation education program that took groups of fifteen people on extended nature expeditions. In affiliation with the National Audubon Society, Cohen and his groups camped and studied nature for periods of several days to six months in the national parks and eighty-four different ecosystems. Over that time, Cohen lived almost continuously in the wilds of nature twenty-four hours a day.

His groups also interacted with and learned from many human communities, including the Amish, outdoorsmen, ecologists, and indigenous peoples. Their goal was to discover how to live in sustainable balance with our natural environment in accord with the United Nations manifesto for environmentally sound personal growth and social justice.

When Cohen turned fifty-five, the "Speed Limit 55" signs along the roadway began to take on a new significance. "I started to realize," he recalls, "that I wasn't going to be able to do this forever." Even organizing several camps at a time, he could only reach a few hundred people per year and he wanted to share the lessons and experiences of relating to nature with large numbers of people no matter where they lived.

While the Internet might not seem to be the most likely place to discover nature, Cohen thought it would be an ideal means for people from around the world to come together to study nature. So at fifty-five, he set out to create *Project Nature Connect*, an on-line educational, counseling and healing program in organic psychology. *Project Nature Connect* offers over three years' worth of courses and classes along with accompanying textbooks, based on the nature activities Cohen used in the travel camps.

The program includes accredited and life-experience courses, cooperating university courses and degree programs, scholarships, professional certification, internships, and occasional on-site workshops. Interested individuals with Internet access anywhere in the world can sign up for specific courses or enroll in a certification, M.A. or Ph.D. degree program.

Participants typically study in e-mail groups of four to six people and do structured nature activities once or twice a week in their own communities, or even in their own backyards. Classes include people from China, Korea, Columbia, Nova Scotia, New Zealand, Australia, coast-to-coast in the USA, or anywhere with access to a computer and Internet hookup.

At seventy-three, Cohen continues to oversee all the course work and, like a modern-day Thoreau, still sleeps outdoors daily near his home base on San Juan Island, Washington.

50. Web Merchant and Auction Trader

Sales over the Internet keep bounding upward as busy schedules and the search for great bargains attract increasing numbers of people on the go. Women now spend more on the Web for both new and used items than men. Businesses are using *eBay* to both buy and sell; *eBay*'s become the place to go for liquidators. So if you have a product to market, anything from used books or CDs to custom-made clothing to specialized exercise equipment, you can make the world your market on the Internet.

There are two primary approaches to selling on the Internet. One is to operate a virtual storefront on a Web site where, like Penny Stewart, you showcase your products. When Stewart became interested in belly dancing as a way to lose weight, she opened a bricks-and-mortar store selling the specialized products needed for this novel form of exercise. Then at fifty-one, she converted her "real" storefront, Crafty Lady, into a virtual one, *www.pinkgypsy.com.* She sells everything from belly dancing costumes and videotapes to elegant body jewelry. As Penny senses new trends, she has added products for other forms of dancing: hula, Tahitian, and Shikira, a Middle Eastern style of dance.

Stewart told us she never has to leave her house now and nets close to $50,000 a year. Even though she sells very specialized wares, by employing a linking strategy, she can draw an audience of people interested in weight loss, health, and nutrition, and even metaphysical ideology. Penny says her most important lessons have been to figure out how to do her Web site maintenance herself so she doesn't have to depend on someone else for her store to be up and working, and to be generous.

Stewart finds that the more generous she is with give-away things, the more exposure she gets. She figures she gets one thousand hits a day, thanks to her practice of giving free links and home pages for craftspeople on a sister site, *craftylady.com.* "It's important to give something away for free. Free home pages have made my site grow. Tons of people will link back to me," declares Stewart.

The other way to sell products on the Internet is through hitchhiking onto auction sites like *eBay, Yahoo Auction,* and *Amazon.com Auctions. eBay,* the largest auction site, has become a primary or supplementary way to sell their wares for all kinds of people from artisans to estate sales specialists. *eBay* estimates 430,000 individuals and small businesses make their livings from *eBay.* This number doubled from 2002 to 2004.

As a seller on an auction site, you pay the site a fee to list your product. The site acts as an electronic intermediary but never actually touches or handles your products. *eBay* works well for so many people because it enables sellers to operate with little overhead and to get a volume of sales one could only otherwise expect in a high-rent, highly trafficked commercial location.

Selling at auction sites, you do not have to maintain a Web site or a database. You simply follow the auction's site instructions to sell anything from antique cars to vintage clothing to used CDs and almost anything you can think of, including yachts, islands, and ferry boats. Not that there's no work involved—you have to create listings to describe your products, manage your inventory, track your sales, and satisfy your customers.

Skip McGrath started selling antiques and collectibles on *eBay* in 1997 when he was downsized from his job shortly before turning fifty. *eBay* sellers like McGrath obtain the goods they sell at antique stores, estate sales, garage sales, pawnshops, flea markets, and thrift shops as well as from buying on line as bidders themselves. They buy on *eBay* and other auction sites, where the bidding is less and the items often go for lower prices. McGrath's own success has inspired him to teach others how to sell on *eBay*.

What you need to sell via an auction site includes a good computer, fast on-line access such as cable, DSL, or satellite, a digital camera with some lights and a backdrop for photographing your products. Skip McGrath recommends shipping priority mail through the post office as it provides free shipping supplies. He finds UPS is only competitive if the item is large, over five pounds.

There are two ways of receiving payment for items sold at auction. One allows people to pay you using a credit card. This requires you to have a merchant account and use a gateway service for which you obligate yourself to paying minimum monthly fees that range from $10 to $60. This is fine if your sales volume is high enough. The other way is to use an on-line third-party banking system, like *Pay Pal*, which is owned by *eBay*, or *Yahoo! PayDirect*, where both seller and the buyer have accounts. A third-party system is more anonymous than using credit cards, and some people prefer it. Still other people who have had a poor experience at some time will not buy from a seller if this is the only means of payment they offer. You'll increase sales if you offer multiple forms of payment.

To help manage the details of auction selling, you can use third-party selling tools like *AuctionWatch* and *Auctionworks*. Basically they automate the auction process, including sending out end-of-auction e-mails and up-loading your photos. They also can track buyers and keep track of inventory. There are plenty of these tools available, so before purchase one, you should take the time to research what they do, if they come with technical support, and what this may cost. Some of them are expensive, so you might ask for a free trial period before purchasing. Skip McGrath uses an auction management service offered through *www.vendio.com*.

It's estimated that 95 percent of *eBay*'s millions of sellers are individuals and small businesses, but some people like Penny Stewart like to do things their way. Stewart tried selling her goods on *eBay* but found people pickier and not as easy to please as shoppers on her own site.

As auction site sales keep growing, new opportunities have emerged. If you don't want to auction your goods, you can try selling on *eBay*'s *Half.com*, where items are sold at a fixed price. You can open an *eBay* storefront or sell from one of the many mall sites, some of which are specialized. You can use consignment stores where you deposit your goods; the store takes over the listing and shipping process and in exchange takes about 40 percent of the selling price. You might also become a Trading Assistant. Unlike a consignment store, you do not take physical custody of the goods and the seller is responsible for shipping to the ultimate buyer. You write the copy for the auction site and manage the sale in return for a sales commission.

Web Merchant and Auction Trader at a Glance

📚 40% 🤝 60%

⊘ 🏪 🌐 📦 📦 🌙 💺 🏠

	Minimal	Moderate	More than most
Start-up cost	X		
Overhead		X	
Potential earnings			X
Computer skills required		X	
Deadline pressures	X		

	Minimal	Moderate	More than most
Flexible hours	X		
Overall stress—relaxing	X		

Likely Transferable Skills, Background, Careers

Anyone with a little computer savvy and a willingness to monitor inflow and outflow of product at the same time can do this business.

What to Charge

Lower prices stand at the top or close to the top of every survey asking people why they shop on the Web. Yet many sellers have found they get better prices than they would get if they sold their wares locally. In the course of doing what they do, auction sites provide an efficient mechanism for finding the price that the market will bear. Many sellers on auction sites shoot for a 100 percent markup, but the key to this is what they pay for what they sell.

Another way to receive payment, particularly when you're getting started with your own storefront or on-line catalogue is to use a payment service, like *catalog.com*. Payment services technically resell your products because merchant account agreements do not allow accepting credit cards for another company.

Best Ways to Get Business

- If you are selling from your own Web site, investing time in researching keyword combinations as they are how someone using a search engine will find you. While everyone's goal is to be at the top of *Google* and the other majors, if you're not in first thirty listings, you'll get no traffic directed to you from search engines. A number of companies provide this service, and some Web designers also will do this kind of research.

- Having a bargain section on your Web site, as Penny Stewart does, offering a 10 percent discount to buyers.

- Keeping in contact with customers, notifying them of sales, promotions, and special newsletters.

- Being quite specific in describing what you are selling. This includes a good photograph. If you are selling something used, candidly describe any flaws or blemishes.

- If auctioning goods, setting a low initial bid and not using a reserve, which means a buyer must meet or exceed a minimum price.

- Making the auction period cover a weekend when traffic is highest.

Marketing Insights

- Convenience, what buyers want that is not available locally, and lower prices drive shopping on the Web. Of course, what's not available locally is available on other Web sites, so what matters to a Web merchant most are convenience and price. Convenience translates into speed of service and ease in buying. Ease in buying comes down to site design, but what you control on a day-to-day basis is speed of service.

- Prompt customer service, including answering queries from prospective buyers immediately, is vital. Delays in answering, shipping, or resolving problems mean a customer will buy elsewhere or not return. Happy customers will be repeat customers.

- The reputation indicated in the ratings on *eBay*, which comes from customer feedback, will make or break an *eBay* seller's business. This is customer service again. Build up your feedback rating as soon as possible.

- Not everything sells on *eBay* or other auction sites; the only way you find this out is to test. On your own site, you will also need to test pricing.

Where Next?

BOOKS

- *eBay for Dummies*, Marsha Collier (For Dummies, 2002). ISBN: 0764516426.

- *eBay Hacks*, David A. Karp (O'Reilly & Associates, 2003). ISBN: 0596005644.

- *The New Basic Seller's Guide to eBay,* Skip McGrath, *www.auction-sellersnews.com.*

- *Starting an eBay Business for Dummies,* Marsha Collier (For Dummies, 2001). ISBN: 0764515470.

- *Sell it on eBay,* Jim Heid and Toby Malina (Peachpit Press, 2003). ISBN: 0321223764.

NEWLETTERS

- Auction Bytes, *www.Auctionbytes.com.*

- Auction Seller News, Vision-One Press, Inc., *www.auction-sellers-news.com.*

- Auction Resources, *http:auction-resources.com/newsletter/news11102003.*

WEB SITES

- *eBay* has scores of *Seller* and *PowerSeller* groups you can join.

From the Home Front

"I only see my business continuing to grow."   —Penny Stewart, fifty-nine

---

Snapshot: Tedde McMillen, On-Line Tea Shops

Tedde McMillen downsized into her fifty-plus home business. In 1994, her daughter Heather Howitt had a special recipe for the Indian beverage, chai, a sweet spicy tea latte. One day she came to her mother and said, "Mom, I think we could sell this stuff." Tedde was ready to help. Coffee and espresso were popular in the Northwest where they lived, so they could see a need for a hot beverage for the other half of the population who don't drink coffee.

Together mother and daughter started Oregon Chai®. Tedde handled the manufacturing; Heather did the sales and marketing. They went from brewing sixteen gallons of tea in a rented kitchen to twenty-thousand gallons a day at a large food-processing plant. Their little company grew so large that they had to hire scientists and engineers to oversee the operations Tedde once managed. "This left me with little to do," she remembers, but after working long, high-stress hours for five years, she was exhausted and ready to work less. Still, she wasn't ready to retire, so she looked around for where else she might fit within the company and found nothing that met her needs, until . . .

One day a customer who lived fifty miles from the nearest big town called to order their chai concentrate. Oregon Chai® had made a strategic decision not to sell direct, wanting instead to focus on marketing through large wholesalers, so, Tedde thought, "Ah ha! This is what I can do. I can sell Oregon Chai® products direct over the Internet to people who can't find it locally."

She dove into learning all she could about on-line sales and three years later has a new business: two thriving on-line tea shops, *www.teddestea.com* and *www.chaiaddict.com*. Her sales have grown 206 percent over the past year. By selling on line, she feels closer to her customers. That had been her greatest pleasure before Oregon Chai® grew so large.

"Life after fifty is good," she says. "I work from home, take my little dog walking every day, play with my grandchildren frequently, volunteer, and exercise."

 ## 51. Wedding Consultant and Planner

If you talk to wedding planners, you'll hear a lot of reasons why more and more couples are choosing to hire them:

- In a down economy, we help people save money; in an up economy, we help them spend more opulently.

- Since more and more couples today both work, they are simply too busy to plan their own weddings, and chances are the bride's mother is working, too.

- Couples want to distinguish themselves among their cohorts, and their wedding is their big chance to make a statement about how they can throw a party.

- The average age of a bride has climbed from twenty in 1982 to twenty-seven in 2002, and the length of the average engagement is now sixteen months. This means couples have more time to save money and plan for the wedding of their dreams.

The fact is, all these reasons are valid and the conclusion is wedding planning can be a profitable business for someone with the right skills and talent. There's plenty of potential business—so far only 1 in 8 of the 2.5 million weddings in the United States hire a wedding consultant. So there's a huge untapped market.

But what exactly do wedding planners do? The answer is nearly anything and everything the bride and groom want them to do. The range of services you can offer is endless.

Roughly a year or more prior to the wedding, the consultant's job usually begins with helping the couple select and reserve a location for their wedding. For many couples, the location is critical to establishing their wedding theme, whether it's at a dedicated wedding chapel, a hotel ballroom, or the increasingly desired "destination wedding" such as at a museum, a lighthouse, a theme park, or a wealthy local estate with a mansion or medieval castle for rent in a faraway country.

Once the location is established, the consultant usually spends months over numerous appointments, assisting the couple in planning and carrying out the specifics of their theme throughout the various elements of the celebration: the invitations, the bridesmaids' dresses and groomsmen's tuxes, the table settings and decorations, the music, the flowers, and the food. The consultant may advise on—or take charge of—helping the couple select their wedding invitations and write the copy; plan their rehearsal dinner; design the wedding cake; rent tents, tables, chairs, and linens; choose a photographer and/or a videotaping service; hire a makeup artist for the bride and other women in the wedding party; select a caterer; hire a DJ or band; reserve a limo service; register for wedding gifts; and even plan their dream honeymoon.

The consultant then helps the couple plan the schedule for the big day, sometimes in minute-by-minute increments. And on the big day itself, many couples want the consultant to be on location, acting as an "event producer" to ensure that the entire affair goes off without a hitch.

As the job description suggests, a successful wedding planner is more than just someone who enjoys giving parties. The profession takes considerable skill and expertise. This includes establishing excellent contacts among other related wedding businesses—venues, caterers, florists, photographers, DJs, and many other services—and negotiating good contracts with them. To succeed in this business, you should be detailed oriented yet creative so you can produce on-time perfect events with so much flair and style that the wedding seems as though it cost more than it did. You must be an expert in wedding etiquette, traditions, and scheduling, as well as diplomatic and good at calming nerves, soothing rumpled feathers, and keeping argumentative relatives from disrupting the joyous event. Finally, you must be a master at juggling your own schedule, as you can often end up with several weddings on the same weekend.

Norma Adelman of the Wedding Casa in San Diego likens the profession to handing a couple a magic wand and asking them, "What is your wish?" Adelman, who began this business at age fifty, confirms that the profession is a lot of "hard work," mentioning that she often gets up at 4:30 in the morning to prepare for an event. "You need to work hard to get business, but I adore it. It makes me feel as high as a kite. Such drama, I just love it. Most people are bored with weddings but they should be legendary, archival events that keep you excited." Adelman beams with pride when she says that one summer, she did eighty weddings, one of them being a nude one!

But, of course, you as your own boss can limit the number of weddings you take on to fit your financial and lifestyle preferences. If you choose you might do only eight, not eighty, weddings a year.

You can begin by organizing a wedding for a friend or relative for free to build your portfolio. Be sure to get pictures from the photographer and letters of recommendation from the bride. We pass along this advice a reader sent to us: "Be wary of courses or seminars that tell you that you can be certified after attending their one- or two-day seminars. A person cannot retain all of the knowledge that is crammed into a seminar like this plus very few, if any, reference materials are given." The Association of Bridal Consultants offers an internship/apprenticeship program for members that can help you learn this business.

Wedding Consulting and Planning at a Glance

 20% 80%

	Minimal	Moderate	More than most
Start-up cost	X		
Overhead	X	With employee	
Potential earnings			X
Computer skills required		X	
Scheduling pressures			X
Flexible hours		X	
Overall stress			X

Likely Transferable Skills, Background, Careers

Other than having planned your own wedding or having been a highly involved mother of a bride, there are several professional backgrounds that are helpful for entering this business, in particular teaching and nursing, because these occupations have taught you how to schedule events and manage people. According to Gerard and Eileen Monaghan, founders of the Association of Bridal Consultants, the profession is maturing, with some practitioners having degrees in business. However, we believe that having a detailed-oriented, sociable, positive personality can be sufficient to get into this business.

What to Charge

Wedding coordinators may charge a flat fee, a per-diem rate, or an hourly rate for their services. Flat fees may be from 10 to 15 percent of the wedding budget, which is now estimated at $22,000 to $27,000. Per-diem rates range from $300 to $1,200. Hourly rates range from $50 to $150. As expected, location influences pricing.

Wedding coordinators should not expect to derive commissions from referrals they make; this is frowned on professionally and discouraged legally. However, coordinators can increase their revenue by providing extra services such as renting tuxedos, printing invitations, and selling accessories like party gifts.

Best Ways to Get Business

- Calling on, networking with, and cross-referring to others providing wedding services: photographers, printers, florists, hotel and banquet-hall managers, bakeries, makeup artists, jewelers, caterers, travel agents, musicians, and disc jockeys. However, some wedding planners indicate that this does not work well for them.

- Joining and participating in professional, community, trade, and religious organizations in your community to make yourself known.

- Listing in the Yellow Pages, which will enable you to be found on Web directories like *switchboard.com* and *anywho.com*. Consider ads on local directory sites like *Yahoo Get Local* and *SuperPages*.

- Advertising in specialty wedding publications or guides and wedding supplements to local newspapers.

- Having a Web site linked to many wedding-related sites. The Web is especially important for wedding coordinators located in destination locations—vacation places where people like to get married.

- Using direct mail to recipients of wedding-planning guides and sending out newsletters to prospective and past clients.

- Offering free consultations for couples, advising them of what will be involved in planning their wedding. Use this time to establish a trusting relationship and to gather information for a written proposal you can submit to them after the meeting.

- Teaching adult education courses on how to plan a wedding.

- Getting repeat business by doing parties and other events such as anniversaries for your clients, their family, and their friends.

- Get listed in directories like *Modernbride.com* and *weddingchannel.com*.

Marketing Insights

- Be aware that the field is increasingly competitive, as thousands of people have joined the ranks of wedding planners. The Association of Bridal Consultants observes that most people take three years to establish their businesses and five to become profitable.

- A full-time wedding coordinator working alone can service forty weddings a year. You should expect June, August, September, and October to be your busiest months, with January your slowest. But be aware that your clients can save significant money by booking their wedding in a slow month.

- Find ways to think outside the box to "niche" your business with new wedding ideas, from having the bride and groom arrive by parachute to planning fireworks displays. Another specialty area are weddings that highlight and pay homage to the couple's ethnic background, particularly Latino.

- Wedding consulting is a glamour business, so you need to spend money on your own wardrobe, makeup, and hairstyling to project your own image to your clientele. You need three types of outfits: (1) business suits for meetings with suppliers; (2) more casual, yet attractive, clothing for meeting with the bride and bridal party in the process of planning the wedding; (3) more formal attire appropriate for attending the wedding.

- You can branch out to plan other types of events such as corporate meetings and bar mitzvahs, particularly in smaller communities, where there may not be enough weddings for a full-time business.

- Exhibiting at bridal shows is expensive but may produce business.

Where Next?

ASSOCIATIONS

- Association of Bridal Consultants—training, accreditation, and professional development programs: (860) 355-0464; *www.bridalassn.com*.

- June Wedding Inc. offers courses: (702) 474-9558; *www.junewedding.com*.

COURSES

- On-line courses: *www.elearners.com.*

- National Bridal Service: (804) 355-6945; *www.nationalbridalservice.com.*

- Weddingcareers: *weddingcareers.com.*

BOOKS

- *Bridal Bargains,* Denise Fields and Alan Fields (Windsor Peak Press, 2002). ISBN: 1889392138.

- *The Complete Outdoor Wedding Planner,* Sharon Naylor (Prima Lifestyles, 2001). ISBN: 0761535985.

- *Emily Post's Wedding Etiquette,* Peggy Post (HarperResource, 2001). ISBN: 0060198834.

- *Goble and Shea's Complete Wedding Planner,* Cecily Shea and Kathleen Goble (Multnomah Publishers). 1999. ISBN: 1576734811.

- *Planning a Wedding to Remember,* Beverly Clark (Wilshire Books, 2002). ISBN: 0934081239.

- *The Perfect Wedding Reception,* Maria McBride-Mellinger (HarperResource, 2000). ISBN: 0060192984.

- *The Ultimate Guide to Wedding Music,* Elizabeth Lluch and Alex Lluch (Wedding Solutions, book and CD, 2002). ISBN: 1887169237.

MAGAZINES

- *Bride's:* (212) 286-2860; *www.brides.com.*

- *Modern Bride:* (800) 777-5786; *www.modernbride.com.*

- *Weddingbells,* U.S. and Canadian editions: (800) 267-5450; *www.weddingbells.com.*

- *Vows:* (303) 776-3798; *www.vowsmag.com*—trade publication.

From the Home Front

"This is one business where wrinkles on your face enhance your salability. We have wisdom about behavior. There's so much pressure on a bride—I'm there to hold it together."   —Norma Adelman, seventy-two

Snapshot: Bev Osbourne, Formal and Evening Dress Rentals

Exasperation inspired fifty-three-year-old divorced fashion consultant Bev Osbourne to develop a novel business idea. A friend was always asking to borrow a designer dress Bev rarely wore herself. "I spent a fortune on that dress," she recalls jokingly, telling her friend, "and you wear it more than I do. I should start charging you $25 every time you borrow it." To Bev's amazement, her friend gladly offered to pay, and she began to wonder if other women might pay to borrow clothing for special occasions.

When Bev saw the prices on mother-of-the-bride dresses while shopping for an outfit to wear to her daughter's wedding, she was convinced, "There's got be to a better way. Men rent tuxes, why not women?" So, she launched Nothing to Wear in the basement rec room of her University Place, Washington, home, renting formals and evening dresses.

Despite skeptics who told her women wouldn't rent dresses, the idea caught on right away and the business grew rapidly. She started with thirty dresses, and during prom season she would have ten people sitting in her living room while others sat outside in their cars waiting to be helped. Ultimately she rented a 400-square-foot space in a nearby building and added wedding gown and tuxedo rentals. With so many well-attired brides and grooms coming into her shop, some also needed a place to get married, so, ever imaginative, Bev became a licensed minister and created a chapel right in the store where she performs wedding ceremonies. In fact she offers a discount on rentals for couples who get married in the chapel.

Bev currently carries 150 to 200 wedding gowns and 300 formals from petite to plus sizes, and says, "Remarriage and mother-of-the-bride dresses are our specialty now." Sixty-three and still upbeat about her business, she likes to encourage older women to stay active.

TURNING YOUR HOBBY INTO INCOME

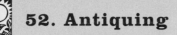

52. Antiquing

D o you delight in rediscovering something old or finding what people thought was nowhere to be found? Do you look at other people's castoffs in a fresh way? Discovering treasures in yard sales, junk shops, or someone's attic can be part of the thrill of antiquing; many people also savor the hunt, particularly on the road to discovering a bargain. As one dealer told us in sharing her feelings about finding a steal, "I love the kill." If you relish antiques and the thought of digging through flea market booths across the United States, Europe, and even Asia, you may very well enjoy a career in antiquing.

With only a simple "shopping cart" software program, some instructions on how to install it, and a little more than a month of eighteen-hour days, Elaine Kula started her on-line antique jewelry business at the age of sixty-five. She sells pieces from the mid 1800s to the 1950s—a stretch of time that she believes produced better-quality jewelry than in later eras. Elaine prefers the clean lines of Art Deco designs and says with the popularity of films like *Chicago* this style is making a comeback. For her, "Finding the good stuff is the real thrill."

While he was working full-time as a principal in a large company designing and furnishing commercial buildings, Peter Beecham began collecting and selling antiques in the Boston area. When he retired at age fifty-nine, he and his wife, Janet, opened Woodbine Antiques in Rockport on Cape Anne, Massachusetts. They wanted to fill a niche they saw was lacking in their region and have fun doing it at the same time. Now they travel to Europe twice a year looking for "unusual quality pieces."

Beecham finds people often now buy antiques as accents rather than to furnish their entire homes, but he also sees the influence on consumers of magazines like *Architectural Digest* that feature entire rooms filled with antiques. He finds his clients are more "interested in selecting one good-quality item than in getting a lot of mediocre pieces." Though the Beechams show their antiques in a store, Peter says, "We control the business; it does not control us" and thus does much of his work at home. He says if the zoning is right, antiques can be sold at home. There are several home-based antique businesses near him. As many as a third of antique dealers appear to be home based.

You can specialize in any one or several of hundreds of categories of antiques. Here are some examples:

Advertising

Architectural

Asian antiques

Bedding

Building and repair materials

Ceiling fans

China and glass

Clocks

Contemporary (1950–now)

Crafting, sewing, art supplies

Decorative arts

Ethnic, tribal jewelry

Fashion jewelry

Floors and windows

Furniture

Garden

Hardware and locks

Holiday, seasonal

Home decor

Housewares and kitchenware

Jewelry supplies

Kitchen, dining, and bar

Lamps, lighting

Lighters and smoking items

Lawn

Loose beads

Maps and atlases

Medical and surgical

Miniatures

Modern (1900–49)

Musical instruments

Necklaces, bracelets

Office furnishings and
    equipment

Pins and brooches

Political paraphernalia

Post-1900 antiques

Postcards and paper

Pottery

Pre-1900 antiques

Primitives

Prints

Rings

Rugs and carpets

Scientific items

Silver and silverware

Textiles, fabrics, and linens

Tools

Transportation

Vanity, perfume, and shaving

Vintage sewing

Watches

Writing instruments

The Internet has been a boon to the antique business. This is true especially for selling smaller items that represent well in a photograph. Elaine Kula, for example, sells antique jewelry. She honed her choice of "key words" so she would get high rankings on search engines, particularly *Google*. She doesn't sell her jewelry on *eBay* because she finds its bargain-hunting customers are not willing to pay the prices she can get on her own site (*www.antiquingonline.com*). Eighty percent of Elaine's business comes from repeat customers. Her secret: high-quality jewelry combined with extraordinary customer service. Her customers include two shops in Amsterdam and Singapore.

Web sites for antique collectors number in the hundreds, but *eBay.com* has emerged as the most popular. Selling via the Web has become so popular it has prompted some antiques dealers to close their stores and move all their business to cyberspace.

But Beecham finds selling his large furniture on the Internet problematic, though he does use *eBay* in the off-season. He prefers to maintain a showroom to provide customers with a hands-on experience with what they are buying. "Antiques are a touchy-feely product, and unless people know who they're dealing with they don't know who they can trust," he says. He gives an example of one snuffbox antiquarian who wanted to sell some of his collection. Beecham took it to an auction house and was told that he had nothing special, maybe $1,000 worth of merchandise. He was advised to put the collection on *eBay* with a $2,000 minimum. He decided to look around a bit more and ended up selling the collection to a New York City dealer for $9,000. Beecham observes, "Even the experts don't always know."

So you need to do your homework in this business not only to price what you sell, but also because consumers are savvy and are discouraged from buying even very good items if the dealer is not knowledgeable. Beecham recommends doing appraisals to educate yourself; others avoid doing appraising for others. You will need to know about quality, materials, and origins before buying something that you want to resell. Kula insists that if the quality is good and the style isn't too outrageous, you will always make money.

Antiquing at a Glance

40% 60%

	Minimal	Moderate	More than most
Start-up cost		X	
Overhead	X		
Potential earnings			X
Computer skills required		X	
Deadline pressures	X		
Flexible hours			X
Overall stress		X	

Likely Transferable Skills, Background, Careers

Being able to recognize quality is a must in this business, as is relating well to often demanding and finicky customers. Elaine Kula attributes her skill to an impoverished childhood that taught her to shop for the diamonds in the rough.

What to Charge

This is the art and the science of this business, but you can see what comparable items are selling for by following the bidding on Web sites like *eBay.* You also can learn what the big auction houses like Sotheby's and Christie's are asking by obtaining their catalogues, which are available from their Web sites.

Best Ways to Get Business

- Selling high-end antiques at antique shows; bargaining at flea markets.

- Selling on your own Web site. You will want to develop repeat customers.

- Selling via antique Web sites and *eBay*.

- Networking with interior designers and decorators who can use you as a source.

- Checking collectors' club newsletters and Web sites that list items members want.

Marketing Insights

- Many people prefer to buy over the Internet. Some of the things Elaine Kula does to serve her customers well include setting up private pages where they can preview merchandise before it's publicly offered, sending twice-monthly newsletters, and guaranteeing satisfaction.

- Collectibles sold on the Internet are typically below dealer prices. In fact, one study of silver coins found that buyers paid 78 percent less than dealer prices for comparable items. But because the Web opens the door to a world of customers a local seller would never see, many items are sold at higher prices than they could get locally.

- The more information you provide about what you're selling, the more apt you are to get favorable prices selling on the Web. When you demonstrate knowledge of what you are selling, people feel greater assurance they'll get what they hope they are paying for.

- The Web also offers an ability to obtain inventory. Because it's difficult for buyers to distinguish quality, sellers often have to accept lower prices for their higher-quality items. Sometimes, however, competitive bidding drives up the prices. Some of the prices people pay can only be accounted for by the shibboleth "One person's junk is another person's treasure."

- Look for inventory in places where there are large numbers of retirees, such as in Florida and Arizona. Be willing to bargain hard with thrift stores where pricing is increasingly inflated by what personnel have seen on *Antique Road Show* and so assume what they have is worth a higher price. But they don't take into account the buyer's cost and the expertise required to clean, polish, sometimes restore, and research the era, value, and history of an item for subsequent sale as an antique, and the skill needed to beautifully display it in their shop or on their site and add creative ideas as to how shoppers might use the item in their own homes.

Where Next?

BOOKS

- *Antiques on the Cheap* James W. McKenzie and Jim McKenzie (Storey Books, 1998). ISBN: 1580170730.

- *Antiques Roadshow Collectibles,* Carol Prisant (Workman, 2003). ISBN: 0761128220.

- *How to Start a Home-Based Antiques Business,* Jacquelyn Peake (Globe Pequot Press, 2000). ISBN: 076270814X.

- *Price It Yourself!,* Joe L. Rosson and Helaine Fendelman (HarperResource; 2003). ISBN: 0060096845.

CERTIFICATION

- If you wish to pursue becoming a certified appraiser, the American Society of Appraisers tests and accredits personal property appraisers in a number of antique specialty areas: (703) 478-2228; *www.appraisers.org.*

WEB SITES

- *www.collect.com—Antique Trader Weekly*'s Web site.

- *www.goantiques.com*—on-line mall with a relationship to *eBay* that enables uploading items from your inventory to *eBay.*

- *www.TIAS.com's* member sites include *www.antiquearts.com,* an on-line mall, and *www.curioscape.com* with links to thousands of antique sites; *www.kovels.com,* which offers a free pricing guide; and *www.asheford.com,* which offers a home-study course.

53. Aromatherapy

A scent revolution has swept the self-care industry and made its way into the home via candles, skin products, cleaning solutions, room fresheners, and fragrant paint. Although *aromatherapy* is a word major manufacturers often use to describe any product with a pleasant scent, it is actually much more. In the strictest sense aromatherapy is an "art," the art of expertly using concentrated essential oils to produce beneficial effects on health and well-being in both the home and the workplace.

Essential oils are made from flowers, leaves, twigs, or bark in a highly concentrated form so they can be inhaled or absorbed through the skin. They're also used to make compresses, burned in diffusers, and added to bathwater. According to Christine Malcomb, a veteran aromatherapist and master perfumer, aromatherapy can be pursued as a business in a variety of ways. You can work one-on-one with individual clients who can afford to pay enough to cover both your time and your essential oils, which are expensive. One aromatherapist, holistic healer in Malibu, California, for example, uses reflexology, the practice of determining ailments in the body by applying pressure to the feet and hands, to decide which essential oils will best benefit an individual client. This kind of practice is largely unlicensed and relies on the reputation of the individual practitioner for success. Or you can work in conjunction with other professionals because aromatherapy complements other practices such as reflexology, chiropractic, and massage. Health practitioners like to augment their treatments with aromatherapy because essential oils can be used to treat a variety of problems including depression, inflammation, lack of energy, issues associated with menopause, and severe back pain.

You can also produce fragrances for retail and wholesale distribution. Helen Stembridge started her aromatherapy business at fifty-five when she saw herself following in her mother's footsteps to ill health. She used specialized blends of essential oils to treat her own poor health. "I started by saving my own life," says Stembridge in a relaxed voice. She now makes customized aromatherapy blends that she sells through specialty shops and on *eBay*. She also conducts seminars at herb shops and exhibits where massage therapy examinations are being given. There she introduces new practitioners to essential oils with the intention that they use them in doing massage therapy. Some of these contacts become long-term clients.

At the age of fifty, Pam Quick began to import a line of organic oils manufactured by hand in Germany. A former sales rep, Quick now distributes oils to professionals who use them in their practices, as well as to some health-food stores. She and her daughter work together, importing 270 different wild-crafted oils which are 70 to 100 percent more potent than the original plant material. Her Web site is *www.aromatherapist.com*.

Using aromatherapy to treat animals is an area with growing potential. Aromatherapy is currently being used with much success in the Denver zoo to treat gorillas and orangutans for anxiety and depression. Frances Fitzgerald Cleveland, an aromatherapist in Littleton, Colorado, specializes in treating pets. She uses essential oils for everything from fleas and itching to arthritis and car sickness.

If you plan to produce aromatherapy products for retail or wholesale distribution, you need to be aware of the Food and Drug Administration requirements for marketing and labeling cosmetic products.

Aromatherapy at a Glance

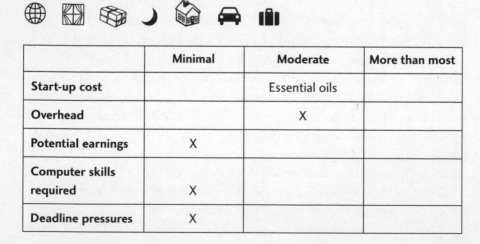

	Minimal	Moderate	More than most
Start-up cost		Essential oils	
Overhead		X	
Potential earnings	X		
Computer skills required	X		
Deadline pressures	X		

	Minimal	Moderate	More than most
Flexible hours			X
Overall stress	X		

Likely Transferable Skills, Background, Careers

Aromatherapists often come from other health-related fields such as massage therapy, chiropractic, psychotherapy, and nursing. Aestheticians and salon or spa professionals also use aromatherapy with their clients.

What to Charge

Hourly rates for individual sessions vary between $70 to $90 for holistic healing catering to a high-income clientele. Making personalized blends ranges from $50 to $130 per bottle, depending on the cost of the oils used.

Best Ways to Get Business

- Advertising in local publications, particularly if you live in or near a health hot spot like Ashville, North Carolina.

- Developing a community of colleagues such as massage therapists, psychotherapists, chiropractors, and reflexologists to refer clients to one another or develop common treatment programs.

- Getting listed in on-line directories such as that of the National Association for Holistic Aromatherapy.

- Selling products on the Internet or your own Web site, through *eBay* and other sites. Develop links with complementary sites.

- Working with salons, spas, and natural-product retail stores to develop referral sources.

Marketing Insights

- People with allergies who normally can't wear perfumes can often wear a fragrance of pure oils. Chances are the product your customer would buy in a department store was synthesized by a

New Jersey chemical plant, according to Christine Malcomb. You create a pure natural substance as well as a unique experience for your customers.

- A pleasing scent and an aesthetic appearance hold the greatest appeal to the two out of every five households who spend discretionary income on fragrances.

Where Next?

ASSOCIATIONS

- The Fragrance Foundation. The site has a page describing the categories of women's and men's fragrances: *www.fragrance.org*.

- National Association for Holistic Aromatherapy: (888) ASK-NAHA, (206) 547-2164; *www.naha.org*. Publishes the *Scentsitivity Quarterly Journal*.

- British associations: The International Federation of Professional Aromatherapists (IFPA), *www.ifparoma.org*, offers extensive links to related sites. Also International Federation of Aromatherapists: *www.ifaroma.org*.

- Handmade Beauty Network. Liability insurance is available to members. (301) 464-4515; *www.handmadebeauty.com*.

BOOKS

- *Becoming an Aromatherapist*, Rhiannon Harris (How to Books, 2001). ISBN: 1857036824.

- *The Complete Book of Essential Oils and Aromatherapy*, Valery Ann Worwood (New World Library; 1991). ISBN: 0931432820.

- *Herbs for Pets*, Mary L. Wulff-Tilford and Gregory L. Tilford (Bowtie Press, 1999). ISBN: 1889540463.

- *Holistic Aromatherapy for Animals*, Kristen Leigh Bell (Lantern Books, 2002). ISBN: 1899171592.

- *Hydrosols: The Next Aromatherapy*, Suzanne Catty (Inner Traditions International, 2001). ISBN: 0892819464.

- *The World of Aromatherapy,* Jeanne Rose, ed. (Frog Ltd., 1996). ISBN: 1883319498. Rose is also the author of 375 *Essential Oils and Hydrosols* (1999), ISBN: 1883319897.

CERTIFICATION

- Aromatherapy Registration Council: (212) 356-0660; *www.aromatherapycouncil.org.*

FDA HANDBOOKS

- *Cosmetic Handbook*—The Food and Drug Administration's handbook summarizing the regulatory requirements for marketing cosmetics in the United States. Available in electronic form at the FDA Web site: *www.fda.gov.*

- *Cosmetic Labeling Manual*—The Food and Drug Administration's handbook summarizing labeling of cosmetics to be marketed in the United States. Available in electronic form at the FDA Web site: *www.fda.gov.*

TRAINING

Using the search phrase "Aromatherapy training," you will find dozens of schools, home-study, and on-line courses. As for any program or business opportunity, we advise you to check references and for instances of consumer complaints at *www.bbb.org.*

From the Home Front

"As an aromatherapist, you spend the entire day handling the most exquisite products in the world. Smell is the most powerful of all senses—the only one that can induce a three-dimensional emotional response."

—Suzanne Catty

Snapshot: Sharon Cox, Herbal Skin Therapies

Sharon Cox of Selah, Washington, had been interested in the healing power of herbs and had been growing organic herbs for over twenty-five years. She'd grown 150 different herbs in her garden and created many poultices, teas, and compresses for family and friends. But this was her passion, not a business. Success, however, would convince her otherwise.

One day coming in from the garden, her inner voice nudged her to make a healing salve from her herbs. That was something Sharon had never done before, but wanting to listen to her "wisdom within," she began collecting herbs she thought might be appropriate. Soon, a very specific recipe came to mind, including every ingredient for a precise formula. "But I don't do recipes!" she thought. Nonetheless, she wrote down the specifics and told a friend about it.

A couple of days later the friend asked Sharon to send some of her new healing salve to a person suffering with an outset radiation rash from cancer treatments. The friend thought the salve might help relieve some of the discomfort and itch. So Sharon made up some salve and shipped it off, urging the patient to take the salve and the formula to her doctor and follow his advice. The doctor said there was nothing harmful in the salve, so to give it a try. Within a few days, the rash disappeared, never to return.

After this glowing success, Sharon created more of her healing herb formula and began giving it away to friends. E-mails, phone calls, and letters began pouring in with reports of positive results for many ailments, like long-term acne, shingles pain, closing diabetic ulcers, burns, itching, rashes, bites, and dry skin.

Continued positive reactions led to frequent suggestions that Sharon start a business, but she was hesitant. She didn't think of herself as a business person, and she feared running a fifty-plus business wouldn't leave time for the things she most enjoyed like taking walks with her husband and playing with their dogs. But, she explains, "I wanted to help more people and be of service if I could." So Azhdarian's Herbal Therapies was born.

Azhdarian's Herbal Therapies now offers a line of healing chemical-free herbal products for soothing muscles, reducing stress and anxiety, and relieving pain and inflammation. And Sharon still has time for walking with her husband and playing with their dogs!

54. Astrologer

Astrology dates back thousands of years to ancient civilizations, probably to about the time humans observed that the moon causes the tides and the sun causes the seasons. Ancient Greek and Chinese sages studied the stars and planets, and decided to correlate their alignment and position in the skies with predictions about the events in people's lives and their fates. The art or science they created is based on interpreting the relationship and position of celestial bodies in the twelve zodiacs to the day a person was born and where those planets and stars are now. Some people who accept astrology believe that personalities and fates are predestined by the cosmos, and that astrological readings help them understand what the heavens have destined for our lives; others believe the cosmos influences our lives and that readings can help us to put those influences to good advantage.

People from all walks of life consult astrologers to get advice on their personal, marital, financial, and business issues. To paraphrase one astrology Web site:

> Astrology reveals your cosmic blueprint, divine intent and cosmic gifts for fulfilling your part in the cosmic plan. Astrology is one of three major factors (cosmic, genetic and environmental) that determine who you ultimately turn out to be. Any one of these can have a dominating influence over our life, so it is very important to know the dominating astrological influences in your life, body, business and world view.

Preparing a person's astrological chart is complicated and until recently time-consuming, in that it requires research and many calculations regarding the position of different stars and planets. The adoption of computers has completely changed how astrologers work because software has been developed that greatly facilitates the mathematical calculations, reducing the time it takes to produce a high-quality forecast from hours to minutes.

The field of astrology is filled with two types of people: those who stick to reporting what the chart reveals and those who take a more interpersonal approach, rendering their readings taking into account their subjective impressions of their clients.

Dell Norwood, for instance, is an astrologer who focuses on natal astrology and two other branches: horary (meaning *of the hour*) and ephemeris (meaning *of the earth*). In each of these cases, she uses different types of charts to perform readings that assess the compatibility between two people or the birth of an idea.

In contrast, Robert Corre works closely with his clients and tries to learn more about who they are and what their goals are. In his mind, astrology is an art, not a science. Much of what he forecasts, he says, lies not only in the chart he prepares but also in the relationship he establishes with his clients. He learns to read his clients using his senses. As he says, "I am good at conjecture, making an educated guess—deducing and speculating what my clients need to know."

Getting started in astrology as a career begins by taking courses at local colleges or hiring a tutor to teach you, as Robert Corre did. There are also various on-line at-home study programs.

Once you have learned the craft, it can take a considerable time to build up a large-enough clientele to make a reasonable full-time income in this business. It took Robert Corre seven years to build up his practice. He points out that now that he's established a reputation, he has access to a steady pool of clientele because he lives in the New York City area.

The range of potential clients you can seek encompasses most areas of human concern. Corre says that most of his clients are women who have similar questions about relationship issues. But all kinds of people consult astrologers for business and personal decisions, such as changing jobs, getting married, moving, making investments, and so on. Parents of newborns want to have their babies' charts done to help them understand their children's personalities and guide them in rearing their children. And you have undoubtedly heard that many entertainment celebrities, politicians, and famous businesspeople consult astrologers in making important career decisions, financial investments, or even for political advice. Some businesses use astrologers to assess the compatibility of new hires with their current employees, for strategic planning, new-product evaluations, team building, and one-on-one management counseling.

Astrology at a Glance

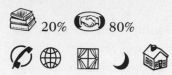 20% 🤝 80%

	Minimal	Moderate	More than most
Start-up cost	X		
Overhead	X		
Potential earnings	X		
Computer skills required	X		
Deadline pressures	X		
Flexible hours			X
Overall stress	X		

Likely Transferable Skills, Background, Careers

Given computerization and software for making charts, astrology is open those with a passion for studying the stars and helping people understand their relationship to their lives.

What to Charge

Initial consultations, usually sixty to ninety minutes, with a comprehensive astrological chart range from $80 to $150, though some "star" astrologers get fees in the thousands. To a great extent, what you charge expresses your confidence in your ability and credentials. It's also common for astrologers to work with clients on the phone by the half hour for $30 to $50. If you attract clients from all over the country for your telephone practice, you may vary your rate according to the cost of living where the caller lives. Charts sold as stand-alone products go from $15 to $75, depending on whether they're natal, compatibility, or forecasting reports.

Best Ways to Get Business

- Networking in community organizations. While you will encounter skeptics, in virtually any gathering of people, chances are that better than one out of every four people believes in astrology, so there usually will be one or more people interested in what you do.

- Giving free readings to begin developing a word-of-mouth business because most clients come through word-of-mouth referrals.

- Giving away free charts can result in their being shown to other people, who decide they want their own charts or wish the greater detail and integration that comes with a personal consultation. So prominently display your name and contact information on charts you create.

- Speaking and teaching classes on topics that attract interest, such as on the charts of celebrities and famous personalities and your interpretation of the news.

- Advertising in local "New Age" publications. Also writing articles or a regular column for such a publication.

- Affiliating with a New Age bookstore that contracts with you to do readings for clients.

- Having a Web site indicating your specialty, experience, and testimonials.

- Offering a discount package, such as two-for-one specials or once-a-month clubs in order to bring clients in and keep them coming back. In addition, you can do group, organization, or family charts and, using a notebook computer and portable printer, do charts at parties and other events.

Marketing Insights

- You can choose a specialization others have forged, such as financial, medical, psychological, relationship, predictive, sun sign, Vedic, and karmic astrology, or you can define one of your own. Some astrologers have found more specialized niches such as horse-racing or stock-market timing, sometimes based on their prior career or industry.

- People are most apt to be interested in a chart at turning points in their lives like birthdays, weddings, and births, or when facing a crisis or ethical quandary. When the economy is down, for example, people are interested in advice on money and jobs.

- Investing in software that allows you to compile a star chart and a forecast in an impressive way along with a color plotter or printer will enhance the perception of your value.

- Resorts and cruise ships are worth pursuing as many are now offering astrology classes and readings for their guests.

Where Next?

ORGANIZATIONS

- American Federation of Astrologers, Inc.: (888) 301-7630 , (480) 838-1751; *www.astrologers.com.*

- International Society for Astrological Research (ISAR): *www.isarastrology.com.*

- Organization for Professional Astrologers provides an e-newsletter and the Career Astrologer, a quarterly forum: *www.professional-astrology.org.*

BOOKS

- *A Handbook for the Self-Employed Astrologer,* Robert P. Blaschke (Earthwalk School of Astrology, 2002). ISBN: 096689782X.

- *The Astrologer's Handbook,* Frances Sakoian (HarperResource, 2005). ISBN: 006272004X.

- *The Creative Astrologer: Effective Single-Session Counseling,* Noel Tyl (Llewellyn Publications, 2000). ISBN: 1567187404.

- *How to Start, Maintain, and Expand an Astrological Practice,* (L.A.B. Professional Publishing, 2001). ISBN: 0970069626. Available from the Organization for Professional Astrologers.

SOFTWARE

Dozens of companies produce astrology software. You can also can get free charts made on a number of Web sites. Astrolabe, which has been producing software since 1979, offers free charts on its site and also links to other sites with free charts: (800) 843-6682; *www.alabe.com.*

TRAINING

Training in astrology can be obtained from a mentor or in scores of schools and on-line courses, such as those offered by:

- Robert Corre, interviewed for this profile, offers an on-line study program, *www.forumonastrology.com.*

- Kepler College of Astrological Arts & Sciences: (425) 673-4292; *www.kepler.edu.*

From the Home Front

"Each horoscope is fascinating and many people say they've gotten more insight into themselves than by going to therapy. It's gratifying because you meet so many people and what I do is looking for a person's highest potentials. It takes work to understand ourselves. A horoscope shows this readily; with no judgment, it helps a person to understand who they are."

—Dell Norwood, sixty-four

---

55. Basket Making and Chair Caning

If you like working with your hands and enjoy looking upon your finished work with pride, basket making or chair caning could be a satisfying career for you. An interesting history and the opportunity to reclaim lost skills gives special life to this type of work.

The many traditions of caning and weaving include making furniture and chairs, as well as beaded, painted, or woven baskets. The skills for making baskets and caning chairs are similar and while some people do both, many specialize in just one, building a reputation for their work through unique or specialized designs like Joe Conroy's Nantucket Lightship baskets.

Basket making is an old skill that's enjoying renewed interest. Joe Conroy, sixty-four, began making traditional Nantucket Lightship baskets when he retired from his job at the age of fifty as a serviceman for NCR. "This is very precise work," he says. "Some people find it difficult, but I enjoy doing it and enjoy showing other people how to do it too." Joe teaches workshops from his studio as well as making his baskets.

Regina Kastler of Seattle began making baskets after injuries from three car accidents left her unable to pursue her first love, weaving cloth on a loom. Kastler's creativity led her to incorporating bits of leather given to her by a friend into some of her basket designs. This gave them a southwestern look. She has also copyrighted a hand-painted sports-motif design. This type of specialization is a way of rising above the low-cost baskets sold through discounters. Kastler sells as many as fifty-five of her baskets a week.

Working with unusual materials is a plus. Pine needles, antlers, peculiar kinds of tree branches, and other nontraditional basket materials like wire or plastic make for exceptional creations that can distinguish your work from that of others.

Antique wicker furniture restoration is another specialty. Cathryn Peters of Wickerwoman in Minnesota specializes in repairing Victorian-era furniture, but she will work with pieces made as late as the 1940s. She forgoes fixing more recent wicker as she doesn't find the craftsmanship or the materials to be of a quality worth restoring; she recommends buying new wicker instead.

Ben Scott, a retired Episcopal priest, had long been interested in early-nineteenth-century history and wanted to pursue chair caning for several years before he retired. He received a grant to get some training and now works with a variety of materials including fiber rushing and natural cattail rushing. Ben has a friend who goes to auctions and when chairs on the block don't sell, he offers the auction house a dollar for each chair. Ben and his friend then restore these chairs by regluing, recaning, and refinishing them. They are then able to sell them at a small profit.

The materials for caning and basket making are not expensive, and the turnaround time can be relatively good. Cane, plastic, or other interesting materials can be used to weave new seats and backs in fine-looking old chairs. Tools required simply include a sharp pair of scissors and the cane.

The materials you need are available from craft stores or supply houses, but excellent materials also can be found growing wild in most areas of the country. Nearly any vine can be used to make a basket and most farmers or property owners are happy, when asked, to have someone help them clear rampant honeysuckle or wild grape from their lands.

Teaching the skills you acquire is a good way to augment your income. Conducting seminars at your own studio or preparing a curriculum for an adult-education program are two ways to offer your services as a teacher.

Chair Caning and Basket Weaving at a Glance

 80% 20%

	Minimal	Moderate	More than most
Start-up cost	X		
Overhead	X		
Potential earnings	X		
Computer skills required	X		
Deadline pressures	X		
Flexible hours			X
Overall stress	X		

Likely Transferable Skills, Background, Careers

The keys for a basket-making and caning business are simply an interest in the craft and the patience to master and perform the detailed work required.

What to Charge

Charges are directly related to the type of materials, the look of the chair or basket, and your own skill level. Figuring your time at between $25 and $65 per hour plus materials' costs is a formula many use, but depending on your specialty and location, you may find your earnings work out to be much less than that. Seat weaving is priced by the hole and varies between $1 and $2 per hole. Repairing the typical chair seat takes six to eight hours.

Best Ways to Get Business

- Entering your best work in craft competitions at juried shows puts your work in the spotlight. Winning a prize provides publicity opportunities and credibility for your work.

- Exhibiting at craft shows results in sales and special orders, and attracts students for courses, should you choose to teach.

- Lecturing and conducting demonstrations based on your specialty for historical and antique groups as well as other local clubs and small business organizations. Telling amusing or colorful stories about your work will spice up your talk and make it memorable.

- Mounting a magnetic sign or decal on your vehicle showing a graphic and your phone number and/or Web site.

- Showing samples of your work, either on your own Web site or on others' sites, like the National Basketry Organization's Gallery of Baskets.

Marketing Insights

- At craft fairs, instead of just exhibiting, do demonstrations of your weaving in your booth. People will stop, watch, and ask you questions, which gives you an opportunity to tell about your work.

- Be careful about spending money on print ads, but some basket makers have found ads in craft magazines like *Craft Report* (*www.craftsreport.com*), *Sunshine Artists* (*www.sunshineartist. com*), and *Shuttle Spindle & Dyepot*, the journal of the Handweavers Guild of America (*www.weavespindye.org*), to be productive.

- Baskets can be decorative or functional art, usable as log or laundry baskets.

- You can develop a specialty by learning and employing largely lost arts, like rosemaling (a flowery Norwegian painting technique), making New England clam baskets or employing Native American beading.

- Gift-basket businesses need baskets and unusual containers, so you may be able to sell wholesale to one or more gift basket makers, developing a regular outlet for your work. If you produce specialty baskets, such as ones with ethnic or topical appeal, you can target gift-basket makers who cater to people with these interests.

Where Next?

ASSOCIATION

- The National Basketry Organization, Inc.: (770) 641-9208; *www.nationalbasketry.org*. You can learn about basket conventions and regional associations and participate in a forum where you can network with others. The site also provides useful links to resources.

BOOKS

- *The Caner's Handbook,* Bruce Miller and Jim Widess (Sterling Publishing,1992). ISBN: 0937274607.

- *Cane, Rush and Willow: Weaving With Natural Materials,* Hilary Burns and Hilary Burnham (Firefly Books; 2003). ISBN: 1552092607.

- *Making Chair Seats from Cane, Rush and Other Natural Materials,* Ruth B. Comstock (Dover Publications, 1989). ISBN: 0486256936.

- *The Craft of Chair Seat Weaving: With Cane, Rush, Splint, and Rope,* George Sterns (Interweave Press, 1991). ISBN: 0934026564.

TRAINING

- Apprentice with someone established who is interested in passing on the craft.

- Community-education and adult-education courses sometimes offer basket-weaving training.

- The Northeast Basketmakers Guild offers retreats with guest teachers, weaving days in their shop, which are not training sessions but opportunities to learn from what other weavers are doing.

- Books and videos.

WEB SITES

- *www.basketmakers.com*: comprehensive informational site for basket makers, basket artists, materials vendors, and others interested in this art.

- *www.caning.com,* the site for the Caning Shop, has one of the largest selections of basketry-related books (especially hard-to-find ones), as well as supplies for basket making, chair caning, and gourd crafting. The owner, Jim Wildess, is the co-author of several caning-related books, an NBO member vendor (800) 544-3373.

- *www.countryseat.com*: links to local guilds and helpful "FAQs."

From the Home Front

Joe Conroy remembers his high-school athlete friends joking about "Basket Weaving 101," as an alternative to algebra. Now Joe believes the joke would be on them as basket weaving is "a heck of a lot more difficult" than people think.

Snapshot: Jeanne and Tony Degatano, The Cape May Teddy Bear Co.®

For Jeanne and Tony Degatano the magical age of fifty brought on a midlife crisis! But they didn't resolve their life crisis in any of the typical ways. No sports cars. No affairs. Instead, having recently built a new home in the historic Victorian style in Cape May, New Jersey, as their "retirement" home, they wanted to open some kind of retail shop in their home featuring something from their own interests that would be fun, interesting, and unique.

Having been teddy bear collectors for a number of years and knowing the smile a teddy bear brings to the faces of children and adults of all ages, and the timeless nature of these cherished cuddly friends, they created the Cape May Teddy Bear Co.®

Jeanne and Tony carry all types of teddy bears from everyday bears from major manufacturers to fabulous collectible bears. But they also wanted to offer a teddy bear that was unique to them. So they designed their own line of bears. "We wanted a huggable bear with classic features," Jeanne explains, so they opted for heirloom soft plush bears in honey or chocolate brown with oversized paws, an extra-long snout, and five-way joints.

Jeanne felt that these stylish bears would not be complete without a sartorial complement, so she has designed hundreds of outfits for their bears from the traditional sweater with ribbon to sports outfits, uniforms from various careers, elegant Victorian wear, holiday attire, and more.

For the serious collector, the Degatanos also personalize their trademarked bear. Specialty bear requests have included a Las Vegas Showgirl, Tinkerbell, Snow White, Dorothy, and even a chicken. They've also reproduced wedding gowns and finery for birthdays and special holiday occasions. Limited-edition bears come with a signed and numbered certificate called a "Bear'er Bond."

Jeanne and Tony knew it can take three years to get a new business under way so, not wanting to be undercapitalized and risk failing, they kept their "day jobs" and hired key people to manage their store. "We thrive on the challenge of designing these one-of-a-kind bears!" Jeanne declares.

56. Cake Baking and Decorating

If you've enjoyed making and decorating cakes for your children's birthdays or other special events, making beautiful confections could be a great way to express yourself creatively and make a nice living. Cakes are used as centerpieces for many kinds of celebrations and parties—birthdays and weddings, quinceañera and bar mitzvah celebrations, christenings, anniversaries, plus retirement, bon voyage, and moving parties. And people are willing to pay to have a memorable one.

Glenda Chavez of Wichita Falls, Texas, spent her career in banking and real estate before becoming a "sugar artist." "It happened quite by accident," she recalls. Her niece was getting married and couldn't find a wedding cake she liked that she could afford. Glenda was drafted to make the cake and her business grew from there, mostly from referrals. Now she is booked up to two years in advance and charges $1,000 or more for some of her cakes.

As Glenda found, this business is simple to start. Once you set up and outfit your kitchen with the equipment you need to bake, you can start with one recipe and expand from there as desire and need compel you. You may make cakes for many types of occasions or you may specialize in cakes for particular events like weddings.

Before starting this business, however, you will need to check with your local health department. State laws regulating what you are permitted to do commercially in a home kitchen vary from state to state. Earlene Moore, a prize-winning cake decorator and practical decorating teacher from Lubbock, Texas, points out, "Some states are very lenient with small home-baking businesses, only requiring you to get legal when your gross sales exceed a specified dollar amount."

In some areas, getting legal may mean doing as Susan Schatz of Tulsa, Oklahoma did when she built an addition onto her house for a state-approved commercial kitchen. But it was worth it, she told us. By baking cakes at home, she could use her creative skills without having to go out at night as she would in a catering business. But having a commercial kitchen in a residence may conflict with the zoning requirements in your area. Most cities have zoning ordinances that limit or prohibit operation of this type of business without a special variance or conditional-use permit. So check with both your health department and local zoning board or department.

If licensing or zoning prevents you from using your home kitchen, you do have alternatives. For example, you may be able to rent a commercial kitchen in its off-hours, such as in a church, fire station, 4-H camp, or state park. Some states offer start-up food businesses the use of incubator kitchens.

Legalities aside, this is a highly creative profession. You can draw inspiration from photos of wedding cakes in bridal and wedding magazines. Your options range from simple and elegant to traditionally opulent, taking care to adjust your style to the desire and budget of your customers. Or you can develop a unique style of your own and make a name for yourself as a culinary artist.

There's also a physically demanding side to this business. Large batter-laden bowls can be heavy. Blending and pouring take stamina. Cakes need to be loaded and unloaded carefully, and some may even require ladders for assembly. The effort to make and put together an exquisite cake requires using hands, back, knees, and legs. As Earlene Moore says, "I have muscles some men would envy." Most bakers do the final assembly of the cake at the site of the event, which means you need to have a vehicle that will accommodate delivery with room to carry any tools you might need at the site. In delivering and assembling your cakes, you may also need the help of an assistant. Spouses are often drafted to play this role.

Cake Decorating at a Glance

50% 50%

	Minimal	Moderate	More than most
Start-up cost	X		
Overhead	X		
Potential earnings		X	
Computer skills required	X		
Deadline pressures			X
Flexible hours		X	
Overall stress		X	

Likely Transferable Skills, Background, Careers

Cake decorators come from every field. *American Cake Decorating Magazine* found that 29 percent of its readership is over fifty. What they share is artistic skill and, because cakes are used for special occasions, the enjoyment of making people happy.

What to Charge

Prices for cakes are generally based on the number of people at the event. They vary by location. Three dollars per person represents a basic price, but in New York City, it is not unheard of to charge $25 per serving. Be sure to not charge less than local bakeries. Undercutting local merchants is a "good way to get yourself turned in" to the health department, says Earlene Moore. Charge at least what they do, but usually more.

Best Ways to Get Business

- Developing referral relationships with florists, caterers, photographers, and salons that specialize in weddings and other events.

- Donating cakes to charities as samples. If the cakes are seen and people like them, they will come to you with future orders.

- Making your cake look as wonderful as the customer imagines, or even more so. Rave reviews and satisfaction are the key to getting word of mouth working for you.

- Obtaining publicity, particularly when your cakes are shown.

- Showing off your cakes on a Web site. Check out Earlene Moore's site at *www.earlenescakes.com* and notice, she doesn't ship cakes.

Marketing Insights

- Make your cakes taste good as well as look great. Referrals won't come your way if people leave their cake on their plates.

- Polish your communication skills so you can work well with emotionally stressed brides and mothers, wedding planners, and sometimes grooms. You need to help them avoid mistakes like choosing cake colors that don't photograph well or choosing a style of cake with a dated look that will generate disapproving comments on the big day. Positive or negative, the comments of the day will be associated with you.

- Grooms' cakes, a tradition in the South, are gaining nationwide popularity. They're often made of chocolate and decorated to reflect the interest or personality of the groom.

- Cake decorating as a home-based business is growing because of the demise of mom-and-pop bakeries. People who want a cake that's more distinctive than what they can buy at a supermarket or the Wal-Mart bakery turn to independent bakers.

- If you're considering making another form of dessert, and perhaps even for cakes, something that can help you establish your name is selling small portions at flea markets and construction sites at lunchtime. Be sure to include your business card or brochure with every slice or piece.

Where Next?

ASSOCIATIONS

- International Cake Exploration Société (ICES): *www.ices.org*.

BOOKS

- *From Kitchen to Market,* Stephen F. Hall (Upstart Press, 2000). ISBN: 1574101382.

- *How to Create a Profitable Cake Decorating Business "From Scratch,"* Stacy Robinson, an ebook, *www.bizymoms.com*

MAGAZINES

- *American Cake Decorating Magazine:* (800) 869-6882; (651) 293-1544; *www.cakemag.com*.

- *Cake Craft and Decoration Magazine*—the U.K. cake magazine:. *www.cake-craft.com*.

From the Home Front

"This is not something I have to do; it's something I want to do. It's fun. I use my artistic ability. It's one of those things I used to say about painting. I'll do that sometime. One of these days I'll get to that."

—Glenda Chavez, fifty-six

Snapshot: Perry A~, Dessert

Perry A~ began her unusual fifty-plus career as Perry Arledge, a southern-raised, well-pampered, lady of luxury whose life took a sudden left turn and landed in dusty West Texas, seventy miles from the nearest McDonald's. The town was Seymour, Texas, and her new role was wife of a cattle rancher. At fifty, her life path began zigzagging again. Newly divorced, she was faced with looking for her very first job in a small town.

"Although I had a college degree, I never really planned to work for a living," she recalls. "I had to resign from my bridge club and my social activities and take care of myself." She applied for what she thought was a secretarial position with the Department of Corrections and found herself wearing a badge and carrying a gun as an adult probation officer.

Her duties included teaching DWI classes to people who didn't want to hear what she had to say, so she used Cajun stories about drunks to take the preaching out of her teaching. Two and half years later she lost that job, but she had discovered that she could motivate people to change their attitudes and she wanted to motivate and inspire others as a professional speaker.

Moving to Wichita Falls, Perry took a job in sales with a major hotel, where she had the opportunity to work with meeting planners and hotel staff. They encouraged her to speak to the local civic clubs. She began by using her Cajun humor to talk about what she called "Obstatunities," chances to turn obstacles into opportunities. A few years later she came upon a novel idea that has become her signature ever since: People are as transparent as their choice of a favorite dessert.

She translated this unique philosophy into a winning keynote speech, "People Are Just Desserts" and has since written a book by the same name. Explaining how everyone in our lives brings a sweet reward, Perry began showing listeners and readers alike how to enjoy the fat-free, zero-calorie, totally delectable benefits of seeing yourself and everyone around you as a scrumptious treat.

Since her name was difficult for people to pronounce, she shortened it to Perry A~ and bills herself as the world's only dessert analyst. Now remarried and living in Austin, with husband, David Smith, Perry is a seasoned master storyteller and humorist. She has spent the past fifteen years taking her audiences on an emotional roller coaster that leaves them refreshed and eager to accept life's challenges. Corporate and organizational meeting planners pay her $8,500 or more for a ninety-minute keynote speech and up to $20,000 for a daylong workshop.

"I learned what I needed one step at a time," says Perry. "My advice to women over 50 is if you don't know you can't, you can. Help is available all along the way. Doors will open when you are ready. Do something you love, be passionate about it and it will happen."

57. Calligraphy

While scribes are no longer highly revered as they were once upon a time, there remains a market for the beauty of variable writing, known as calligraphy. Computers, of course, have taken over the way most documents are created today, cutting into the demand for calligraphers. "But the computer is too rigidly invariable to compete with the individuality of italic handwriting for certain special uses such as on invitations, resolutions, proclamations, quotations, place cards and place mats, poetry, name tags, and special-event announcements," says self-taught calligrapher Bill Bostick.

During World War II, Bostick was in charge of the cartographic unit that made the chart maps of Omaha Beach and Utah Beach for the invasion of Normandy. When he returned from the war, he worked in the commercial printing industry until, at the age of fifty, Bostick established La Stampa Calligrafica, his own calligraphic press. As a working calligrapher for forty years, he has taught and taken all manner of calligraphy commissions, including being called on to letter what will become historic documents.

Risa Gettler studied graphic design in school and was exposed to calligraphy through her studies. During her years working for an ad agency, she used calligraphy to personalize certain projects. When she retired in 1995, she joined a calligraphy guild and has enjoyed a steady flow of work through this affiliation.

Bostick says, "Individual craftsmanship is expressed in its variation." Not only is the writing itself varied, but so is the need for calligraphy. For example, Gettler's projects have included personalizing family stories or genealogies, breast cancer awareness literature, and printing on surfaces that a computer printer can't handle. Some calligraphers create their own papers that are well suited to the inks used in calligraphy.

Calligraphy at a Glance

 75% 25%

	Minimal	Moderate	More than most
Start-up cost	X		
Overhead	X		
Potential earnings	X		
Computer skills required	X		
Deadline pressures		X	
Flexible hours		X	
Overall stress	X		

Likely Transferable Skills, Background, Careers

Commonly, calligraphers have art or graphic-design training or backgrounds but with practice, practice, practice, calligraphy can be mastered by many people.

What to Charge

Calligraphy work is typically priced by the piece, which can vary with the amount of copy and detail the client wants. For example, typical prices for addressing invitations with inner and outer envelopes are from $1.50 to $3.00 each, for place cards, $1.25 to $1.50.

If you are getting work as a subcontractor or for a printer or another source, expect to discount your prices by 35 to 40 percent. Search the Web for calligraphy pricing in your area.

Best Ways to Get Business

- Designing your business card to reflect the style of your work. Build relationships with local printers, reprographic shops, and stationery stores. Since they rarely have an in-house calligrapher, they routinely send this work out.

- Contacting restaurants about having a custom-designed, hand-lettered menu. While most will print their menus, they will require an original that can be provided. Of course, menus need updating, which can mean ongoing business.

- Contacting clubs, civic groups, schools, churches, libraries, local governments, and any other organizations that might want to have certificates, special awards, or proclamations that would be enhanced by calligraphy.

- Joining a local calligraphy guild. You can find a master list at *www.calligraphicarts.org/guilds.html,* or you can usually locate one in your area through this Web site.

- Incentivizing your customer. Risa Gettler has designed flyers for free but charged for hand-addressing the envelopes.

- Making a portfolio with samples of the kinds of calligraphy you do to show to prospective clients.

- Displaying your work on a Web site.

Marketing Insights

- Calligraphy appeals to people who want something individual and handmade and are willing to pay the premium this costs.

- Change your own everyday handwriting so that it becomes a billboard for your ability. Then handwrite notes so people will see what you can do. You will get commissions for work from people who see checks or other documents you sign.

- The clients you serve can provide you with prestige. You can compete in contests such as those sponsored by the Smithsonian. If you win, you can, as Risa Gettler has been able to do, say her work is "in the Smithsonian."

- You may be able to sell your own hand-created note cards, quotations, bookmarks, and the like at craft fairs or by wholesale through card and gift shops.

Where Next?

ASSOCIATIONS:

- Association for the Calligraphic Arts: (574) 287-2189; *www. calligraphicarts.org*. This international association has two categories of membership: individuals and local guilds.

- International Association of Master Penman, Engrossers and Teachers of Handwriting: *www.iampeth.com*. Has links to teachers and sources of calligraphic supplies.

TRAINING

- Community-education programs often offer courses in calligraphy.

- *www.calligraphyonline.com/learning*.

BOOKS

- *Back to the Second Basic R*—Ritin. Bill Bostick's kit is a self-teaching aid. ISBN: 0-9606630-3-7. Available at: *www. bookmasters.com/marktplc/calligraphy.htm*.

- *Complete Idiot's Guide to Calligraphy*, Jane Eldershaw (Alpha Books, 2001). ISBN: 002864154X.

From the Home Front

Risa Gettler, now fifty-eight, sees herself doing calligraphy for a long time: "God willing, if there's no arthritis, there's no end to it."

---

58. Candle Making

Two out of five people spend disposable income to buy candles for celebrations, ceremonies, romantic occasions, home decorations, and stress relief. People also use candles to create ambience, mask odors, and as gifts. Handmade items in general and candles that make an impression on people in particular are in demand. Candle making can be a profitable business, whether you focus on simple colored-wax versions scented with high-quality blends of oils and perfumes, or decide to make unusual customized designs that go beyond the more common manufactured types like tapers, straight-sided dinner candles, columns, pillars, and votives.

Lois Morin started making candles as something to do with her time when her husband was stationed in the forests of Maine. She became inspired one day when she unwrapped a candle from Sicily that smelled as good as the day it was given to her years before. Soon friends were urging her to sell the candles she was making. Morin started frequenting craft shows where people would even bring their own containers for her to fill with her wax. Now she is planning to put out a line of aromatherapy candles that uses pure soy wax and no dyes.

At age fifty, Louise Robidas, now fifty-four, dreamed of having her own business. She was looking for something to make for Christmas gifts and found candle making on the Internet. Her friends and family loved her candles, and she decided to open a small business based in her backyard shed. Because her home is in an area with a favorable zoning situation, she's able to sell her candles out of her workshop. Neighbors can smell wonderful fragrances as her candles are being made. Customers are drawn to the handmade quality of her products. She created a Web site (*www.Kountrypeddler.com.*), where she shows off her candles. She's become so successful that this year she hired a sales rep to take her candles to the wholesale market.

The wax and fragrance you use must be of equal quality, Morin advises. "It is best to use the purest, uncut product," she states. If you use too many additives like sterin or fibar, you get a candle that doesn't burn well. Morin finds her work to be fairly scientific, as there are plenty of things to test when blending wax and fragrance and finding the best products to make her complex three-dimensional constructions. "I'm not just waxing a wick," she says, emphasizing all the experiments she must conduct to make safe, high-quality candles.

Many candle makers are working with soy-based waxes now as they burn cleaner, take scent well, and work like beeswax without difficulties with wicking. Parafin waxes are dangerous as they give off black smoke and soot.

There are some initial start-up costs. You need something safe in which to melt wax, and it should have a thermostat. A commercial melter with a faucet costs around $300. It will melt several hundred pounds of wax at a time and makes transferring the hot wax to molds much easier. Using molds to hold the melted wax will help make a safe candle. You can buy molds from distributors, adapt candy molds, or make your own. Despite there being over a thousand different fragrances available, it's best to start with just three or four until you get your technique down. While you're usually standing while candle making, it can also be done from a wheelchair.

Because you are working with potentially dangerous materials, you will need to carry product liability insurance. You'll need to do some searching to find a policy that best suits your situation. You also need to provide warning labels on your candles that provide information about how they burn and reminding the user never to leave burning candles unattended—one out of six people do.

Candle Making at a Glance

 90% 10%

	Minimal	Moderate	More than most
Start-up cost		X	
Overhead	X		
Potential earnings		X	
Computer skills required	X		
Deadline pressures		X	
Flexible hours			X
Overall stress		X	

Likely Transferable Skills, Background, Careers

Candle makers as well as candle buyers are overwhelmingly female and come from all walks of life. The craft requires creativity, curiosity, and a willingness to experiment and find a pleasing product for your customers.

What to Charge

In pricing your candles, use the following rule: Double your costs for wholesale customers and double it again for retail customers. Expect approximately a 500 percent markup as you place value on your time as well as your materials. Keep in mind that you're not competing with the small 50¢ votive candles people can get at a discount store. Specialty candles can cost as much as $200.

Best Ways to Get Business

- Giving away samples. By giving a candle to her gas man, Louise Robidas got favorable word of mouth and repeat sales.

- Providing your candles to organizations for door prizes.

- Getting exposure at craft fairs and shows where you can display new products and give away samples with purchases. Be able to tell a story about your candles.

- Developing your own Web site, or subscribing to co-op-style Web sites with other candle makers or high-quality craft sellers. A Web site is like an electronic brochure and a twenty-four-hour gallery for your candles. When the appeal of your candles is mostly visual, this is a great way to have constant exposure.

- To increase your reach into wholesale distribution, hiring a sales rep who will work on a commission, typically 15 to 20 percent.

Marketing Insights

- The key reasons people buy candles are for their smell, the mood they create, the romantic feelings they invite, the comfortable/cozy feelings they bring to a room, and the odors they mask. Candlelight immediately comes to mind whenever people think about how to create a soothing, relaxing environment.

- Research by the candle industry shows that fragrance is by far the most important consideration in purchasing a candle. Color, cost, size, and shape come next, in that order.

- More candles are sold prior to and during the Christmas season than at any other time of year. Going along with this, winter is the most popular season for using candles, but half of candle consumers use them all year round.

- You'll do better with premium candles. So avoid selling in flea markets where people seek bargains and haggle over prices.

- In terms of ingredients, keep in mind that combining the best and worst ingredients doesn't work. Wax and fragrance must go hand in hand. The premium waxes, particularly for health-conscious consumers are soy, beeswax, and bayberry wax, but you'll discover each type of wax has its own advantages and disadvantages.

- The market for handmade candles varies geographically. For example, Florida is not a hot market for candles. If you're going to be relying on sales in your area, check the demand before you invest. Selling on the Web, of course, is an alternative, particularly for candles with a strong visual appeal.

Where Next?

ASSOCIATION

- International Guild of Candle Artisans, *www.igca.net*. The guild has a chat room where you can network with others.

BOOKS

- *The Candlemaker's Companion: A Complete Guide to Rolling, Pouring, Dipping, and Decorating Your Own Candles,* Betty Oppenheimer (Storey Books, 2001). ISBN: 1580173667.

- *Candle Making for Fun and Profit,* Michelle Espino (Prima Lifestyles, 2000). ISBN: 0761520406.

- *Candle Making: A Step-by-Step Guide from Beginner to Expert,* Bob Sherman (M Evans & Co, 2002). ISBN: 0871319683.

From the Home Front

In answer to the question "How long do you see yourself making candles?" Lois Morin (*www.stregamoon.com*) said, "As long as I can stand up. A lot of candle makers are quite old—in their seventies."

59. Ceramics

Maybe you took ceramics as an elective in college or signed up for a ceramics workshop and savor memories of handling the clay and watching something creative, exquisite, or otherwise, rise up from under your hands. Certainly if you like creating things others can enjoy for years to come and don't mind getting your hands dirty, you might want to become a ceramic artist.

Many people enjoy the look of handmade pottery, whether it's a simple cup for water or a tall, incredibly glazed vase. So as a ceramic artist, you can focus on making simple, useful items like cups, bowls, and plates. Or if you are looking for a challenge, teapots, large platters, and tall urns or vases used for home décor can sell for higher prices if the venue and the workmanship are right. Usually you would be working with a wheel, but some artists fabricate their pieces from slabs or make them with coil constructions.

Anne Testa of the Association of Clay and Glass Artists of California points out that people are primarily drawn to ceramics as a creative outlet. Artists range from those who want to make a living from their work to those who treat it more like a hobby, working part-time. There are two approaches to making ceramics, according to Testa: hand built and wheel thrown or mold poured. Clearly wheel-thrown work takes more time; nevertheless the practice is a precise one and takes study and experience to perfect. "Potters," Testa explains, "tend to be pragmatic, and patient."

Lee Mittleman was vice president of research and development with a San Francisco Bay area technology firm when he decided to change. He looked at the high-tech job market but felt frustrated with the pace that the high salaries demanded. So at fifty-two, he decided to change directions and enrolled in a concentrated series of ceramics courses, studying thirty hours a week until he found his own way of working with clay.

Now Lee combines his ceramics business with his love of travel. He has spent two months researching the origins of his art in Japan and Korea. "I've found clay to be a common bond with people all over the world." For Lee ceramics is a road to his own personal growth. "I am nowhere near the limits of what I can do."

Earthenware, stoneware, and porcelain are the most general types of ceramics, but there are many ways to specialize such as with particular glazes or ways of treating the surface like corrugating, incising, polishing, punching with tools, scoring, smoothing, using painted elements, applying decoration, and combining clay with baskets, to name just a few.

Some people, like Mittleman, steer clear of glazing technology. But if you want to work with glazes, you can buy commercial glazes that you mix and stir with water. Or, like Otto Heino, you may develop your own glaze from scratch.

At fifty-seven, Otto Heino committed himself to ceramics and began developing a specialized raku glaze. This is a difficult technique seen on costly pottery from Japan. It took Otto two years and two months to perfect it. Still for four years he didn't sell a single piece, but then people in Japan got wind of his beautiful ochre coloration and were crazy about it. Now, at age eighty-eight, Otto makes more than a million dollars a year thanks to what he calls "developing a better mousetrap someone wanted in the worst way." He personally staffs his gallery in Ojai, California, and teaches seminars on how to make a living in the ceramic arts.

As you can see, getting started in this business is as simple as taking a class and as complicated as perfecting a technique and inventing a style. You need sufficient physical strength to handle twenty-five- to fifty-pound bags of clay. Maintaining the strength to be a ceramic artist, says Otto, is "like a musician with an instrument. You must keep practicing."

You will need access to a kiln, which means either purchasing one yourself or by associating with a gallery or workshop that will let you rent time for firing your pieces. Investing in a kiln of your own will give you control over all that goes into the kiln, and that means more control over the results. You'll also need a wheel and a slab roller.

Ceramic Arts at a Glance

 60% 40%

	Minimal	Moderate	More than most
Start-up cost			X
Overhead—travel		X	
Potential earnings		X	

	Minimal	Moderate	More than most
Computer skills required		X	
Deadline pressures	X		
Flexible hours			X
Overall stress	X		

Likely Transferable Skills, Background, Careers

An art background is helpful but not necessary in this field.

What to Charge

As with most art, prices for ceramics range widely. Certainly you will want to charge more than manufactured pieces sold as housewares. When you sell locally, the local market determines what you can charge. For example, San Francisco supports higher prices than the Sacramento Valley. When you sell through a gallery, they will help you price your work. Studying prices of pottery sold on the Web will help you establish prices.

Best Ways to Get Business

- Exhibiting at craft shows. Retail shows are geared toward the consumer, and there is no commission on the sale. Sometimes you will get requests for custom-made items. Lee Mittleman does up to forty weekend craft shows a year. Wholesale shows are a way to sell a lot of products.

- Joining a craft guild where you can network to obtain leads to venues where you can sell your work.

- Attracting people to your studio. In some regions there are open studio associations that sponsor events to bring people into members' studios. This could bring people to your studio who would never otherwise see your work. You can also explore attracting members of a collector's guild like an auxiliary organization of a museum to come to your studio.

- Selling from your own studio, if your zoning permits.

- Getting a gallery to sell your work. Galleries' commissions range from 30 to 50 percent.

- Selling from the Web. You can create your own site or use a service like *http:www.internet-art-marketing.com,* which enables you to get your work up with as little as a digital camera or a scanner. You can also collaborate with other artists, as Ann Testa does at *www.clayartgallery.com,* or sell on *eBay* and other Internet auction venues.

Marketing Insights

- Since you can't compete on price with items manufactured offshore, the uniqueness of what you make matters. Lee Mittleman puts it this way: "Everything does not have to be cheaper, faster, or better." Otto Heino says, "It's not how many you make; it's how many good ones you make." So not only do you get to set the pace of production and control the creativity of the product; you need to do this.

- To achieve the success of the people interviewed for this profile, consider specializing in a lost type of ceramic or treatment that will appeal to a specific market or taste.

- Entering competitions will generate publicity in journals like *Ceramics Monthly,* as they feature the winners and other artists the editors find interesting.

- You can create publicity for your work by inviting schools to bring classes of students to your workshop to see an artist at work.

Where Next?

ASSOCIATIONS

- American Ceramic Society: (614) 890-4700; *www.acers.org.* Publishes *Ceramics Monthly:* (614) 794-5890, *www.ceramicsmonthly.org* and *Pottery Making Illustrated,* (614) 890-4700; *www.potterymaking.org.*

- American Craft Council: (212) 274-0630; *www.craftcouncil.org.* Publishes *American Craft Magazine.*

- National Council for Ceramic Arts: (866) 266-2322; (303) 828-2811; *www.nceca.net*.

BOOKS

- *Clay and Glazes for the Potter*, Daniel Rhodes and Robin Hopper (A & C. Black,1988). ISBN: 0713630078.

- *The Complete Potter's Companion*, Tony Birks (Bulfinch. 1998). ISBN: 0821224956.

- *Functional Pottery: Form and Aesthetic in Pots of Purpose*, Robin Hopper (Krause Publications, 2000). ISBN: 0873418174. Robin Hopper has several other books, including *The Ceramic Spectrum: A Simplified Approach to Glaze and Color Development*, and *Staying Alive: Survival Tactics for the Visual Artist*.

- *How to Make Money in Your Ceramic Business*, Dale Swant (Scott Publications,1993). ISBN: 0916809633.

- *The Kiln Book: Materials, Specifications and Construction*, Frederick L. Olsen (Krause Publications, 2001), ISBN: 0873419103.

From the Home Front

At eighty-eight, Otto Heino states ever so eloquently that we're "going to be under the ground forever. You might as well make what you can while you're on top."

Snapshot: Sherry Nelson, Metal Artist

A totally unexpected change led Sherry Nelson of Beaverton, Oregon, to create her own business shortly after age fifty. Sherry had been an art director for twenty-seven years when her position was eliminated in a corporate restructuring. With Oregon having the highest unemployment rate in the country, she was unable to find a job and, to make matters worse, six months later her husband, Delbert, was laid off from his position as a welding teacher. That's when Sherry decided to go to welding school, get her construction contractor's license, and join her husband in business as a metal artist.

Together they formed Delbert Nelson Designs, creating custom metal doors, gates, and functional art. Their motto is "Make a personal statement . . . let our unique vision enhance your home or business for decades to come." Sherry created a four-color brochure and mailed it to local architects and builders. Within two weeks they had their first project: fences with two gates and a stainless-steel sculpture for an outdoor fireplace.

Sherry now meets with clients, designs the jobs and does the drawings, estimates the cost, draws up the contracts, makes full-size patterns, buys the metal, does plasma cutting and some welding, grinding, and finishing work. The Nelsons personally deliver and install their work or arrange surface delivery for projects outside the Beaverton area.

"I haven't worn a suit or carried a briefcase in twelve months," she reports. "Instead, I carry a five-gallon bucket with welding gear in it!"

Snapshot: Jan Fixsen, Jewelry for the Feet

For Jean Fixsen 2001 was a year of surprises, love, sorrow, and new beginnings. She got married, lost her job, endured the nation's shock and grief of 9/11, suffered the stock market crash with her husband, and launched her dream business, designing jewelry for the feet.

Like artists and cultures throughout the ages, Jan had always been fascinated with the grace and beauty of the human foot. From her background in fashion and law, she knew her market for her unique jewelry would be boutiques, salons, and gift stores, but to make her dream a reality, she first had to find manufactures to reproduce her fine gold and beaded ankle bracelets and toe rings. Then she had to locate suppliers for her materials, research market locations, and make retail contacts throughout the region where she could place her jewelry. All on a limited budget.

A major economic downturn in the Pacific Northwest posed an additional hurdle for Jean. So she made two key decisions: first, to put her business, Ankles and Toes, onto the Internet; and second, to move from Oregon to Arizona, where her husband would rebuild his construction business. Both in their mid-fifties, the couple decided to move forward and never look back.

Jean now has several new lines of jewelry. Large companies are interested in her jewelry collection, and new calls come in every day from customers wanting her pieces.

"We have overcome adversity with great resolve and determination." And, she adds with confidence, "There are a lot of feet out there."

60. Chair Making

"Completely handmade" is an anomaly in the twenty-first century. The notion of heirlooms and quality has, in large part, been replaced by numbers and affordability. This is true for most products in our lives, including the chairs we spend hours sitting on. But some real purists still exist who are willing to take the time and effort to craft a chair that won't be found at a driveway yard sale or in the back room at the Goodwill store ten years from now.

There's a growing cadre of artisans making Windsor, Shaker, or other classic chairs designed before the Industrial Revolution. You won't get rich doing this work, but you can make a decent living and enjoy the pride of continuing a tradition that began centuries ago.

Developing the craftsmanship needed to make a sellable classic chair takes time, but once you master the techniques and hone your skills, you can reinterpret traditional designs if you wish to create something with its own unique personality. Jeff Trapp of Madison, Wisconsin, makes Windsor chairs. He harvests his own trees, splitting the wood by hand to retain the quality of the grain. "Cutting down the trees," he says, "is part of the mystique."

Once the wood is harvested, it must be dried before it is workable. While Trapp could kiln-dry his wood to reduce shrinkage, he prefers to air-dry the wood to retain the natural oils that accompany moisture that stays in the wood for a time. Jeff could also purchase some parts like legs from a factory, but he prefers to make each piece individually, even leaving a few tool marks to speak to the authenticity of the woodworking.

Each element that goes into constructing such a chair is unique, and the work is relatively slow thanks to the demands of fitting and making structural decisions distinctive to each chair. Making effective decisions about fitting comes with experience and patient craftsmanship.

Some chairs are painted and often milk paints are used as they employ a nontoxic binder made from casein, which occurs naturally in milk. The paint comes in powder form and is mixed with water. Linseed oil, varnish, or mineral spirits finish the surface. Old colors and earth tones, like brick reds, muted greens, and black are customary. Variations in technique and application are not limited, though, and different combinations can result in pleasing, unusual patinas.

Mike Dunbar began making Windsor chairs in the early eighties. Now he operates the Windsor Institute in Hampton, New Hampshire, where he teaches people how to make chairs plucked from the annals of history. Over the last ten years, Dunbar has taught 6,500 people in courses consisting of nine classes over ten weeks, which allows students time for practice in between classes.

While the focus of this profile is on Windsor chairs, Shaker chairs and twig chairs are also popular. They include dining-room and kitchen chairs, rocking chairs, bar stools, and other stools. Slat-back chairs are also popular with buyers.

Making chairs is, of course, physical work. But Dunbar says, "It's not so much arduous as aerobic." It requires fluid movement, but he's even had handicapped students who have been successful working on their hands and knees. "They're especially clever with clamps," he says.

Handmade chairs are expensive compared to machine-made Windsor knockoffs. Trapp says you can go to "Oak Express and buy a machine-made chair for $75, but what do you have?" With a meticulously made chair, you're getting something that's made to last two hundred years or longer.

Chair Making at a Glance

50% 50%

	Minimal	Moderate	More than most
Start-up cost		X	
Overhead	X		

	Minimal	Moderate	More than most
Potential earnings			X
Computer skills required	X		
Deadline pressures	X		
Flexible hours			X
Overall stress	X		

Likely Transferable Skills, Background, Careers

Carpenters, cabinetmakers, and others who have professionally worked with wood as well as hobbyists who enjoy working with wood are particularly well suited to this business, especially if they're already making cabinets and tables. But Dunbar has taught people with all kinds of blue-collar and white-collar backgrounds.

What to Charge

Prices depend on the type of chair, the wood, and the region of the country. They range from $350 to $2,500. Accomplished craftsmen can produce about two chairs a week.

Best Ways to Get Business

- Selling what you make from your own Web site. This provides you with an international market while enabling you, if you choose, to live in a lower-cost, scenic, or remote area.

- Producing a color-printed catalogue or sell sheet to disseminate at antique shows and to interior designers.

- Exhibiting at high-end shows at which furniture is shown, particularly ones associated with historic buildings or preservation areas. However, Mike Dunbar advises avoiding run-of-the-mill craft shows, calling them a "setup for failure," as people won't pay the price for a handmade chair. Keep in mind that transporting chairs to show can result in damage.

- Forming or joining a woodworkers' guild to mutually refer business, have a Web site, and be a source of support.

- Testing advertising in magazines that target colonial styling, such as *Early American Life*.

- Getting publicity that shows off your chairs.

Marketing Insights

- People who buy handmade chairs are more like people who want a signed painting instead of a print. Some of these people will save for years to buy handmade furniture.

- Customers west of Pennsylvania are not as familiar with the style or value of chairs from past eras; so sometimes, to get a high price, you will need to educate your prospective buyers.

- The 9/11 terrorist attacks raised the interest in items from the American past, not only antiques from earlier periods, but also the styles of those times, including handmade chairs.

- Jeff Trapp finds people are willing to wait up to a year for their handmade chairs, but "it's pushing a rock uphill to get people to wait longer than that."

Where Next?

ASSOCIATIONS

- American Society of Furniture Artists: *www.asofa.org*.

- The Furniture Society: (434) 973-1488; *www.furnituresociety.org*.

BOOKS

- *The Chairmaker's Workshop: Handcrafting Windsor and Post-and-Rung Chairs*, Drew Langsner (Lark Books, 2003). ISBN: 1579902308.

- *Chairmaking and Design*, Jeff Miller (Taunton Press, 1997). ISBN: 1561581585. Book relates to a separate video by the author.

- *Traditional Windsor Chair Making with Jim Rendi*, Jim Rendi (Schiffer Publishing, 1993). ISBN: 0887405037.

- *Making Classic Chairs: A Craftsman's Chippendale Reference*, Ron Clarkson and Leigh Keno (Fox Chapel Publishing, 1997). ISBN: 1565230817.

- *Making Classic Country Chairs*, David Bryant (Trafalgar Square, 2002). ISBN: 1570762007.

- *The Shaker Chair*, Charles R. Muller, Timothy D. Rieman and Stephen Metzger (University of Massachusetts Press, 1992). ISBN: 0870237950.

- *Windsor Chairs*, Wallace Nutting (Dover, 2001). ISBN: 0486417255.

TRAINING

- Windsor Institute, Hampton, New Hampshire: (603) 929-9801; *www.thewindsorinstitute.com*.

- Kentucky Rustic Furniture, the Moffett Family, Danville, Kentucky: *www.moffetts.biz/classes.htm*.

From the Home Front

"I'm not trying to make a fortune; I fell in love with Windsor chairs . . . making the chairs is the easy part."

—Jeff Trapp, fifty-one, *http:jefftrappwindsors.com*

 ## 61. Dog Walking

If you're looking for a way to combine exercise and earning a living, love dogs, and can toss a stick or a ball with just a bit of skill, a dog-walking service may be just the ticket for you. Dog walkers are in demand in urban areas where everyone in the household works or is otherwise busy. If their dogs need more exercise than a high-rise or home with a small yard can provide, someone's got to take them out for their daily romp. Large dogs may need twice-daily jogs.

Dog walking requires a love of animals, the ability to manage their behavior, and the patience to satisfy their sometimes picky owners. Owners have different requirements. Some owners have strict instructions about where they want their dogs walked, whether their pets are to be given snacks and what kind, where they are allowed to be in the house when you return them, and security precautions and procedures you must follow.

Other owners will let you use your judgment as to how their dogs are exercised. So you need to establish the parameters for what each client wants and what you are comfortable doing. Some owners also may ask you to do small errands or bring in the mail. You should decide ahead of time if you will do these kinds of things as part of your service.

If you live in an area like Los Angeles and you need to transport the dogs to a place where they can run around without a leash, you'll have to accept the fact that your vehicle is always going to be dirty and hairy and will quickly come to smell like a kennel. So having a separate vehicle like a station wagon or small SUV for the dogs will not only serve you well taxwise but will enable you to have a conveyance suitable for a human social life. If you decide to walk the dogs around their own neighborhoods, then this is not an issue.

Some dog walkers prefer to walk each dog individually, and a very large dog needs to be walked alone since you are responsible for controlling it. Other dog walkers walk as many as six at one time; some take even more if they can take the dogs somewhere they can safely run off leash. The size of the dogs and where you are walking them should determine how many you can take on each excursion, if they will be on leash or off, and what you will do in case of an emergency, like a fight or a foxtail in the nose. Pam Gibson started a dog-walking business at age fifty-one, and since her Pittsburgh area clients are far apart, she walks one dog at a time. Some she has to walk twice daily; so she has a busy route and a growing client base.

Gibson, who calls herself the "Dog Nanny" says, "It's mandatory that you love dogs." It's like being a baby-sitter, she asserts. "The pet owner wants to meet me and see how I relate to their dog. Then if they find that I'm good with their dog, they'll give out my name to their friends." Letting owners know about medical and behavioral problems will help demonstrate your care for the owners and their dogs.

Dog Walking at a Glance

 50% 50%

	Minimal	Moderate	More than most
Start-up cost	X		
Overhead		X	
Potential earnings		X	
Computer skills required	X		
Regular schedule			X
Flexible hours		X	
Overall stress	X		

Likely Transferable Skills, Background, Careers

Lots of us have an affinity for dogs and a lifetime of raising and interacting with them. That's what this business requires, along with a desire to be outdoors and enjoy a lot of physical activity.

What to Charge

Price varies with the service you provide and the clientele you serve. Fifteen to $25 per dog for one half-hour walk per day is typical. Some owners want their dogs walked several times a day. Surcharges are common for weekend work.

Best Ways to Get Business

- Having your card or flyer posted in vet offices and animal hospitals.

- Face-to-face networking inside business and trade organizations, all of whose members work and many of whom own dogs.

- Having business cards handy to give to people you meet while dog walking who express interest in your services. If you have a Web site, people can easily learn more about you.

- Developing relationships with other dog walkers so you can back one another up in case of emergencies. This will also lead to referrals when another dog walker doesn't have an opening or doesn't want to walk a particular dog.

- Posting flyers in high-traffic areas, such as by computers in libraries.

- Having your brochure and a discount coupon as part of a new homeowner's welcoming package.

- Having a Web site with client endorsements and listing your services and fees.

- Listing your cell phone in the Yellow Pages so you can be reached while you're servicing your clients.

Marketing Insights

- You can encourage your clients to refer by giving some free walks when you get a new client from a referral.

- Letting owners see how you interact with dogs is a big part of demonstrating your skill. Having insurance, being bonded, supplying background information about you, and supplying references willing to be phoned will also help give them the confidence to put their beloved friends in your care. Be sure to get the name and number of each dog's vet and have it with you at all times.

- You can enhance your service by offering wilderness excursions or runs on the beach.

- Your target customers are people who want their dogs walked regularly every day. Frequent travelers, such as celebrities, who board their dogs while traveling, do not provide steady income unless you negotiate to be paid anyway.

Where Next?

ASSOCIATION

- National Association of Professional Dog Walkers. Offers liability insurance and bonding coverage: (866) 899-3633; *www.napdw.com.*

BOOK

- *Starting a Pet Sitting Career (and loving it!),* Kristin Webb Walker, *www.sitmypet.com.*

From the Home Front

Pam Gibson, fifty-three, laughs when her uncle says, "So your parents sent you to school for four years to be a dog-sitter." But she doesn't mind. "Most of my life I wanted to do something like this and I'll keep doing it as long as I can. I love dogs."

 ## 62. Gardening and Growing Flowers, Food, and Herbs

If you're one of the one in four Americans for whom gardening is a hobby or interest, you'll be glad to know that people have turned their backyards, basements, and small parcels of a few acres into growing an income as well as flowers, foods, and herbs they love. In part, this is possible because over the past thirty years, people have demonstrated a burgeoning interest in exotic and new foods for their kitchen table and an increasing desire to eat healthily.

As a result, upscale grocery stores, health-food stores, mainstream supermarkets, farmers' markets, roadside stands, and gourmet restaurants are doing a booming business selling a wide range of organic produce, specialty foods, edible flowers, fresh herbs, and unique mixtures of condiments.

In fact, according to the Organic Trade Association, the organic food industry is growing between 20 and 25 percent a year, with sales expected to exceed $30 billion by 2007, up from a mere $1 billion in 1990.

You can tap into this profitable "green" economy without owning acres of land. For vest-pocket, or micro, farming, all you need is a small parcel such as your own backyard or perhaps a few acres in the country to plant edible flowers or specialty fruits and vegetables like zucchini blossoms, blue fingerling potatoes, white asparagus, blood oranges, or exotic varieties of melons, or you can grow many herbs and vegetables like mushrooms and sprouts in your basement, in window planter boxes, or on your roof.

The popularity of farmers' markets has given a significant boost to very small growers, especially those who are certified as organic, since more and more people are seeking out locally grown, nonchemically treated produce. Farmers who offer the perfect organic head of lettuce or tomato can charge more than supermarkets and still have buyers standing in line.

Of course, becoming a vest-pocket grower is easiest if you already live-in—or are willing to move to—the warmer southern or western states, where just a small parcel of land often allows you to grow several crops a year, enough for a decent income. But even if you live elsewhere in the United States, you can grow during your climate's growing season and make a part-time income. People who live in areas that have very short growing seasons can grow year-round, too—cultivating flowers, herbs, and produce in greenhouses. Greenhouse nurseries have become the sixth-largest source of agricultural commodities in the United States as the interest in tropical plants, trees (for woody ornamentals), medicinal herbs, and hydroponically grown vegetables (especially tomatoes) has created a year-round demand.

Leigh Humphries has been profitably gardening since the age of fifty. Leigh makes a part-time income selling vegetables, herbs, and flowers through a co-op and two other stores. She also participates in a Maine Consumer Supported Agriculture (CSA) program to feed low-income seniors and improve their diets. She is paid $100 per senior, which entitles them to come to her farm stand and receive a certain amount of produce each week.

If you already own some land, your start-up costs will be minimal, but if you're starting from scratch, you may need to invest as much as $10,000 to get your business going. Here are some parameters to consider:

- Land—The amount of land you will need to earn a full-time living depends on what you intend to grow, the time your crops need for maturity, and the extent of crop rotation you will need to do. Where crops can be grown year-round, a quarter of an acre can be profitable. In most parts of the country with a winter season, you need two to ten acres. Be sure to find out if your zoning ordinance allows you to grow crops for sale. If you don't have zoning problems, or if you outgrow your backyard, find out if your city will rent low-cost land, or lease land from a friend or neighbor who has a large yard.

- Supplies—You will need seed, fertilizers, growing pots, planting boxes, hoses, and other supplies. Expect to invest from $500 to $2,000 at first. Building a small greenhouse requires $500 to $1,000 for a wood structure or $2,000 to $20,000 for a steel structure, depending on size and materials used.

- Delivery Vehicle—The type of vehicle you need also depends on your crops and where you intend to sell. To keep your start-up costs down, you can buy a used van or truck.

Russell Libby, an agricultural economist in Maine, points out that it is important to size up your land and your market when you begin business. You need to be prepared to spend money improving the quality of your soil and your water distribution.

If you are not sure what to grow, visit your local farmers' markets and natural-food stores and talk to gourmet chefs to find out what they are purchasing from local farms. Some of the most popular items being sold today include herbs used for cooking, teas, medicines, condiments, perfumes, aromatherapy, and even for pet digestion; fresh-cut flowers sold as decoration for the home or office, and dried flowers for sale in country shops, gift stores, and catalogues; edible flowers, such as carnations, bachelor's buttons, borage, calendula, pansies, and rose petals (some bars use borage and other blooms in mixed drinks); and heirloom varieties, such as tomatoes, melons, and roses, whose seeds have been passed down over generations.

If you intend to sell what you grow to restaurants, ascertain how many of the top fifty restaurants in your vicinity will buy from local growers and what they buy. Before making a final decision, it's a good idea to contact the horticultural and agricultural departments of universities and the state or county agricultural extension offices in your area. There you should be able to meet with a horticulturist and ask about what will grow in your area and the best ways to grow it. If you are near an agricultural university, check out what services it offers for very small farms.

You also need to check federal, state, and local regulations. If you have decided to process or can what you grow, you may need special permits. Some items such as flowers may require you to collect sales taxes. If you use a scale, it will need to be certified by the local agency that regulates weights and measures.

To become an organic farmer you need to either obtain federal certification, or if you sell less than $5,000 per year, you can call yourself an organic farmer without registering. However, many states require you to register with their agricultural agency, so be sure to check into your state's regulations.

If you are fascinated with organic farming, you may want to explore other new trends in sustainable agriculture. For example, one movement called "permaculture" refers to a holistic design system for creating sustainable human environments, by completely integrating food production, housing, appropriate technology, and community development. As an example, permaculture systems emphasize standard organic farming and gardening techniques utilizing cover crops, green manures, crop rotation, and mulches.

Whether your taste runs to garlic or ginger, mushrooms or marigolds, oregano or lavender, there's probably a way for you to turn your love of the earth, healthful food, and beautiful flowers into a new career or some extra income.

Gardening and Growing Flowers, Food, and Herbs at a Glance

	Minimal	Moderate	More than most
Start-up cost			Land, van
Overhead		X	
Potential earnings		X	
Computer skills required		Bookkeeping	
Deadline pressures	X		

	Minimal	Moderate	More than most
Flexible hours			X
Overall stress	X		

Likely Transferable Skills, Background, Careers

Growing things takes a passion for being close to the earth. While anyone can get into farming, it is not a no-brainer activity. It takes knowledge of chemistry, botany, insects, and agricultural techniques to maximize and preserve your crop production, so be prepared to read and even take courses at your local agricultural colleges or through your state horticultural agency.

What to Charge

A general rule of thumb is to set the retail price at four times the cost of what a crop costs you to grow. However, organic foods sell at higher prices, on average about 30 percent more than nonorganic foods and sometimes as much as four times supermarket prices.

If you intend to sell in farmers' markets, average sales are $1,000 a day, according to a survey conducted by *Growing for Market* newsletter. In smaller markets, sales range from $200 to $700. Expect to pay between $25 and $75 a day for a space at a farmers' market, though some are now charging a percentage of gross receipts.

If you are growing in a greenhouse, the rule of thumb is that a 30-by-96-foot greenhouse holding 10,000 six-inch pots can produce $2.50 profit per pot, or about $20,000 in ninety days.

Best Ways to Get Business

- Selling retail at:

  - Farmers' markets and swap meets, as well to local restaurants, groceries, health-food stores, and exporters. Chefs may shape their menus based on unusual foods you grow. Schools, colleges, and universities are also good markets.

  - Farm stands.

- Selling wholesale to:

  - Food cooperatives or co-ops, which are owned by members.

  - Supermarkets that like to offer locally grown foods.

  - Local restaurants, particularly upscale ones.

  - Gift basket makers and stores.

  - Herbalists.

- Selling through Community Supported Agriculture projects (CSAs). Sometimes a group of farmers will band together to serve 350 to 700 member households. Customers pick up their food at a drop point, such as a farm stand or natural-food store.

- Letting people pick directly from your property. If your land is located near a well-traveled roadway, charge people to harvest their own food for a 30 to 40 percent discount. Called "U-Picks," fruit goes over best with consumers.

Marketing Insights

- Growing something that isn't available from others locally may give you a market to yourself. For example, instead of growing basil, you can grow Thai basil. Also consider growing crops that will serve untapped or underserved markets.

- By staying on top of food trends, you may spot something new happening in consumer tastes, such as a new sauce or a trend toward an ethnic cuisine that requires a certain herb. Then you can be among the first to grow the ingredients needed to support that trend. "In" crops, however, sometimes attract large agribusinesses, which are now entering niche markets, pushing out smaller growers. This means being ready to follow a new trend.

- One way to boost your profit margin is to add value to what you grow. For example, you can wash, cut up, and mix varieties of lettuce and charge a premium price for the resulting prepackaged salad greens; you can process basil for pesto sauce; or you can arrange flowers and sell them as bouquets. If you specialize in certain flowers or produce, you may be able to repackage what you grow by bottling, pickling, drying, or making body-care products, aromatic pillows, or just about anything you can think of that has a market.

Where Next?

ASSOCIATIONS

- Association of Specialty Cut Flower Growers: (440) 774-2887, *www.ascfg.org.*

- Hobby Greenhouse Association: *www.theamateursdigest.com/ hga.htm.*

- International Herb Association: *www.iherb.org*

- North American Farmers' Direct Marketing Association: (888) 884-9270, (413) 529-0386; *www.nafdma.com.*

- Organic Trade Association: (413) 774-7511; *www.ota.com.*

BOOKS

- *Ball Redbook: Greenhouse Growing,* Vic Ball (Ball Publishing, 1997). ISBN: 1883052157.

- *Flowers for Sale,* Lee Sturdivant (San Juan Naturals, 1994). ISBN: 0962163511.

- *Gaia's Garden,* Toby Hemenway and John Todd (Chelsea Green Publishing, 2001). ISBN: 1890132527.

- *Growing Your Herb Business,* Deborah Balmuth (Storey Books, 1994). ISBN: 0882666126.

- *The Flower Farmer,* Lynn Bycznski (Chelsea Green Publishing, 1997). ISBN: 0930031946.

- *Herbs for Sale,* Lee Sturdivant (San Juan Naturals, 1994). ISBN: 096216352X.

- *The New Organic Grower,* Eliot Coleman (Chelsea Green Publishing, 1995). ISBN: 093003175X.

- *Secrets to a Successful Greenhouse Business,* T. M. Taylor (Green-earth Publishing, 2003). ISBN: 0962867802.

WEB SITES

- ATTRA National Sustainable Agriculture Information Service, funded by the U.S. Department of Agriculture: (800) 346-9140; *www.attra.org.*

- Community Supported Agriculture Center (CSA): *www.csacenter.org.*

- FoodRoute: *www.foodroutes.org.*

- Great Places to Find Information about Farming Alternatives: *www.nal.usda.gov/afsic/AFSIC_pubs/findinfo.htm.*

- Herb World Online: *www.herbworld.com.*

- Slow Food movement: (212) 965-5640; *www.Slowfood.org.*

- U.S. Department of Agriculture lists farmers' markets at *www.ams.usda.gov/farmersmarkets.*

From the Home Front

"I find growing food for people who really appreciate it to be very satisfying. I used to be in music, so I see this profession as giving a performance. I am also proud and committed to keeping my property a farm. Otherwise, it would just be more lots for houses. This way, I help to maintain the local food supply instead."   —Leigh Humphries, fifty-eight

---

Snapshot: Elena Shermata, Garden Tools

"Start a business after I retire! That's the last thing I'd ever do," Elena Shermata of Clyde Hill, Washington, said to herself when her employer offered a course on how to go into business for the employees like her who were being laid off. Instead, at sixty-two Elena took a job teaching English as a second language and devoted her spare time to working in her garden, where her ingenuity led to a business of her own.

Continually frustrated with the weeding tools she had, Elena jury-rigged a foot-long metal tent stake that was skinny enough to get between the good and the bad roots. One day, her son, a mechanical engineer, suggested he should put a handle on it. Elena shrugged off the idea, but eventually a bigger idea began to sprout in her mind: "Why not make a marketable tool out of it?" she proposed to her son. "It should have a brilliant red handle, so it won't get misplaced. We'll call it Diggit."

After months of experimentation with various and sundry handles, they finally had a galvanized steel blade attached securely to a brilliant soft red handle. With a minimum order of 5,000 handles in his garage, her son began making Diggits and Elena was in business. Because the tool was new and unusual, it quickly attracted publicity from garden writers, and orders started coming in from a chain of hardware stores in seven Western states. Later a tiny article in *Sunset* magazine catapulted Diggits into a national business.

Elena says her greatest satisfaction comes from listening to and talking with gardeners and providing them with long-lasting tools they love.

Snapshot: Allison Weeks and Dave Paulson, an Urban Eco-Community

One lovely autumn day after teacher Allison Weeks turned fifty, she was sitting in her product-laden dream home on Camano Island, Washington, with her dream car in the driveway, when she came face-to-face with the horrifying awareness that her "dream come true" was contributing to the death of our planet. Worse yet, she realized that as telecommunications spread our materialistic values around the globe, growing masses of humanity are also beginning to seek the gratifications of our consumer-driven lives, further perpetuating a worldview that favors Newer, Bigger, Better, and More.

"I began to wonder about a lot of other things about the American Dream that afternoon," Allison remembers. "I started questioning whether our material pleasures and comforts are actually giving us the 'good life' they promise. And if so, then why are our children, including many from affluent neighborhoods, killing one another in our schools? Why," she began to ask "in spite of modern technology and medical advances, are anxiety, asthma, environmental illness syndrome, obesity, cancer, and life-threatening stress-related conditions like hypertension, stroke, and heart disease on the rise?"

Allison had been studying ecopsychology, which examines the psychological roots of the environmental crisis—and from that autumn day on began to imagine another way of life, one in which we live more simply and more respectfully of the Earth's natural resources. Seeing the possibilities, she wasn't content to just imagine how different life could be. She wanted to create an alternative. After long conversations with her partner, Dave Paulson, the couple began planning a retreat community in a remote rustic locale.

They soon realized, however, that attracting a few people to an idyllic country setting wouldn't really effect a change in our society—but demonstrating how people can live in harmony with nature right in the heart of the city just might. So that became their goal. Allison continued to work as a part-time teacher and Dave pursued a private counseling practice while they created the EcoIntegrity Center of Bellingham, or ECO Bell for short, a sustainable urban intentional community.

They purchased property with two houses in Bellingham, started a permaculture-based organic community garden and a research center, and have recruited initial residents into a budding eco-centered community that's on its way to being financially self-sustaining through classes, workshops, and other offerings.

Snapshot: Carol Biggs, Nature Consultant

Carol Biggs had worked seventeen sessions for the Alaska Legislature when chronic fatigue syndrome forced her to resign. But Juneau's oxygen-rich air drew her outdoors for extended time periods on a daily basis. Spending so much time in nature not only restored her health but inspired her to return to graduate school and enter a new career after fifty as a nature consultant.

Carol operates Alaska Nature Connection in Juneau, Alaska. She speaks on the lecture circuit and takes her clients into nature to discover its healing and restorative powers. Drawing on her more than twenty-five-year avocation of studying native plants of the Pacific Northwest rain forests and her love of photographing them,

Carol has also written a series of four-color pocket trail guides called *Wild Edible and Medicinal Plants of Alaska, Canada and the Pacific Northwest.*

Pocket guide in hand, visitors to Alaska's rain forests can identify the beautiful flora around them and learn of their healing as well as culinary values.

Of her career change, Carol says, "Nature has shown me how to be true to myself—and now my work life and personal life are no longer separated, but continually and richly expanding in the larger web of life."

63. Pet Party Service

Parties are about celebrating, marking a day or occasion in some special way. One way to make a party memorable is to feature some creatures. Pet party services provide the creatures. There are two approaches to this service. One is where you are the center of the show as a clown or magician and you use animals in your show. The other is where the animals are the stars and you are the MC, coordinating the event. Either way operating a pet party service can mean your life will be going from party to party.

The types of animals you feature depend only on what you like and the permits you can get. Everything from arctic foxes to chocolate skunks to tarantulas are enthralling to someone. Nearly everyone, kids and adults alike, is fascinated by reptiles and amphibians. An educational exhibit of snakes, lizards, and frogs can enrich a birthday party (as long as there aren't any escapees!). You can offer "Petting Zoos That Come to You," with small pigs and goats or llamas and furry kittens. Interesting birds, pony rides, and dog shows are all ways to feature animals in a pet party. If you have a magician act, a dog can be your assistant. If you are clown, perhaps a talking bird or python can add to the show.

While children's birthday parties are the most probable venues for party animals, they're not the only ones. Party animal services are used for Scout, 4-H, and church functions; country club and corporate events; business openings and promotions; Christmas, bar mitzvahs and bat mitzvahs, communion, and quinceañera parties; school assemblies, and TV commercials.

André Ricaud, who operates Party Pets.com, in New York describes what he does in this way: "We provide the opportunity to many children and adults to experience hands-on contact with animals that they would otherwise never have." Many of his animals are rescued pets, "unwanted or on death row because of ignorance from people who are not properly educated about animals."

Ricaud offers a number of services in making his business a full-time endeavor. In addition to his party service, which he makes fun and educational, he provides animals for exhibits at schools, nursing homes, family occasions, child-care facilities, and special events and does animal education. He also offers pet therapy for persons of any age. Ricaud is adamant about teaching people about animals and wants to help his clients understand that pets are part of the family and deserve fair treatment.

The United States Department of Agriculture regulates the commercial display of animals to the public and for conducting performances featuring animals. You must become a licensed exhibitor. This involves submitting paperwork stating the number and species of animals you are exhibiting. There are different classes of license based on the type of animals you are using. The regulations are stricter for handling wild animals. To learn about USDA licenses and the rules governing animal welfare, either contact a regional office of the United States Department of Agriculture or go its Animal Care Web site, *www.aphis.usda.gov/ac/*.

You can conduct the parties at your own facility if you have the room and provide refreshments and party favors as additional sources of revenue. You may also travel regionally as Ricaud does. He travels from New York to Connecticut, offering on-site pet therapy for seniors as well as a forty-five-minute educational "nature" show. He keeps his services diverse, stressing the educational aspect, to allow for a wide range of possible venues.

Pet Party Service at a Glance

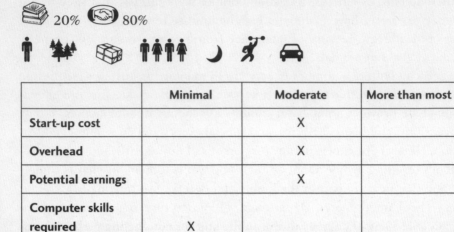

20% 80%

	Minimal	Moderate	More than most
Start-up cost		X	
Overhead		X	
Potential earnings		X	
Computer skills required	X		
Scheduling pressures		X	
Flexible hours		X	
Overall stress		X	

Likely Transferable Skills, Background, Careers

Growing up with animals disposes people to doing something like this, but fascination with animals and the willingness to learn about them and entertain are the key attributes.

What to Charge

Pet party services can be priced by the hour or by the show. Charged by the hour, prices range from $75 to $200 for the first hour, depending on the type of show; for a second hour, from $30 to $75. Some services charge a show price like $250 for up to twenty children and adults plus $8.50 for each additional person. A show will provide two hours of entertainment. Prices for weekend shows may be higher than weekday ones. Prices, of course, vary from region to region.

Best Ways to Get Business

- Contacting principals, administrators, and managers of schools, churches, and other organizations that deal with kids and discussing possible events.

- Developing referral relationships with local bakeries and party stores.

- Doing free assembly presentations at schools and church events and handing out fliers and business cards to kids, parents, and school employees.

- Getting listed on local area Web sites that feature entertainment and party services.

- Handing out fliers in front of pet stores or stores that cater to children like toy or clothing stores. In malls, you will need to get permission.

- Having a Web site that produces feelings of good cheer.

Marketing Insights

- Surprise and novelty to make a party or event stand out are your stock-in-trade.

- You can increase your revenue by using subcontractors to provide caricature drawing, face painting, gift packs, decorations, linen tablecloths, cake, and ice cream at events you book.

- Parties have themes, and so either focusing your animals on a popular theme or having a number of party themes to suggest to clients can help your book sales.

Where Next?

BOOK

- *The Birthday Party Business: How to Make a Living as a Children's Entertainer,* Bruce Fife and William A. Landes (Piccadilly Books, 1998). ISBN: 0941599272.

WEB SITE

- For information about USDA licenses and rules governing animal welfare see *www.aphis.usda.gov/ac/*.

From the Home Front

"So many kids don't get to go to zoos."   —André Ricaud

Snapshot: Al Jacobs and Family, Home-Created Party Games for Children

Nearly twenty years ago, Al Jacobs of Santa Ana, California, created a children's game called Pin the Horn on the Unicorn and had a modest success at making a lot of children and parents happy. But like so many of us, Jacobs found day-to-day needs can intervene in his plans to earn a living from his creative ideas.

He put the game aside and worked for twenty-five years as a piano salesman before pulling it out of storage one day to play with his grandson. While they were playing the game Al had created so long ago, he realized it was time to follow his dreams. He decided to rename and repackage the game and bring it back to life.

"Not only did my grandson love the game, he named the unicorn Happy," Al explains, and the Jacobs family concluded there was still a need for a really fun, beautiful game children could play at birthday parties. "Donkeys and clown games are fine," Al points out, "but they're not very exciting and we knew many people who were making up their own games."

So Happy the Unicorn Party Game became the first in a line of home-created party games from the Jacobs family's new home business, Atomic Gold Creations. They're finally realizing their dream of many years ago—to earn a living creating products that make people happy.

Snapshot: Frank Lima, Costumed Accordionist

Frank Lima says he went about retirement backward. He retired at the age thirty-five after eighteen years as a successful stockbroker. But after traveling the world, remodeling his home, and hanging around for nineteen years, he found retirement got boring. "I could choose to do anything," he explains, "but I had lost my purpose."

Reading about a street performer one day in the local newspaper, he thought to himself, "I could do that!" So at the age of fifty-four, he picked up the accordion he hadn't played in nearly twenty years and headed to downtown Santa Cruz, California, to perform. But Frank was never just an accordionist. He is the Great Morgani, performing in colorful, dramatic, and imaginative costumes that he designs and creates himself to attract and entertain his listeners.

Now at sixty, he draws people who come from across the city just to see what elaborate costume he's performing in that weekend. He has thirty-two accordions, twenty top hats, one hundred regular hats and caps, seventy-five costumes, and, he says, "more shoes than Imelda Marcos ever had, and mine are prettier."

In addition to street theater, Frank also performs for private parties, weddings, art and wine festivals, and upscale corporate events, as well as for nonprofit organizations where he does 180 performances a year at retirement facilities and convalescent hospitals in the Santa Cruz area.

"I'm having the time of my life," he says, "venting my creative energies and dazzling the masses musically and visually."

---

64. Pet-Sitting

A higher percentage of American households have pets than have children. This includes cats, dogs, fish, birds, reptiles, rabbits, small pigs, plus more exotic creatures. Unlike in the past when animals were work animals or yard dogs, today in most homes they're part of the family. In fact, three-quarters of pet owners consider their pets akin to children.

Since it is usually inconvenient to take pets to work or along for most travel, many pet owners are using pet-sitters rather than boarding their beloved creatures. Many animals need extra attention, like house training for puppies and medication for older dogs. Although some board facilities have come to be more like hotels than kennels, most facilities don't offer the level of service devoted owners want their pet to get.

So if you love animals, your pet-sitting businesses could take several forms that vary in how physically demanding they are:

- Daily or twice-daily home visits to the animals.

- A combination of pet-sitting and house-sitting where you stay at the client's home while they're away—especially important for pets with separation anxiety.

- Taking animals into your own home as a boarding or day-care service.

- Acting as an agency to prescreen and schedule sitters for your client base.

The average person starting a pet-sitting business is female, between forty-one and sixty years of age, and involved in her second or third career, according to Ellen Price of Pet Sitters International, an organization for professional pet-sitters.

Marjorie Eubanks was somewhat older when she started Nanny Grams in Los Angeles at seventy-five years of age. She was working part-time for a school board when she saw an ad for a pet-sitting training course. She took it and learned CPR for animals. Having been a waitress all her life, she was used to hard work and didn't have any trouble translating her skills into animal care.

Marjorie visits the pets twice a day. She feeds and waters them, cleans up the yard, the cage, or the tank as required, and if they need medication, whether pill, cream, or injection, she administers it. She offers whatever it takes to make her clients feel comfortable about leaving town. She takes care of turtles, fish, birds, dogs, and cats. She also offers other services like watering the lawn and picking up mail. She is bonded, as she finds this makes people more comfortable with leaving their pets and homes in her hands. "I'm the pets' grandma, and they behave. I wish everyone took care of animals as well as I do," she declares.

If you have some expertise with a particular kind of animal, you can specialize in its care. While the largest demand is for dog and cat care, if you are up to the level of physical stamina required to care for larger animals, you might consider livestock such as horses and llamas. If you wish to limit the physical demands, you can stick to caring for small dogs and cats.

If you would like to take animals into your home for "doggie day care," you need to find out if there are zoning or homeowner-association restrictions that would stand in your way. Also, although your neighbors may be away during the day, you should make sure there will be no conflict with them with respect to parking and noise. Some pet day-care services add to their appeal and revenue by offering additional services, like nail trimming, ear cleaning, wing trims for birds, and obedience training, though you may wish to contract with a specialist to provide these services.

Pet-Sitting at a Glance

50%   50%

	Minimal	Moderate	More than most
Start-up cost	X		
Overhead	X		
Potential earnings		X	
Computer skills required	X		
Schedule pressures			X
Flexible hours		X	
Overall stress			X

Likely Transferable Skills, Background, Careers

Most people entering pet-sitting have administrative or management backgrounds or have worked as veterinary technicians or assistants, but anyone with an interest in animals who attends to details, assumes responsibility, and interacts with animals can consider pet-sitting.

What to Charge

Prices vary from region to region, but home visits generally run $15 to $20 for up to three pets. If there are additional animals, if the owner wants pets exercised or walked, and for holiday and after-hour service, a higher price is justified. Two visits a day range from $20 to $35 per day; additional visits, more. Doing household chores or providing other services, like key pickup and return, picking up dry cleaning, collecting mail and newspapers, alternating lighting, or watering plants justify a per-service or hourly charge.

While most people just want safe, reliable, consistent care for their pets, some pet owners have quite specific demands for their animals' care, so it's important for you to communicate clearly what services you provide and if you're willing to provide extra levels of services. Negotiate a fee that will cover the additional work.

Best Ways to Get Business

- Advertising in local papers, offering a 5 percent or 10 percent discount for first-time customers.

- Placing ads on local Web community sites, such as *www.petwalk.com* in San Diego.

- Listing in the Yellow Pages and having incoming calls directed to your cell phone so you can be reached while you're servicing your clients.

- Establishing active referral relationships with veterinarians, travel agents, cleaning services, pet groomers, pet-food and -supply stores, or any place pet owners might ask about finding someone to mind their pets. You can offer reciprocal referral services to them.

- Developing relationships with other pet-sitters so you can back one another up in case of emergencies. This will also lead to referrals when another pet-sitter doesn't have an opening or doesn't want to take on a type of animal.

- Having a Web site with client endorsements and listing your services and fees.

- Getting referrals from organizations like Pet Sitters International, through which you can also obtain bonding and liability insurance.

Marketing Insights

- "The dogs can be happy, but they're not writing the checks," says Ellen Price. Of course, the best way to build your business is with repeat customers, and that means keeping both pets and owners happy.

- Specialization possibilities include providing particular services like caring for postsurgery pets, or sitting for large animals, exotic birds, reptiles, or whatever new pet is in vogue. Caring for pets while owners are hospitalized is another specialty.

- Because a rising number of people truly treat their pets like children, getting them braces for their teeth, treating them to day spa excursions, and giving them antidepressant medication in lieu of a long walk in the park, you may find a market for organic or luxury services designed to make the pet and the pet owner feel pampered.

Where Next?

ASSOCIATIONS

- National Association of Professional Pet Sitters (NAPPS): (856) 439-0324; *www.petsitters.org*.

- Pet Sitters International: (336) 983-9222; *www.petsit.com*.

BOOKS

- *Pet Sitting for Profit,* Patti Moran, (Howell Book House, 1997). ISBN: 087605596X.

- *The Reality of Professional Pet Sitting,* Suzanne M. Roth (Xlibris Corporation, 1999). ISBN: 0738802964.

From the Home Front

"I love it and I like the money. I'll do it until I'm eighty-five at least."
—Marjorie Eubanks, seventy-six

65. Pet Training

Everyone appreciates a well-behaved dog who minds, and it's usually the interaction between the family and the pet that determines whether the animal behaves or not. Pet trainers and behavioral consultants work with pet owners to help them teach their pets how to be better members of the household and avoid contributing to the reported nearly five million dog bites each year and the many more noise complaints from neighbors.

In addition to obedience training, behavioral consultants help solve problems of aggressive and antisocial behavior, barking, chasing cats, destroying the owner's possessions and home (usually due to separation anxiety), exaggerated fear in stormy weather, going to the bathroom in the house, herding people, incessant licking, jumping on people, phobias about riding in a car, self-mutilation, and yanking on a leash.

One can transfer a range of career experience into this field, including psychology, teaching, and animal-handling knowledge. Formerly a marriage and family counselor, Lynn Hoover is now the president of the International Association of Dog Behavior Consultants. She started her animal-behavior practice at the age of fifty when she decided to relate her professional experience working with families to working with people and their pets. Despite her background, she describes herself as "more like a teacher than a psychotherapist." She is committed to using positive methods that are both flexible and compassionate.

Hoover assesses the dog's position in the context of the family and applies her research and experience with dog training to the problems she observes. She says she doesn't just train the pet; she trains the family. "This is an exiting way to be self-employed. You are helping a dog function at its personal best. This result is fewer 'throw away pets.' My dentist says he would even love to be doing this."

Using a behavior program she developed, Judith Levy, fifty, of Pittsburgh, calls her work Canine Behavioral Consulting. She offers a polite-puppy program but can individualize the training to the dog, just as she did with children when she was teaching special education. Her background in behavioral studies helped her figure out how she would approach her training practice.

Ian Dunbar holds a doctorate in animal behavior from Berkeley and is an experienced pet trainer in Northern California. Formerly a veterinarian, he teaches trainers and provides the much-needed service of puppy training. "Dogs are social and need to be socialized," he asserts, but he also provides information on how to train cats, who are pets who prefer to stay at home. He thinks it's important to work with the pet owners as re-inforcing behavior at home makes the training experience stick longer. He finds that even when the economy is down, his business is up.

Even if you develop your own training tactics or follow an existing program, you still will need some training. It's not mandatory to have cer-tification in this field, but it is certainly easier to develop referral sources and to attract clients if you do, and the training you get in the process will give you a base of training methods from which to work.

Some in this field, like Lynn Hoover and Judith Levy, work individu-ally with dogs and their families; others, like Ian Dunbar, hold classes. Most trainers prefer to go to the pet's home, although a few have the pet and its owners come to theirs.

Classes are generally one to four days a week and run for six weeks. Training sessions last an hour a week. Since few yards will accommodate classes, you'll need to find an open space to train. Usable facilities include dog parks and school playgrounds, but doggie day-care facilities that are closed at night, community centers, and police academies are possible, too.

How about cats? Yes, contrary to the expression "like herding cats," kitties can be trained, too. Cats are trained in their owners' homes. Birds and, of course, horses also can receive training.

Pet Training at a Glance

 10% 90%

	Minimal	Moderate	More than most
Start-up cost	X		
Overhead		insurance, lures, and treats	
Potential earnings		X	
Computer skills required	X		

	Minimal	Moderate	More than most
Scheduling pressures			X
Flexible hours	X		
Overall stress		X	

Likely Transferable Skills, Background, Careers

Because dogs rely more than any other nonhuman species on the emotional messages conveyed by our tone of voice, posture, and facial expressions, having a way with dogs is the primary qualification. People come from a range of backgrounds including teachers, military personnel involved with canine units, former police officers, and psychotherapists. Ian Dunbar asserts that "anyone with a smart brain and good people skills can be a puppy trainer." He finds that many of the people he teaches to become trainers are women, often retired from corporate backgrounds, who are looking to pursue something they enjoy doing.

What to Charge

With pricing varying considerably by location, training and consulting on an hourly basis in the home ranges from $30 to $100, with $60 an hour being a popular rate for experienced trainers. Classes range from $30 to $300 for six sessions with $165 a popular price point. Some consultants offer a $125 package consisting of a training plan with a 60- to 90-minute visit.

Best Ways to Get Business

- Conducting classes in a park where people are watching. Ian Dunbar makes almost every training exercise into a game. Observers watching the class think it looks like fun and want to try it with their dogs and spread the word.

- Developing referral relationships with veterinarians. Vets refer behavioral problems to specialists. We were referred to a specialist in barking problems in Virginia whom we consulted by phone from our home in California.

- Having a Web site that tells your approach along with client endorsements and listing your services and fees.

- Listing in the Yellow Pages with your calls being forwarded to your cell phone so you can be reached while you're servicing your clients.

- Making presentations at which you use educational materials as handouts.

- Placing ads on local directory sites like *Yahoo Get Local* and *SuperPages* and getting listed in directories that refer dog trainers.

- Writing about your approach or specialty for local papers.

Marketing Insights

- One trainer told us, "Most people's brains shut down when it comes to dogs." That's when they call you. This includes first-time pet owners, people who buy breeds of dogs known for behavior problems, people adopting dogs from shelters with unknown backgrounds or rescuing dogs with known behavior problems, people with small children, and retired persons acquiring a dog for the first time.

- Advertising in general circulation media risks drawing the wrong kind of clients.

- Specialization possibilities include particular behavior problems or psychological disorders, particular types of dogs, like hunting dogs who won't hunt, or cats, birds, or horses.

Where Next?

The pet world is filled with organizations, books, and Web sites. The resources cited are selected for someone considering dog training as a business.

ASSOCIATIONS AND CERTIFICATION

- American Dog Trainers Network. *www.inch.com/~dogs.*

- Association of Companion Animal Behavior Counselors: *http://animalbehaviorcounselors.org.*

- Association of Pet Dog Training: (800) 738-3647; *www.apdt.com.*

- National Association of Dog Obedience Instructors, Inc.: *www.nadoi.org.*

- International Association of Dog Behavior Consultants: *www.iadbc.org.*

BOOKS

- *Culture Clash,* Jean Donaldson (James and Kenneth Publishing, 1997). ISBN: 1888047054. Also from this author: *Dogs Are from Neptune,* ISBN: 0968420710.

- *Don't Shoot the Dog,* Karen Pryor (Bantam, 1999). ISBN: 0553380397.

- *Excel-Erated Learning,* Pamela J. Reid, Ph.D. (James and Kenneth Publishing, 1996). ISBN: 1888047070.

- *Handbook of Applied Dog Behavior and Training,* vol. 1, Steven R. Lindsay and Victoria Lea Voith (Iowa State University Press, 2000). ISBN: 0813807549.

- *So You Want to Be a Dog Trainer,* Nicole Wilde (Phantom Publishing, 2001). ISBN: 0966772628. Also by this author: *It's Not the Dogs, It's the People! A Dog Trainer's Guide to Training Humans,* ISBN: 0966772636.

TRAINING

- Dr. Ian Dunbar Dog Behavior & Training Seminars: (707) 745-4237; *www.puppyworks.com.* Dr. Dunbar has also developed a series of video training courses: (800) 419-8748; *www.siriuspup. com.* And booklets on puppy and dog training, such as *How to Teach an Old Dog New Tricks.*

- Each of the organizations listed in Association and Certification above either provide training leading to certification or list schools whose training qualifies.

WEB SITE

- DogProblems.com: discussion group and loads of links—*http:dogproblems.com.*

From the Home Front

"I don't consider myself a dog trainer. It's more like family therapy with people and their dogs. I work with the family and the dog as a unit. I'm doing exactly what I was meant to do for my life's work, and it's been a very spiritual journey for me."
—Judith Levy, fifty

66. Photographer

For more than half a century, photography has played a part in the lives of most people—from baby pictures to snapshots of bar mitzvahs and graduations; wedding albums we treasure for a lifetime or fine art to adorn our homes. For important life and business events each year, millions of individuals and companies hire photographers to take the top-quality photos they cannot take. So if you've always had a passion for photography, perhaps it's time to use to your creative spirit to launch your next career.

As a professional photographer, you can be a generalist or you can specialize in areas that are of particular interest to you. For example, if you enjoy interacting with people, you might specialize in:

- Portraits, addressing the needs of the more than one in five American households that have professional photographs taken during the course of a year. You might choose an even more specialized niche like taking pictures of pregnant moms or newborns.

- School photos, which include class pictures, and may extend to sports-team photos that you sell to parents and class reunions.

- Wedding and bar mitzvah photographs, which involve lots of contact with clients and their families.

- Publicity and portfolio photos for models, artists, actors, and actresses.

If you are not good at photographing people or feel is not for you, there's still a wide world of specialized photography you can do, including:

- Product photos—taking photographs for advertisements, catalogues, and sales materials.

- Pet photos—if you love animals, you can spend your days capturing the victory poses of purebred championship dogs, cats, or horses.

- Livestock photos of cattle, horses, and hogs are needed for the covers of agricultural trade magazines, auctions, stud services, and for ads for selling semen.

- Nature photography—you can focus on landscapes, rivers, mountains, sunsets, sunrises, and other natural phenomena.

- Storm photography—you might enjoy the excitement of shooting hurricanes, tornados, or lightning storms for newspapers and magazines.

- Sports photography—you can capture the excitement of extreme sports such as hang gliding, skydiving, big-wave surfing, and auto racing, or stick with the more tame sports such as auto, motorcycle, or boat racing.

- Architectural photography—if you like stationary things such as buildings, architectural photography is another specialty.

- Photojournalism—you can take documentary photographs, telling stories with your photos and selling them to book and magazine publishers.

- Business and travel magazine photography—you can cultivate a working relationship with publications that need photos from locations you like to explore.

- Legal, medical, scientific, or insurance work—you can specialize in taking shots of crime scenes, accidents, or scientific experiments.

- Local, state, and federal governments—you can work for various government agencies that need aerial photographs and forensic photo evidence of crime scenes, fires, and evidence.

If meeting deadlines for assignments is not to your taste, you can participate in the $800 million-a-year stock photography field. Stock photography is distinguished from assignment photography and other specialized fields like fashion photography in that you take photos of virtually any subject you please and sell them to agencies who resell them to people needing photos for books, promotional materials, documentaries, advertising, and corporate or government publications.

Another choice is fine-art photography, in which you emphasize creating a timeless masterpiece of any subject as a piece of art rather than as a personal memento for a client. If you wish to pursue photography as a fine art, you might seek to capture highly charged or emotional human experiences, or you might travel the world photographing the beauty of nature or foreign cultures, selling your work as salon prints through galleries, exhibits, and art fairs or published in books.

You may be wondering how someone can make a living at photography these days after the invention of digital cameras and simple printers that allow anyone to print beautiful four-color photos. Indeed, many professional photographers were worried that digital cameras would damage their business, but the opposite appears to be true. Stacey Friedlein, a teacher and photography expert, points out that digital photography has actually created a need for more specialized work that only professionals can usually do. There's more need to manipulate and adjust photos using software, for example, as well as learning the sophisticated new types of printing. Most people don't want to learn how to do all this, as it takes time and skill. "Digital photography," Friedlein says, "has actually opened doors to second careers for people with technical backgrounds."

Friedein also points out that digital photography has not changed the skills required to be in the photography business today; you still need a good eye for composition and artistic ability. In his view, family and portrait photography are growing, in part because of the resurgence of the family after September 11, 2001. The trend in wedding photography is to sell the couple an album that truly reflects the experience of their wedding, rather than just a potpourri of photos.

Another photographer, Paul Schaufler of Olympia, Washington, began a professional photo business at age fifty-three after retiring from the forest service—and he is now seventy-four years old. Fascinated by black-and-white photos, he switched from 35mm film to a 4-by-5 format to capture his love of exteriors—where architecture and the sun form interesting patterns. He used to sell his photos to stock agencies, until those agencies began producing CDs with thousands of stock photos on them. He then switched to doing large prints in silver gelatin, in the manner of Ansel Adams. He also photographs artwork for artists who need color slides of their work.

The Internet has also drastically improved the market for many photographers who can now sell their work to anyone anywhere.

Photography at a Glance

The types of photography are so varied that no particular icons apply.

	Minimal	Moderate	More than most
Start-up cost		X	
Overhead		X	
Potential earnings			X
Computer skills required			X
Scheduling pressure			For some
Flexible hours			For most
Overall stress		X	

Likely Transferable Skills, Background, Careers

Artists and designers can use their knowledge of color and composition to move into photography. However, a prior youthful interest and passion for photography is the best background to have. As discussed earlier, since digital photography is making the business much more technically oriented, people who have had job or life experience with computers, software, and printers may have knowledge and skills that will help them enter the field.

What to Charge

In commercial photography, the photographer sets the price. For work away from home, hourly, daily, and weekly location rates are used. Adding special film and materials costs as separate charges helps with overhead. Since negotiating rates is common, having or developing negotiating skills is important for photographers. Also, photographers are frequently unaware of their overhead, so it's not reflected in their pricing. To determine your prices, we recommend consulting with experienced photographers and using a book like *Pricing Photography* by Michael Heron, which has pricing charts for assignment and stock photography.

Best Ways to Get Business

- Bartering your services in exchange for free advertising with publications read by your target market.

- Cold-calling potential clients by telephone or in person. You can literally start with the letter "A" in the Yellow Pages and call right on down the list to "Z." Or you can be more focused and seek out only car dealers, manufacturing companies, or some other specialization in your local area.

- Creating a large portfolio to show prospective clients. Show either the variety of work you do or the specialization you have mastered.

- Gaining publicity from donating prints for benefits, auctions, and prizes in exchange for a list of the attendees and their addresses, which you can use to build a mailing list for your own direct-mail advertising.

- Handing out business cards with your Web site address where people can see your images and order them.

- Listing your specialty in the Yellow Pages, which will also enable you to be found on Web directories like *switchboard.com* and *anywho.com*. Consider enhanced ads on local directory sites like *Yahoo Get Local* and *SuperPages*.

- Participating in business-referral organizations or in trade or community associations that have potential clients, such as arts organizations in your city.

- Participating in professional associations, such as the Professional Photographers Association of America, which has state organizations and local chapters virtually everywhere.

- Selling your images on your own Web site or on sites like Photographers' Portfolios at *www.vsii.com/portfolio/homeport.html*, Portfolios Online at *www.portfolios.com*, and Sell Photos at *www.sellphotos.com*.

- Volunteering your time to photograph events for organizations that can give your work good visibility, such as charity events that attract the well-to-do.

Marketing Insights

- For many, the convenience of having someone else take the photos will keep photography a viable business despite the growing popularity of low-cost digital cameras. As of this date New York publishers still accept conventional photographs. However, increasing numbers of businesses use digital cameras costing under $1,000 to take photos they can use on the Web but that would not be of high enough quality for print. Commercial advertising, on the other hand, demands digital photos at a quality level that can be printed on paper. Cameras capable of taking those photos cost in the thousands, an investment that professional photographers are willing to make.

- As more and more photo buyers take advantage of searching for their specific photo needs on the Web, individual stock photographers are able to sell directly to the buyer from their own Web sites, without going through a stock agency, so having a Web site that represents your art and is listed on the major search engines is now a tool of the trade.

- Many photographers create products from their images, such as mugs, clothing, postcards, posters, and even dolls.

Where Next?

ASSOCIATIONS

- Advertising Photographers of America: (800) 272-6264; *www.apanational.com*.

- American Society of Media Photographers: (609) 799-8300; *www.asmp.org*.

- American Society of Picture Professionals: (703) 299-0219; *www.aspp.comOutdoor*.

- Writers of America: (406) 728-7434; *www.owaa.org*.

- North American Nature Photographers Association: (303) 422-8527; *www.nanpa.org*.

- Photographic Society of America: *www.psa-photo.org*.

- Photo Marketing Association International: *www.pmai.org*.

- Professional Photographers of America: (404) 522-8600; *www.ppa.com.*

- Society of American Travel Writers: (919) 861-5586; *www.satw.org.*

BOOKS

- *The Art of Wedding Photography:* Bambi Cantrell, Skip Cohen and Denis Reggie (Watson-Guptill, 2000). ISBN: 0817433252.

- *ASMP Professional Business Practices in Photography,* American Society of Media Photographers (Allworth Press, 2001). ISBN: 1581151977.

- *Business and Legal Forms for Photographers,* Tad Crawford (Allworth Press, 2002). ISBN: 158115206X.

- *Digital Photography,* Derrick Story Hacks, (O'Reilly, 2004). ISBN: 0-596-00666-7.

- *The Law (in Plain English) for Photographers,* Leonard D. DuBoff (Allworth Press, 2002). ISBN: 1581152256.

- *The Photographer's Guide to Marketing and Self-Promotion,* Maria Piscopo (Allworth Press, 2001). ISBN: 1581150962.

- *Pricing Photography,* Michal Heron and David MacTavish (Allworth Press, 2002). ISBN: 1581152078.

- *SellPhotos.Com: Your Guide to Establishing a Successful Stock Photography Business on the Internet,* Rohn Engh (Writers Digest Books, 2000). ISBN: 0898799449. Engh has other books, including *Sell and Re-Sell Your Photos,* ISBN: 0898797748.

WEB SITES WITH ARTICLES, COURSES, FORUMS

- BetterPhoto.com: *www.betterphoto.com.*

- *Outdoor Photographer* magazine: *www.outdoorphotographer.com.*

- Photography Discussions Group: *www.rit.edu/~andpph/photolists.html.*

- Photographers News Network: *www.photonews.com.*

- Rohn Engh's Photosource International: (715) 248-3800, (800) 624-0266; *www.photosource.com.*

FRANCHISES

- Lil' Angels Photography. Preschool and day-care photography. (800) 358-9101; *www.lilangelsphoto.com.*

- The Sports Section. Youth and sports photography. (866) 877-4746; *www.sportssection.com.*

From the Home Front

"I've always loved taking photos while climbing mountains. I will continue doing photography as long as my legs hold out. I'll backpack with my cameras weighing 60 lbs. until I can't handle that anymore."

—Paul Schaufler, seventy-four

Snapshot: Ed Blunk, Wild Images

When Ed Blunk of Fairview, Oregon, lost his job at fifty-one, he concluded he was at a point in life when you just about have to have your own business to carry you over into the retirement years. So he turned to his two loves: art and wildlife.

When Ed was taught to hunt and fish as child, he became so adept at stalking game that by the time he reached his teens he could sneak up on a deer without it even knowing he was nearby. But after graduating from the North American School of Conservation and Wildlife Management, he began to see nature from an ecological perspective and from then on he's done his hunting with a camera, taking photographs and later transforming them into wildlife portraits and outdoor scenes.

Many years of studying and living up close and personal with wildlife—sometimes as near as ten feet away—enables Ed to capture the eyes, fur, features, and expressions of his wild subjects at a level of detail few people are privileged to observe. So he decided to turn his unique artistic perspective and distinctive style into a business. A self-taught artist, he has sold over three hundred major pieces, including ones featuring a cougar sipping unaware from a stream, a mountain goat holding forth nobly on a slope, and a snow owl fiercely staring down the viewer.

"My art," he explains, "allows us to enter harmlessly into the an-

imals' natural habitat and appreciate its splendor." Ed creates origi-
nals, prints, greeting cards, and bookmarks, ranging in price from $1
to $2,000 plus.

67. Quilting

Quilting is an old art that some once had thought was lost, but it's acquired new life, spurred by features on home-decorating television
shows and a renewed interest in old-fashioned "nesting." In the process,
it's become a two-billion-dollar industry. People of every age are getting involved in making and acquiring handmade items for their homes. Craft
stores are declaring profits instead of losses, and quilting societies nationwide are experiencing growth in their memberships. So if you are a person
desiring to break free from a digital lifestyle, you might find a recreational
craft like quilting relaxing as well as a source of income.

According to quilting business expert Sylvia Landman growing areas
for quilters are art quilting for walls and museums; being paid for designs
by publishers and fabric manufacturers; and teaching and writing about
quilting. So popular has quilting become, says Landman, that "clothing
manufacturers are simulating a quilted look on wearables, stamping the
patterns onto the cloth."

Elaine Van Dusen began quilting to help her relax and to pass the
time while caring for a mother with Alzheimer's disease. A former coro-
nary nurse, Van Dusen started her quilting business at sixty-two. Now
seventy-five, she teaches, gives lectures, and sells her quilts all over the
world from her Web site (*quiltsbyelaine.com*). She hand-quilts custom
quilts, wall hangings, memory quilts, and children's quilts though she uses
machine quilting for some patterns. To meet the demands of her business,
Elaine calls on the services of seven independent quilters and uses four
rooms of her Vermont home.

There are many types of quilts one can create from simple patchwork
to elaborate intertwining patterns with mitered edges and solid color with
pattern changes, and therefore many ways to specialize. Some designs are
very old and packed with traditional meaning. Others are more contemporary. Most people prefer traditional designs. "The appeal is for things
that are homey," states Sandi MacDonald of the National Quilting Association. "People want things that connect them with past generations."

Van Dusen claims most of her customers are in their forties and early fifties. She describes them as often being professionals who are looking for something unusual for their homes, something that will be an heirloom. "Remembrance quilts," dating from the Civil War era, have a big following. "A lot of families cannot give up the clothing of someone they lost," says Van Dusen. So she makes the pieces of cloth into memory quilts. People also are saving their children's clothing and using it for memory quilts.

Lately, Van Dusen has seen a rise in orders for her machine-quilted pieces. They are more affordable but still a customized product, since most of her work is special ordered. Sometimes she makes a traditional pattern using contemporary cloth for a unique look. She also combines Norwegian hand cutwork with quilted pieces for beautiful wall hangings.

According to Sandi MacDonald, many quilters are hobbyists who begin to take on consignment work and quilt for other people. Some quilters focus on finishing complete quilt tops by bringing together the top, the batting, and the back, completing it by tying or stitching.

When Elaine Goodchild moved to a remote mountain community, for example, she began feeling "restless and bored" after a while. So at fifty-four she bought a long-arm quilting machine and now serves the growing number of amateur quilters in her community. "They bring all the top batting and backing; I put it in the machine and stitch in whatever style they want. This machine has filled a niche for me."

Because of its popularity, a passion for quilting can become a source of income by producing salable quilts, teaching others to quilt, selling designs, writing about quilting, or, as Elaine Goodchild is doing, using her quilting machine to help other quilters.

Quilting at a Glance

 50% 50%

	Minimal	Moderate	More than most
Start-up cost	Sewing machine and frame		Long-arm quilting machine
Overhead	X		
Potential earnings	X		

	Minimal	Moderate	More than most
Computer skills required		X	
Deadline pressures	X		
Flexible hours			X
Overall stress	X		

Likely Transferable Skills, Background, Careers

Any experience with needlework is a great plus but not necessary as there are quilting guilds and inexpensive courses through quilt shops that will take you from beginner to intermediate as quickly as you want to go. It does take patience, dexterity, and an eye for detail.

What to Charge

Quilts are usually priced by the square foot. Less common is pricing by the square inch, by spools of thread, or establishing an hourly rate and pricing your quilts based on the time it takes you to make them. Complexity of the quilt is an important factor in its price. In establishing your prices, talk with other quilters, both in person and in the on-line chat groups; see how quilts are priced at shows and on the Web; and read what the experts say in books and magazines.

Best Ways to Get Business

- Advertising in upscale resort area magazines and dining guides.

- Generating income from teaching and writing for magazines.

- Having a Web site, which becomes your gallery. Elaine Van Dusen gets 80 percent of her orders from her Web site.

- Selling at quilt shows where you can generate commissioned work.

- Selling designs to manufacturers at major quilting shows.

Marketing Insights

- Join a quilting guild and benefit from the networking you will do.

- You must educate many customers as to what makes up a really good quilt because you're competing with quilts coming in from overseas. Help them to understand what they're getting, and they are more apt to pay the price you ask.

- Says Van Dusen, "You have to use good fabric." It must be top of the line."

- As in most businesses, customer service is your best asset.

- Being able to take credit cards via a toll-free number will increase your sales.

Where Next?

Quilting organizations, publications, and Web sites number in the thousands. We've selected some key ones for orienting you to the business aspect of quilting and getting you into the field.

ASSOCIATIONS

- American Quilter's Society On Line: (800) 626-5420; *www.aqsquilt.com.*

- The National Quilting Association, Inc.: (410) 461-5733; *www.nqaquilts.org.*

BOOKS

- *Quilting for Fun and Profit,* Sylvia Ann Landman and Barbara Brabec, (Prima Lifestyles, 1999). ISBN: 0761520376.

- *Make Money Quilting,* Sylvia Ann Landman (Allworth Press, 2004). *www.sylvias-studio.com/quilterspage.htm.*

- *Making Your Quilting Pay for Itself,* Sylvia Ann Landman (Betterway Publications, 1997). ISBN: 1558704469.

- Reviews of over 100 quilting books on the Quilt University site: *www.quiltuniversity.com/reviews.htm.*

- Quilt Books USA provides links to the major publishers of books and patterns: *www.quiltbooksusa.com/*.

WEB SITES AND GROUPS

- Planet Patchwork hosts four mailing lists, including one for people in the quilting business: *http:planetpatchwork.com/quiltbiz.htm*.

- QuiltTeach, a Yahoo group for professional quilting teachers: *quiltteach@yahoogroups.com*.

- Quilt Designers, a Yahoo group for professional designers: *Designers@yahoogroups.com*.

- Information on copyrighting quilts: *www.sylvias-studio.com*.

TRAINING

- Because of its popularity, quilting is widely taught. Check with your local guild about venues and shows in your area. You can find local guilds at *www.quiltprofessionals.com* or *www.ttsw.com/QuiltGuildsPage.html*.

- Quilt University—over a hundred on-line courses from quilting's stars: *http:www.quiltuniversity.com*.

From the Home Front

"My love of quilting has never diminished, and I am finding this to be an exciting and busy time in my life. I love exploring new and unusual techniques. Quilting does not hurt me. I have no desire to quit. It's fascinating and rewarding."
—Elaine Van Dusen, seventy-five

---

68. Sewing and Specialty Seamstress

If you love to sew, you have a new career right at your fingertips. While the repetitive movements and deadlines of sewing can be physically demanding, you'll find there are more specialized ways to turn your passion into a profit.

While working in the nursing and health-care field, Norrie MacIlraith took up quilting for stress relief, but she soon saw that sewing presented many income possibilities. So she opened a sewing business and now makes everything from Renaissance Faire costumes to business attire. She also fashions window treatments and reupholsters furniture. She thrives on the variety. "Every person who comes along brings a different challenge," she declares.

Wendy Miller, San Francisco chapter president of the Professional Association of Custom Clothiers (PACC), specializes in designing and sewing custom, one-of-a-kind clothing for her clients. She worked for years as a paralegal before she decided to combine her creative skills with her professional ones in a clothing business. Still, she emphasizes that sewing is hard work. "Homemade is only good if it's professional," she states. "To produce a truly professional job," she adds, "you have to be able to combine design and negotiation skills with your sewing skills." She emphasizes both design and quality in her work.

Miller asserts that her clients don't want to spend money on retread fashions or clothes that will be out of style in a week. "They don't want to feel like cattle," she insists. They're looking for something unique and custom fit for them, and that's what she provides.

Even in the realm of custom clothing, though, you can specialize according to the customers you serve, such as:

- Clothes for the very tall or small person.

- Custom clothing for members of religious groups with specialized dress customs.

- Professional or career wear for people with unusual proportions.

- People with special physical needs like mastectomy patients, Down's syndrome children, people with curvature of the spine, and wheelchair-bound people.

For example, several years ago at a speech we gave in South Dakota, we met Lucille Birkholitz and Sandra Neuberger, who established a successful business employing farm wives to help them fill the demand people with disabilities have for clothing that's easy to put on and take off. They have since sold their business, Specially For You. The demand for clothing serving people with various disabilities is certain to increase as boomers age into their eighties and nineties and beyond.

You can also specialize in what you sew:

- Bridal clothing made from scratch, including gowns for theme weddings such as Victorian or Renaissance styles, or altering heirloom gowns.

- Dance costumes.

- Expedition clothing.

- Garments that are wearable art.

- Home-decorating items, such as slipcovers, draperies, valences, duvets, pillows, shams, and other items for the household.

- Pet accessories, such as sweaters, outdoor wear, party outfits, and horse blankets.

Then there's the realm of alternations and tailoring, as well as custom embroidery and monogramming of shirts, hats, and jackets for bowling teams and for specific occupations, particularly ones that are growing like the casino industry.

Beyond custom sewing, some people have done well with designing fabric products that need to be manufactured, but usually these soon grow beyond home businesses.

In her third career after age sixty-five, Shirley Adams has manifested her love for sewing in a different way. She has designed master patterns with pattern pieces that can be combined to make any design you want. "Anything you see commercially you can copy with my patterns," says Adams, a former college design teacher and PBS television sewing show host, who travels nationwide doing sewing seminars. She also offers sewing lessons on her Web site, *www.sewingconnection.com.*

To sew professionally, you must be able to fit people, which means both being fearless in expressing yourself and intuitive enough to know how to communicate with each customer. Many customers will not give you much lead time. They need clothing or clothing alterations for trips, formal events, or a change of their seasonal wardrobes. And they need it tomorrow. Meeting their scheduling needs may be inconvenient for you. One seamstress told us, "Clothing for bridal parties is all about deadlines." Particularly under these circumstances, sewing can be physically exhausting. Many clients need to come for fittings in the evening, so you need to schedule your day to stay fresh for them.

Specialty Sewing at a Glance

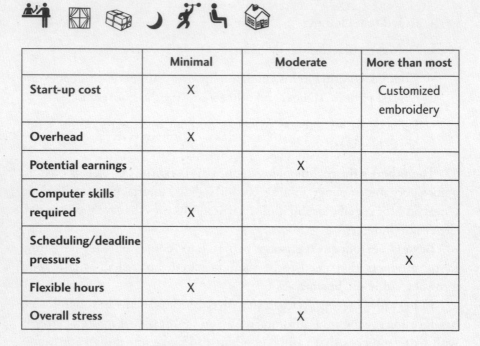

25% 75%

	Minimal	Moderate	More than most
Start-up cost	X		Customized embroidery
Overhead	X		
Potential earnings		X	
Computer skills required	X		
Scheduling/deadline pressures			X
Flexible hours	X		
Overall stress		X	

Likely Transferable Skills, Background, Careers

People who have been sewing all their lives for the love of it will find it easier to switch to sewing professionally as the skills are not easy to master. Anyone self-taught or mentored and those with a proclivity for geometry or with an engineering-type mind can also translate these skills into specialty sewing. It is important to be willing to correct mistakes and work with the client to make something really special. "It's got to be better than what they can buy in the store. Good enough is not enough," insists Wendy Miller.

What to Charge

While taking into account what competitors charge in your area, keep in mind that your prices need to account for what it costs you to operate and pay yourself an acceptable hourly wage. Customers prefer an all-inclusive fixed price, including fittings and pattern alterations you make. However, if you shop for special fabrics or notions, consider charging extra for your shopping time: figure costumes and evening gowns in the hundreds of dollars; wedding gowns, being the most complex, in the thousands. Alterations can range from under ten dollars to over fifty dollars for resizing a garment. If you sell wearable art through a gallery, the gallery will help you price the work, but will take a commission.

Best Ways to Get Business

- Face-to-face networking in organizations whose members suit your specialty.

- Giving business cards to clients and asking for referrals; sending thank-you notes when you get referrals.

- Listing in the Yellow Pages, which will enable you to be found on Web directories like *switchboard.com* and *anywho.com*.

- Posting flyers/business cards on community bulletin boards and at local fabric and craft stores.

- For alterations, getting work from local dry cleaners.

- For custom clothing, getting referrals from the Web by being listed with the Professional Association of Custom Clothiers.

- If you make home decorating items, advertising in local newspapers and getting referrals from interior designers and decorators.

Marketing Insights

- Wendy Miller suggests going shopping with the client so you know who your competition is. Are they looking at clothes they can buy at Ross or Marshall's? Then they won't be able to afford your fees. If your client prefers Neiman Marcus and Nordstrom then she will love what you have to offer and will take full advantage of your creativity without debating about the price.

- Offering some small amount of work as an incentive to refer can stimulate referrals.

- If you make wedding gowns, consider increasing your revenue per customer by offering to make a doll-sized version of the bridal gown as a keepsake. You can make it from fabric leftovers.

Where Next?

ASSOCIATIONS

- National Network of Embroidery Professionals: (800) 866-7396, (330) 678-4887; *www.nnep.net*.

- Professional Association of Custom Clothiers: (877) 755-0303, (443) 755-0303; *www.paccprofessionals.org*. PACC has chapters.

BOOKS

- *Power Sewing,* Sandra Betzina (Taunton Press, 2000). ISBN: 1561583634.

- *Sew Up a Storm,* Karen L. Maslowski (Sewstorm Publications, 1995). ISBN: 0964872919.

- *The Business of Sewing,* Barbara Wright Sykes (Collins Publications, 1992). ISBN: 0963285750.

MAGAZINES

- *Sew News:* (800) 289-6397; *www.sewnews.com*.

- *Stitches* magazine, for embroiderers, links to *Profitable Embroiderer* magazine: *www.stitches.com*.

WEB SITES

- The Home Sewing Association: *www.sewing.org*.

- American Sewing Guild: *www.asg.org*.

From the Home Front

When asked how long she plans to continue sewing professionally, Norrie MacIlraith, sixty-one, unhesitatingly replied, "Indefinitely. Sewing's one of my favorite things. It's very creative. Every project is new from start to finish."

Snapshot: JoAnne Bock, Preemie Baby Clothing

Cervical spine surgery forced JoAnne Bock to leave her career in nursing, but the birth of her first granddaughter shortly thereafter led to a rewarding new career.

Like her own two children, the newborn granddaughter was premature and when her daughter was advised to find doll clothes for the baby to wear, JoAnne quickly put her lifelong sewing skills to work creating tiny preemie outfits. It soon became apparent that many other preemies needed clothing, too, so she began placing a few of her outfits in children's stores. Just six months after her fiftieth birthday, JoAnne was in business.

The business, Oh So Small, has been profitable from day one and now at seventy-three JoAnne is still going strong. The business has always been based in her home in Puyallup, Washington. "From the start my intent was to keep things small enough so I could do the parts I like the best," she says, "designing, sewing, and having personal contact with my customers."

Income from her business has enabled her to travel worldwide acquiring and maintaining new accounts, and she's able to make donations to her favorite causes. "I'm doing something I love that people need," she says, and she has no plans to quit.

JoAnne's advice to others: Start small and build up slowly. Maintain a consistent good-quality product. Be honest with your customers and don't promise a delivery if it's not possible. Keep track of money flow and focus. Don't try to do everything you're asked."

Snapshot: Carolyn and John Grace, Blanket Weavers

Close your law practice in the city, move to a remote island, and become weavers. Sounds a like a scene from a movie, right? But that's exactly what Carolyn and John Grace did. Their adventure began with four children, successful Boston law practices, and summer trips to Swans Island, Maine.

"From the very beginning," John recalls, "we had fantasies of moving here. But it was just wonderful, wishful thinking." John and Carolyn didn't want to disrupt the children's schooling, and they had no idea how they could earn a living on the island. "We were making lawyers' money," says Carolyn, "but we never lived that way." They were saving for their dream, pulling together enough resources to start a new life and finance a business. No easy undertaking while raising four kids.

After twenty years of summer vacations on Swans Island, the dream seemed more realistic. The kids were growing up; three were through college, and one was in boarding school. They had a small summerhouse on the island and the twenty-eight-acre parcel it sat on. Now all that remained was to find a way to support themselves on the island.

Law was not an option. John and Carolyn were both ready for something new, and there was something they had always dreamed of doing. For years the Graces had cherished the few summer-weight wool blankets that had been passed on to them by John's family. These were vintage blankets of a quality that simply wasn't available anymore. The Graces suspected that others, too, remembered such blankets and missed them as much as they did. As it happened there were already enough sheep on the island to produce plenty of wool.

Everything looked good, except for one last problem. The Graces had no idea how to weave blankets. So, they began touring wool mills in the United States and in Ireland. Later, John left his practice in Boston and headed to Maine to apprentice at a small cotton blanket mill. He knew right away he was making the right move. "I loved it," he says. "I knew I would be very happy and comfortable working with the looms."

To develop his technique he took classes in design and studied textiles, color, weaves and patterns, wanting to establish the look and feel of the vintage blankets they remembered. He was looking for the perfect weave, a fabric with a wonderful drape, a perfect edge, and a comforting feel. Once John mastered the technique he wanted, the Graces went to a country fair in Blue Hill, Maine, with their samples. Without a loom and without ever having made a blanket before, they took eight orders, went home, bought a state-of-the-art hand loom, and began weaving the first Swans Island blankets in their Boston dining room. The Atlantic Blanket Company was born.

Today John and Carolyn live on Swans Island and continue to sell blankets at craft shows, through their catalogue, on Swans Island, and via the Internet. Their hard work and creativity has won them a blue ribbon for excellence in the 1996 Smithsonian Craft Show, and their business has grown to the point where four island weavers now work with them.

69. Soap Making

The soaps of old were made with lye or animal products and even though they could remove virtually any kind of stain, they were difficult to produce and smelled repulsive. Now soap formulations include coconut and other vegetable oils or glycerin, essential oils with pleasing fragrances, and a range of colors from soft to vibrant. Fifty percent of U.S. households spend discretionary income on special soaps, so there's a huge market, and filling it requires little initial outlay for those who would enjoy combining science and art into a soap-making business at home.

According to Sandy Maine of Sun Feathers, a trainer and soap maker for twenty-three years, there are few impediments to starting this business. Getting started is not difficult. You can do it in your kitchen. You need some large pots and pans to cook and then pour out the soap. "Your growth depends on how hard you're willing to work," Sandy says. There are no special licensing or FDA regulations, and it's possible to do it in any kind of space with a cooking ring and a work surface. "It's clean and fun," adds Maine, who offers mentoring and guidance as well as soap products on her Web site, *www.sunsoap.com*.

After Dollie Cooksey retired as a school-bus driver in Arleta, Texas, her cousin taught her how to make soap. Soon, at age fifty-four, Dollie started a soap business in her kitchen where she wondered if someone might mistake her soap for a snack. Four years later she has rented a friend's cottage next door to her home and uses that as her workshop and business base. Her husband helps with the production of her all-vegetable soaps. Over the last four years, she has gone to many tourist spots and craft fairs to sell her wares. From these, she has gained a following of repeat business from all over the country, especially from those who buy her Christmas soaps as gifts.

Because of the strong demand for soap and the ability to develop repeat customers, a soap-making business can grow larger than you might think or want. Sandy Maine has been in business since 1979 and employs twenty women at her upstate New York facility. She provides training as well as expertly made products and wholesale supplies. With a million dollars a year in sales, Maine declares, "This is a very simple business."

About the only limit to the number of soap recipes and formulations you can create is your imagination. Scores of books are available to help you master soap making, from the simplest melt-and-pour how-tos to specialized formulating guides. The Internet is a good resource as well, although soap makers tend to guard their recipes like grandchildren. As you become creative, you need to be alert to chemistry safety issues. Fortunately, a ready resource to help you do this is available on the Web in the MSDS (Material Safety Data Sheets) database produced by the U.S. Government Department of Defense. It contains instructions and guidelines for blending chemicals and what protective measures you should take in using them. It's also a good idea to consult with colleagues with more experienced hands.

Soap making at a Glance

50% 50%

	Minimal	Moderate	More than most
Start-up cost		X	
Overhead	X		
Potential earnings		X	
Computer skills required		Making labels	
Deadline pressures		To be ready for shows	
Flexible hours		X	
Overall stress	X		

Likely Transferable Skills, Background, Careers

Your background isn't as important as your interest in soap, experimenting, problem solving, and using your sense of design in combination with an attention to detail.

What to Charge

Check the Internet and specialty shops to see what competitors in your area are charging. Compare the soap you're making with what you see out there already and price accordingly. Soap is usually sold by the bar, like $4 for one bar or four for $15, but some sell it by weight. Your price needs to reflect the time and materials you have put into it, but at the same time remain affordable.

Best Ways to Get Business

- Demonstrate soap making at museums, restoration societies, and botanical gardens, which are happy to have soap makers doing their thing. In return, your soaps are sold in their gift shops. Negotiate for them to be sold all the time, as people who see you may come back for more and for gifts for others.

- Developing a Web site and taking orders directly from the site, offering a toll-free number for people to phone with orders.

- Selling at farmers' markets and craft shows. Sandy Maine says, "It's easy."

Marketing Insights

- You can private-label your soap and wholesale it to stores, but this may entail producing volumes that require you to go into mass production, usually not a home business.

- A variation or addition to soap making is making natural home-cleaning and pet-care supplies using essential oils to make them special.

Where Next?

ASSOCIATIONS

- Handcrafted Soap Makers Guild, Inc.: (866) 900-7627; www.soapguild.org.

- Handmade Beauty Network. Liability insurance is available to members. (301) 464-4515; *www.handmadebeauty.com.*

BOOKS

- *The Naturally Clean Home: 101 Safe and Easy Herbal Formulas for Non-Toxic Cleansers,* Karyn Siegel-Maier (Workman, 1999). ISBN: 158017194X.

- *Soapmaking for Fun and Profit,* Maria Nerius (Prima Lifestyles, 1999). ISBN: 0761520422.

- *The Soap Book,* Sandy Maine (Interweave Press, 1995). ISBN: 1883010144. Sandy Maine has another book on making soaps, *Creating an Herbal Bodycare Business.*

- *The Soapmaker's Companion,* Susan Miller Cavitch (Storey Books, 1997). ISBN: 0882669656. Susan Miller Cavitch is also the author of *The Natural Soap Book.*

WEB SITES

- Glossary for the Modern Soap Maker: *www.ccnphawaii.com/ glossary.htm.*

- Soap Naturally, an international forum for natural soap makers: *www.soapnaturally.org.*

- *Saponifier Magazine,* an on-line magazine for the handcrafted soap and toiletry industry: *www.saponifier.com.*

From the Home Front

"I like how different using our vegetable-based soaps feels. Our soaps feel different from manufactured soap made with chemical compounds that are mainly petroleum based."   —Dollie Cooksey, now fifty-eight

70. Travel Services

Ore thing is clear about most people over fifty: We love to go places and have the wanderlust bug deeply ingrained in our spirit. Whatever the world political or economic situation, few of us are about to give up traveling, as there are still plenty of parts of the world we want to explore.

If you are part of this crowd, consider that it is possible to combine your interest and desire to travel with making money—and occasionally getting deeply discounted "familiarization rates" for your own travel or tours and at hotels that want you to talk positively about them. You may also be able to get a tax deduction for travel expenses you personally incur in association with operating your travel business, though to enjoy these benefits, you may be asked to demonstrate that you're serious about making a profit from your travel business.

Unfortunately making money in the travel business is more challenging than as it used to be. First, the Internet has altered the way people make and buy their travel and tourism arrangements, with airline tickets and popular tours now being a commodity. Second, you cannot process and prepare airline tickets from a home office. Finally, the profit margins on many travel packages are so minimal that it's difficult to make much money as a travel agent.

Nevertheless, there are at least three approaches a home-based travel aficionado can pursue to make money at travel.

Tour Packager

Tour packagers put together specialty niche tours that you require some kind of special expertise to create. For example, perhaps you have traveled extensively in a region of Germany and have become familiar with various hotels, walking tours, restaurants, and other amusements there that would be of interest to a wide range of people. If so, why not work with those establishments and guides in Germany to set up your own tour? Once you establish a schedule and fees for your private tour, you can advertise it via your own Web site or print up some brochures to mail out upon request. Although your participants will need to purchase their own airline tickets to and from the starting and ending points of your destination, you can mark up the tour package price of hotels, food, and guide services about 18 percent to 25 percent. Or you can save the cost of a guide by doing this yourself. Actually, you can buy the tickets for your client, getting the frequent-flyer mileage yourself but you are taking on a risk when you do this, such as having the customer's check bounce.

Kelly Monaghan, who authored one of the most noted books on being a home-based travel agent, is an expert on Hadrian's Wall, a classic Roman ruin in Great Britain. Kelly used to lead tour groups there, until one day while he was there, he met a tour guide for another group. Kelly now hires that tour guide for his tours, which allows him to make money on the tours he books without having to go there. (For another example of tour packaging, see the snapshot on page 417 about Ray and Shirley Harris who operate a travel tour packaging business inside the United States.)

Traveling Adult-Education Courses

A related concept to tour packaging is selling traveling adult-education courses. As for a tour, you undertake to organize the entire voyage including lodging and meals. However, educational tours are focused on a topic that you have the ability to teach people about as they travel. Where you go may or may not be related to your topic.

For example, say you are an expert in watercolor painting, digital film-making and editing, karate, or salsa dancing. Or maybe you had a business doing something other people want to learn. Why not put together a week to anywhere in the world that people might enjoy visiting while they learn what you have to teach? You could rent a farmhouse in Ireland, a villa in Italy, or a beach house in the Virgin Islands from which to conduct your classes, giving people time during each day to go exploring on their own. Or why not teach on ship, taking your group on a cruise while they learn? As with tour packaging, it is up to the participants to book and pay their airfare to your destination, but once there, your tour includes arrangements for their food, accommodations, and the classes you teach.

Your fees will need to reflect both the value of what participants will be learning and the fact that you have found the accommodations for your customers and possibly made advance deposits using your own money to get group rates for them. Of course, you will also have the cost of promoting and marketing your course via your own Web site, brochures, bulletin boards, chat rooms, and other places where potential attendees might learn about it. So you will need to calculate the fees to ensure that you have built in enough to compensate you for all your costs as well as your role in organizing the trip and teaching the programs.

Travel Writing and Publishing

Despite the fact that the Web is full of free travel information, hundreds of thousands of people still buy travel magazines, newsletters, and books, especially those that cover unusual destinations or that contain tips on unique sightseeing ideas and money-saving tips.

You can get into travel writing in any of several ways. The traditional route is to write a query letter to travel magazines about an idea you have for an article along with published samples of your travel writing, then waiting for an assignment. While there are well-paid travel writers, magazines and newspapers are difficult to break into and many expect you to cover your own travel expenses.

Another way to do travel writing is to write for Web sites. The key is to search for sites related to your travel interests that need better editing and writing and propose to provide this. Chances are you'll need to promise to help to attract visitors to the client's site to read your work.

Many people are choosing to go the self-publishing route, creating their own Web sites, newsletters, and books about their travel experiences. For example, if you are expert enough to write a guidebook about a travel destination, a successful model is placing that quality and quantity of information on a Web site and providing it free. You earn your income by allowing Google-style ad words on your pages that relate to the destination, selling sponsored pages of hotels and other vendors wanting to reach people your site attracts. You also earn because some people invariably have questions or want confirmation of their decisions, and you can charge for telephone consultations at about a dollar a minute. However, the challenge with self-publishing is promoting and marketing your Web site or publication.

For example, Patty Wilson founded her company, the Evergreen Bed & Breakfast Club, and profits from the publication of her directory. A home-style self-published B&B guide, Patty's directory lists the addresses and phone numbers of people around the world who are willing to open their homes to travelers as informal bed-and-breakfast hosts. Patty charges $75 per year for membership fees, and she now has 2,000 members who receive the directory. (See the snapshot of Patty Wilson on page 418.)

Self-publishing can also be done on your own Web site with the goal of creating a highly trafficked site in your area of interest that will draw sponsors; this involves developing Web skills and a lot of marketing.

Travel Services Businesses at a Glance

50% 50%

	Minimal	Moderate	More than most
Start-up cost		X	
Overhead		X	
Potential earnings	X		
Computer skills required			X
Deadline pressures		X	
Flexible hours			X
Overall stress		X	

Likely Transferable Skills, Background, Careers

If you had a career in sales, marketing, advertising, or promotion, these skills are highly transferable to a travel tour business. It also helps to have extensive experience traveling and knowledge of unique travel locations or to possess a unique skill or background others will pay you to learn about while traveling.

What to Charge

People who put together tour packages often receive 18 to 25 percent of the total package price. Alternatively, you can arrange the pricing of a tour so that your travel is free, whereby the participants pay a fee that essentially covers all your expenses.

Best Ways to Get Business

- Creating brochures and fliers that sell your tour or trip. Be sure to include testimonials from satisfied clients.

- Generating referrals from satisfied clients. You may wish to offer discounts when one client helps you sign up others.

- Having a creative, fascinating Web site that describes your tour, course, or travel guide for sale.

- Networking in organizations, including business-referral organizations, to develop a tour business drawing on area residents.

- Speaking to organizations with members likely to be interested in your travel specialty.

Marketing Insights

- Whichever of these approaches you take to making money from your passion for travel, all involve marketing and sales skills, whether you are selling the public to take your tour, attend your overseas class, buy your book or newsletter, selling an editor or Web site owner, or generating traffic for a Web site, but equally important is the passion and expertise you share with other people.

- Travel is basically a customer-service business. Everyone we've ever interviewed who does well in a travel field is a star at making people happy.

- You will be most successful if you know your product. While you don't need to go on every cruise down the Danube, you need to have done it at least once if that is what you are selling in your tour package.

Caveats

- Beware of "card mills"—advertisements claiming you can become a home-based travel agent by paying a few thousand dollars to obtain an affiliation with a travel agency. Kelly Monaghan told us, "They have zero credibility in the industry." The Federal Trade Commission has cracked down on a number of such agencies that have been charging individuals for the privilege of independently working through them.

- If you operate tours, you will want to include in your cost the price of both trip insurance for your clients and errors and omissions insurance for you.

Where Next?

ASSOCIATIONS

- Association of Canadian Travel Agents: (613) 237-3657; *www.acta.net.*

- National Association of Commissioned Travel Agents (NACTA) for home-based and cruise-oriented agents: (703) 739-6826; *www.nacta.com.*

- The American Society of Travel Agents, (703) 739-2782. *www.astanet.com*

  The National Tour Association, operators of escorted bus tours: (800) 682-8886, (859) 226-4444; *www.ntaonline.com.*

- United States Tour Operators Association (USTOA) has a client insurance program: (212) 599-6599; *www.ustoa.com.*

BOOKS

- *Home-Based Travel Agent,* Kelly Monaghan (The Intrepid Traveler, 2001). ISBN: 1887140352. Telephone: (212) 569-1081. Monaghan also publishes *The Travel Agent's Complete Desk Reference,* ISBN: 1887140360. His site is *www.intrepidtraveler. com.*

- *How to Start a Home-Based Travel Agency,* Tom Ogg and Joanie Ogg (Tom Ogg and Associates, 1997). ISBN: 1888290056. The Oggs also publish *Selling Cruises,* ISBN: 188829003X.

- *Internet Marketing for Your Tourism Business,* Susan Sweeney (Maximum Press, 2000). ISBN: 1885068476.

- *Start Your Own Specialty Travel and Tour Business,* Rob Adams and Terry Adams (Entrepreneur Media, 2003). ISBN: 189198473X.

- *The Travel Guru,* Bill Reitter. ISBN:1401024971. Book and CD on how to become a tour operator. Reitter, who has been an independent tour operator for over twenty years, offers other products at *www.gurupublishing.net.*

MAGAZINE AND NEWSLETTER

- *Marco Polo* magazine, a travel magazine geared to adventure travelers who are over fifty. Welcomes queries at 1299 Bayshore Blvd., Ste. B, Dunedin, FL 34698; *www.marcopolomagazine.com*.

- *Travelwriter Marketletter:* (208) 988-7672; *www.travelwriterml.com*.

WEB SITES

- Institute of Certified Travel Agents (ICTA) has a distance learning program and lists schools with weekend programs: (800) 542-4282, (781) 237-0280; *www.icta.com*.

- *Travelwriters.com,* operated by *Marco Polo* magazine.

FRANCHISES

- Cruise Planners: (800) 817-5729, (888) 582-2150, (410) 257-6594; *www.cruiseagents.com*.

- CruiseOne Inc.; (800) 892-3928, (954) 958-3648; *www.cruiseonefranchise.com*.

From the Home Front

"The travel field requires humility and a willingness to be patient, to learn and change."   —Patty Wilson, who started her business in 1982 at fifty-two

---

Snapshot: Ray and Shirley Harris, Tour Operators

Ray and Shirley Harris, of Twin Falls, Idaho, started their business by accident. When Ray left his management position of thirty-one years to retire at the age of fifty-two, he began driving for a local bus company in order to "have something to do." Meanwhile Shirley was volunteering as a travel coordinator for the women's organization at her church.

Because the Harrises had traveled quite a bit over their forty years of marriage, friends began asking them to set up a tour to Branson, Missouri. Branson bills itself as the "The Live Music Show Capital of the World." It's located in the Missouri Ozarks and is thriving. After hedging at first, they finally decided they would do it on a "cost only" basis. Ray reserved the bus and Shirley started making plans for the trip, estimating costs and printing brochures. Friends spread the word and everyone had so much fun that after the last bill was paid, the group was so appreciative of the Harrises' efforts that they gave Shirley and Ray the remaining funds as a "tip," and pleaded for more trips.

Future trips were such a success that one day Ray and Shirley looked at each other and said, "Hey, this was really fun! We could do this as a business!" So, they opened Harris Tours.

They don't advertise their business. It's all word of mouth. Their clientele is composed of people who know each other or have mutual friends, and thus have a lot in common and become like a large family when they travel together. That's why Harris Tours specializes in creating itineraries that are much like family vacations. They travel on secondary roads when possible to avoid freeway "sameness" and find unusual scenic and historical, places to stop along the way.

In addition to repeat trips to Branson, the Harrises have taken groups to the Oregon coast, the Portland Rose Festival, Mount St. Helens, the Redwoods, most of Utah's many national parks and monuments, the Black Hills and Mount Rushmore, Yellowstone National Park, Laughlin, Nevada, Seattle, Washington and Victoria, British Columbia, as well as arranging short trips to nearby places.

Ray and Shirley soon discovered their "accidental" business could grow bigger than they really want it to. So they can spend more time with their grandchildren, they now limit their trips to four or five a year. Even making fewer trips, though, the business still provides a nice supplement to their retirement income.

Best of all, the Harrises travel in a style they couldn't otherwise afford and get paid to do it! "In sharing your own skills and interests," they report, "you can not only enhance your own enjoyment of something you love to do, but also build a lucrative way to share your interests with others!"

Snapshot: Patty Wilson, Bed and Breakfast Club

Patty Wilson of Falls Church, Virginia, was forty-nine when her husband passed away, so just when she was beginning to think about retirement planning, she found herself instead with a child still at home and debts to pay.

After working at two jobs for a couple of years, Patty finally had all the debts paid with $80 left over. Momentarily, she thought of using it to open an IRA with an eye once again to planning for retirement. Instead, she decided she would use the $80 to start a business if she could do it in her spare time, have it pay its own way and grow on its own earnings.

While reading an article about the World's Fair in Knoxville, Tennessee, Patty had a business idea that met those criteria. The article reported that European bed-and-breakfast accommodations were beginning to catch on in the USA and she remembered how much she and her husband had enjoyed staying in B&Bs when they traveled in England and Ireland.

With these memories in mind, she created the Evergreen Bed & Breakfast Club, a truly over-fifty business. Not only was Patricia over fifty when she started the club, but all the members must be over fifty too and must be willing to host each other in their own homes for a small gratuity. Beginning with only sixty-eight members, the Evergreen Bed & Breakfast Club recently celebrated its twentieth anniversary with more than two thousand members throughout North America and beyond.

This simple concept has proven to be a boon for both Patricia and budget-minded seniors who love to travel, enjoy making new acquaintances, and prefer the comfort of a home to a hotel. "The advantage of this business for me," she says, "has been the simplicity and economy of operation it affords."

At one point Patricia considered selling her business, but now in her seventies, she says, "I wouldn't sell under any circumstance. It's an absolute joy to own a growing, going concern that affords me such freedom."

Snapshot: Harry and Lela Schitz, Educational Dog Sled Programs

Who in the world would think you could start a sled dog business in Southern California? But that's exactly what Harry and Lela Schitz did after they turned fifty. Like so many others, the Schitzes' lives were turned upside down when Harry lost his job to downsizing. With no buy-out options, they were left wondering "What now?"

Lela's job as a public-school teacher provided Harry with the security to start looking for a new career he would enjoy. Actually, without knowing it, they'd both already begun exploring a new career. They'd always loved dogs and had been reading and learning everything they could about wolves and working dogs. First their interest drew them to visit guide-dog programs for the blind. Then, a trip to Mammoth Mountain provided them with the opportunity to take their first dog sled ride behind sixteen dogs.

They returned to their own mountain community of Blue Jay, California, exhilarated from the experience and the seeds of a business idea took form. They would start a dog sled company and give people rides in conjunction with a nearby ski resort in Snow Valley. They loved the idea, saved $5,000, and bought five dogs. Mountain Mushers was born.

But Snow Valley is in Southern California, not exactly a snow capital. On most weekends Lela would have to run out in front of their lead dog while Harry pushed the sled from behind to get it through the mushy, uneven snow. Fortunately fate intervened and took their business in a better direction.

"As luck would have it," Lela remembers, a teacher at the school where she worked came for a dog sled ride and suggested that Harry bring the dog sled team and equipment to the school as an educational experience. A week later, Harry and the team had a classroom of fourth-graders enchanted with dog sledding and Mountain Mushers became California's only touring edcuational dog sled team!

That was eleven years ago. Over that time Harry and the team of dogs, Zack, Squaw, Jake, Mary, and Star, have traveled to over 1,000 schools and libraries throughout Southern California, teaching about the famed Iditarod and Yukon Quest sled dog races and how man first visited the North and South Poles. He and the dogs also teach children the importance of teamwork and animal care.

Lela, now retired from her job, spends her time feeding, hugging, and caring for the dogs and well as teaching and writing about their experiences. She admits it was a tough sell at first to get people to envision a dog sled company in Southern California, but now most of their business comes from repeat customers and word of mouth.

"We're always ready to share our excitement about what we do," she adds and tells others, "Follow your dreams."

Snapshot: Evelyn Zivetz, Senior Healthy Lifestyle Exchange

Evelyn Zivetz was living in Japan where her husband worked for the American Embassy, doing research in her field of gerontology, when she stumbled onto the idea for her fifty-plus business. In interviews with older Japanese, she was frequently asked "How do older American stay young?" She thought the best way for them to discover the answer would be to live with older Americans right in their own homes.

Evelyn knew there are many international exchange programs for youth, but people over fifty have had few such opportunities, even when they were younger. So she presented the idea of an exchange program to Japanese contacts at the embassy, but they were skeptical. "Japanese our age don't speak English," she was told. "Japanese our age don't invite Westerners into their homes." She pointed out that they themselves spoke English and had Westerners into their homes. Why wouldn't others?

Point made, the idea was accepted and a story about Evelyn's program appeared in the newspaper. It drew inquiries from all over Japan. The first group of twenty fifty-plus Japanese traveled to the United States for their "homestays" and Evelyn's business, Seniors Abroad, was born. The primary goal of the program is for seniors to learn alternative ways to stay active by participating in the lives of active people over fifty from other cultures. Hosts in the United States and Japan volunteer to welcome couples or single seniors to stay in their homes for six days. Hosts and guests are matched and correspond with one another six to seven weeks before they meet.

Seniors Abroad has expanded to include New Zealand and Australia and celebrated its twentieth anniversary in 2003. Says Evelyn, now seventy-seven, "I love receiving letters from hosts and guests describing the life changes that result from experiences abroad. We have much to learn from each other."

ABOUT THE AUTHORS

Paul and Sarah Edwards are award-winning authors of sixteen books, including *Working From Home,* the first commercially published book on the topic. They operate the Pine Mountain Institute from their home office in a mountain community in California from which they provide coaching and teach online courses based on the theme that motivates all their writing—living the life you want to live while doing the work you want to do. They also broadcast a live radio show from their home office.

Paul and Sarah are columnists for *Entrepreneur, Entrepreneur's BYOB, Homeofficemag.com,* and *Costco Connection* and were named as Speakers of the Year by *Sharing Ideas* magazine in 1996.

They operate two Web sites where they can be contacted directly, *www.workingfromhome.com* and *simplegoodlife.com.* Updates and added content for this book will be found on the *WorkingFromHome.com* Web site or can be accessed directly at *www.50pluscoaching.com.* Paul and Sarah welcome learning about resources they can add or updates you have for the information in the book.